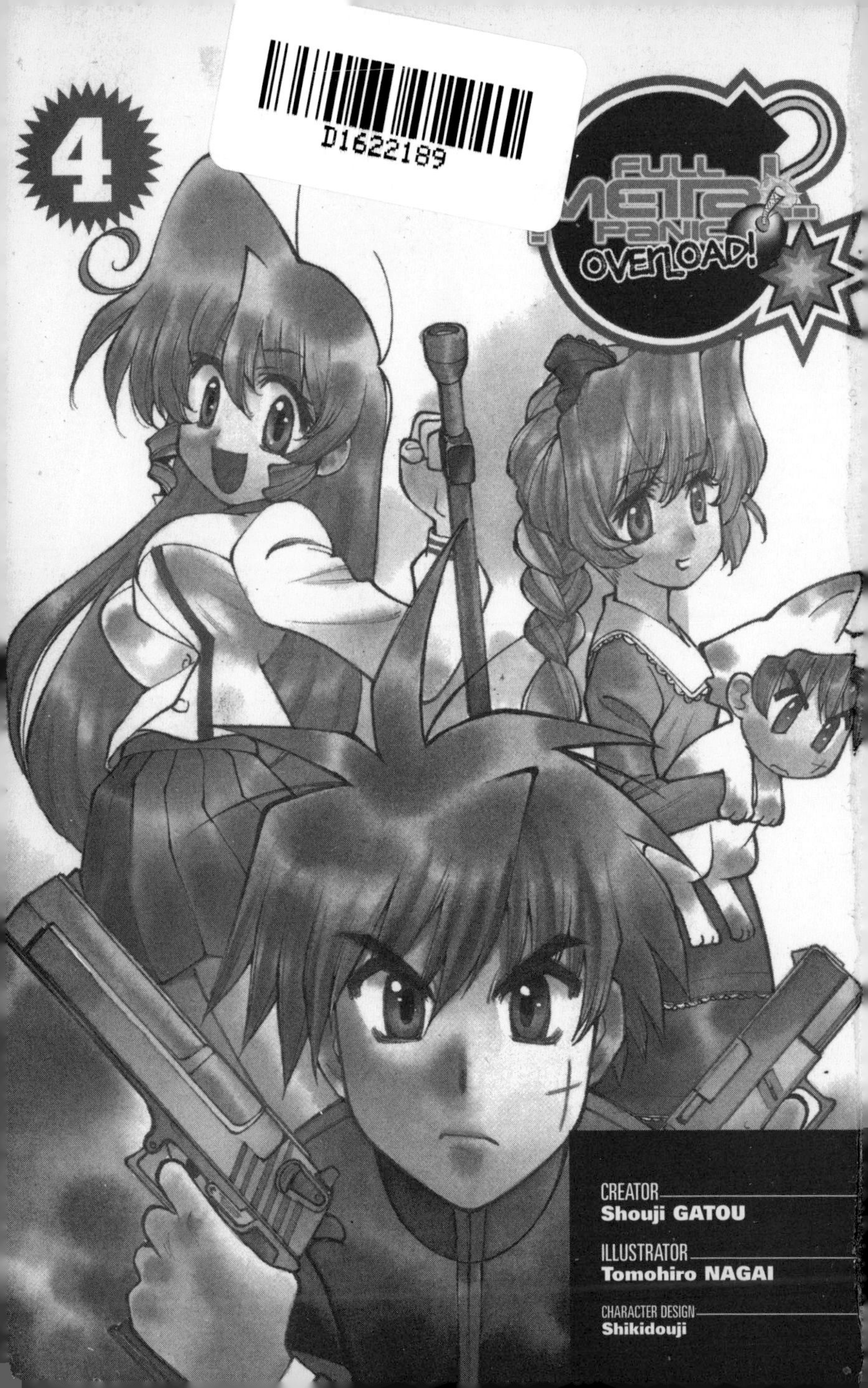
D1622189
4
FULL METAL PANIC
OVERLOAD!
CREATOR
Shouji GATOU
ILLUSTRATOR
Tomohiro NAGAI
CHARACTER DESIGN
Shikidouji

CONTENTS

BOMB 19 STORM WARNING—BEWARE OF RAIN AND EXPLOSIONS

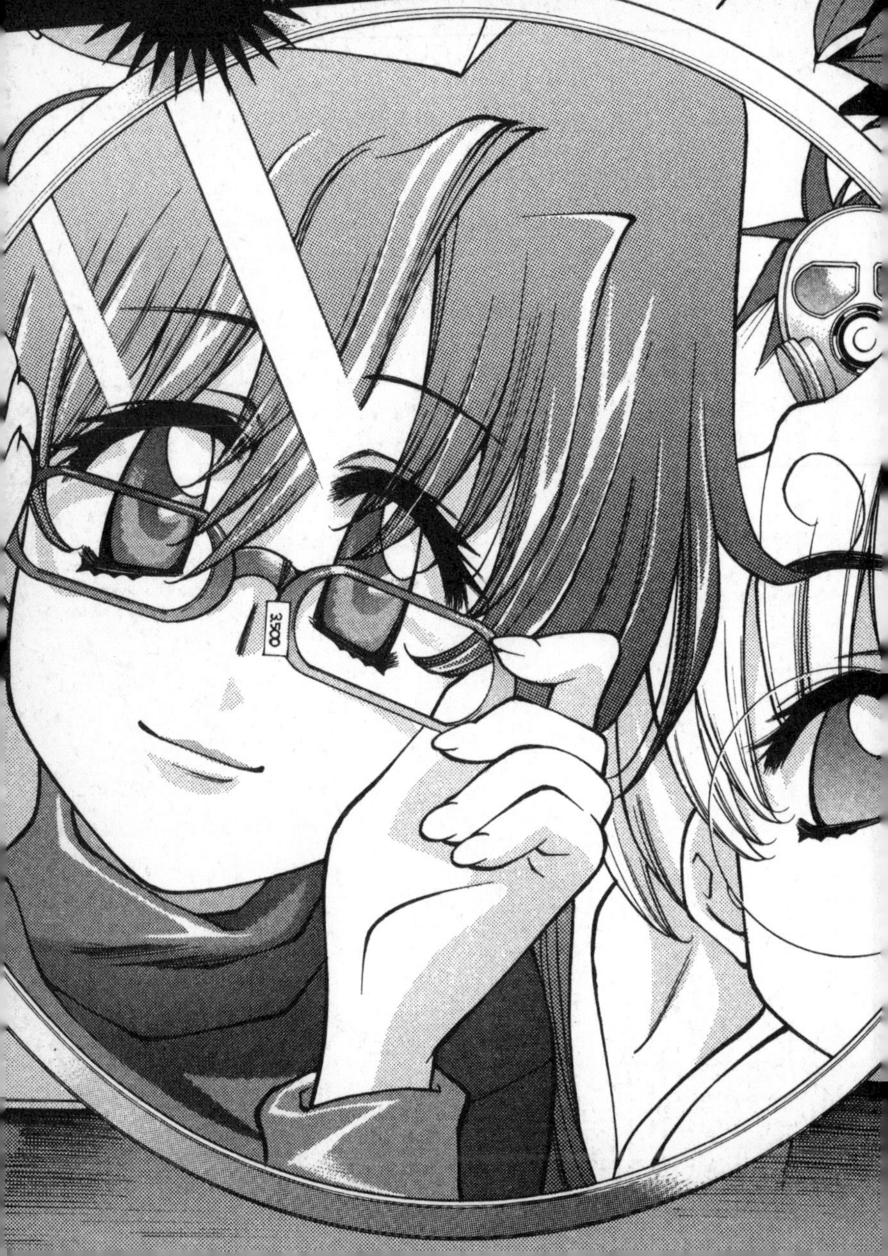
3,500

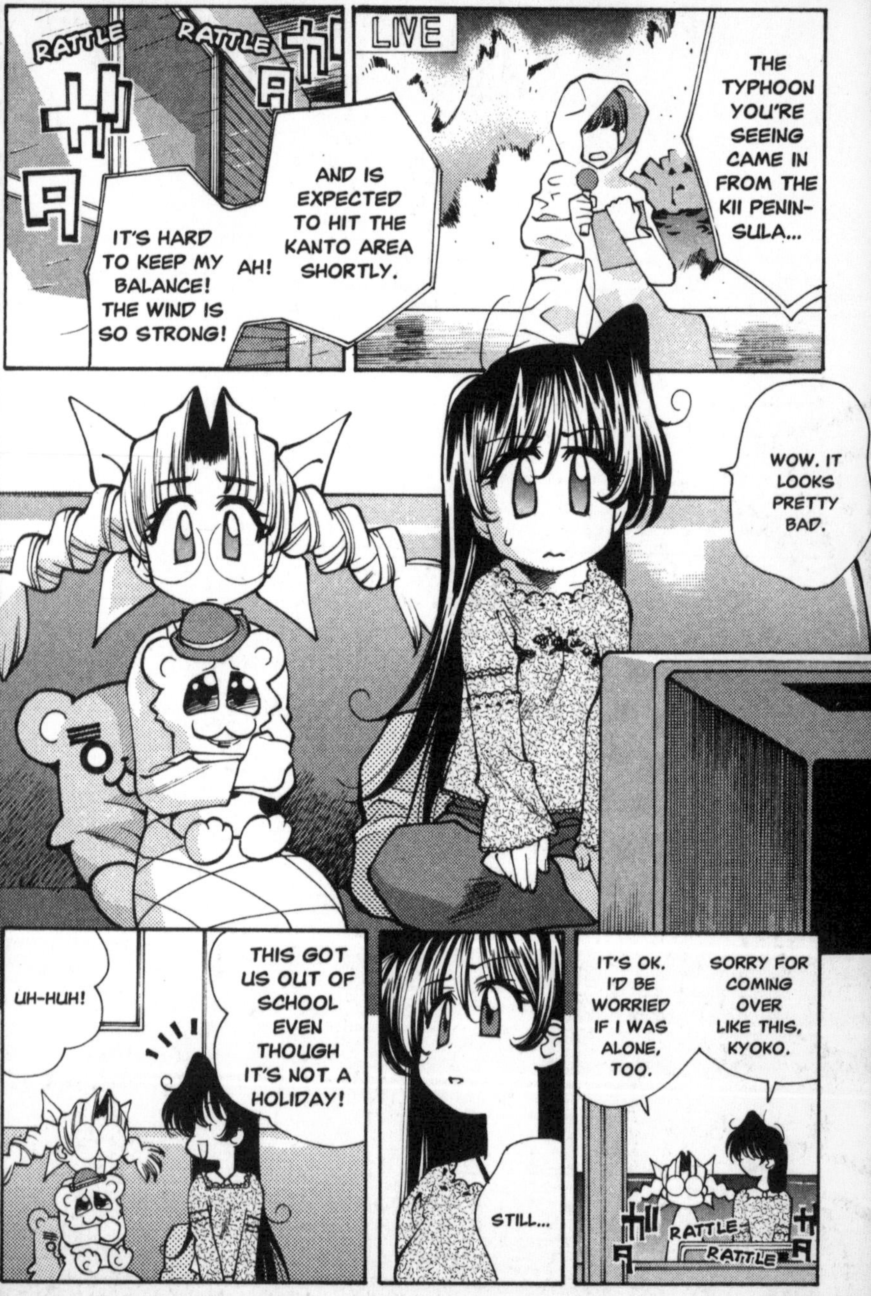
LIVE
THE TYPHOON YOU'RE SEEING CAME IN FROM THE KII PENIN-SULA...
AND IS EXPECTED TO HIT THE KANTO AREA SHORTLY.
AH!
IT'S HARD TO KEEP MY BALANCE! THE WIND IS SO STRONG!
RATTLE
RATTLE
WOW. IT LOOKS PRETTY BAD.
SORRY FOR COMING OVER LIKE THIS, KYOKO.
IT'S OK. I'D BE WORRIED IF I WAS ALONE, TOO.
RATTLE
RATTLE
STILL...
THIS GOT US OUT OF SCHOOL EVEN THOUGH IT'S NOT A HOLIDAY!
UH-HUH!

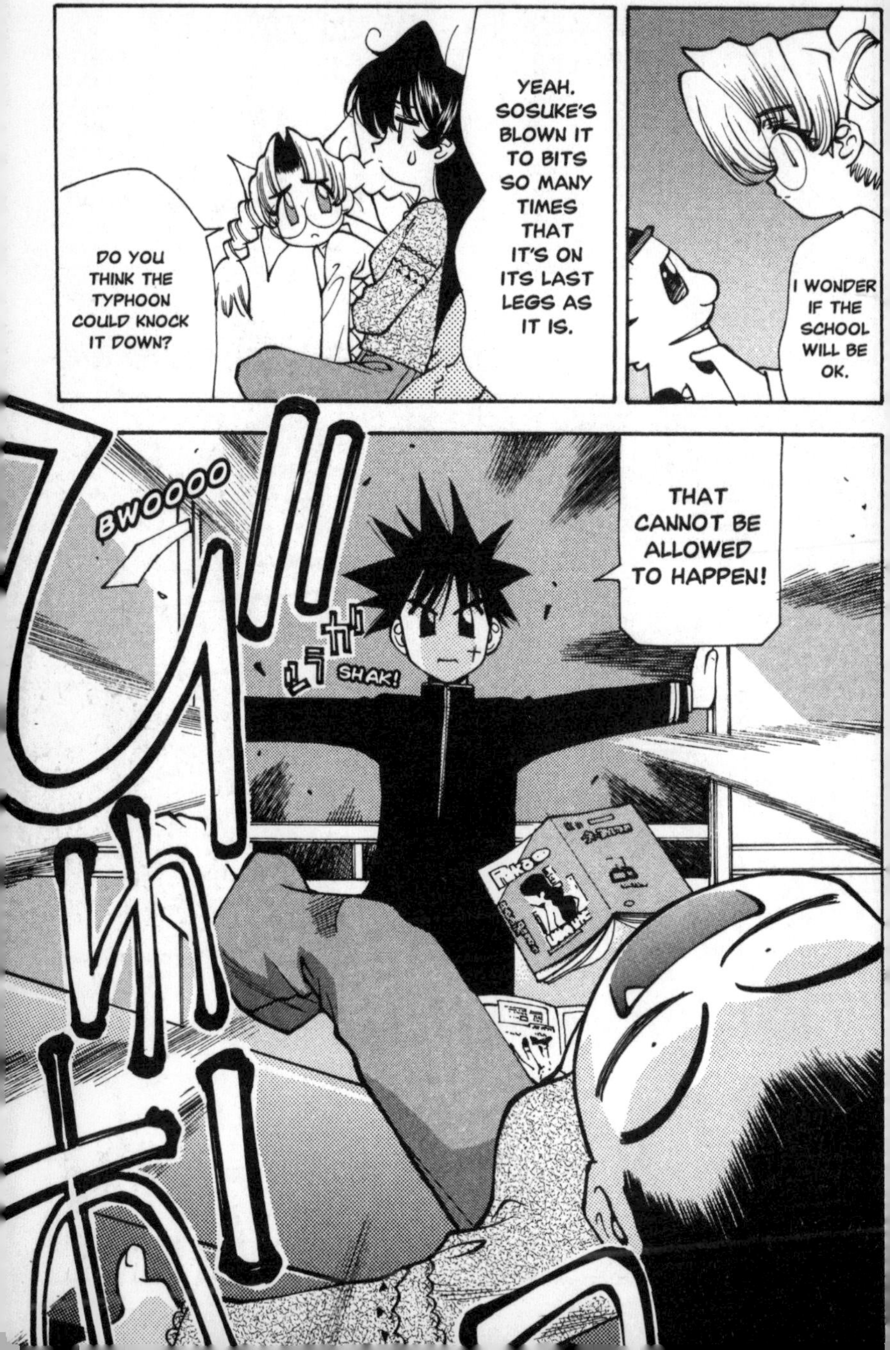
I WONDER IF THE SCHOOL WILL BE OK.
DO YOU THINK THE TYPHOON COULD KNOCK IT DOWN?
YEAH. SOSUKE'S BLOWN IT TO BITS SO MANY TIMES THAT IT'S ON ITS LAST LEGS AS IT IS.
THAT CANNOT BE ALLOWED TO HAPPEN!
SHAK!
BWOOOO

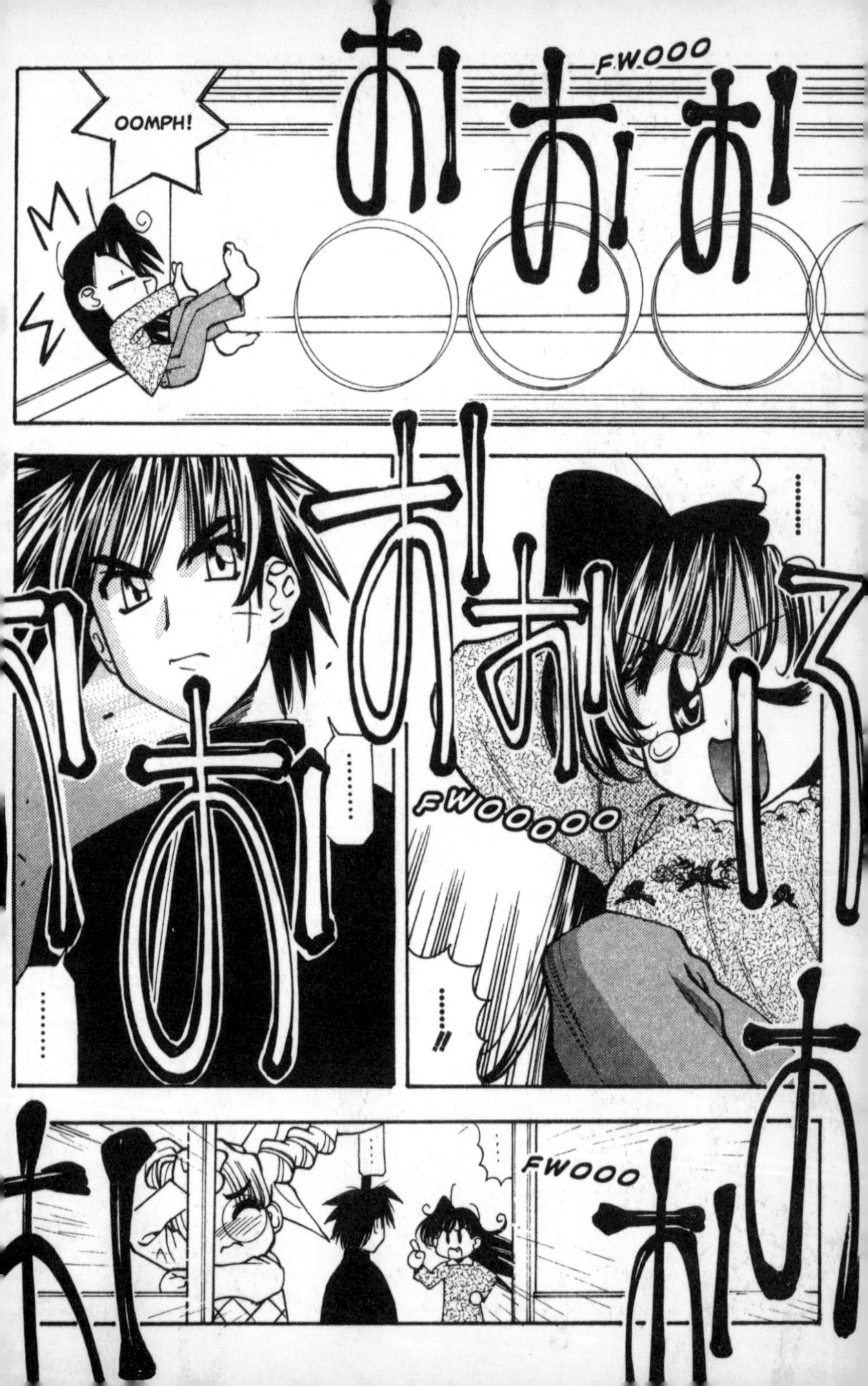

FWOOO
OOMPH!
......
FWOOOOO
......!!
......
......
FWOOO

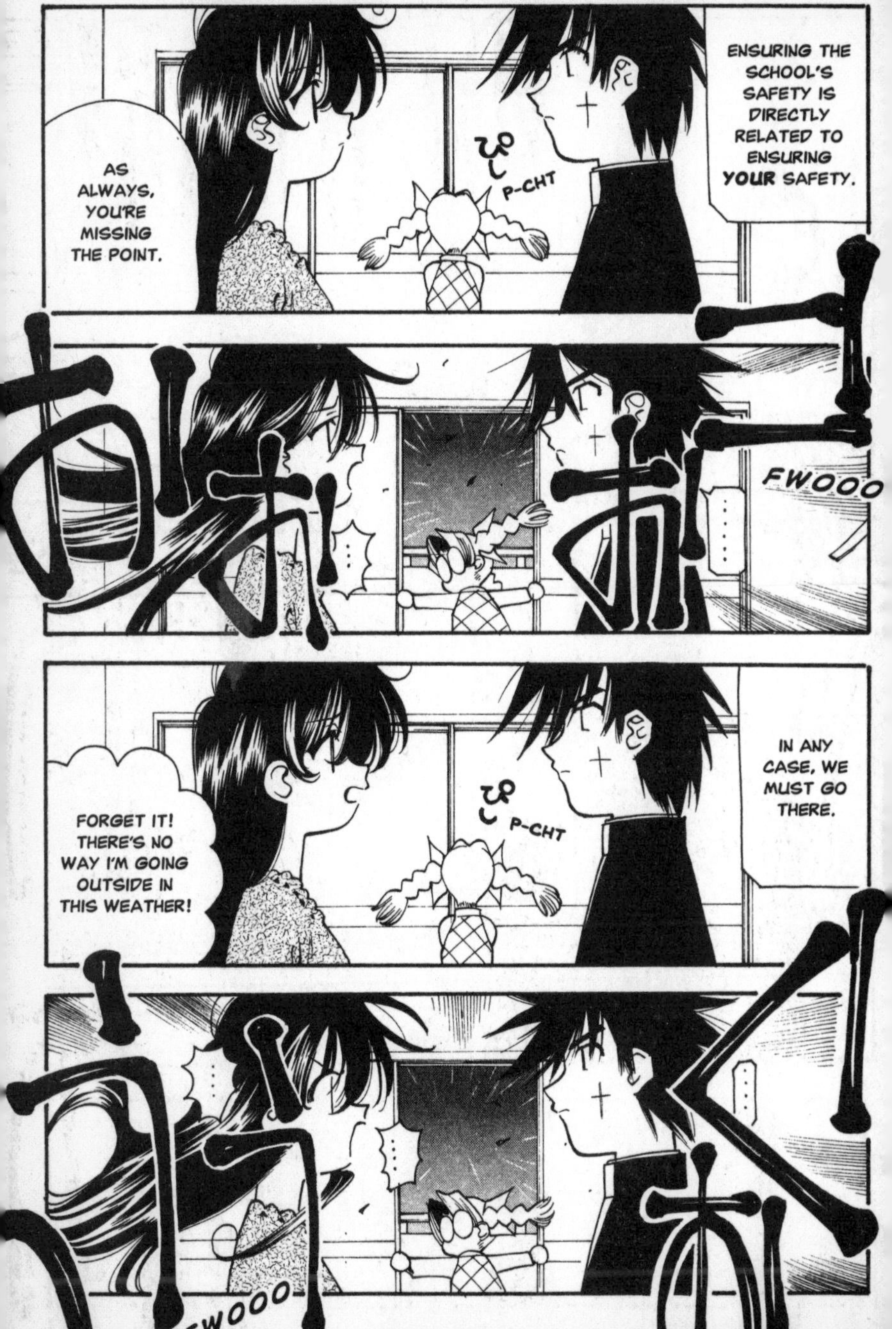
ENSURING THE SCHOOL'S SAFETY IS DIRECTLY RELATED TO ENSURING YOUR SAFETY.
ぴ
P-CHT
AS ALWAYS, YOU'RE MISSING THE POINT.
FWOOO
...
...
IN ANY CASE, WE MUST GO THERE.
ぴ
P-CHT
FORGET IT! THERE'S NO WAY I'M GOING OUTSIDE IN THIS WEATHER!
...
...
...
FWOOO

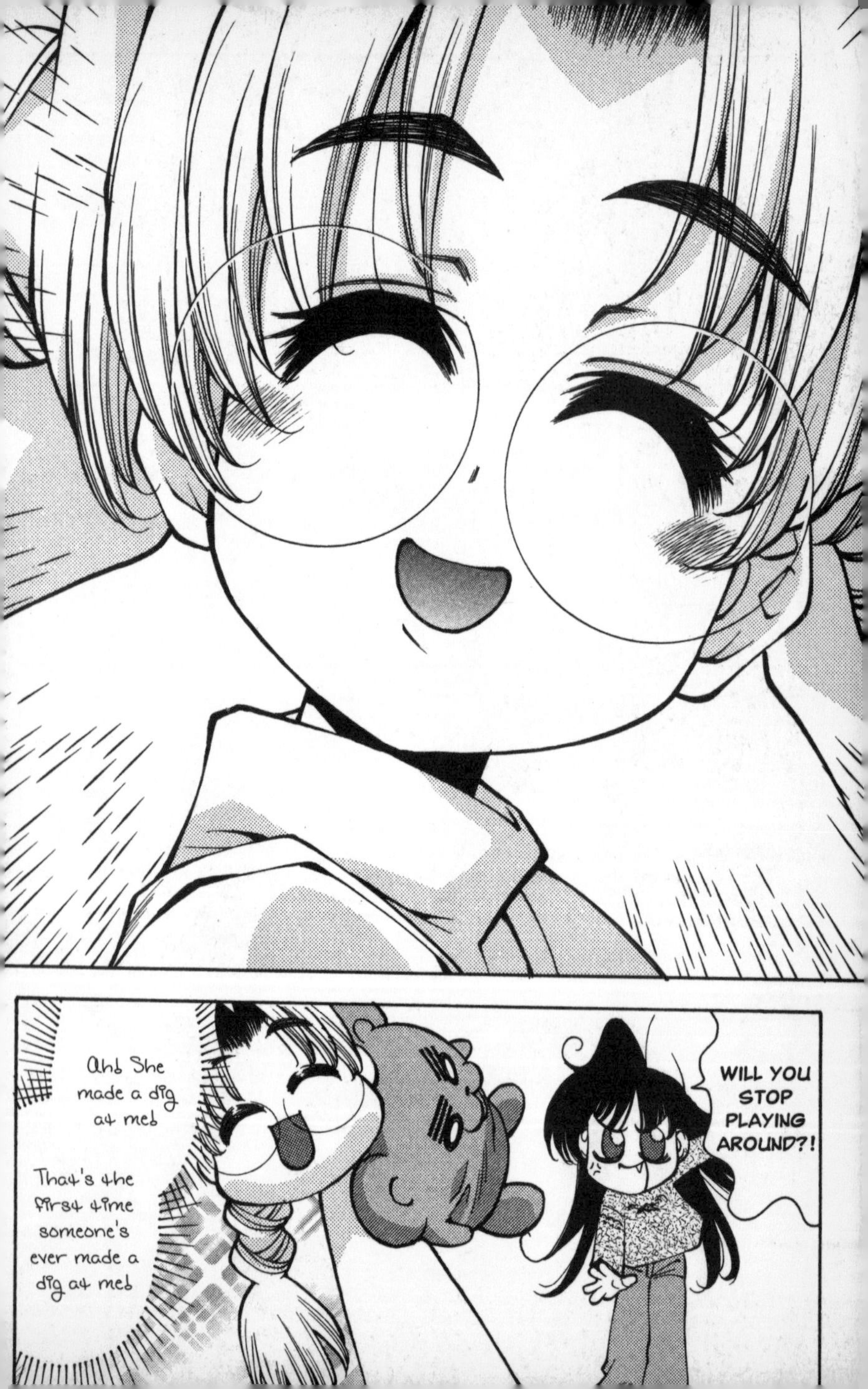

WILL YOU STOP PLAYING AROUND?!
Ah! She made a dig at me!
That's the first time someone's ever made a dig at me!

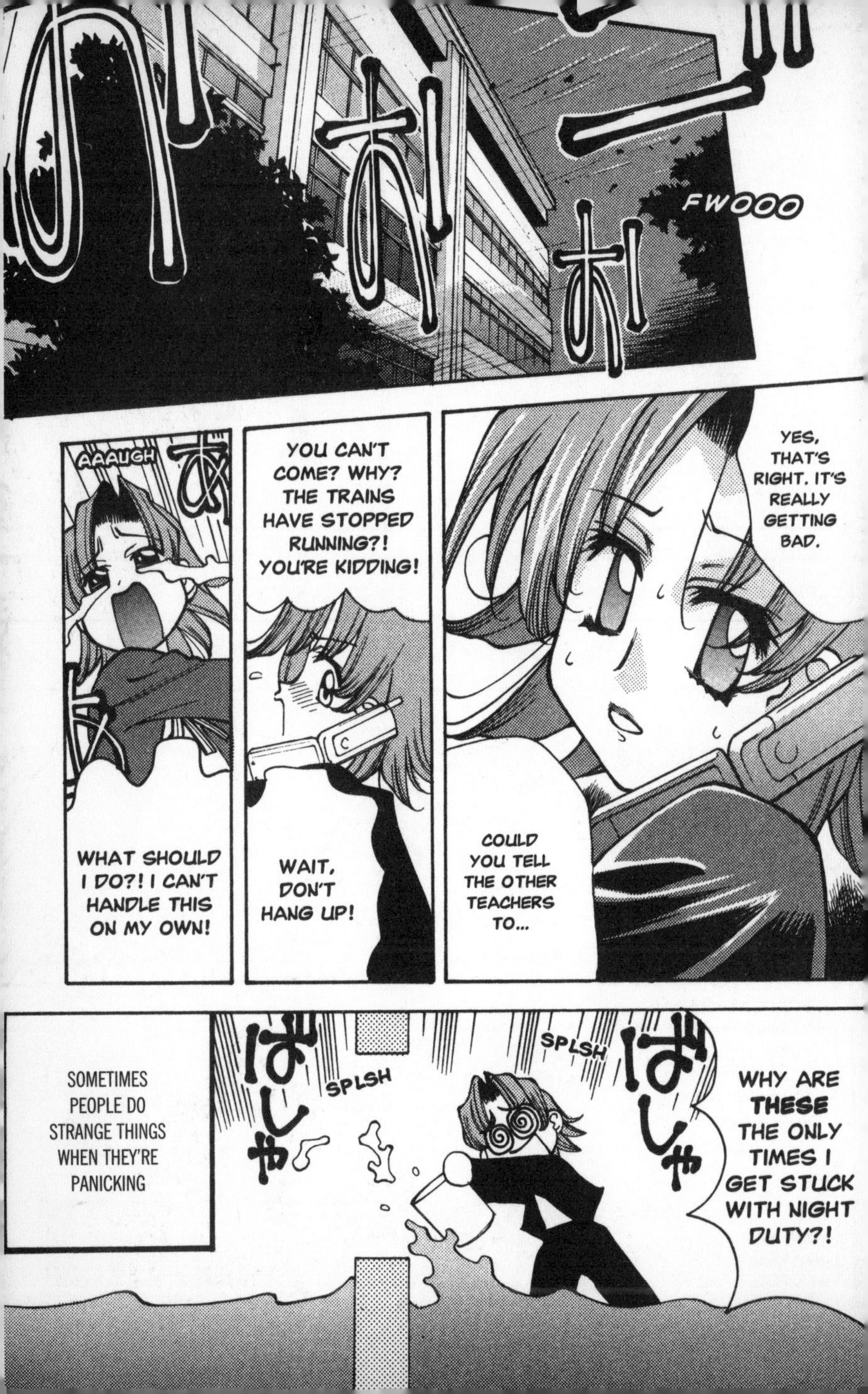
FWOOO
YES, THAT'S RIGHT. IT'S REALLY GETTING BAD.
COULD YOU TELL THE OTHER TEACHERS TO...
YOU CAN'T COME? WHY? THE TRAINS HAVE STOPPED RUNNING?! YOU'RE KIDDING!
WAIT, DON'T HANG UP!
AAAUGH
WHAT SHOULD I DO?! I CAN'T HANDLE THIS ON MY OWN!
WHY ARE **THESE** THE ONLY TIMES I GET STUCK WITH NIGHT DUTY?!
SPLSH
SPLSH
SOMETIMES PEOPLE DO STRANGE THINGS WHEN THEY'RE PANICKING

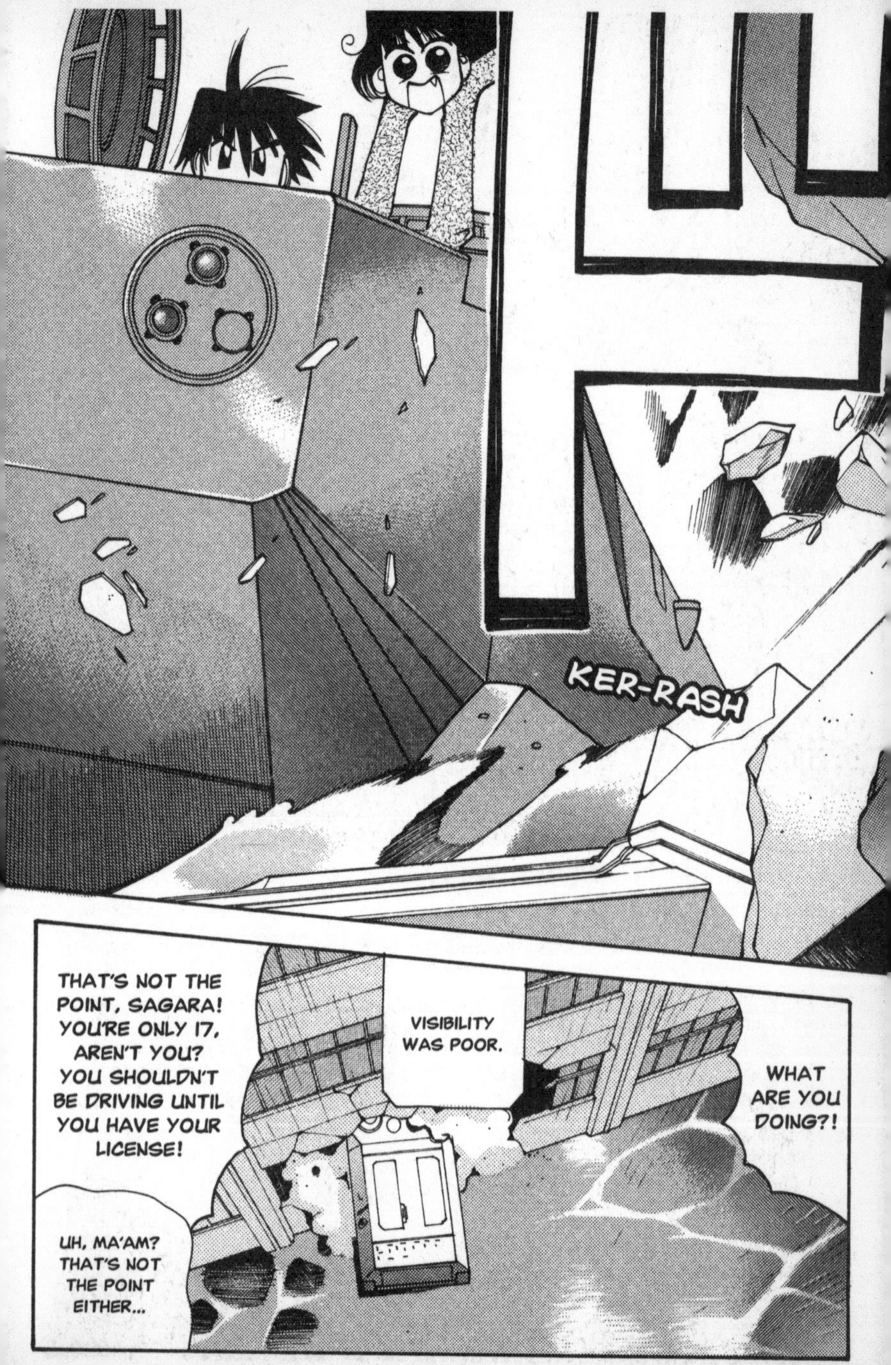
KER-RASH
WHAT ARE YOU DOING?!
VISIBILITY WAS POOR.
THAT'S NOT THE POINT, SAGARA! YOU'RE ONLY 17, AREN'T YOU? YOU SHOULDN'T BE DRIVING UNTIL YOU HAVE YOUR LICENSE!
UH, MA'AM? THAT'S NOT THE POINT EITHER...

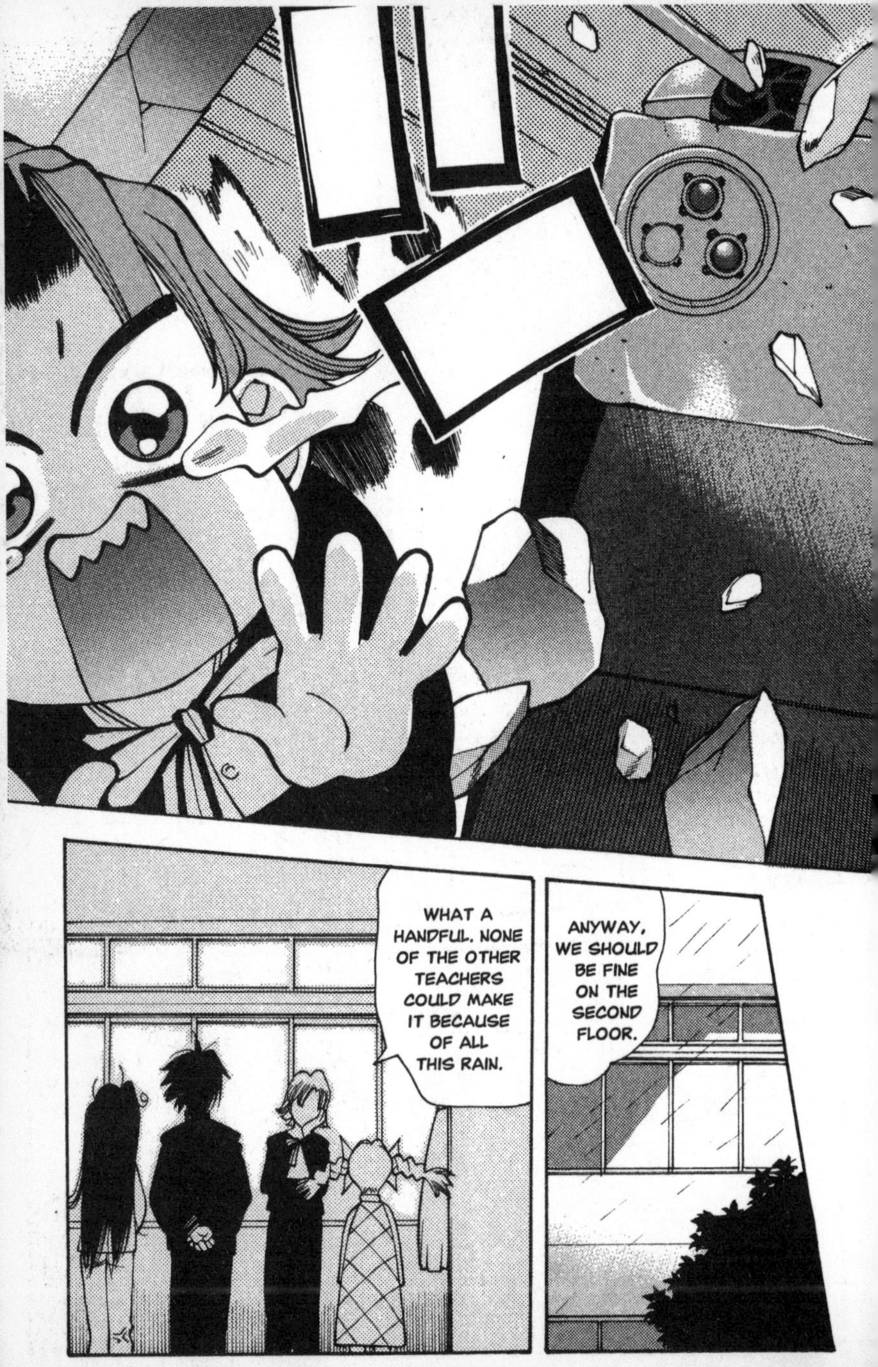
ANYWAY, WE SHOULD BE FINE ON THE SECOND FLOOR.
WHAT A HANDFUL. NONE OF THE OTHER TEACHERS COULD MAKE IT BECAUSE OF ALL THIS RAIN.

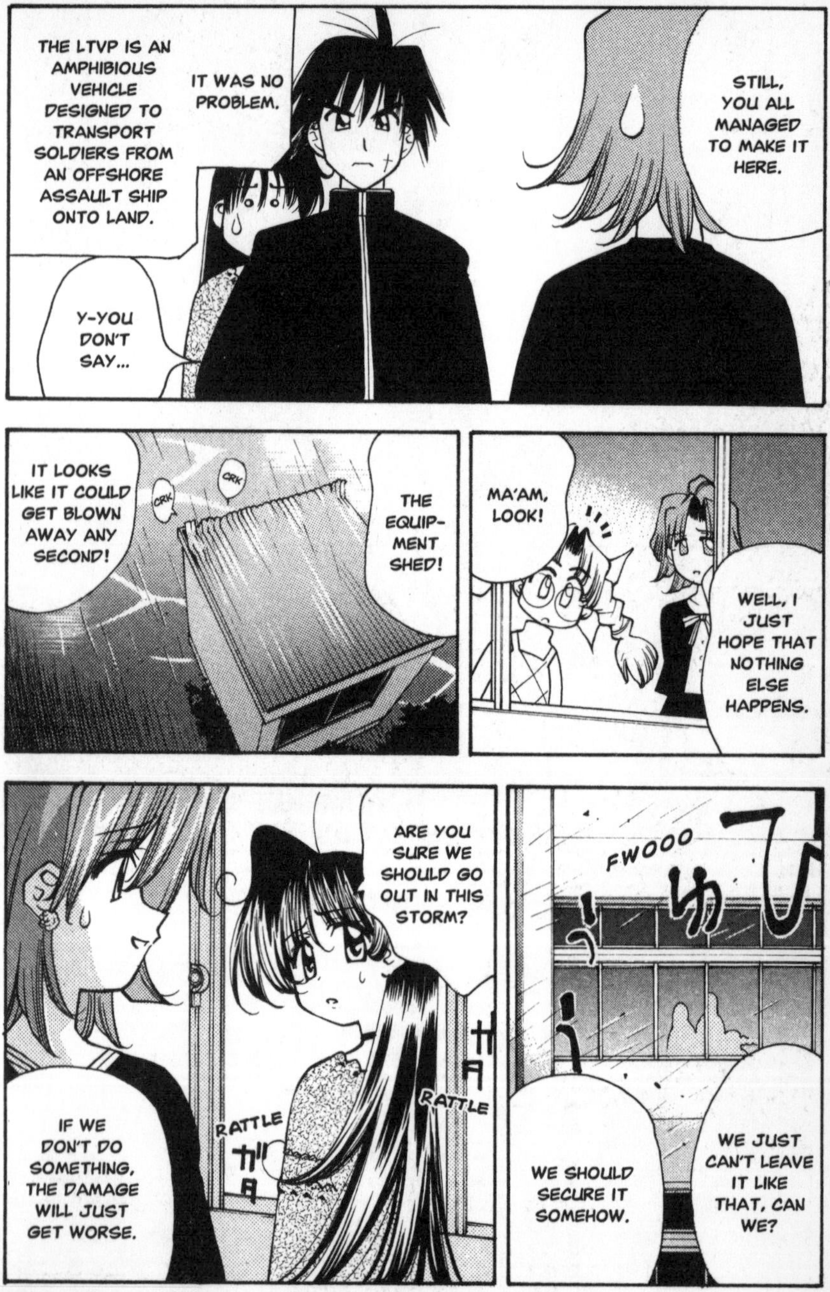
STILL, YOU ALL MANAGED TO MAKE IT HERE.
IT WAS NO PROBLEM.
THE LTVP IS AN AMPHIBIOUS VEHICLE DESIGNED TO TRANSPORT SOLDIERS FROM AN OFFSHORE ASSAULT SHIP ONTO LAND.
Y-YOU DON'T SAY...
WELL, I JUST HOPE THAT NOTHING ELSE HAPPENS.
MA'AM, LOOK!
THE EQUIPMENT SHED!
CRK
CRK
IT LOOKS LIKE IT COULD GET BLOWN AWAY ANY SECOND!
FWOOO
WE JUST CAN'T LEAVE IT LIKE THAT, CAN WE?
WE SHOULD SECURE IT SOMEHOW.
ARE YOU SURE WE SHOULD GO OUT IN THIS STORM?
RATTLE
RATTLE
IF WE DON'T DO SOMETHING, THE DAMAGE WILL JUST GET WORSE.

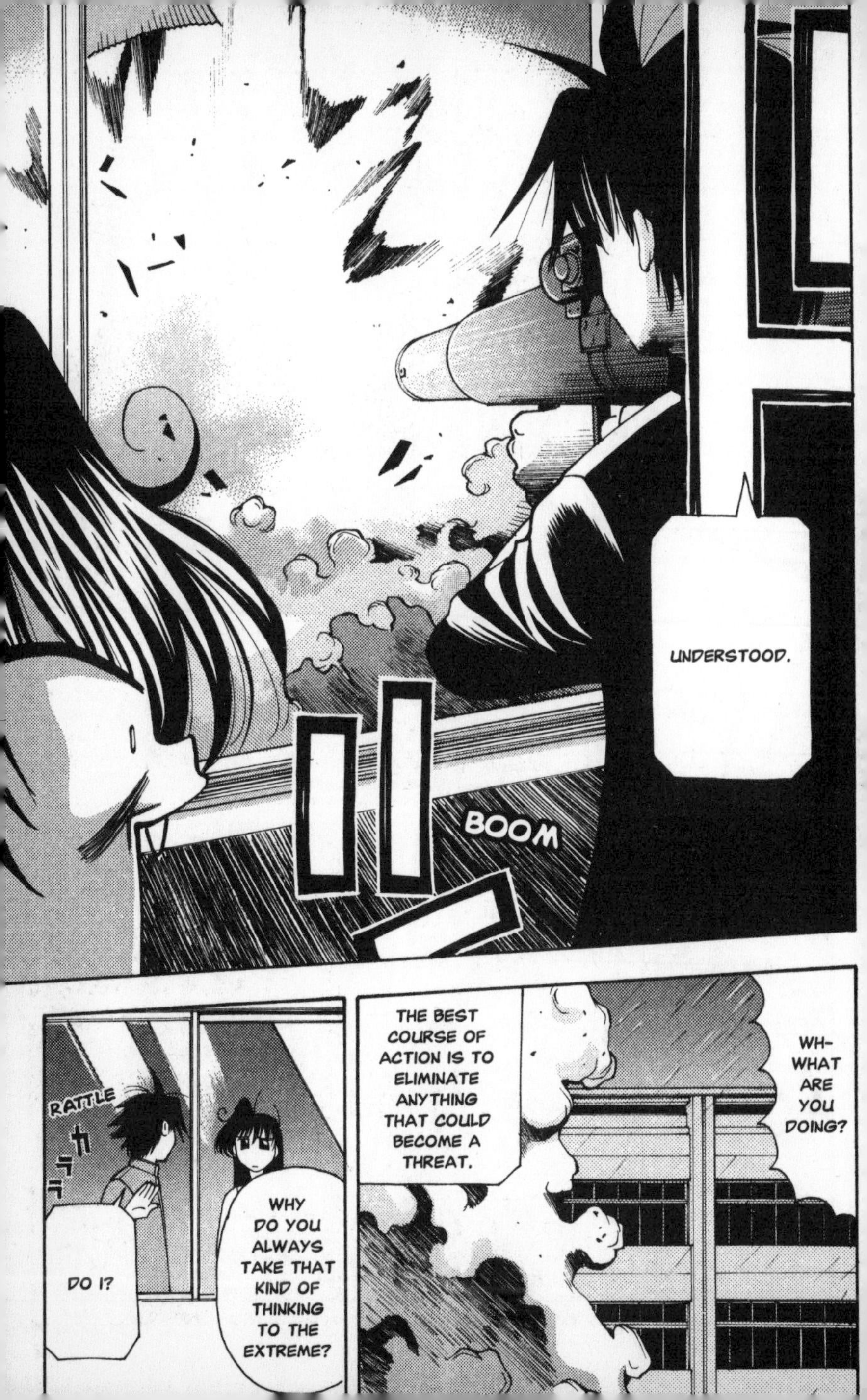

UNDERSTOOD.
BOOM
WH- WHAT ARE YOU DOING?
THE BEST COURSE OF ACTION IS TO ELIMINATE ANYTHING THAT COULD BECOME A THREAT.
RATTLE
カララ
WHY DO YOU ALWAYS TAKE THAT KIND OF THINKING TO THE EXTREME?
DO I?

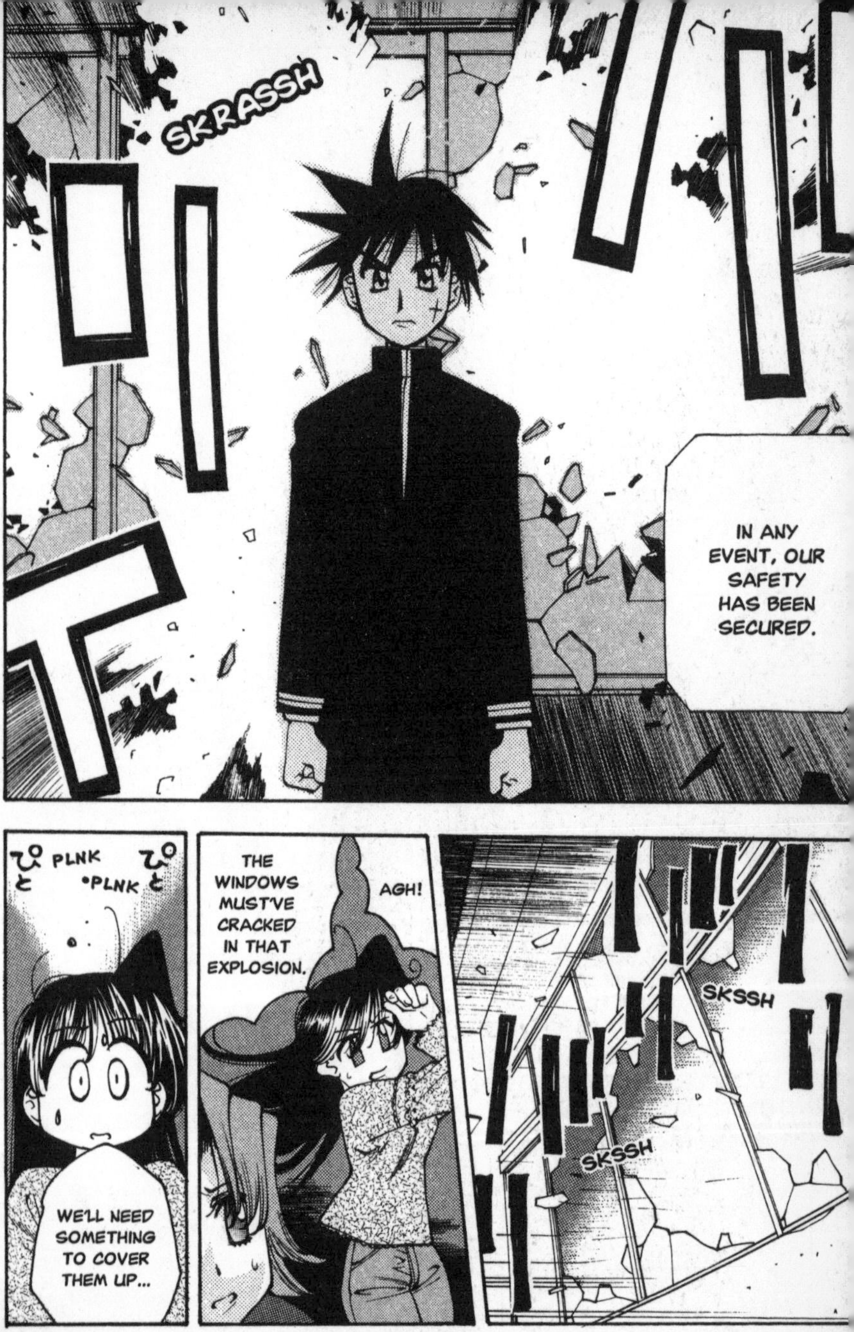
SKRASSH
IN ANY EVENT, OUR SAFETY HAS BEEN SECURED.
SKSSH
SKSSH
AGH!
THE WINDOWS MUST'VE CRACKED IN THAT EXPLOSION.
ぴと PLNK
ぴと •PLNK
WE'LL NEED SOMETHING TO COVER THEM UP...

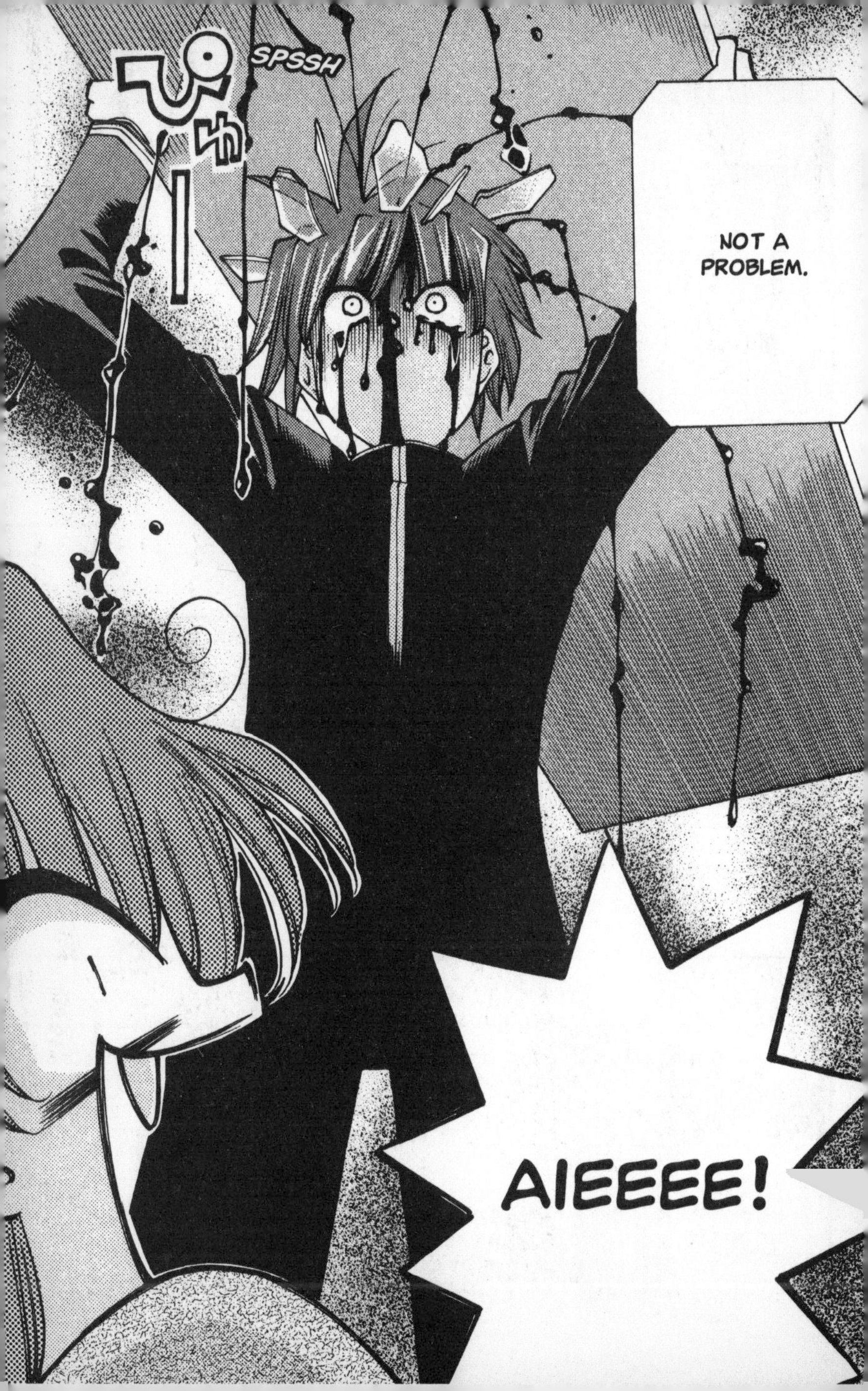
NOT A PROBLEM.
ぴゅー
SPSSH
AIEEEE!

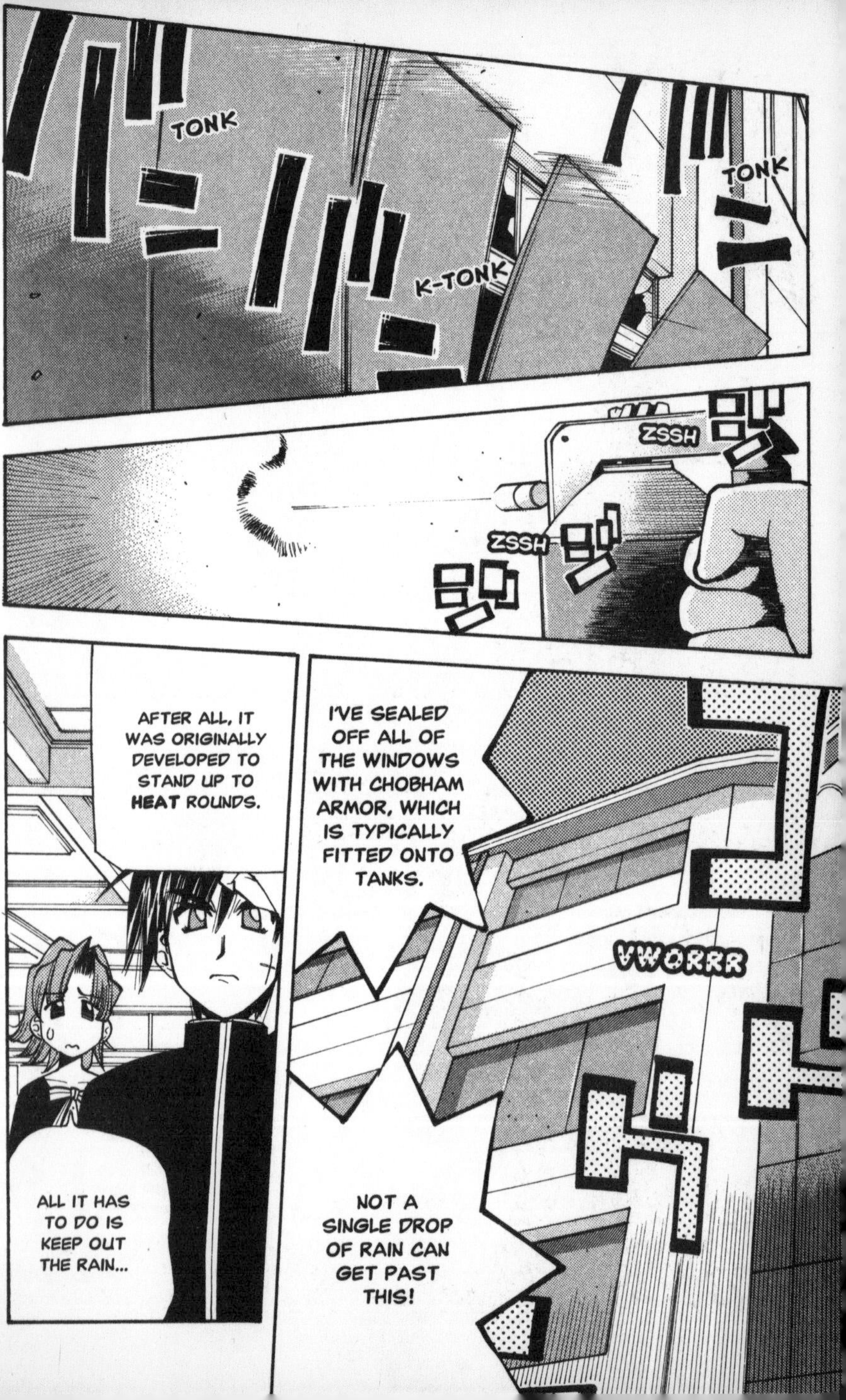
TONK
K-TONK
TONK
ZSSH
ZSSH
I'VE SEALED OFF ALL OF THE WINDOWS WITH CHOBHAM ARMOR, WHICH IS TYPICALLY FITTED ONTO TANKS.
VWORRR
NOT A SINGLE DROP OF RAIN CAN GET PAST THIS!
AFTER ALL, IT WAS ORIGINALLY DEVELOPED TO STAND UP TO HEAT ROUNDS.
ALL IT HAS TO DO IS KEEP OUT THE RAIN...

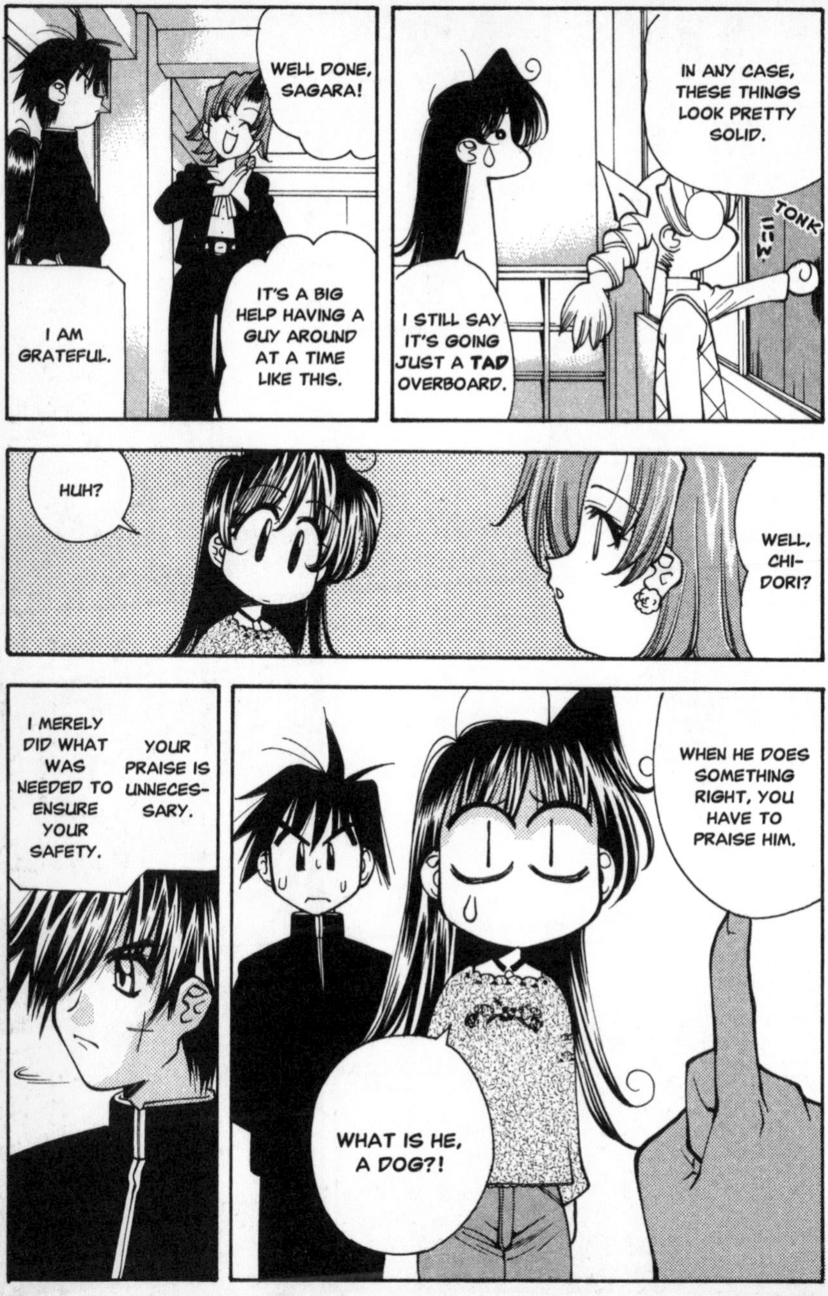
WELL DONE, SAGARA!
IT'S A BIG HELP HAVING A GUY AROUND AT A TIME LIKE THIS.
I AM GRATEFUL.
IN ANY CASE, THESE THINGS LOOK PRETTY SOLID.
TONK
I STILL SAY IT'S GOING JUST A **TAD** OVERBOARD.
WELL, CHI-DORI?
HUH?
WHEN HE DOES SOMETHING RIGHT, YOU HAVE TO PRAISE HIM.
I MERELY DID WHAT WAS NEEDED TO ENSURE YOUR SAFETY.
YOUR PRAISE IS UNNECES-SARY.
WHAT IS HE, A DOG?!

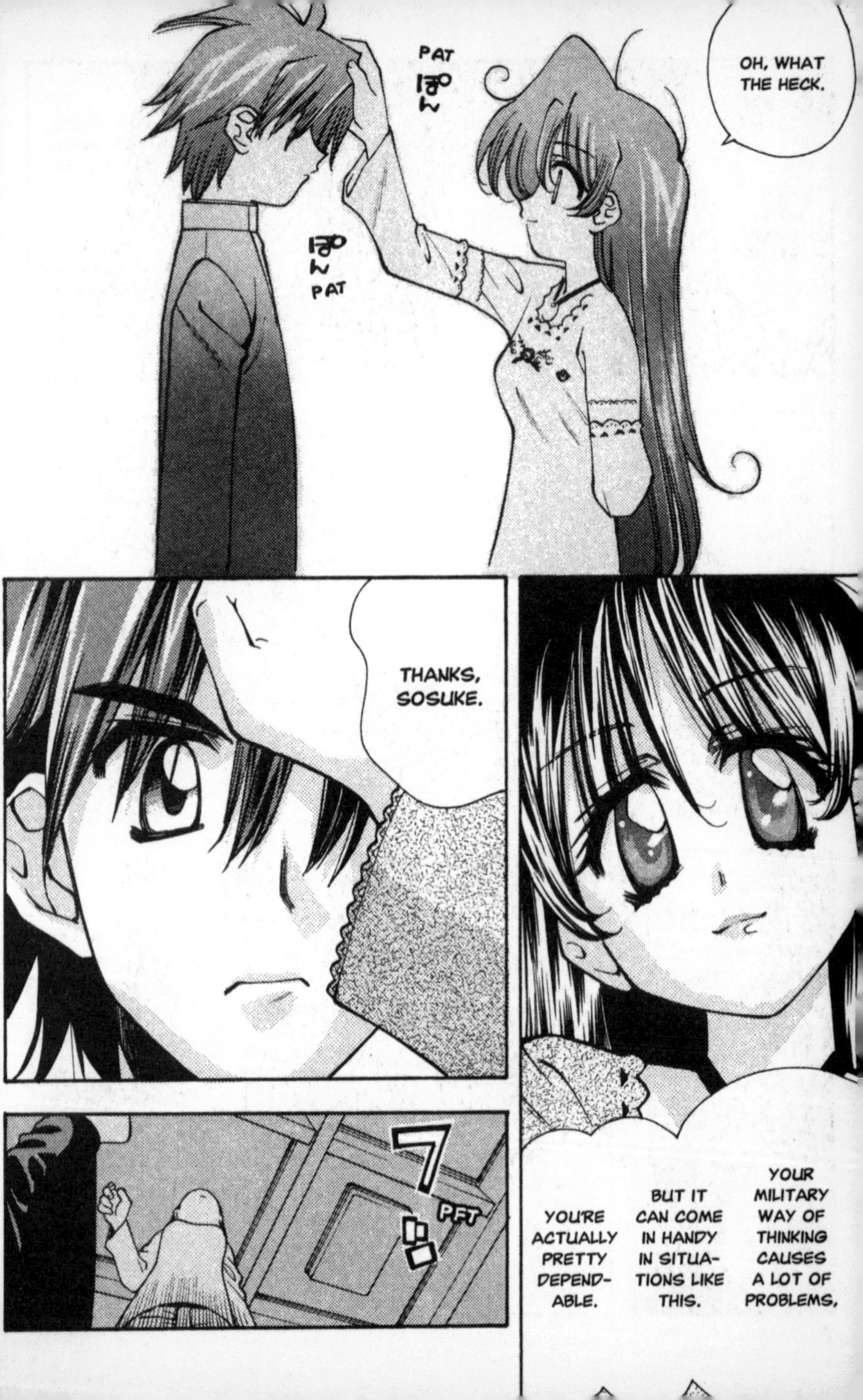

OH, WHAT THE HECK.
PAT
ぽん
ぽん
PAT
THANKS, SOSUKE.
YOUR MILITARY WAY OF THINKING CAUSES A LOT OF PROBLEMS,
BUT IT CAN COME IN HANDY IN SITUATIONS LIKE THIS.
YOU'RE ACTUALLY PRETTY DEPENDABLE.
PFT

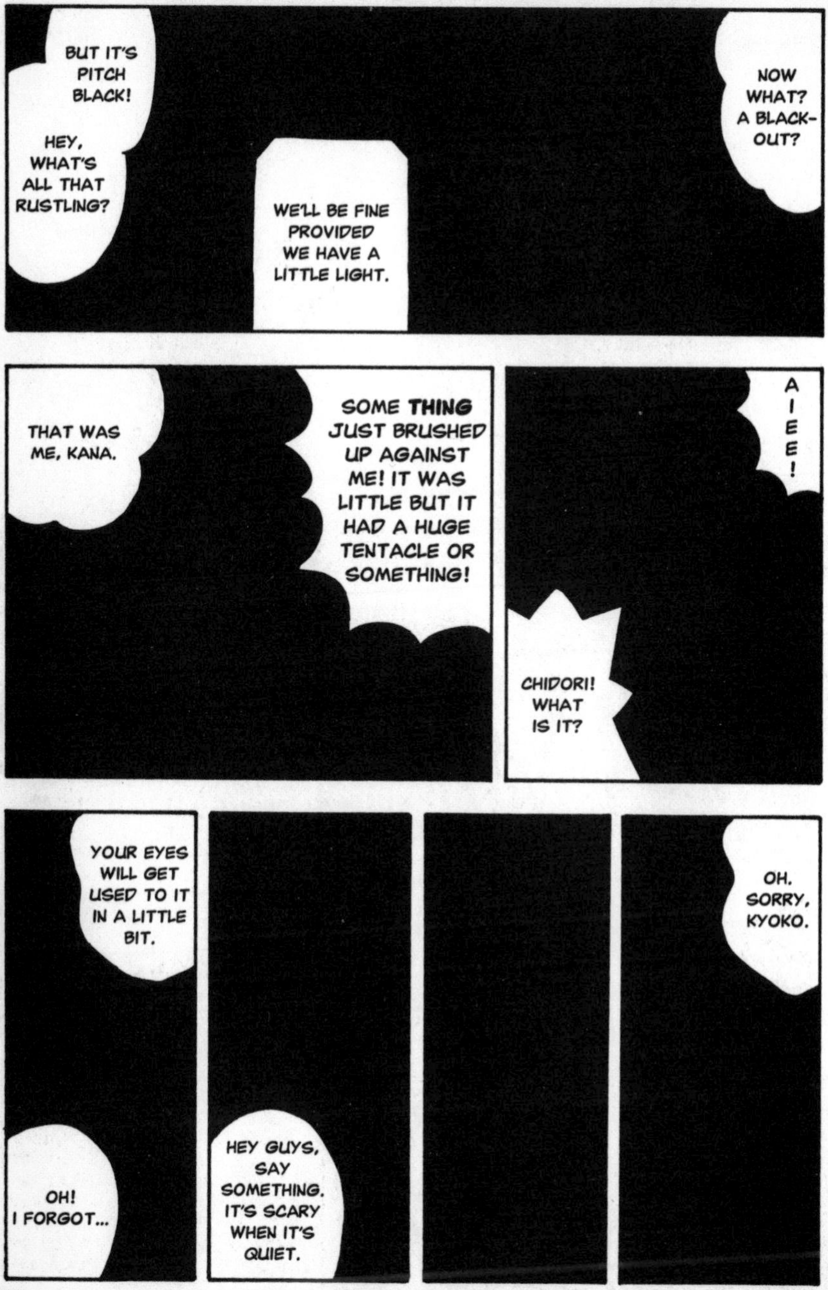
NOW WHAT? A BLACK-OUT?
WE'LL BE FINE PROVIDED WE HAVE A LITTLE LIGHT.
BUT IT'S PITCH BLACK!
HEY, WHAT'S ALL THAT RUSTLING?
AIEE!
CHIDORI! WHAT IS IT?
SOME **THING** JUST BRUSHED UP AGAINST ME! IT WAS LITTLE BUT IT HAD A HUGE TENTACLE OR SOMETHING!
THAT WAS ME, KANA.
OH. SORRY, KYOKO.
HEY GUYS, SAY SOMETHING. IT'S SCARY WHEN IT'S QUIET.
YOUR EYES WILL GET USED TO IT IN A LITTLE BIT.
OH! I FORGOT...

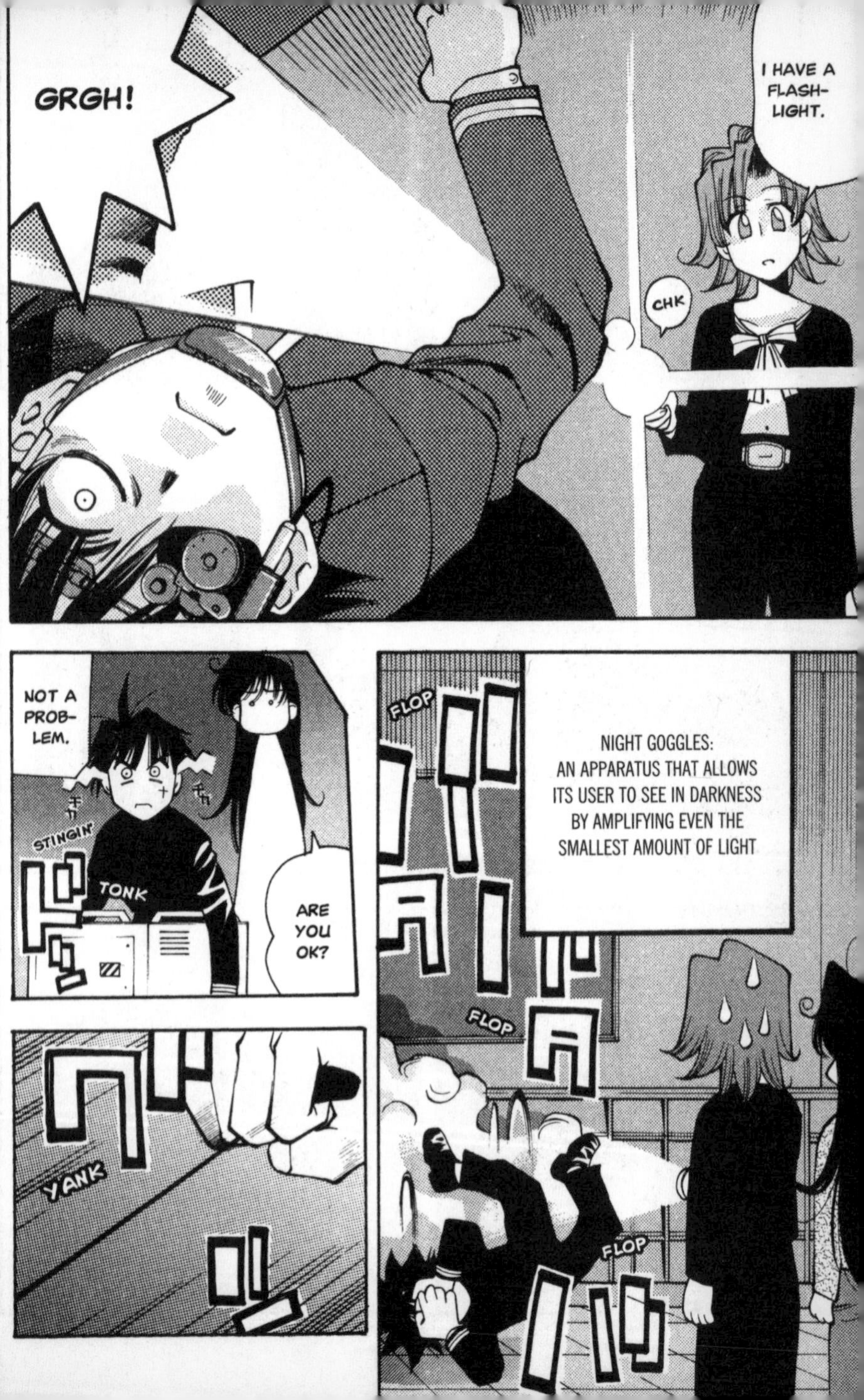
I HAVE A FLASH-LIGHT.
CHK
GRGH!
NIGHT GOGGLES:
AN APPARATUS THAT ALLOWS ITS USER TO SEE IN DARKNESS BY AMPLIFYING EVEN THE SMALLEST AMOUNT OF LIGHT
FLOP
FLOP
FLOP
ARE YOU OK?
NOT A PROB-LEM.
STINGIN'
TONK
YANK

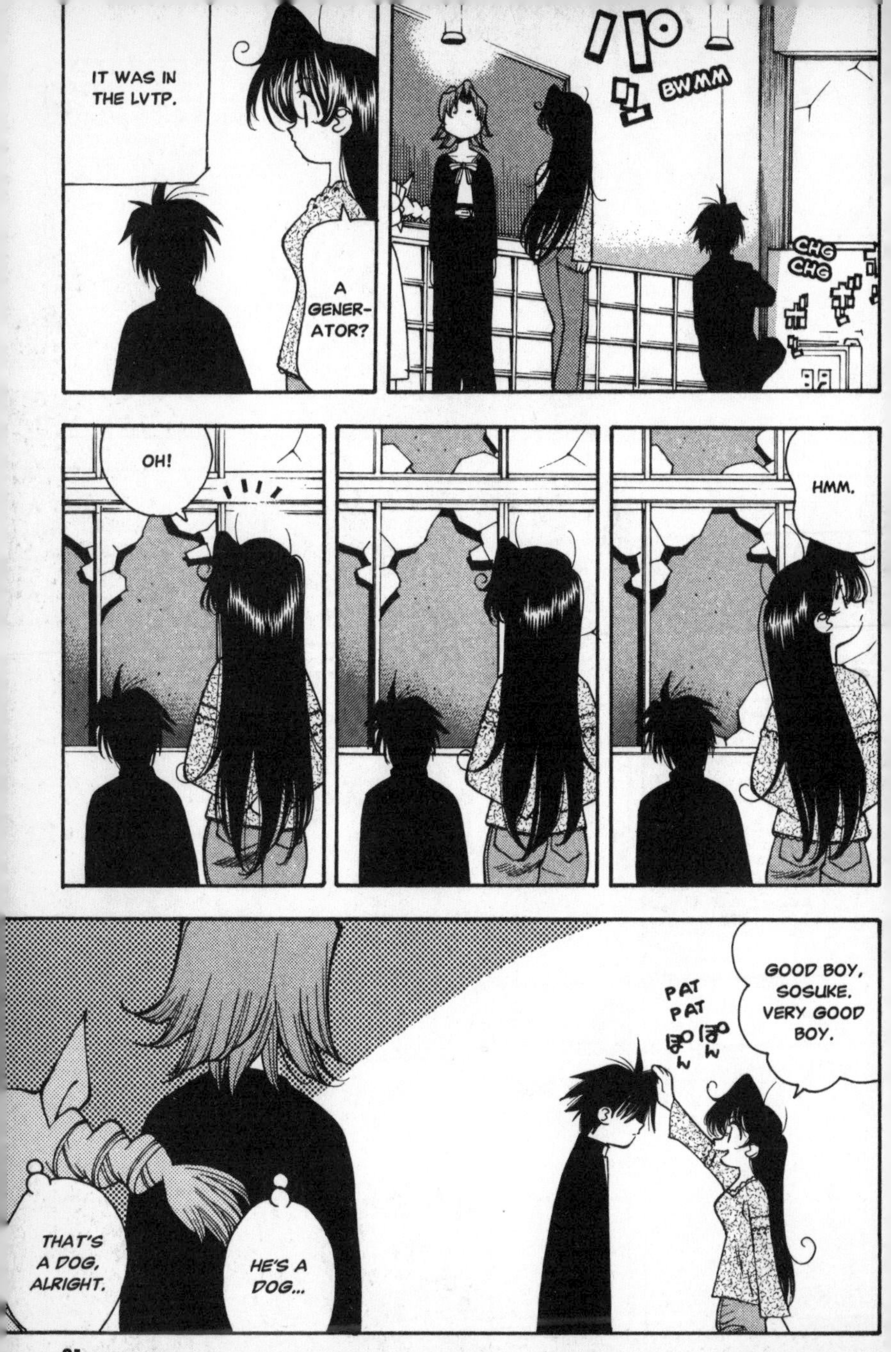
IT WAS IN THE LVTP.
A GENERATOR?
BWMM
CHG CHG
OH!
HMM.
GOOD BOY, SOSUKE. VERY GOOD BOY.
PAT PAT
HE'S A DOG...
THAT'S A DOG, ALRIGHT.

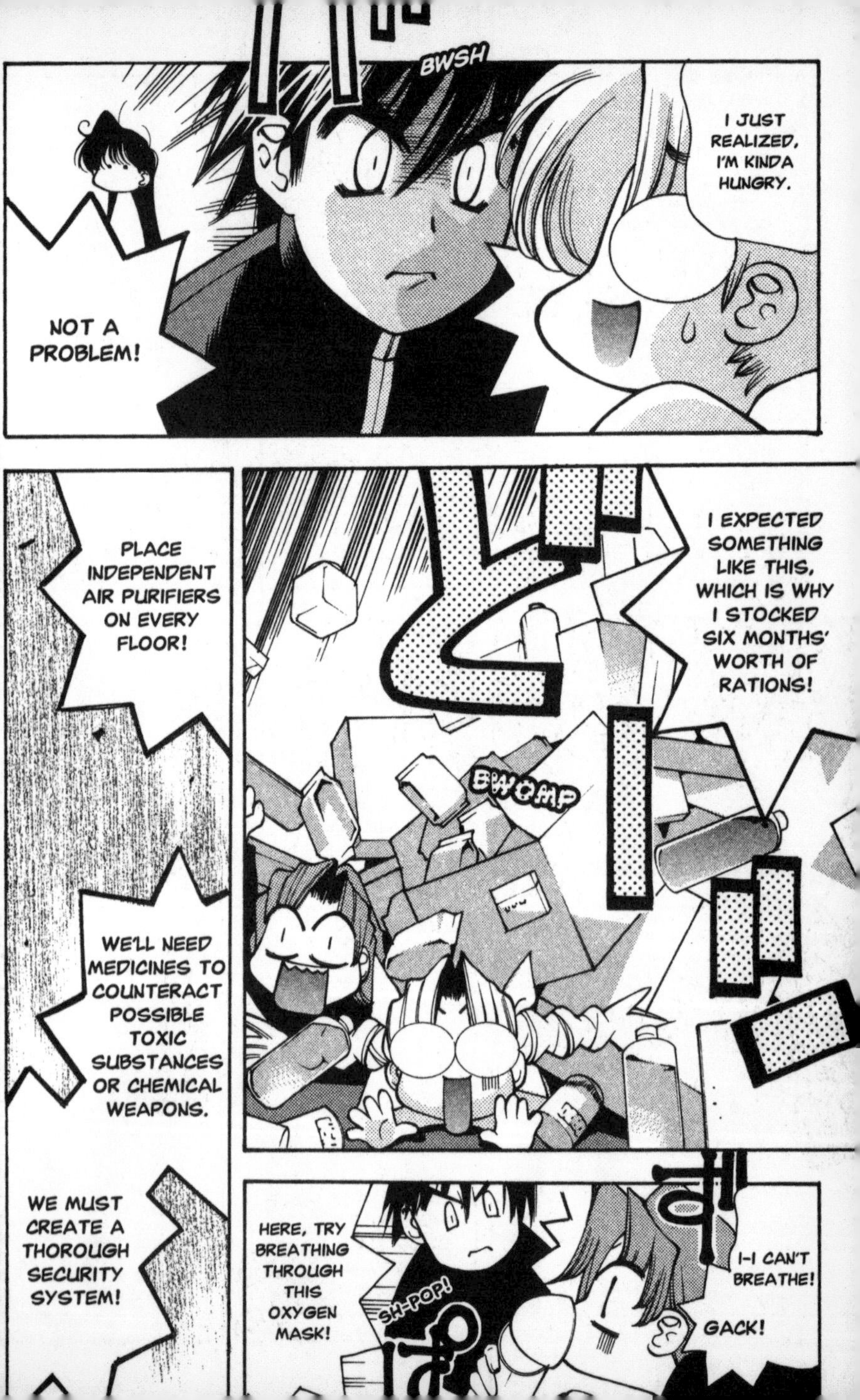
BWSH
I JUST REALIZED, I'M KINDA HUNGRY.
NOT A PROBLEM!
I EXPECTED SOMETHING LIKE THIS, WHICH IS WHY I STOCKED SIX MONTHS' WORTH OF RATIONS!
BWOMP
PLACE INDEPENDENT AIR PURIFIERS ON EVERY FLOOR!
WE'LL NEED MEDICINES TO COUNTERACT POSSIBLE TOXIC SUBSTANCES OR CHEMICAL WEAPONS.
I-I CAN'T BREATHE!
GACK!
HERE, TRY BREATHING THROUGH THIS OXYGEN MASK!
SH-POP!
WE MUST CREATE A THOROUGH SECURITY SYSTEM!

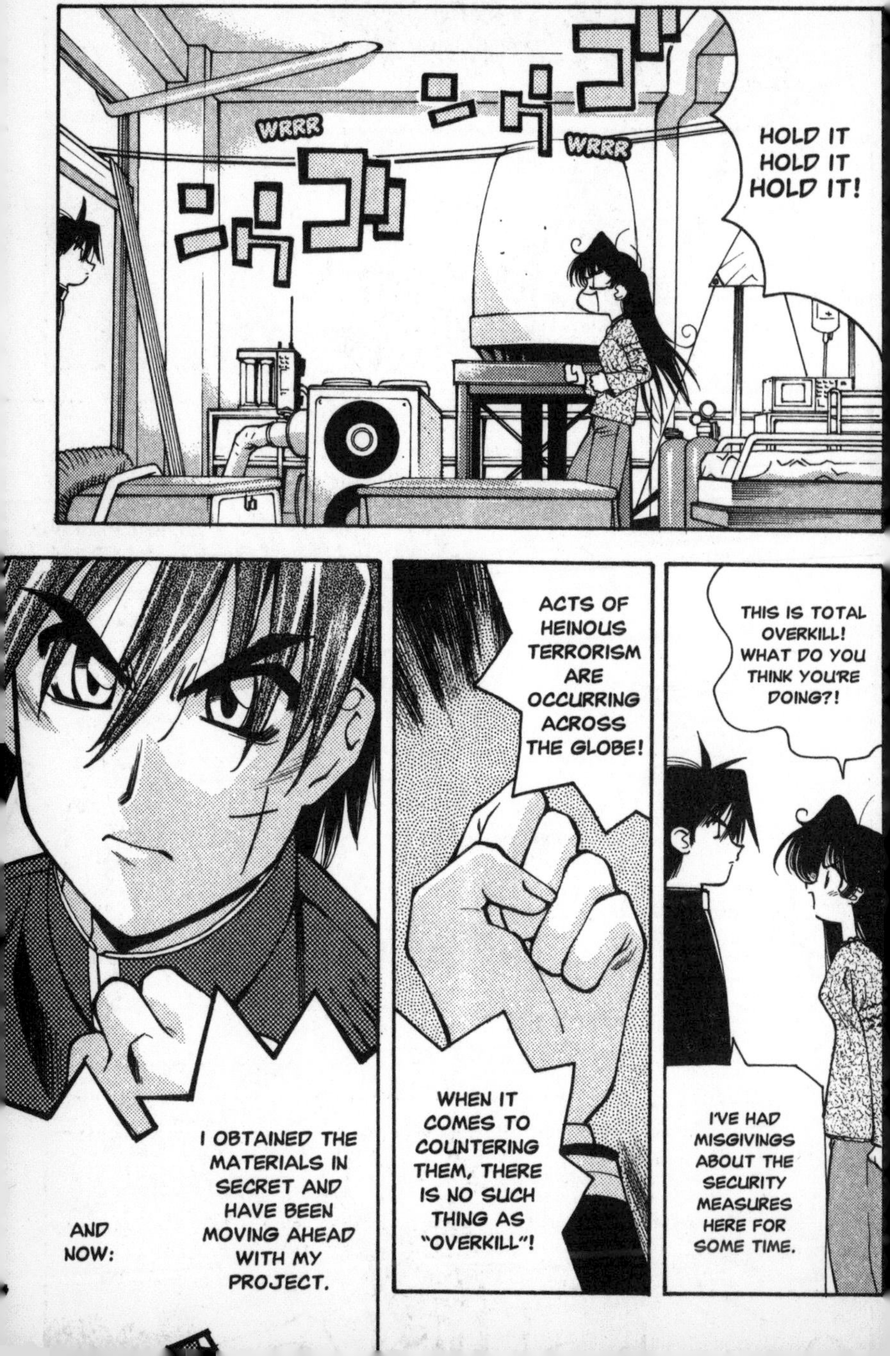
HOLD IT HOLD IT HOLD IT!
WRRR
WRRR
THIS IS TOTAL OVERKILL! WHAT DO YOU THINK YOU'RE DOING?!
I'VE HAD MISGIVINGS ABOUT THE SECURITY MEASURES HERE FOR SOME TIME.
ACTS OF HEINOUS TERRORISM ARE OCCURRING ACROSS THE GLOBE!
WHEN IT COMES TO COUNTERING THEM, THERE IS NO SUCH THING AS "OVERKILL"!
I OBTAINED THE MATERIALS IN SECRET AND HAVE BEEN MOVING AHEAD WITH MY PROJECT.
AND NOW:

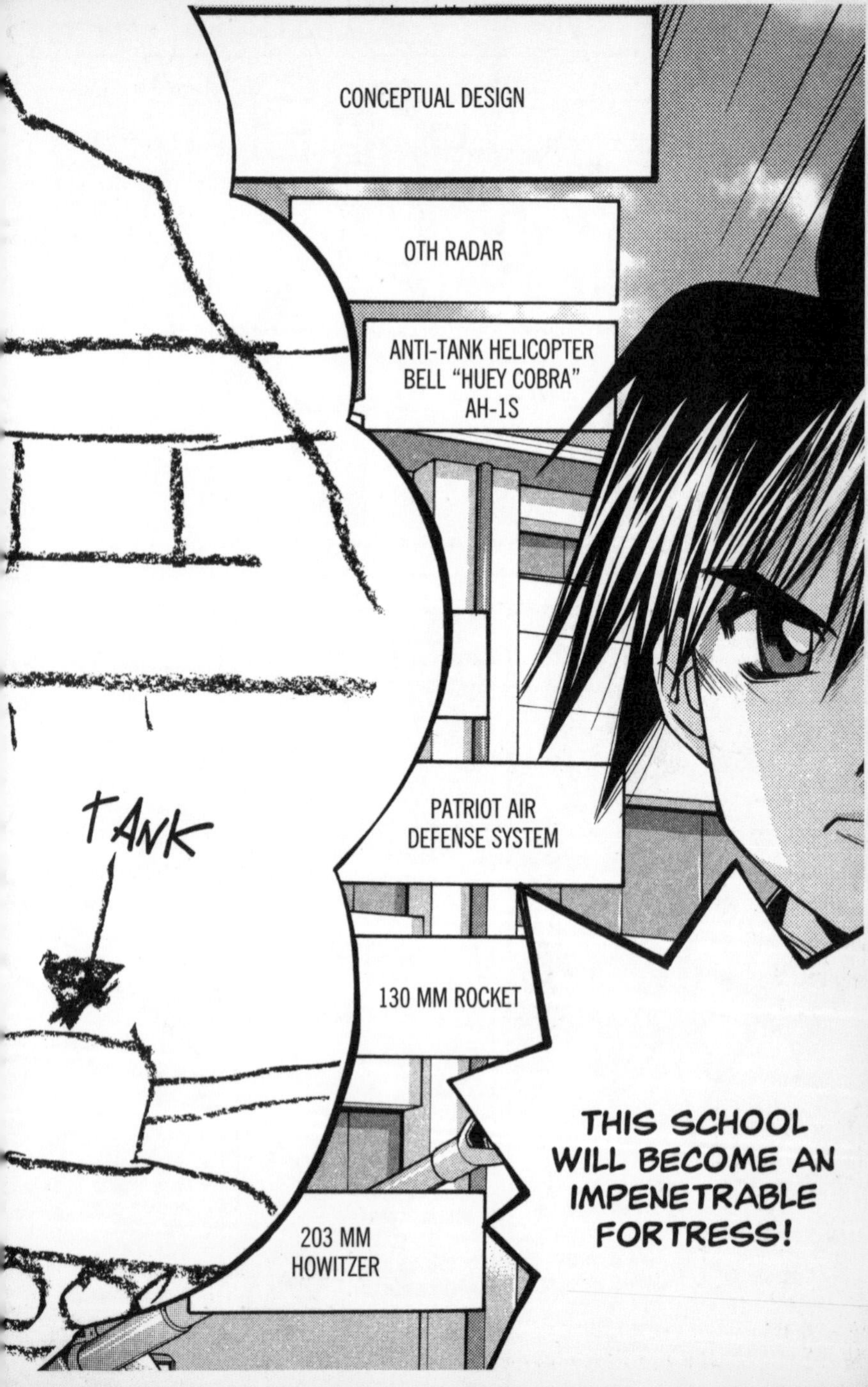
CONCEPTUAL DESIGN
OTH RADAR
ANTI-TANK HELICOPTER BELL "HUEY COBRA" AH-1S
TANK
PATRIOT AIR DEFENSE SYSTEM
130 MM ROCKET
THIS SCHOOL WILL BECOME AN IMPENETRABLE FORTRESS!
203 MM HOWITZER

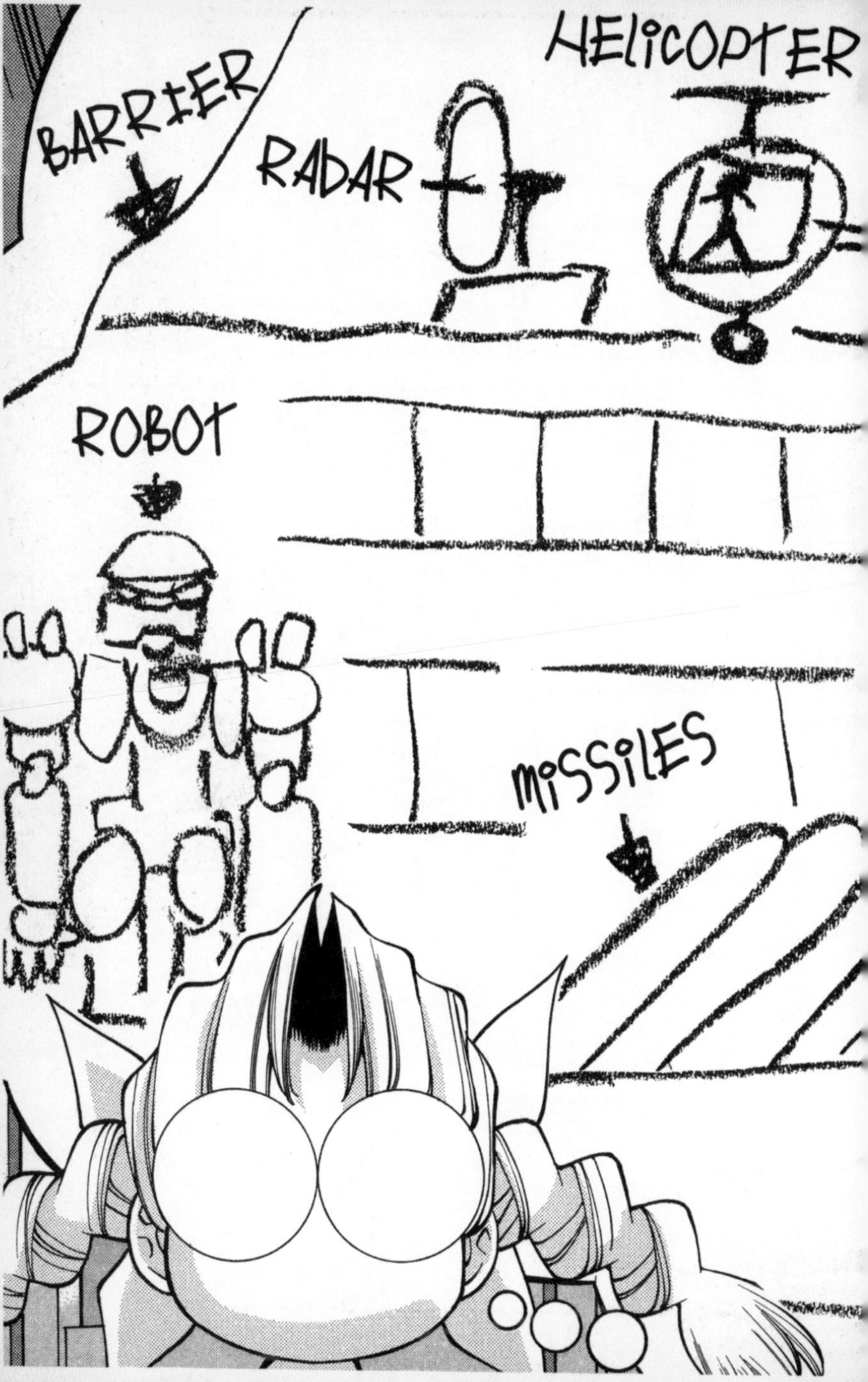
BARRIER
RADAR
HELICOPTER
ROBOT
MISSILES

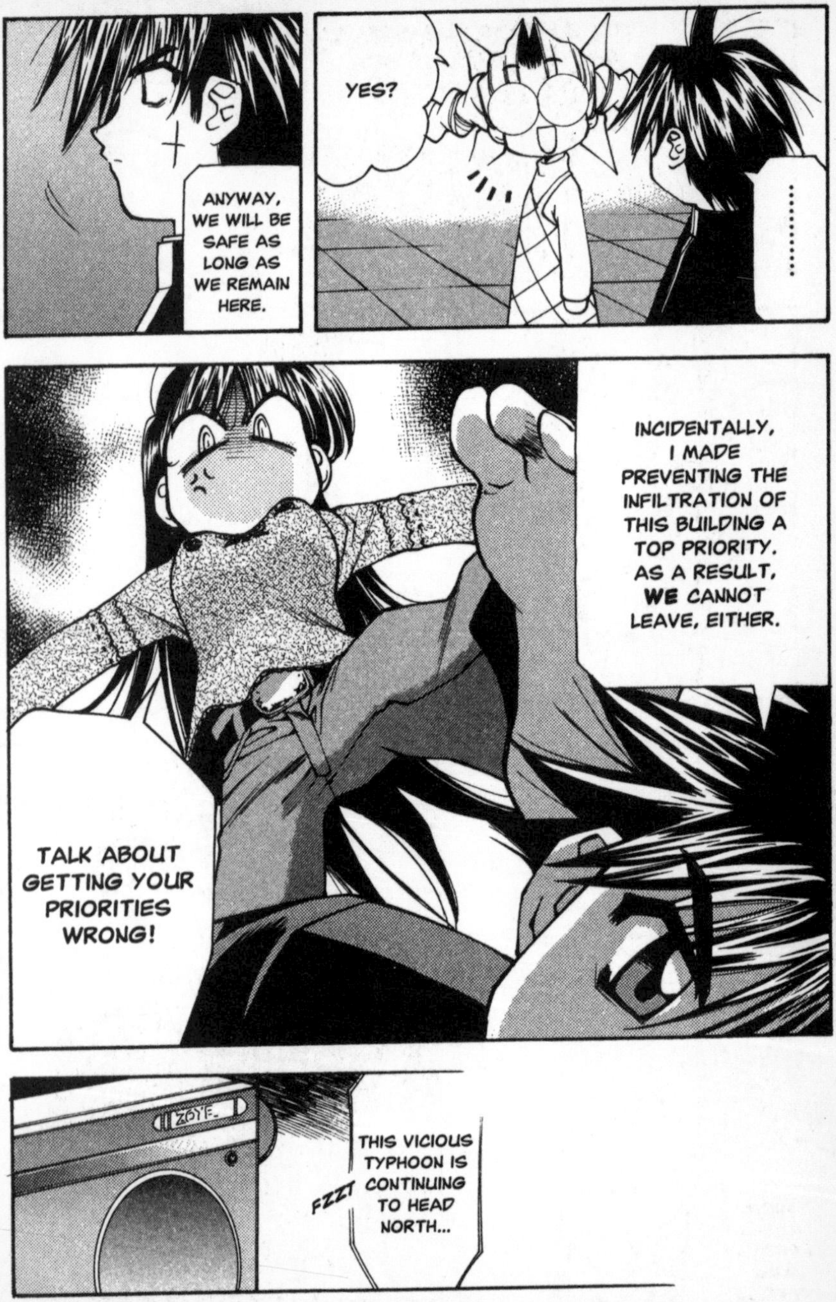

......
YES?
ANYWAY, WE WILL BE SAFE AS LONG AS WE REMAIN HERE.
INCIDENTALLY, I MADE PREVENTING THE INFILTRATION OF THIS BUILDING A TOP PRIORITY. AS A RESULT, **WE** CANNOT LEAVE, EITHER.
TALK ABOUT GETTING YOUR PRIORITIES WRONG!
THIS VICIOUS TYPHOON IS CONTINUING TO HEAD NORTH...
FZZT

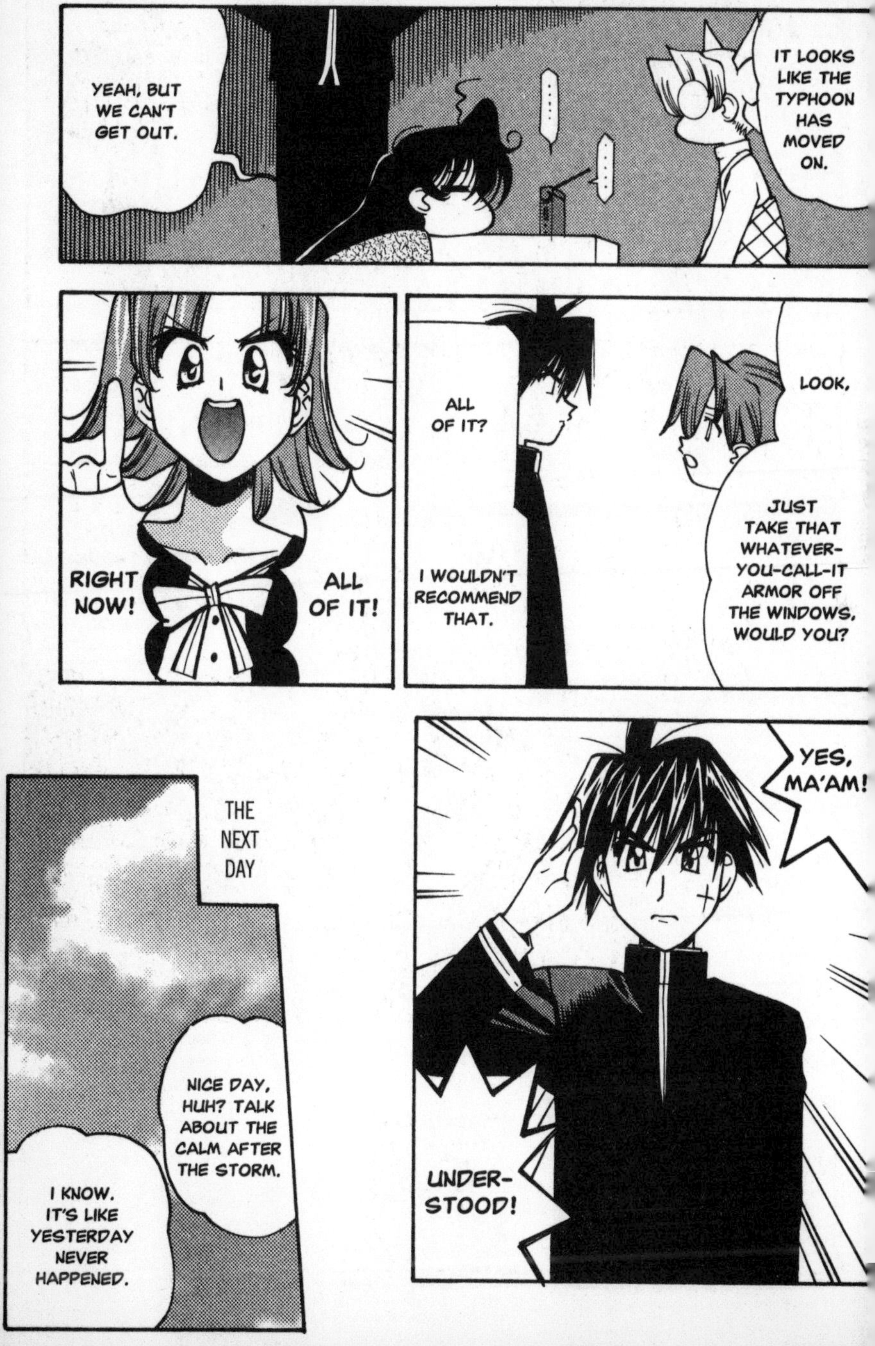
IT LOOKS LIKE THE TYPHOON HAS MOVED ON.
...
...
YEAH, BUT WE CAN'T GET OUT.
LOOK,
JUST TAKE THAT WHATEVER-YOU-CALL-IT ARMOR OFF THE WINDOWS, WOULD YOU?
ALL OF IT?
I WOULDN'T RECOMMEND THAT.
ALL OF IT!
RIGHT NOW!
YES, MA'AM!
UNDER-STOOD!
THE NEXT DAY
NICE DAY, HUH? TALK ABOUT THE CALM AFTER THE STORM.
I KNOW. IT'S LIKE YESTERDAY NEVER HAPPENED.

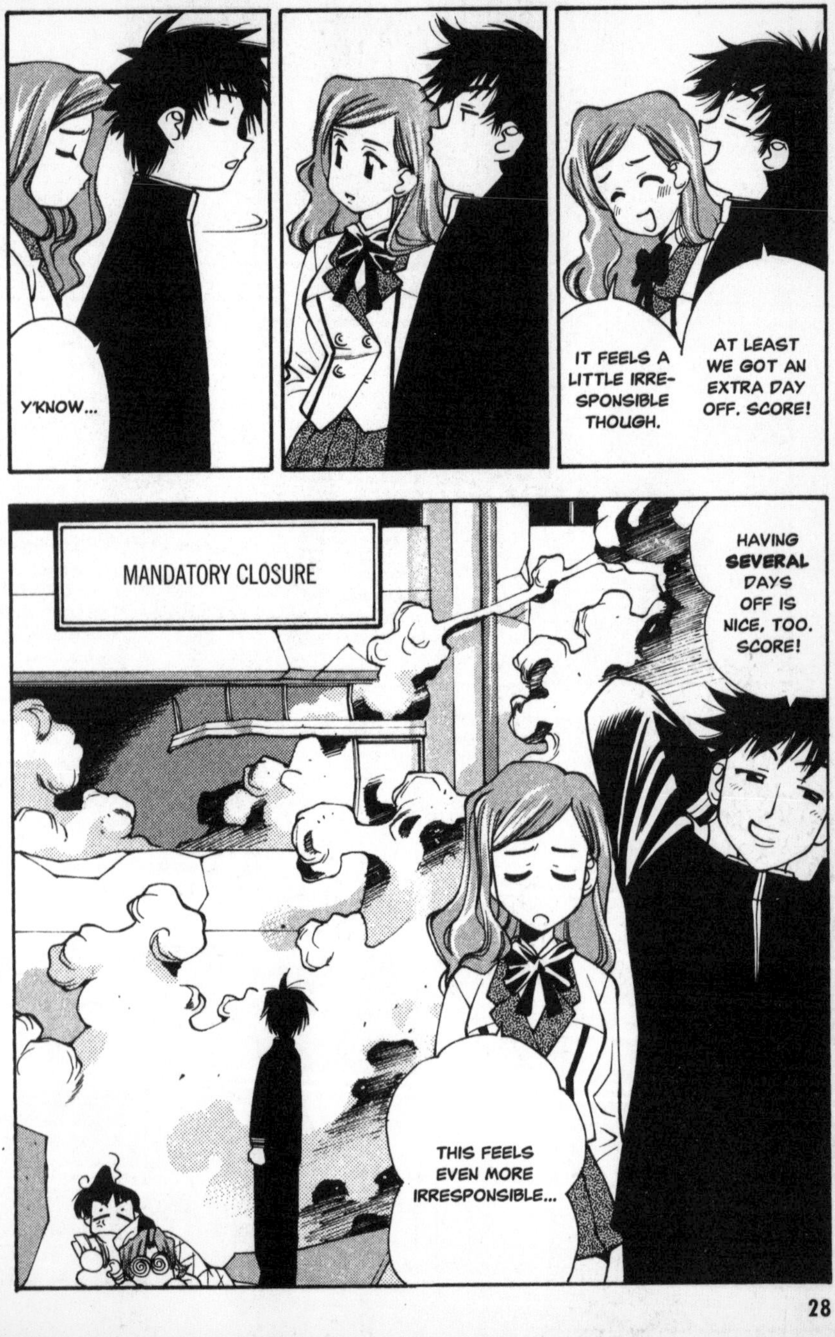

Y'KNOW...
IT FEELS A LITTLE IRRE-SPONSIBLE THOUGH.
AT LEAST WE GOT AN EXTRA DAY OFF. SCORE!
MANDATORY CLOSURE
HAVING SEVERAL DAYS OFF IS NICE, TOO. SCORE!
THIS FEELS EVEN MORE IRRESPONSIBLE...

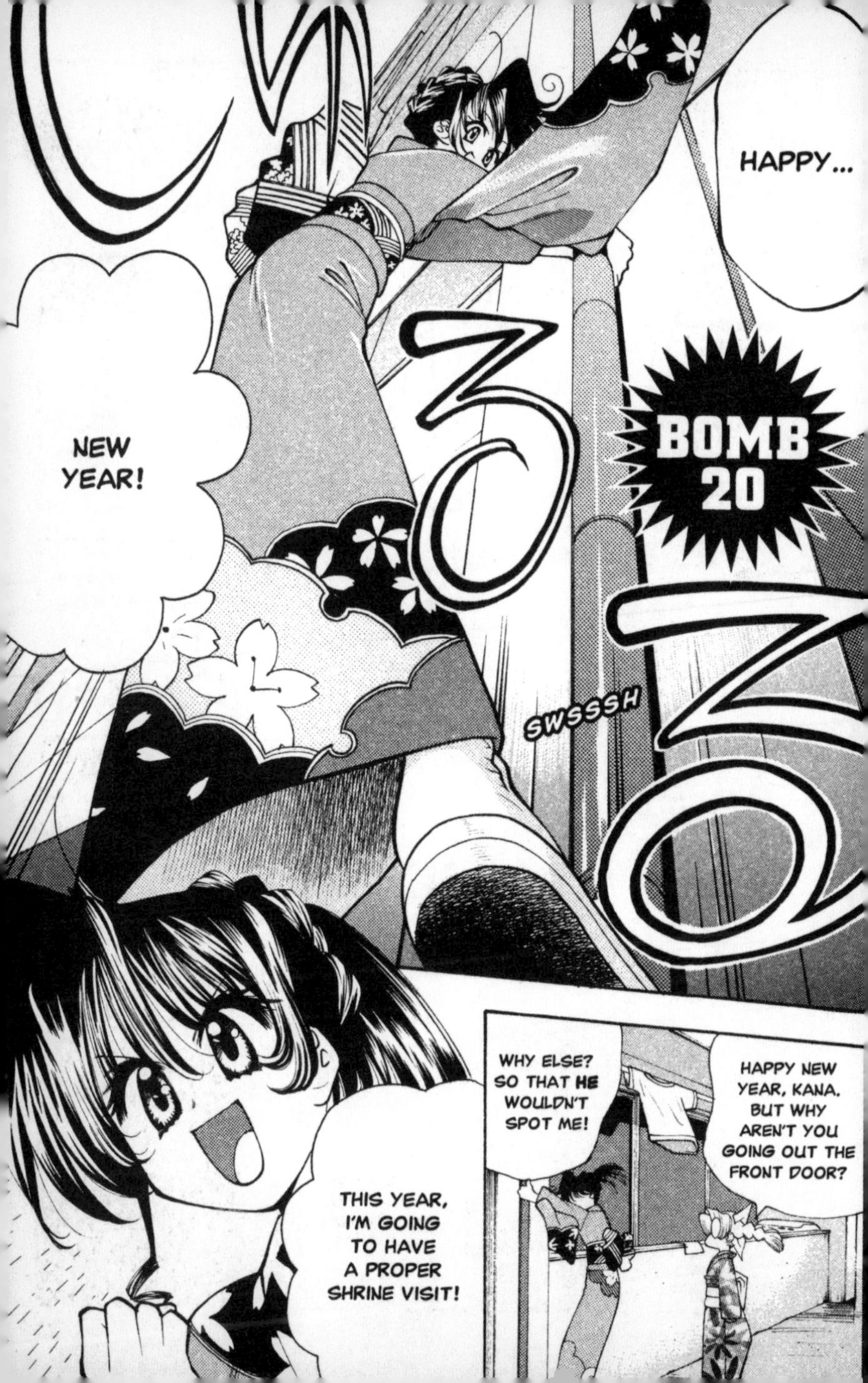
HAPPY...
NEW YEAR!
BOMB 20
SWSSSH
HAPPY NEW YEAR, KANA. BUT WHY AREN'T YOU GOING OUT THE FRONT DOOR?
WHY ELSE? SO THAT HE WOULDN'T SPOT ME!
THIS YEAR, I'M GOING TO HAVE A PROPER SHRINE VISIT!

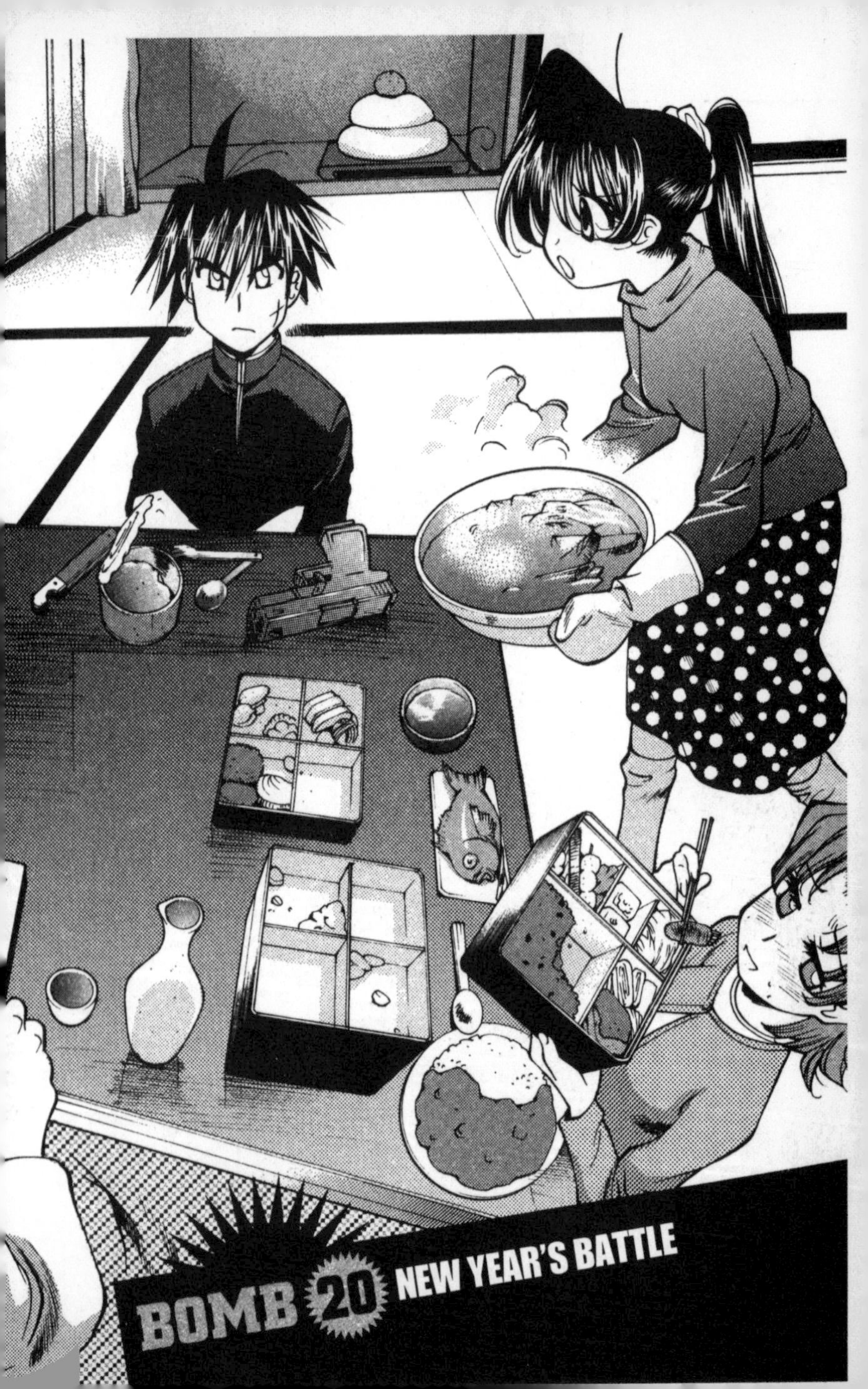
BOMB 20 NEW YEAR'S BATTLE

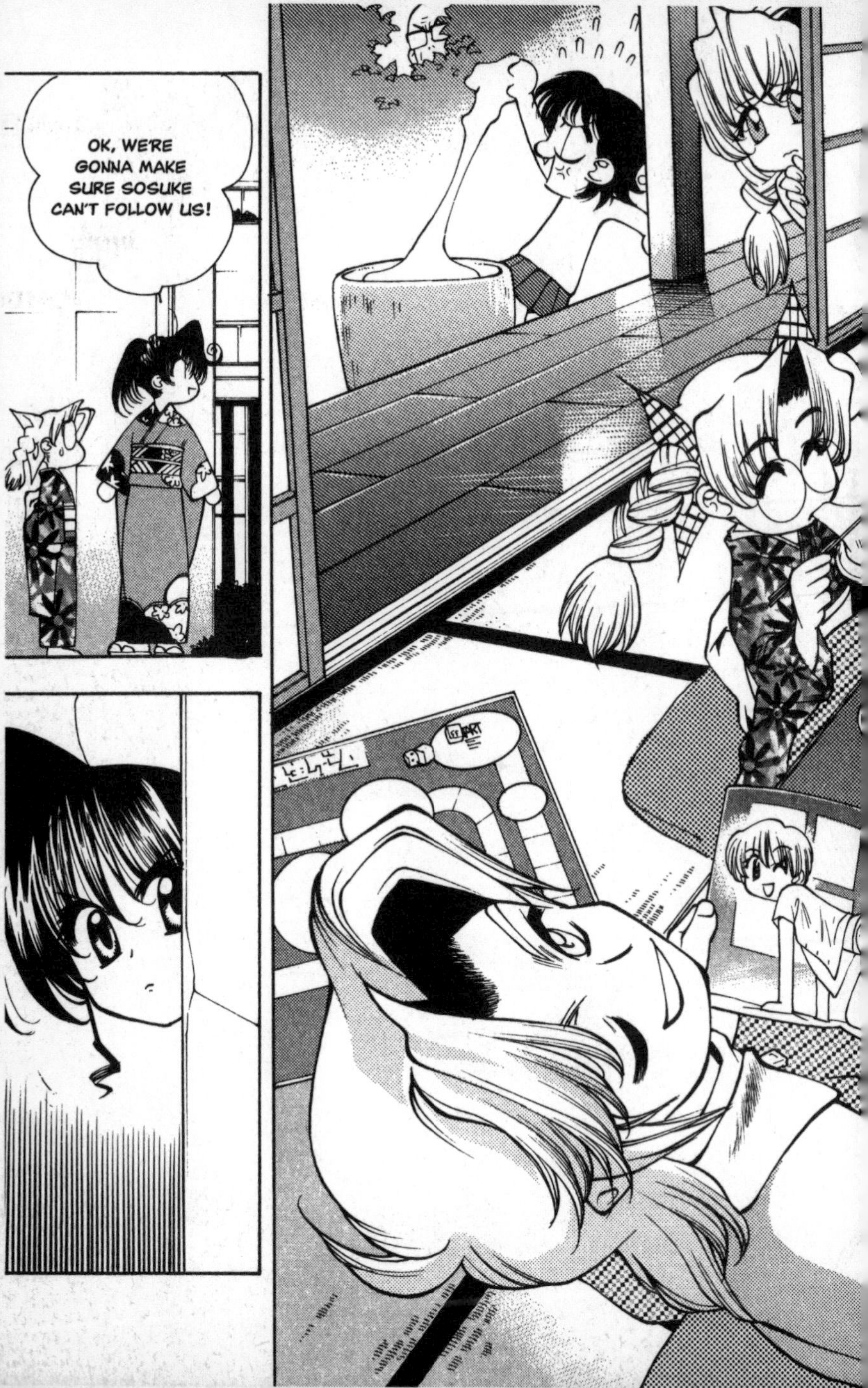
OK, WE'RE GONNA MAKE SURE SOSUKE CAN'T FOLLOW US!

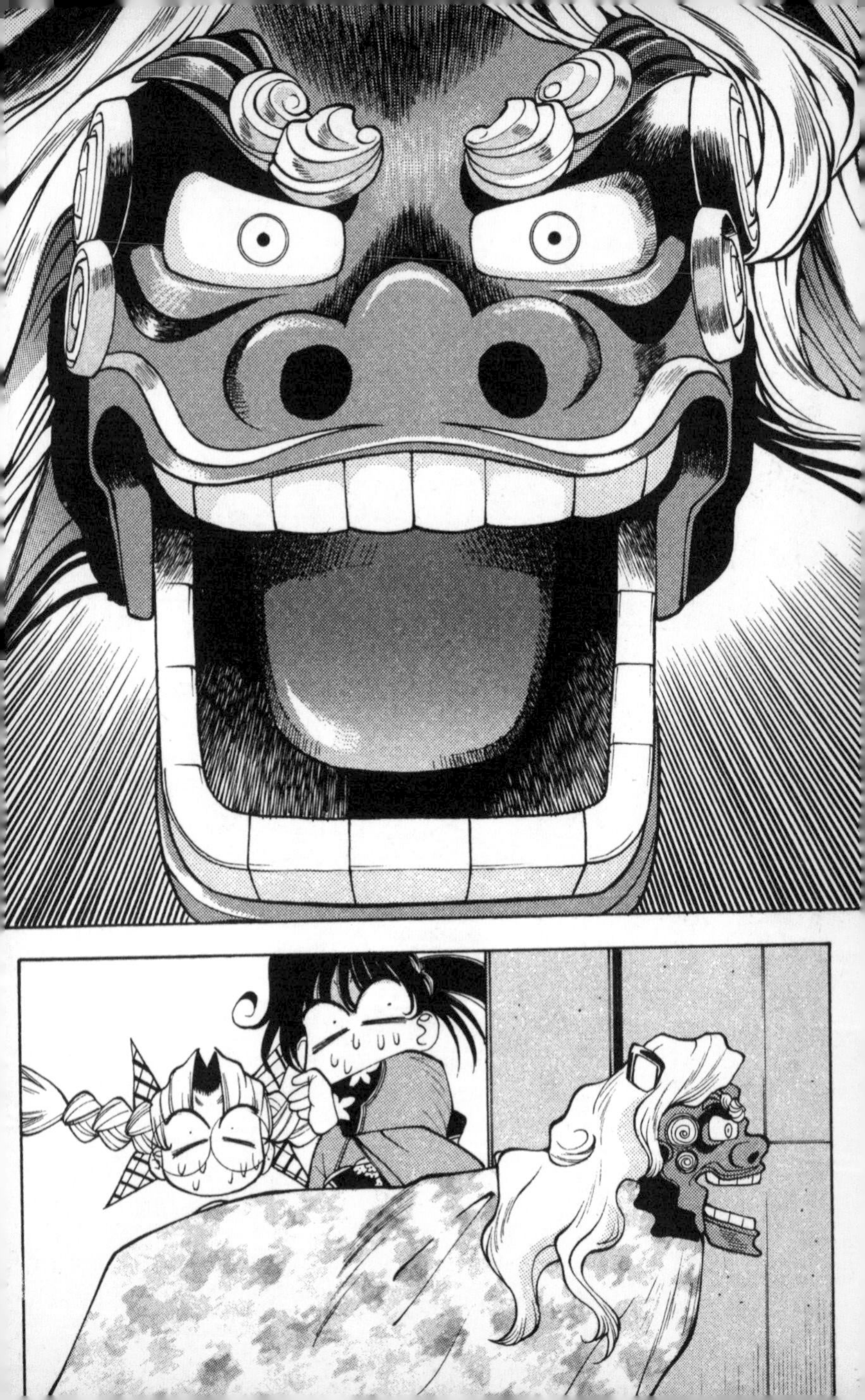

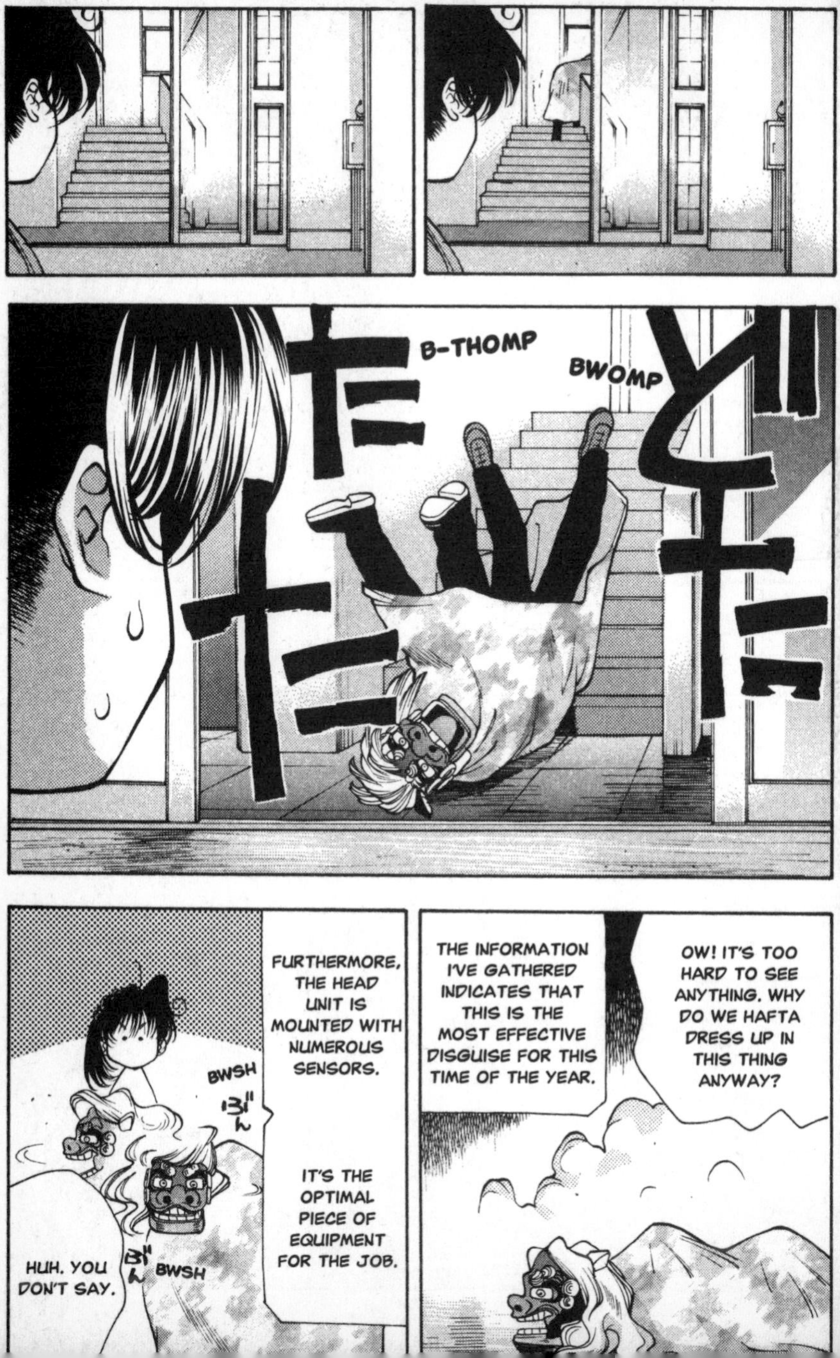
B-THOMP
BWOMP
OW! IT'S TOO HARD TO SEE ANYTHING. WHY DO WE HAFTA DRESS UP IN THIS THING ANYWAY?
THE INFORMATION I'VE GATHERED INDICATES THAT THIS IS THE MOST EFFECTIVE DISGUISE FOR THIS TIME OF THE YEAR.
FURTHERMORE, THE HEAD UNIT IS MOUNTED WITH NUMEROUS SENSORS.
BWSH
IT'S THE OPTIMAL PIECE OF EQUIPMENT FOR THE JOB.
BWSH
HUH. YOU DON'T SAY.

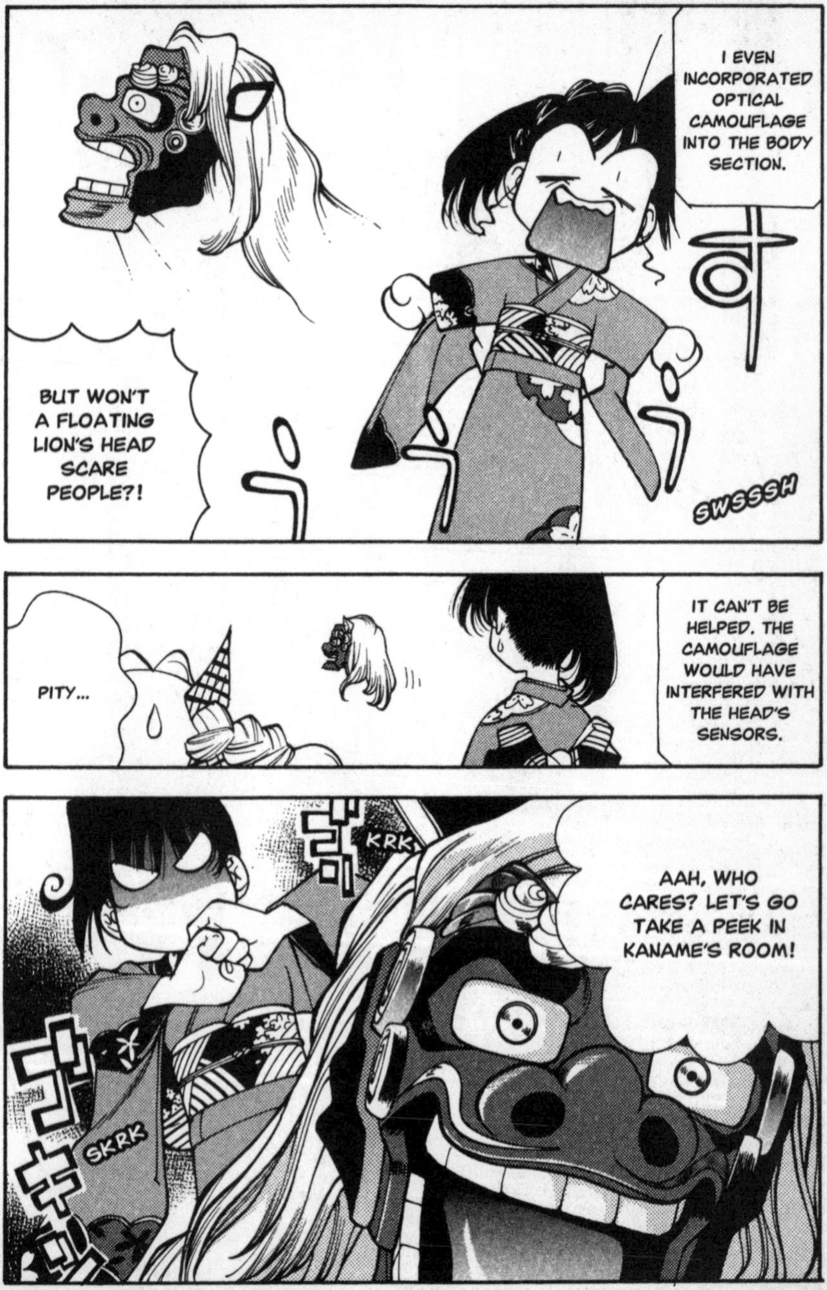
I EVEN INCORPORATED OPTICAL CAMOUFLAGE INTO THE BODY SECTION.
す
BUT WON'T A FLOATING LION'S HEAD SCARE PEOPLE?!
SWSSSH
IT CAN'T BE HELPED. THE CAMOUFLAGE WOULD HAVE INTERFERED WITH THE HEAD'S SENSORS.
PITY...
AAH, WHO CARES? LET'S GO TAKE A PEEK IN KANAME'S ROOM!
KRK
SKRK

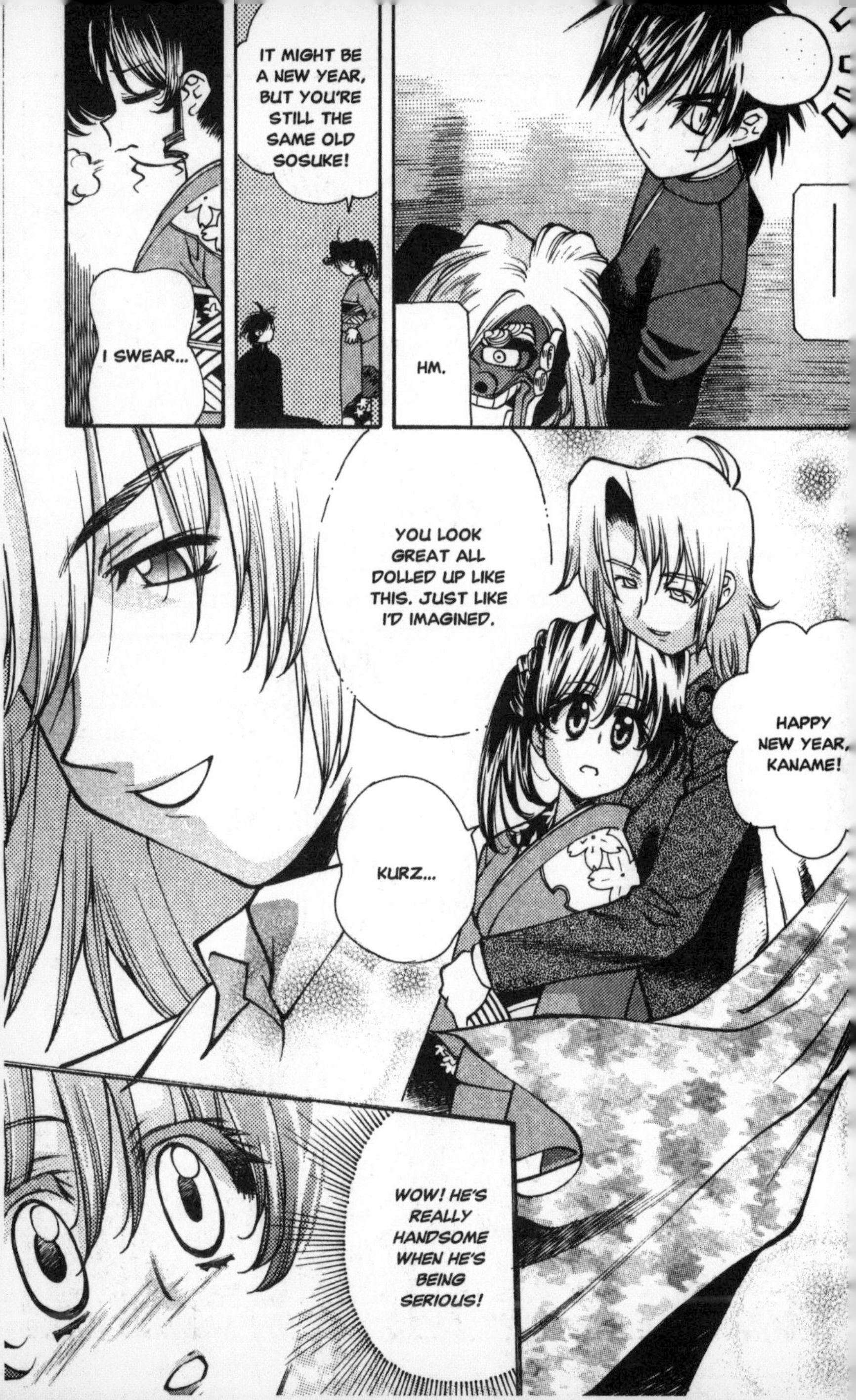
HM.
IT MIGHT BE A NEW YEAR, BUT YOU'RE STILL THE SAME OLD SOSUKE!
I SWEAR...
HAPPY NEW YEAR, KANAME!
YOU LOOK GREAT ALL DOLLED UP LIKE THIS. JUST LIKE I'D IMAGINED.
KURZ...
WOW! HE'S REALLY HANDSOME WHEN HE'S BEING SERIOUS!

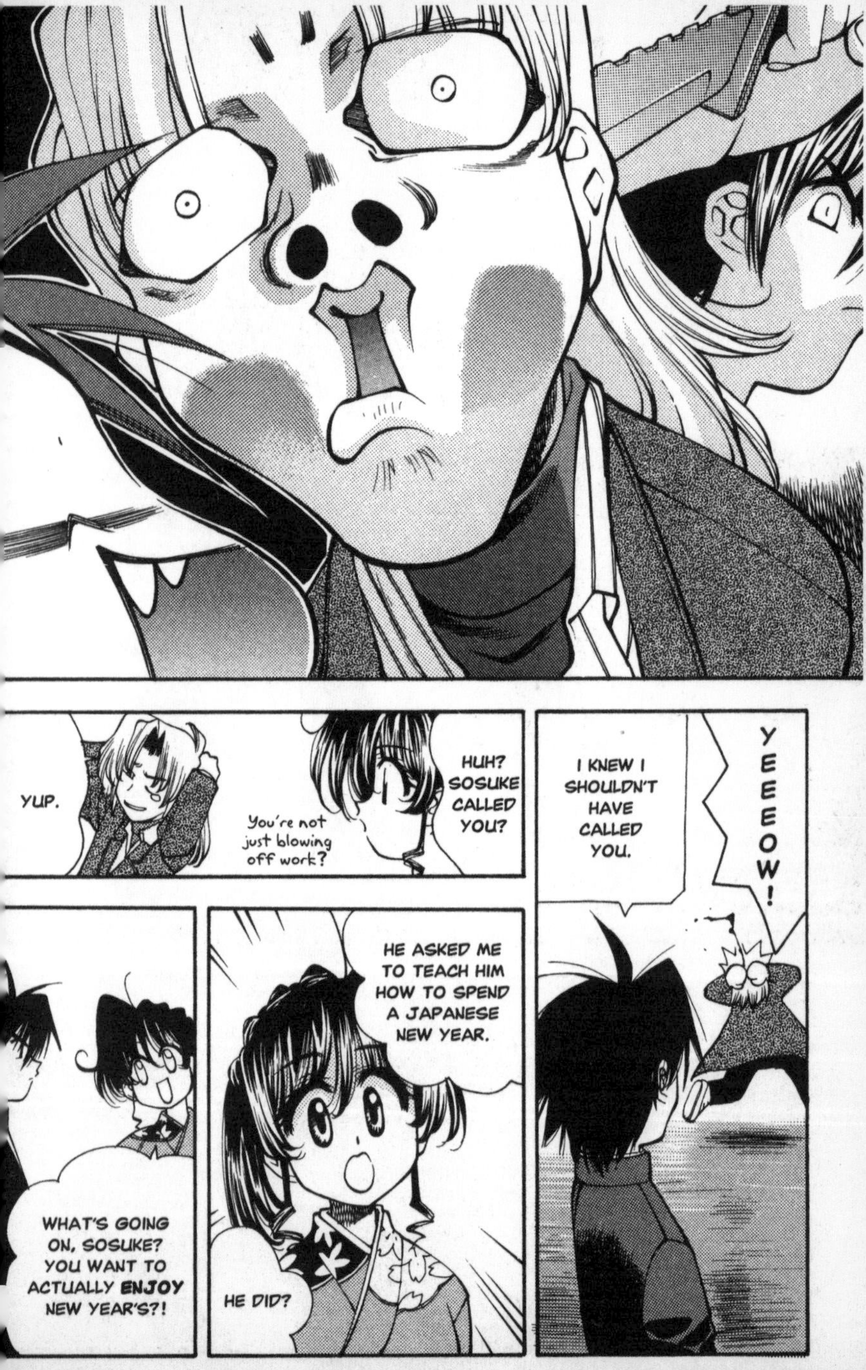
YEEEOW!
I KNEW I SHOULDN'T HAVE CALLED YOU.
HUH? SOSUKE CALLED YOU?
You're not just blowing off work?
YUP.
HE ASKED ME TO TEACH HIM HOW TO SPEND A JAPANESE NEW YEAR.
HE DID?
WHAT'S GOING ON, SOSUKE? YOU WANT TO ACTUALLY **ENJOY** NEW YEAR'S?!

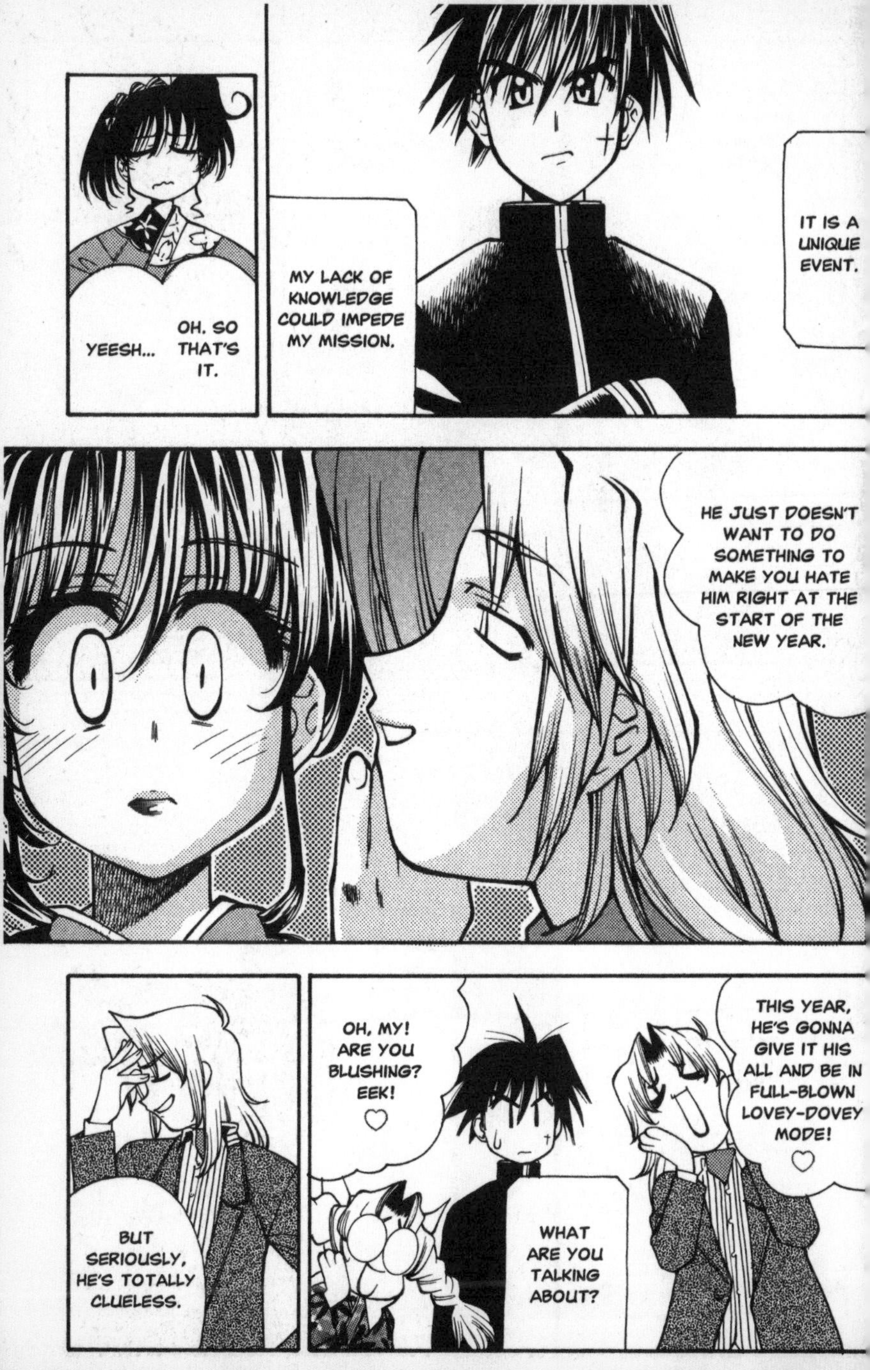
IT IS A UNIQUE EVENT.
MY LACK OF KNOWLEDGE COULD IMPEDE MY MISSION.
OH. SO THAT'S IT.
YEESH...
HE JUST DOESN'T WANT TO DO SOMETHING TO MAKE YOU HATE HIM RIGHT AT THE START OF THE NEW YEAR.
THIS YEAR, HE'S GONNA GIVE IT HIS ALL AND BE IN FULL-BLOWN LOVEY-DOVEY MODE! ♡
WHAT ARE YOU TALKING ABOUT?
OH, MY! ARE YOU BLUSHING? EEK! ♡
BUT SERIOUSLY, HE'S TOTALLY CLUELESS.

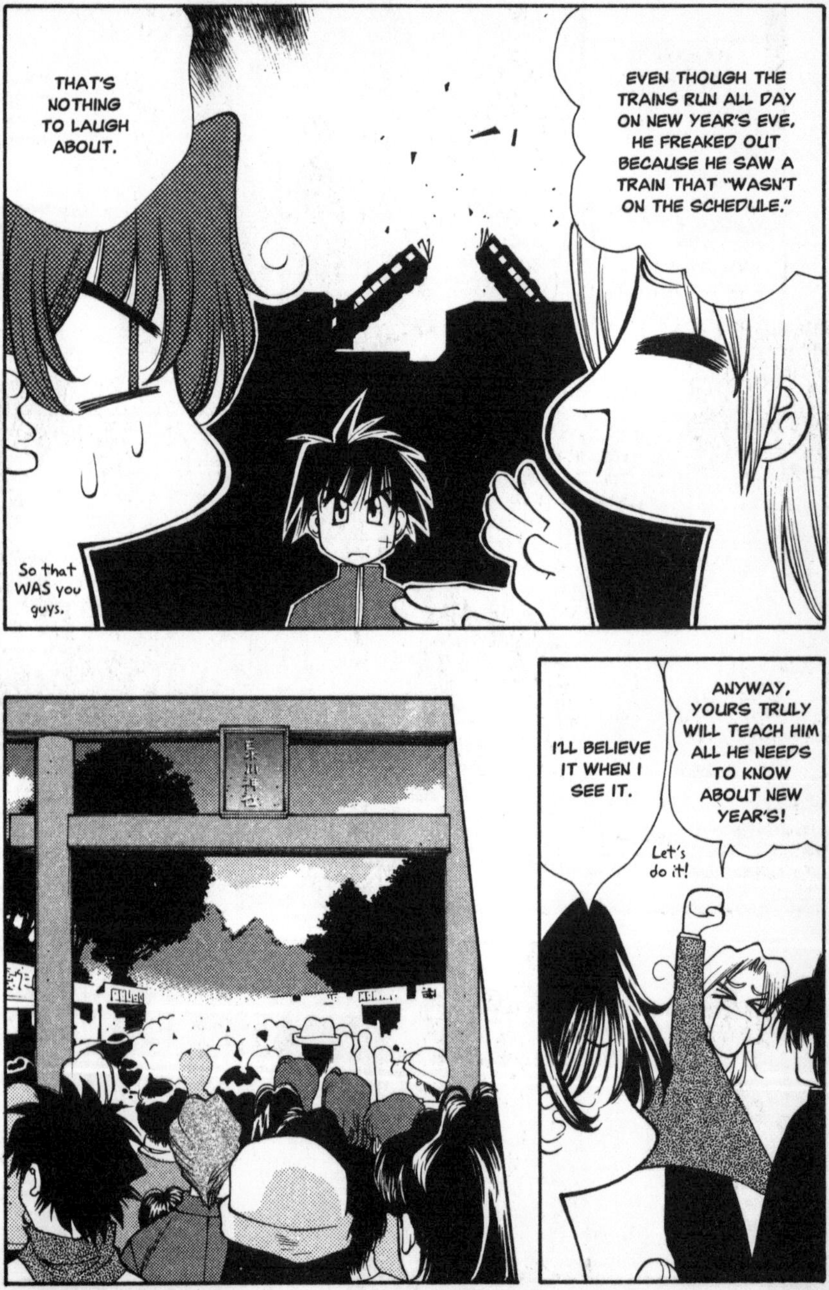
EVEN THOUGH THE TRAINS RUN ALL DAY ON NEW YEAR'S EVE, HE FREAKED OUT BECAUSE HE SAW A TRAIN THAT "WASN'T ON THE SCHEDULE."
THAT'S NOTHING TO LAUGH ABOUT.
So that WAS you guys.
ANYWAY, YOURS TRULY WILL TEACH HIM ALL HE NEEDS TO KNOW ABOUT NEW YEAR'S!
Let's do it!
I'LL BELIEVE IT WHEN I SEE IT.

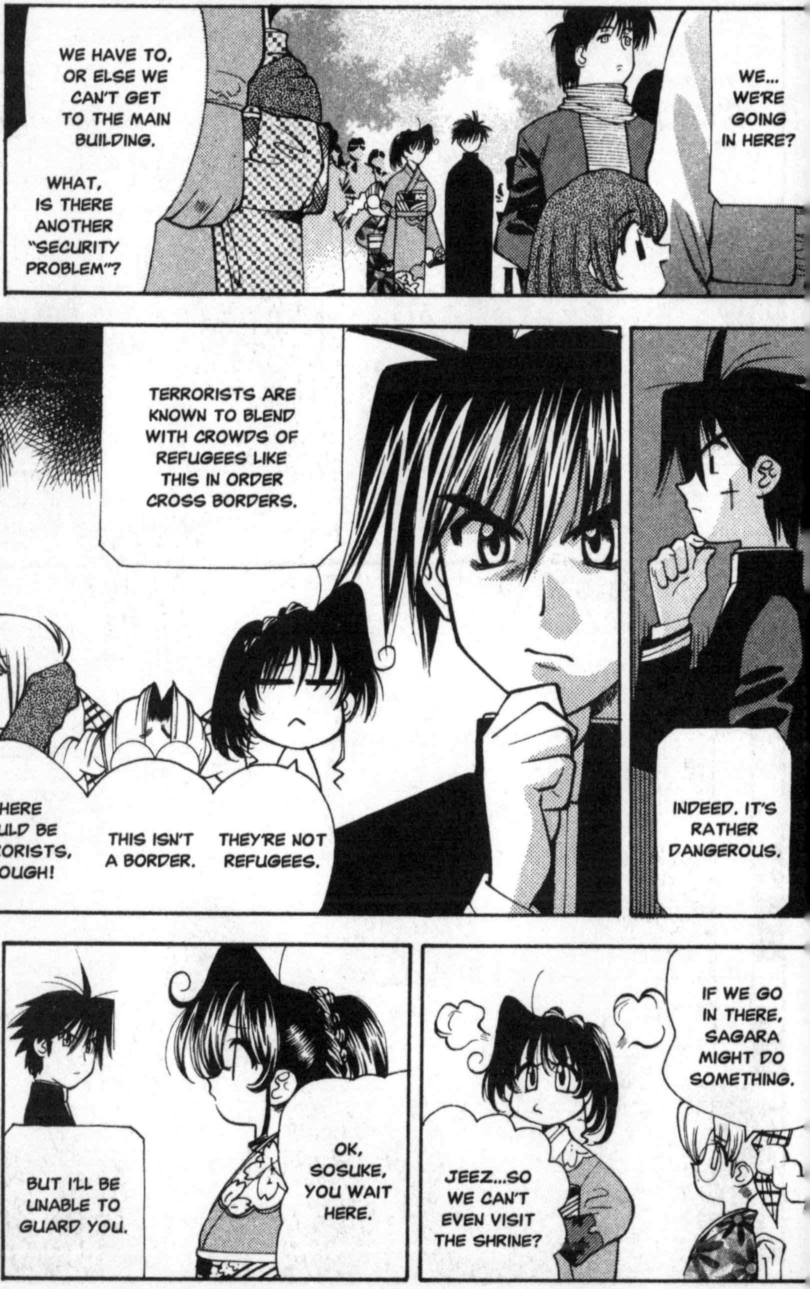

WE... WE'RE GOING IN HERE?
WE HAVE TO, OR ELSE WE CAN'T GET TO THE MAIN BUILDING.
WHAT, IS THERE ANOTHER "SECURITY PROBLEM"?
TERRORISTS ARE KNOWN TO BLEND WITH CROWDS OF REFUGEES LIKE THIS IN ORDER CROSS BORDERS.
INDEED. IT'S RATHER DANGEROUS.
THEY'RE NOT REFUGEES.
THIS ISN'T A BORDER.
THERE COULD BE TERRORISTS, THOUGH!
IF WE GO IN THERE, SAGARA MIGHT DO SOMETHING.
JEEZ...SO WE CAN'T EVEN VISIT THE SHRINE?
OK, SOSUKE, YOU WAIT HERE.
BUT I'LL BE UNABLE TO GUARD YOU.

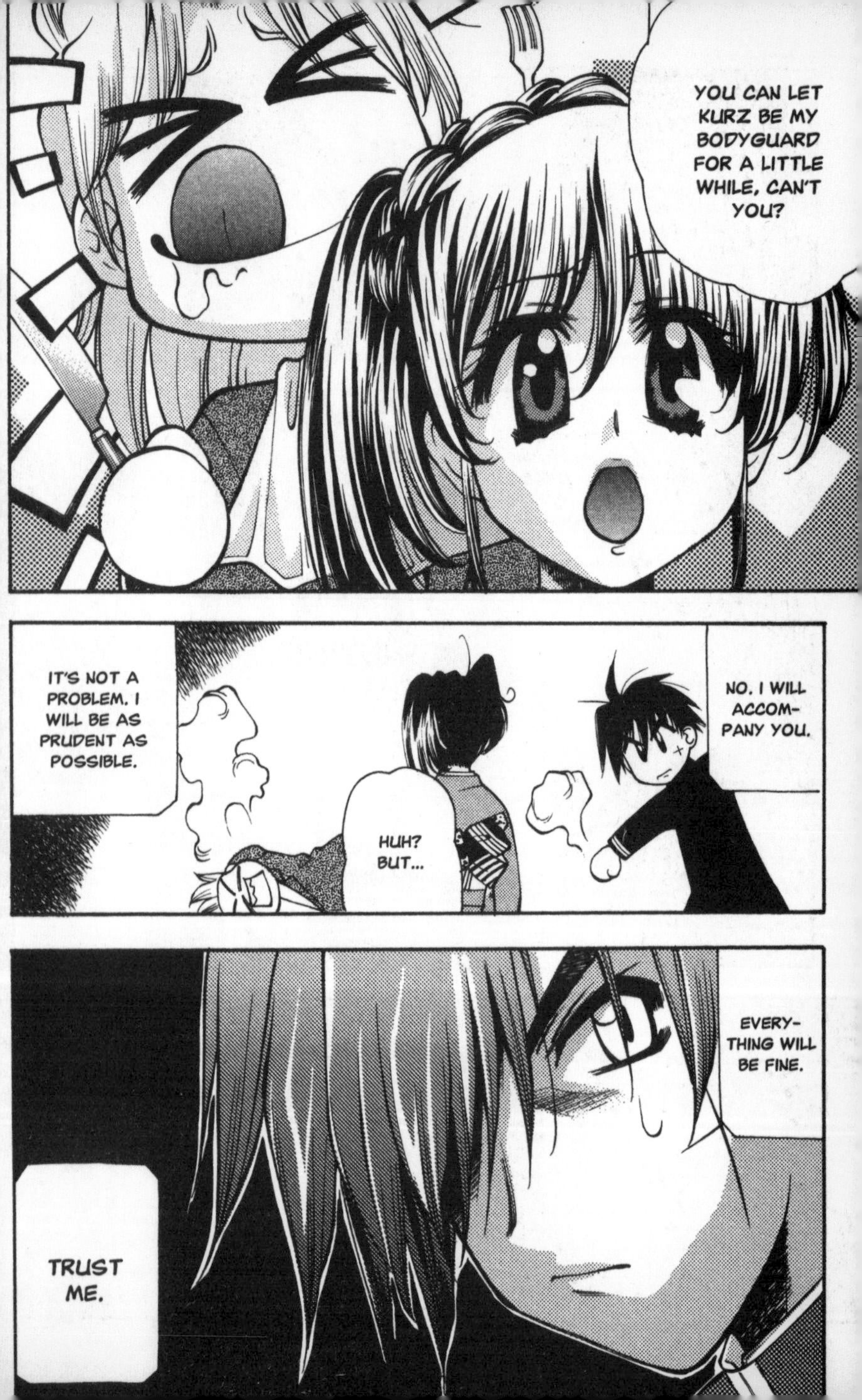
YOU CAN LET KURZ BE MY BODYGUARD FOR A LITTLE WHILE, CAN'T YOU?
NO. I WILL ACCOMPANY YOU.
IT'S NOT A PROBLEM. I WILL BE AS PRUDENT AS POSSIBLE.
HUH? BUT...
EVERYTHING WILL BE FINE.
TRUST ME.

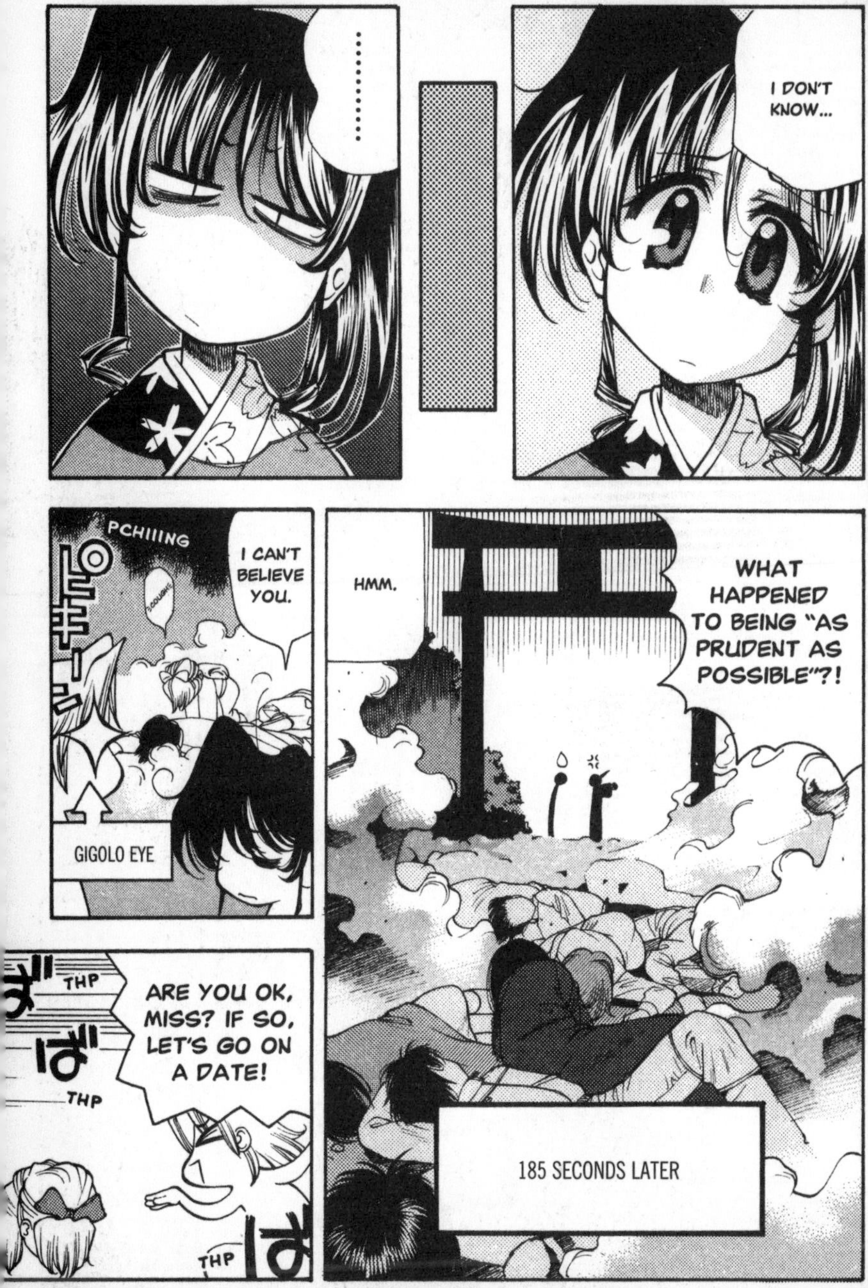
I DON'T KNOW...
......
WHAT HAPPENED TO BEING "AS PRUDENT AS POSSIBLE"?!
HMM.
PCHIIING
I CAN'T BELIEVE YOU.
GIGOLO EYE
185 SECONDS LATER
ARE YOU OK, MISS? IF SO, LET'S GO ON A DATE!
THP
THP
THP

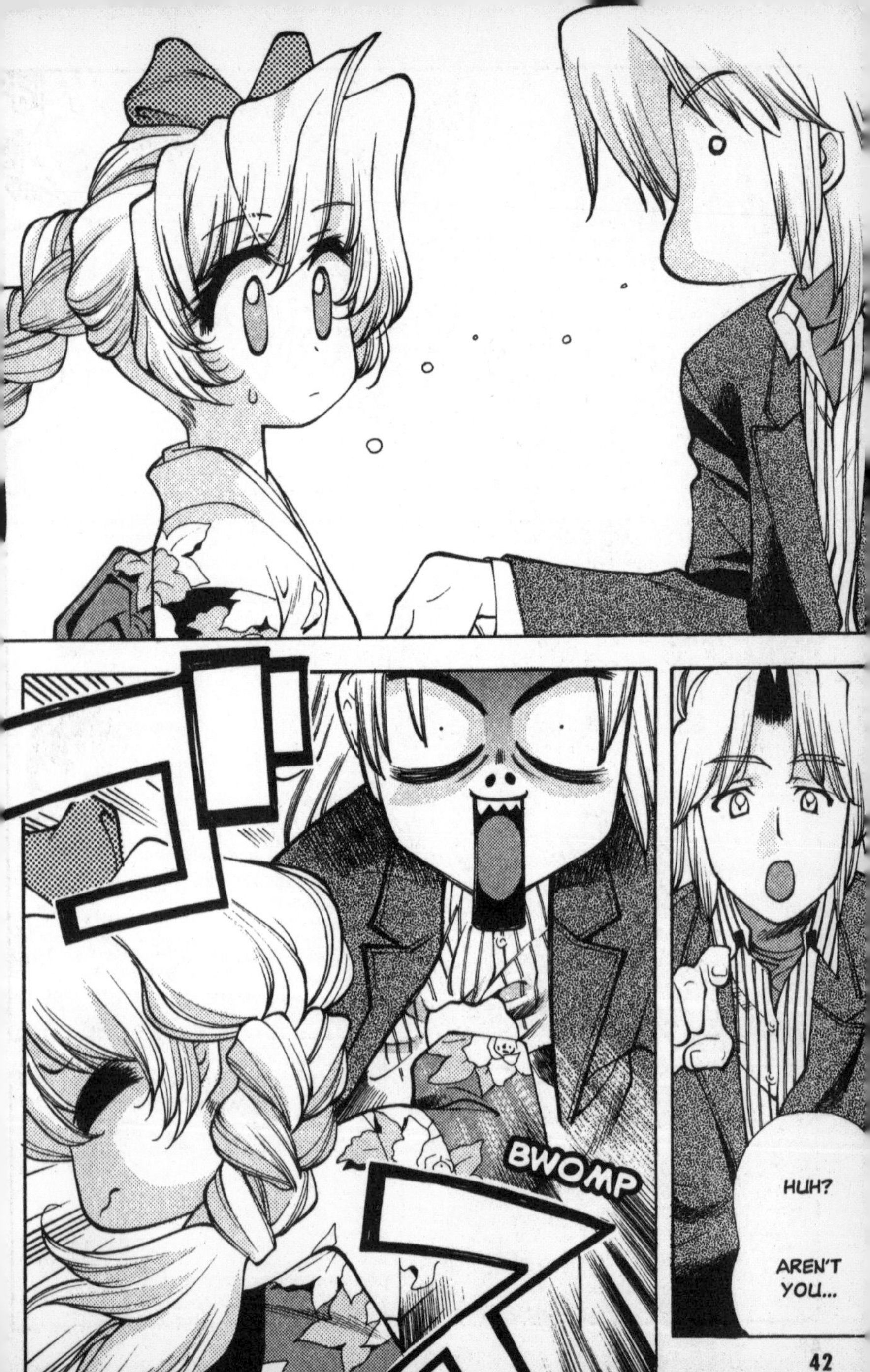
BWOMP
HUH?
AREN'T YOU...

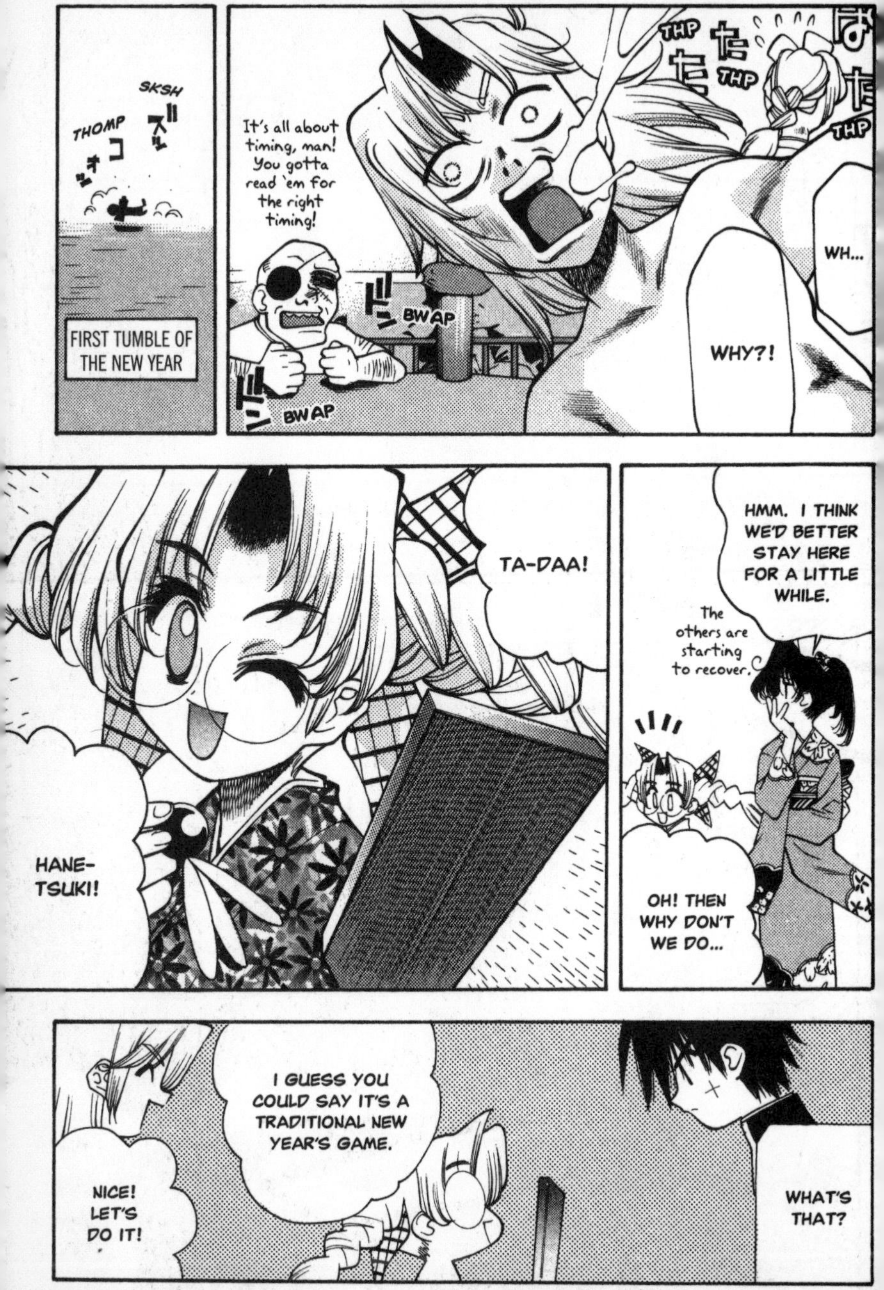
THP
THP
THP
WH...
WHY?!
It's all about timing, man! You gotta read 'em for the right timing!
BWAP
BWAP
SKSH
THOMP
FIRST TUMBLE OF THE NEW YEAR
HMM. I THINK WE'D BETTER STAY HERE FOR A LITTLE WHILE.
The others are starting to recover.
OH! THEN WHY DON'T WE DO...
TA-DAA!
HANE-TSUKI!
WHAT'S THAT?
I GUESS YOU COULD SAY IT'S A TRADITIONAL NEW YEAR'S GAME.
NICE! LET'S DO IT!

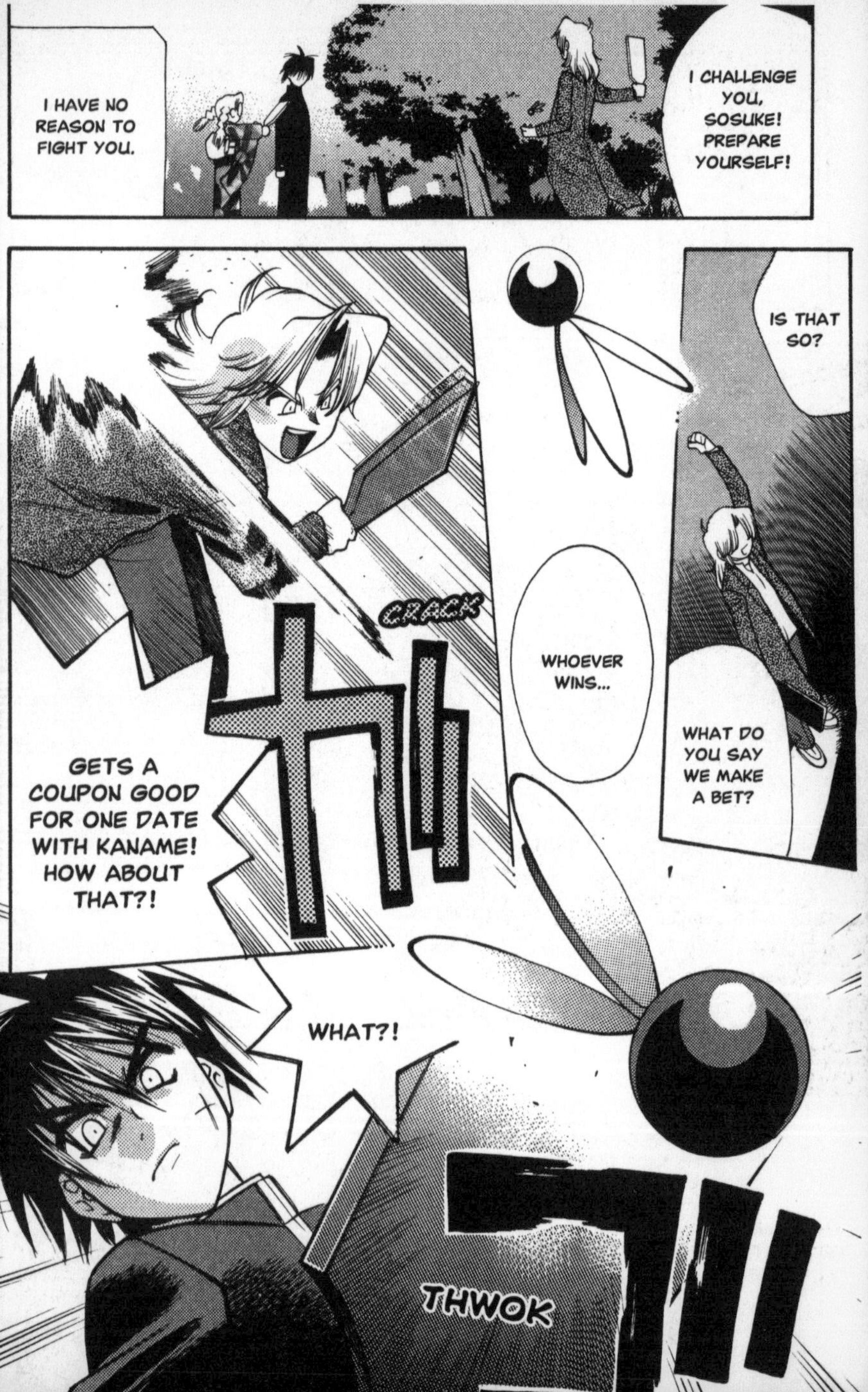
I CHALLENGE YOU, SOSUKE! PREPARE YOURSELF!
I HAVE NO REASON TO FIGHT YOU.
IS THAT SO?
WHAT DO YOU SAY WE MAKE A BET?
WHOEVER WINS...
GETS A COUPON GOOD FOR ONE DATE WITH KANAME! HOW ABOUT THAT?!
CRACK
WHAT?!
THWOK

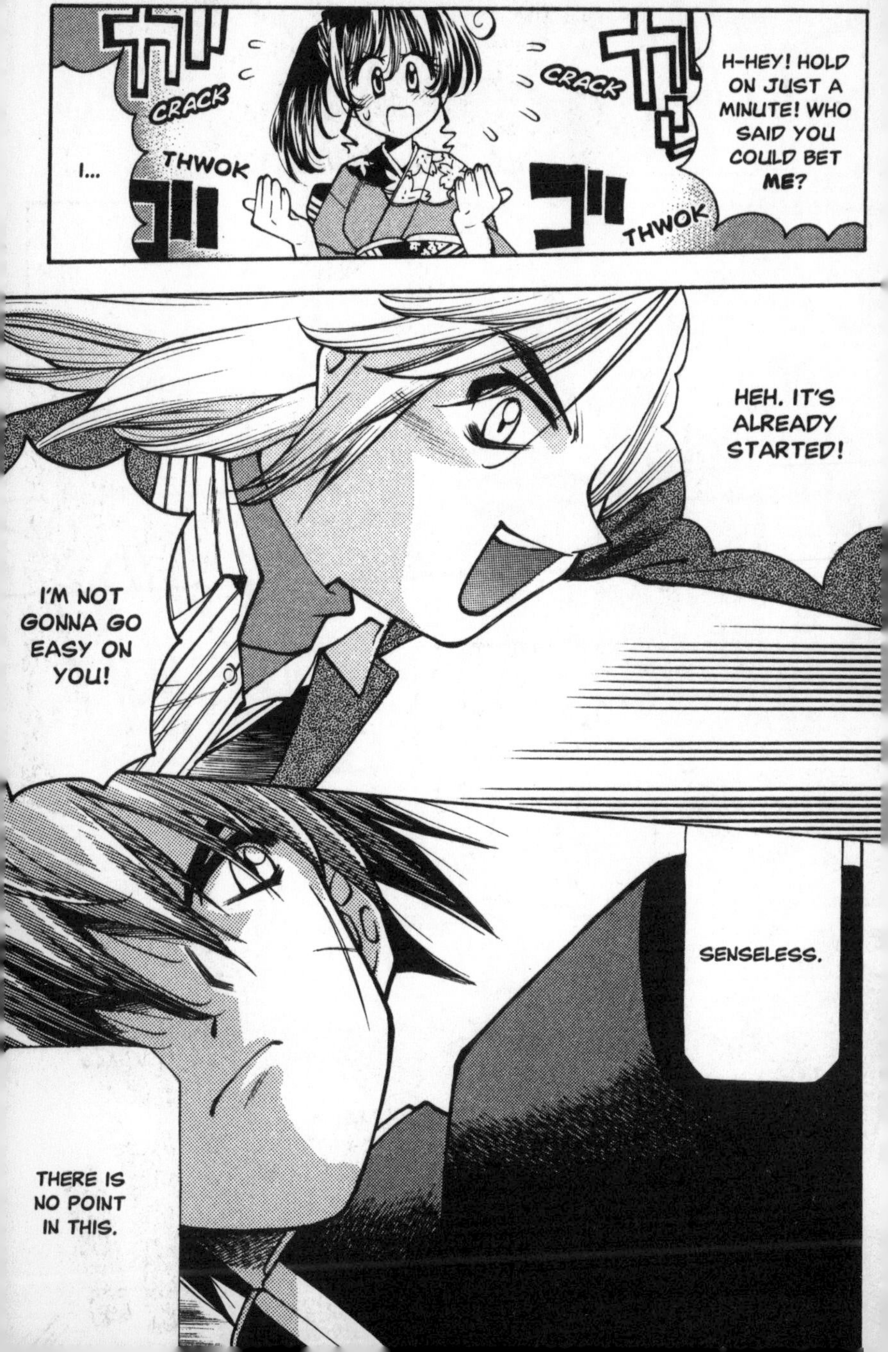

H-HEY! HOLD ON JUST A MINUTE! WHO SAID YOU COULD BET ME?
CRACK
THWOK
CRACK
THWOK
I...
HEH. IT'S ALREADY STARTED!
I'M NOT GONNA GO EASY ON YOU!
SENSELESS.
THERE IS NO POINT IN THIS.

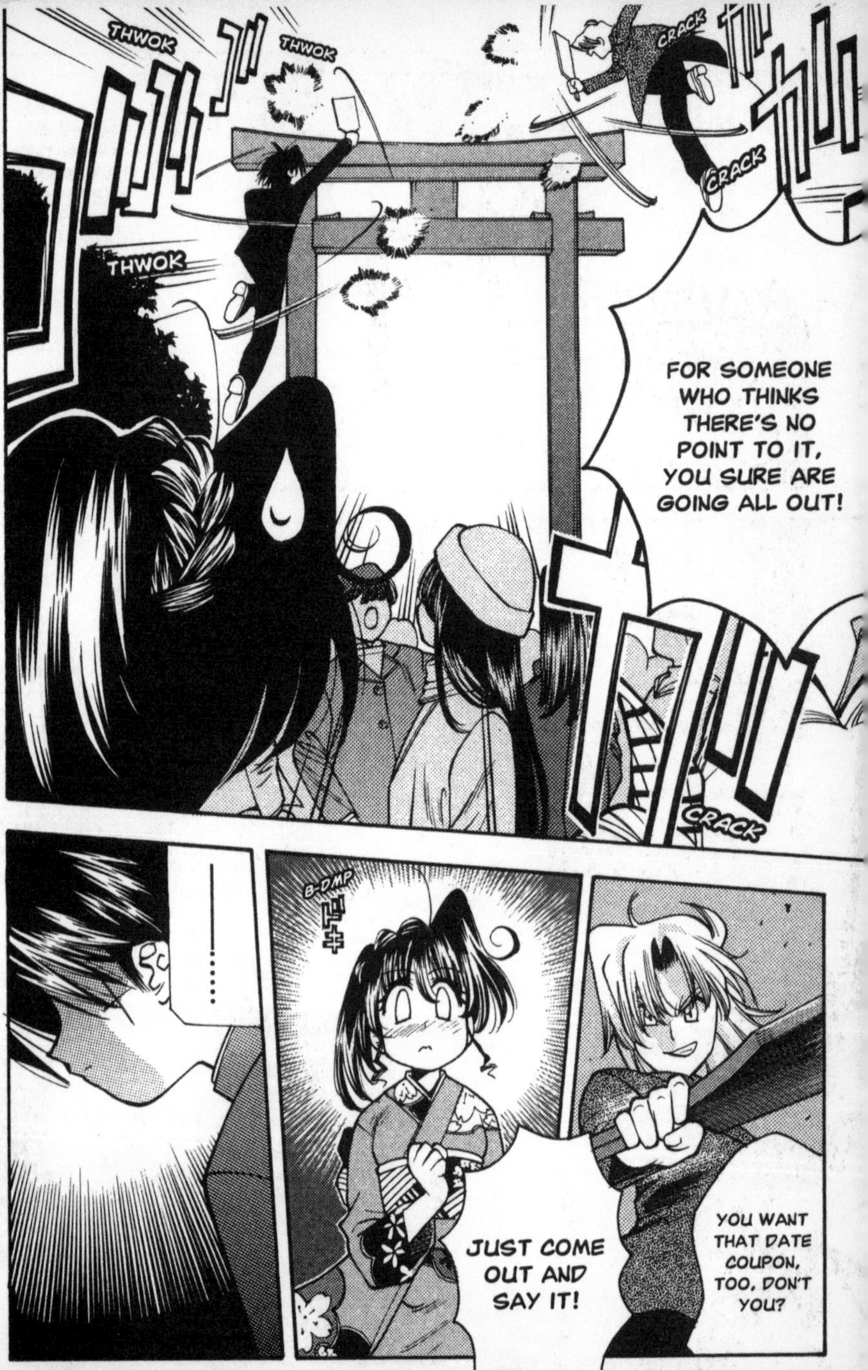

THWOK
THWOK
CRACK
CRACK
THWOK
FOR SOMEONE WHO THINKS THERE'S NO POINT TO IT, YOU SURE ARE GOING ALL OUT!
CRACK
......
B-DMP
YOU WANT THAT DATE COUPON, TOO, DON'T YOU?
JUST COME OUT AND SAY IT!

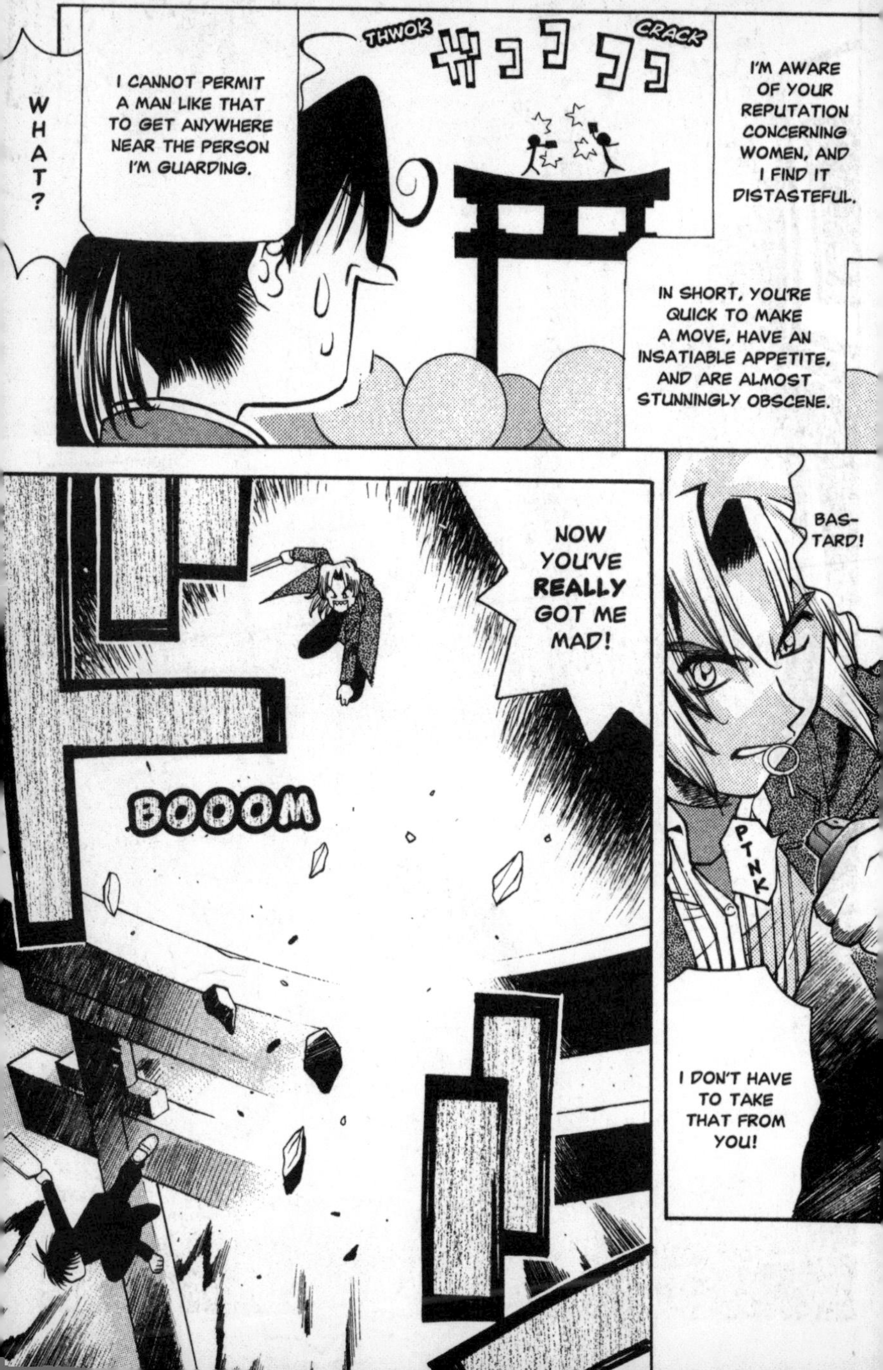
I'M AWARE OF YOUR REPUTATION CONCERNING WOMEN, AND I FIND IT DISTASTEFUL.
IN SHORT, YOU'RE QUICK TO MAKE A MOVE, HAVE AN INSATIABLE APPETITE, AND ARE ALMOST STUNNINGLY OBSCENE.
CRACK
THWOK
I CANNOT PERMIT A MAN LIKE THAT TO GET ANYWHERE NEAR THE PERSON I'M GUARDING.
WHAT?
BAS-TARD!
PTNK
I DON'T HAVE TO TAKE THAT FROM YOU!
NOW YOU'VE REALLY GOT ME MAD!
BOOOM

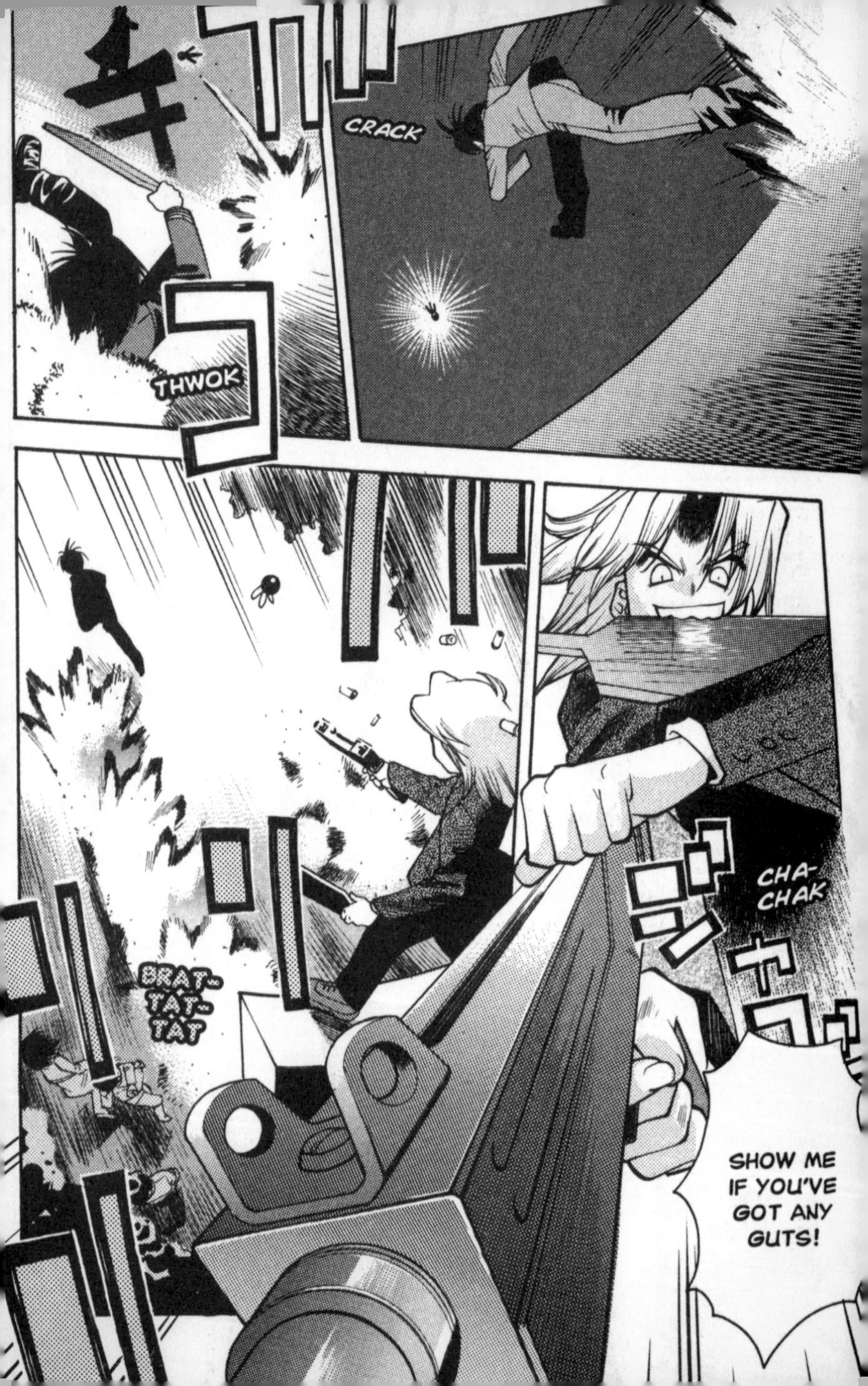
CRACK
THWOK
CHA-CHAK
BRAT-TAT-TAT
SHOW ME IF YOU'VE GOT ANY GUTS!

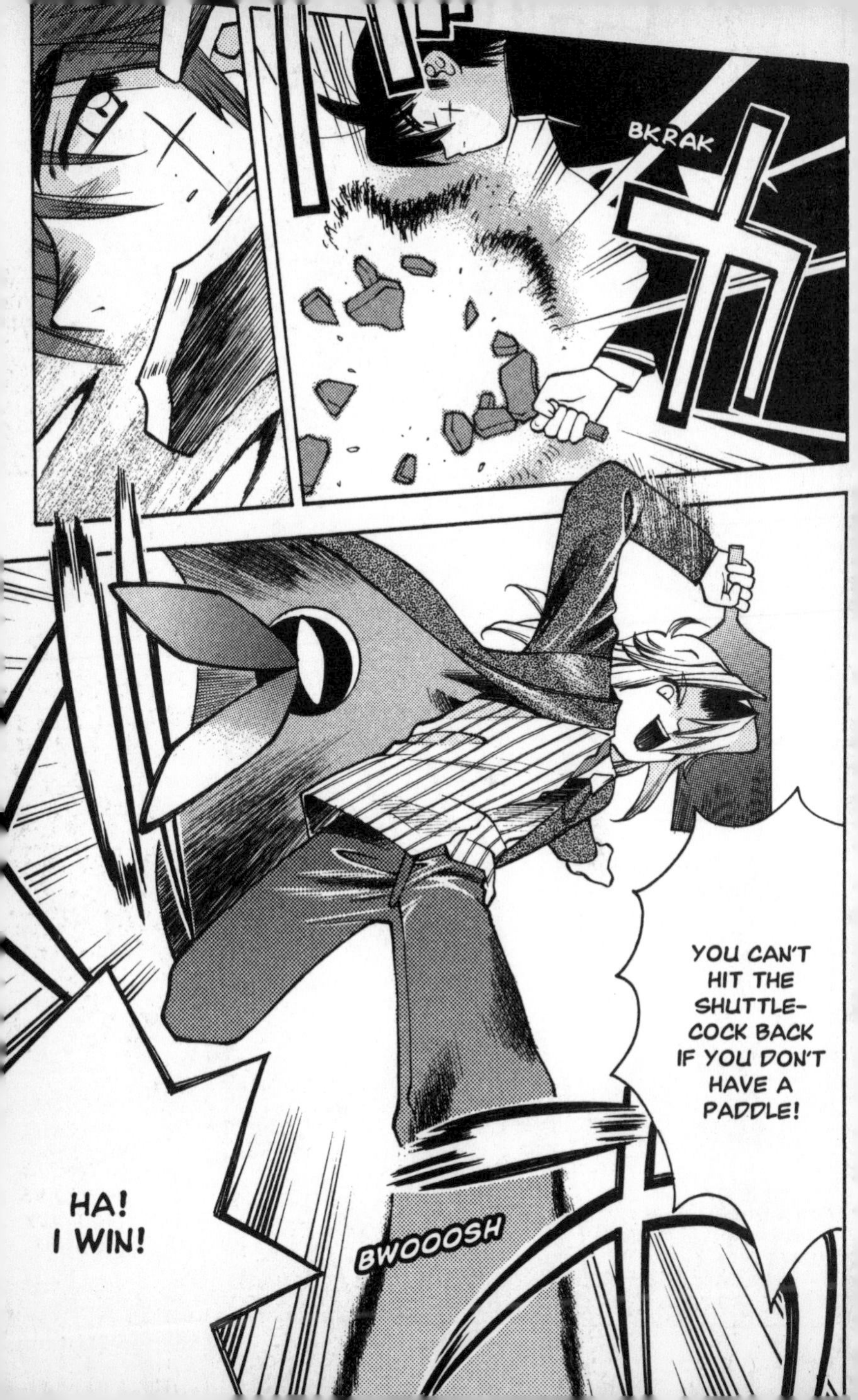
BKRAK
YOU CAN'T HIT THE SHUTTLE-COCK BACK IF YOU DON'T HAVE A PADDLE!
BWOOOSH
HA! I WIN!

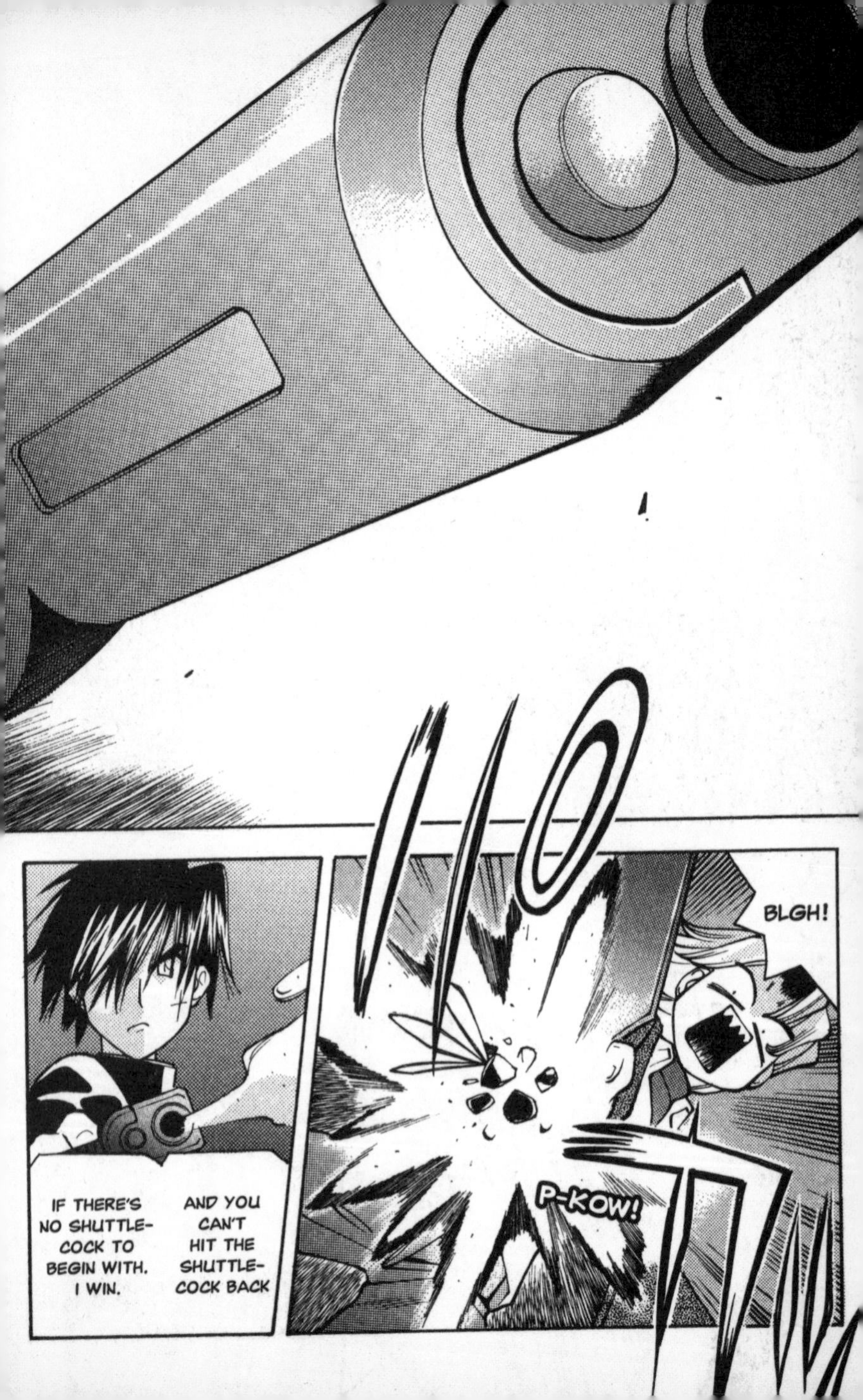
BLGH!
P-KOW!
AND YOU CAN'T HIT THE SHUTTLE-COCK BACK
IF THERE'S NO SHUTTLE-COCK TO BEGIN WITH. I WIN.

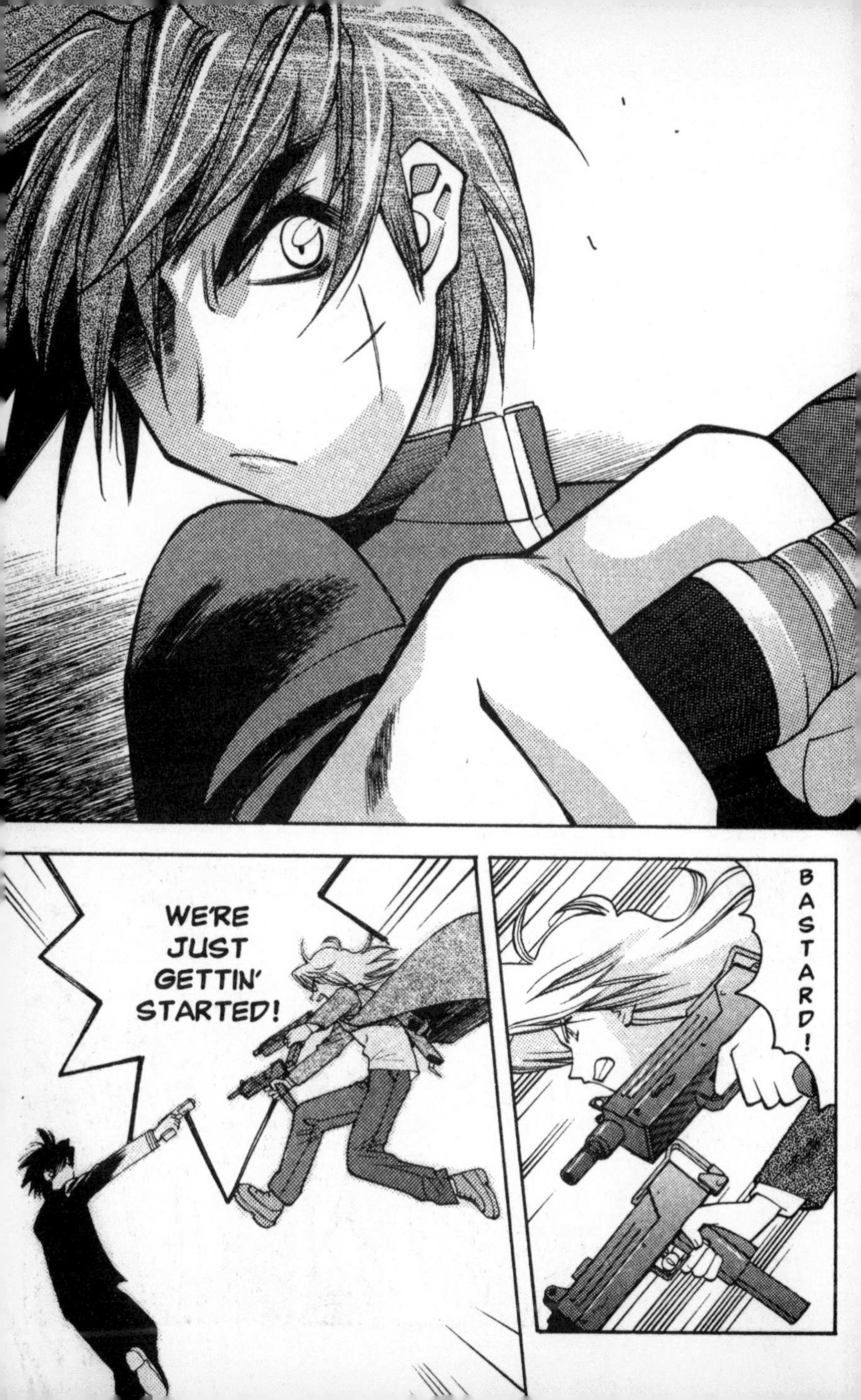
BASTARD!
WE'RE JUST GETTIN' STARTED!

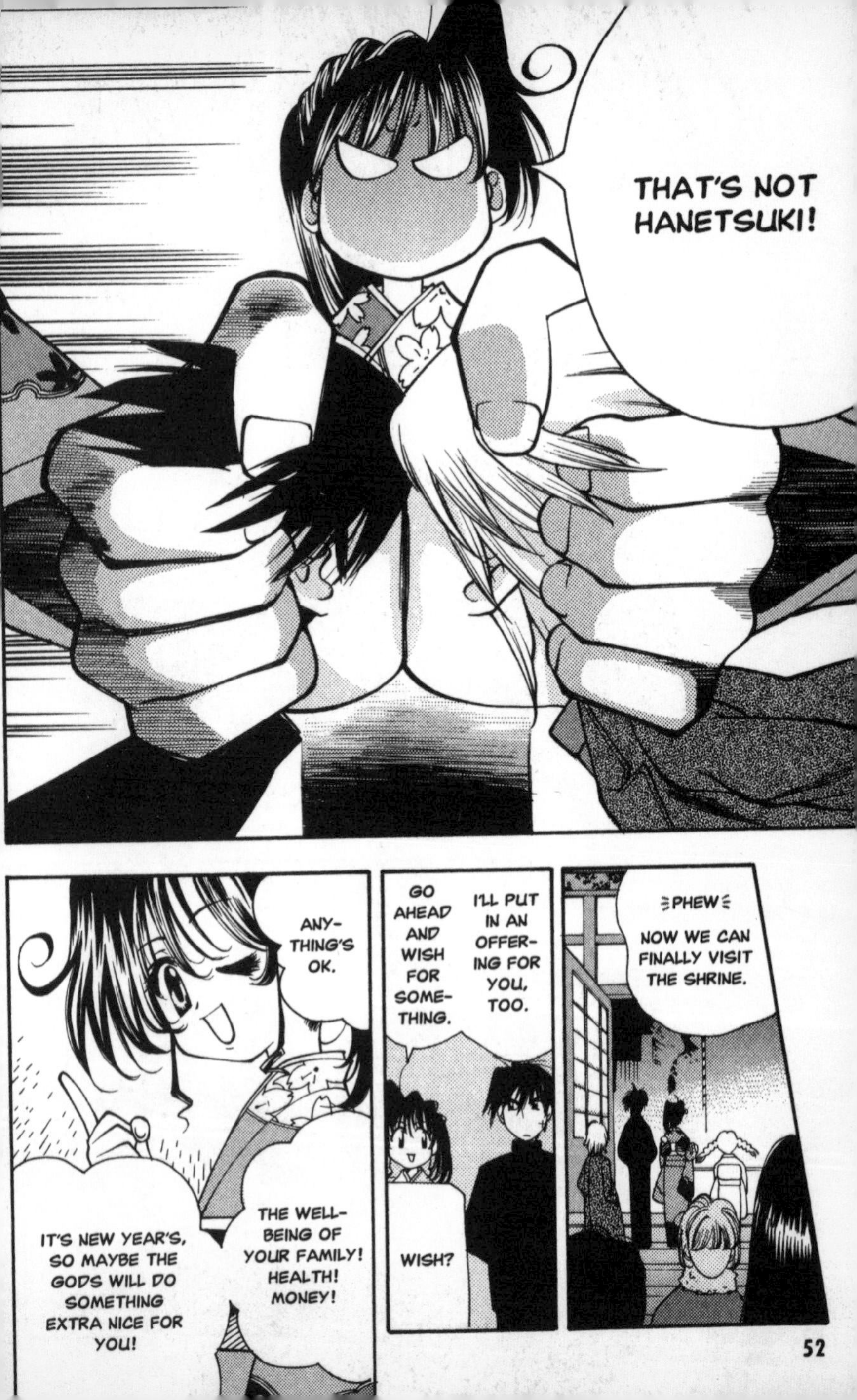
THAT'S NOT HANETSUKI!
≡PHEW≡
NOW WE CAN FINALLY VISIT THE SHRINE.
I'LL PUT IN AN OFFERING FOR YOU, TOO.
GO AHEAD AND WISH FOR SOMETHING.
WISH?
ANY-THING'S OK.
THE WELL-BEING OF YOUR FAMILY! HEALTH! MONEY!
IT'S NEW YEAR'S, SO MAYBE THE GODS WILL DO SOMETHING EXTRA NICE FOR YOU!

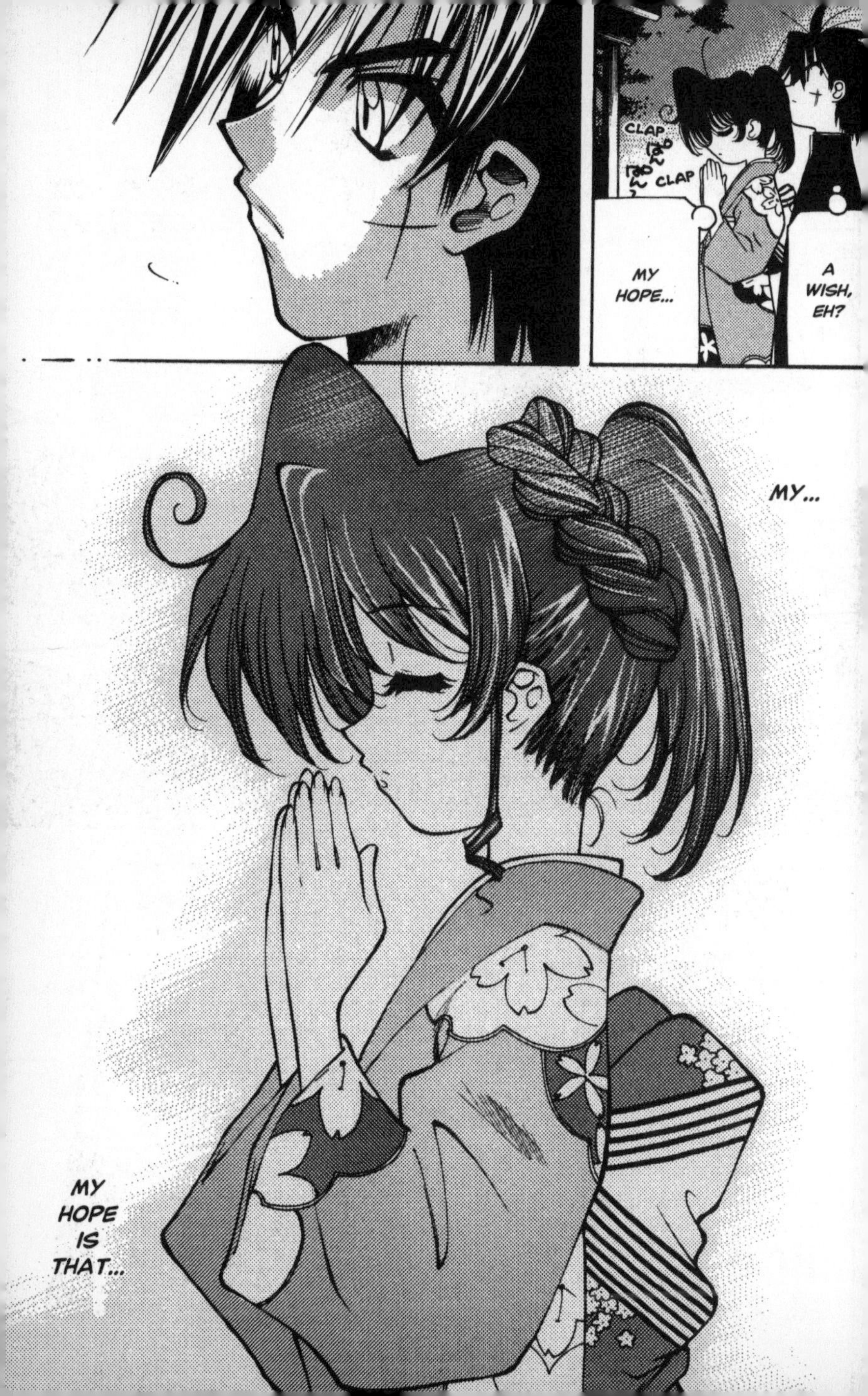
A WISH, EH?
CLAP
CLAP
MY HOPE...
MY...
MY HOPE IS THAT...

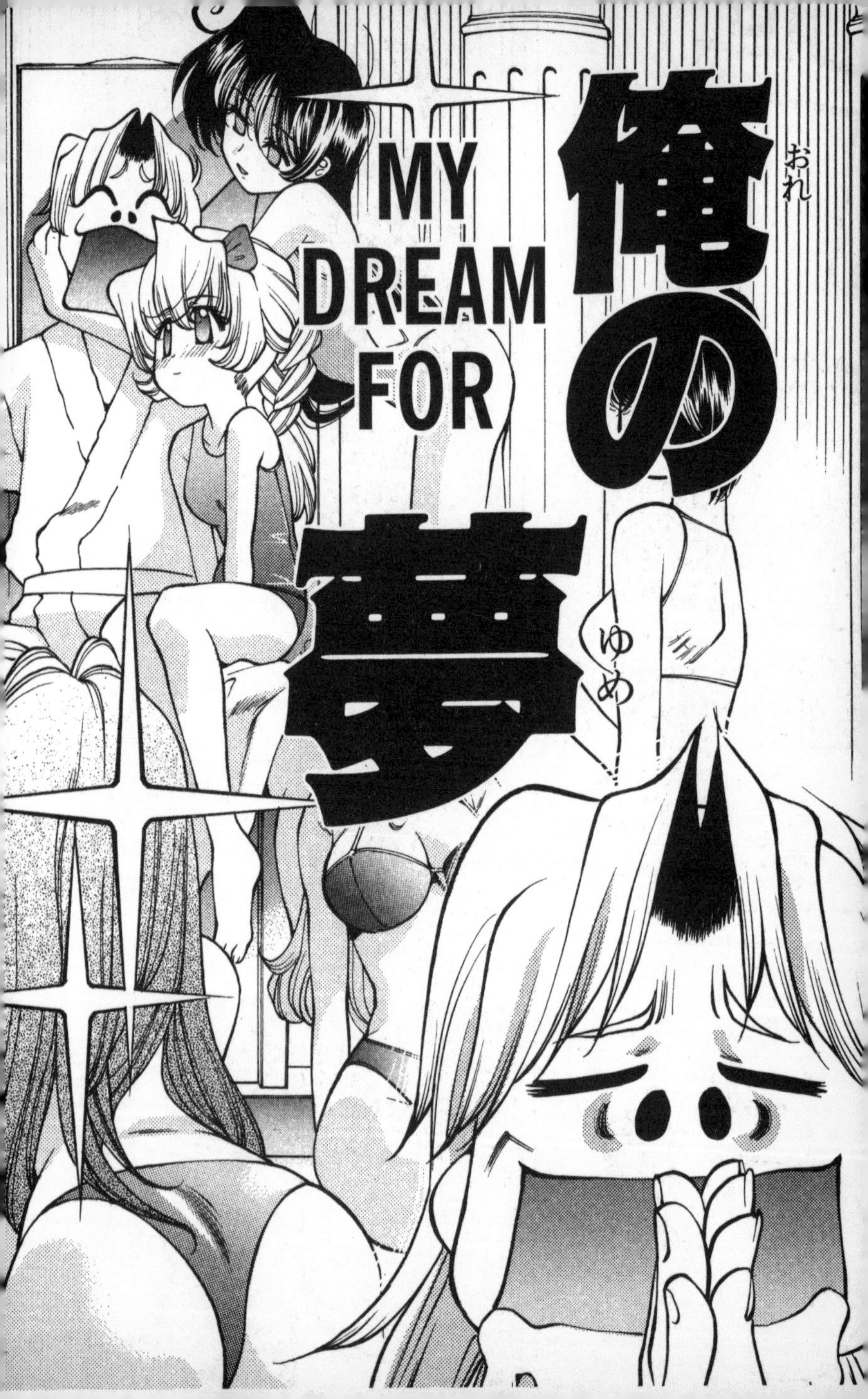
俺の夢
おれ
ゆめ
MY DREAM FOR

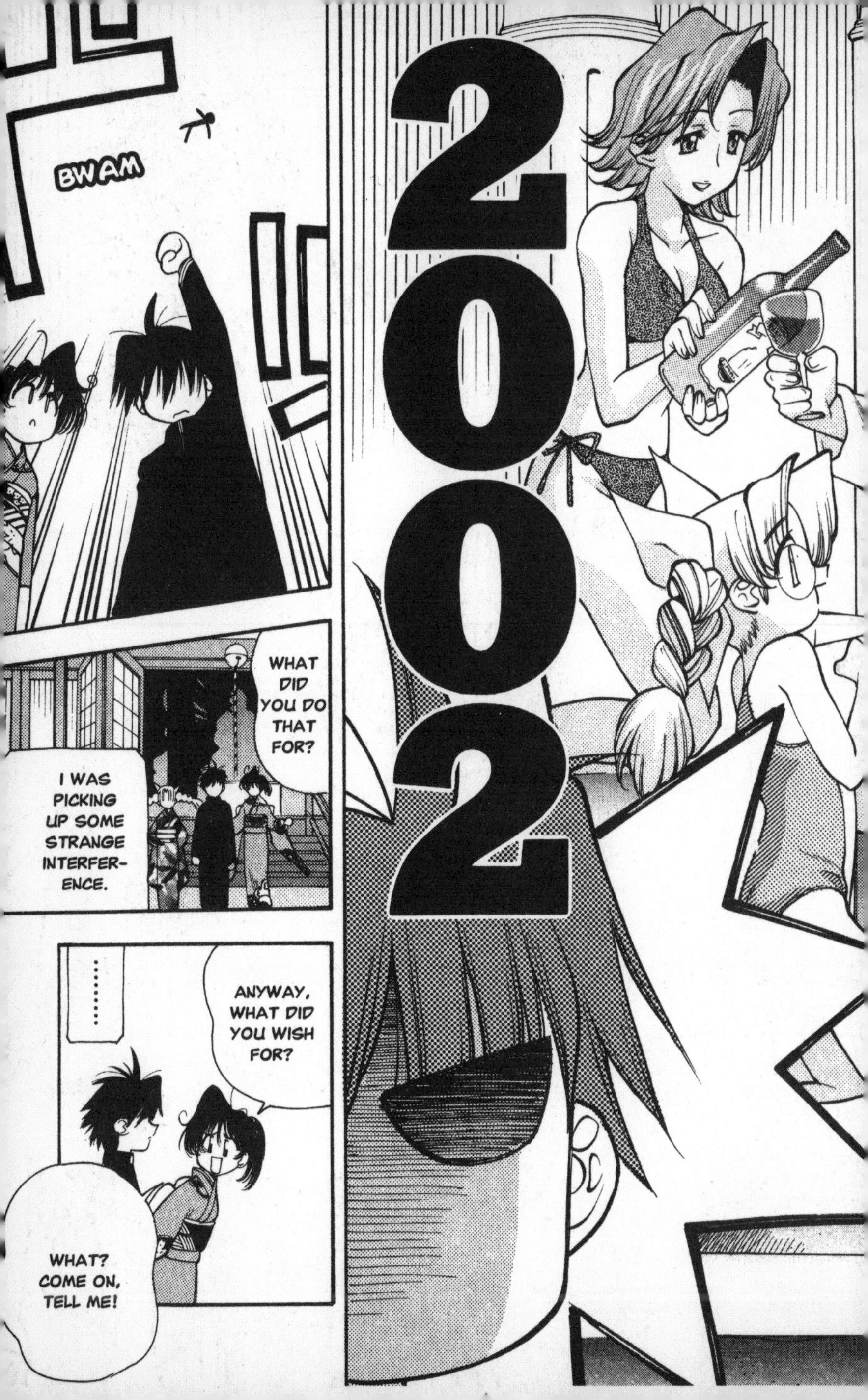
2002
BWAM
WHAT DID YOU DO THAT FOR?
I WAS PICKING UP SOME STRANGE INTERFERENCE.
....
ANYWAY, WHAT DID YOU WISH FOR?
WHAT? COME ON, TELL ME!

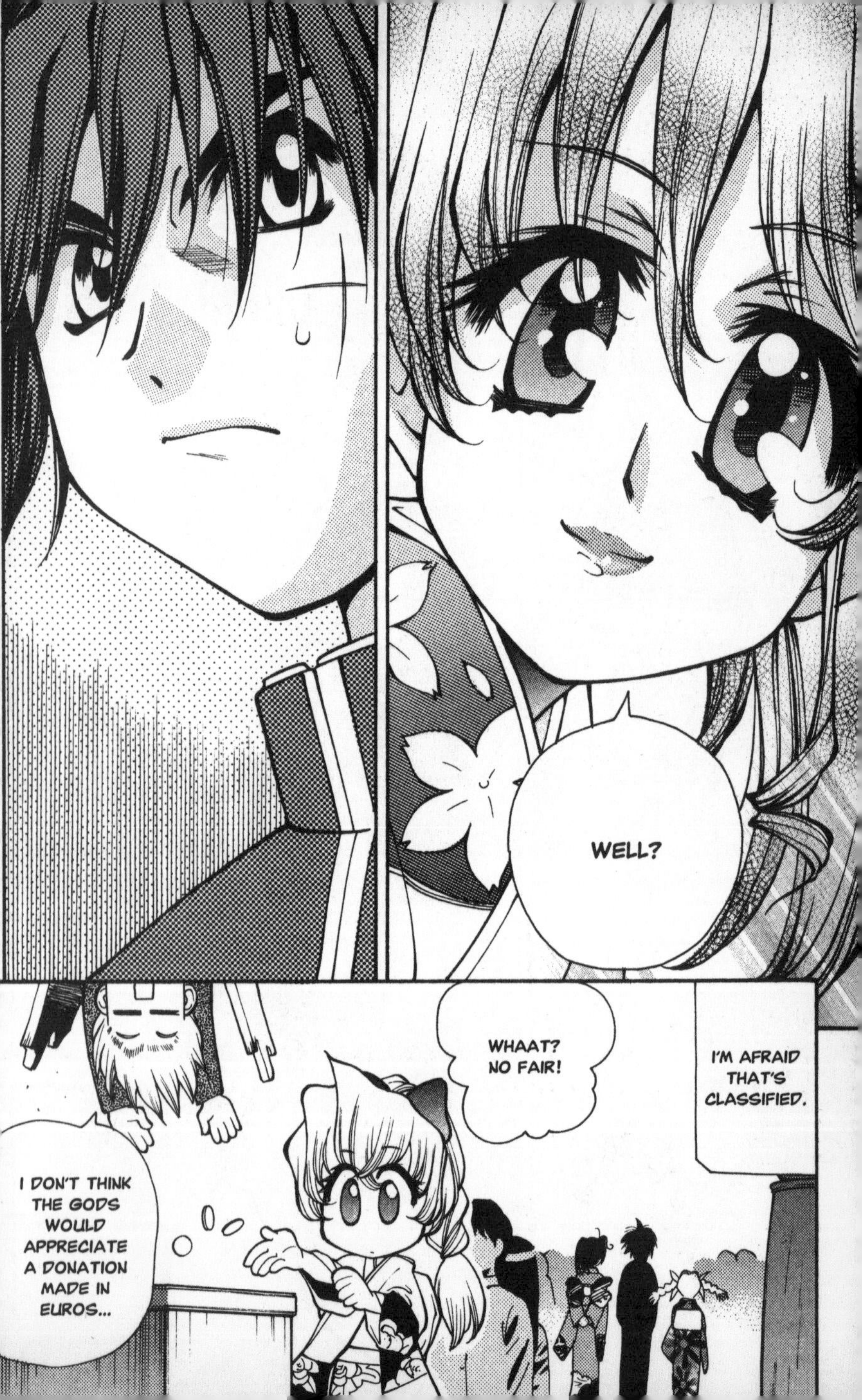
WELL?
I'M AFRAID THAT'S CLASSIFIED.
WHAAT? NO FAIR!
I DON'T THINK THE GODS WOULD APPRECIATE A DONATION MADE IN EUROS...

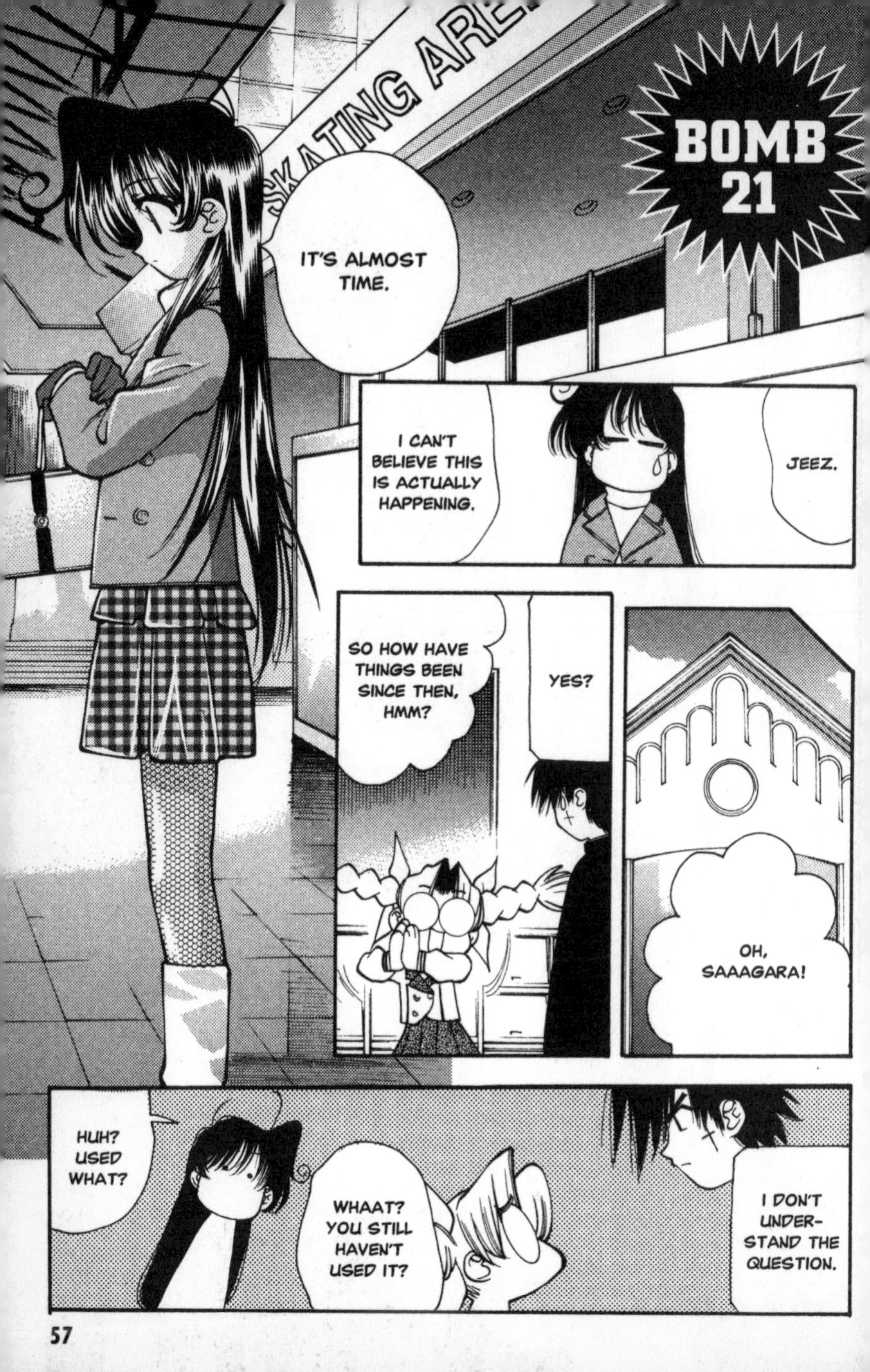
BOMB 21
SKATING ARE
IT'S ALMOST TIME.
JEEZ.
I CAN'T BELIEVE THIS IS ACTUALLY HAPPENING.
OH, SAAAGARA!
YES?
SO HOW HAVE THINGS BEEN SINCE THEN, HMM?
I DON'T UNDER-STAND THE QUESTION.
WHAAT? YOU STILL HAVEN'T USED IT?
HUH? USED WHAT?

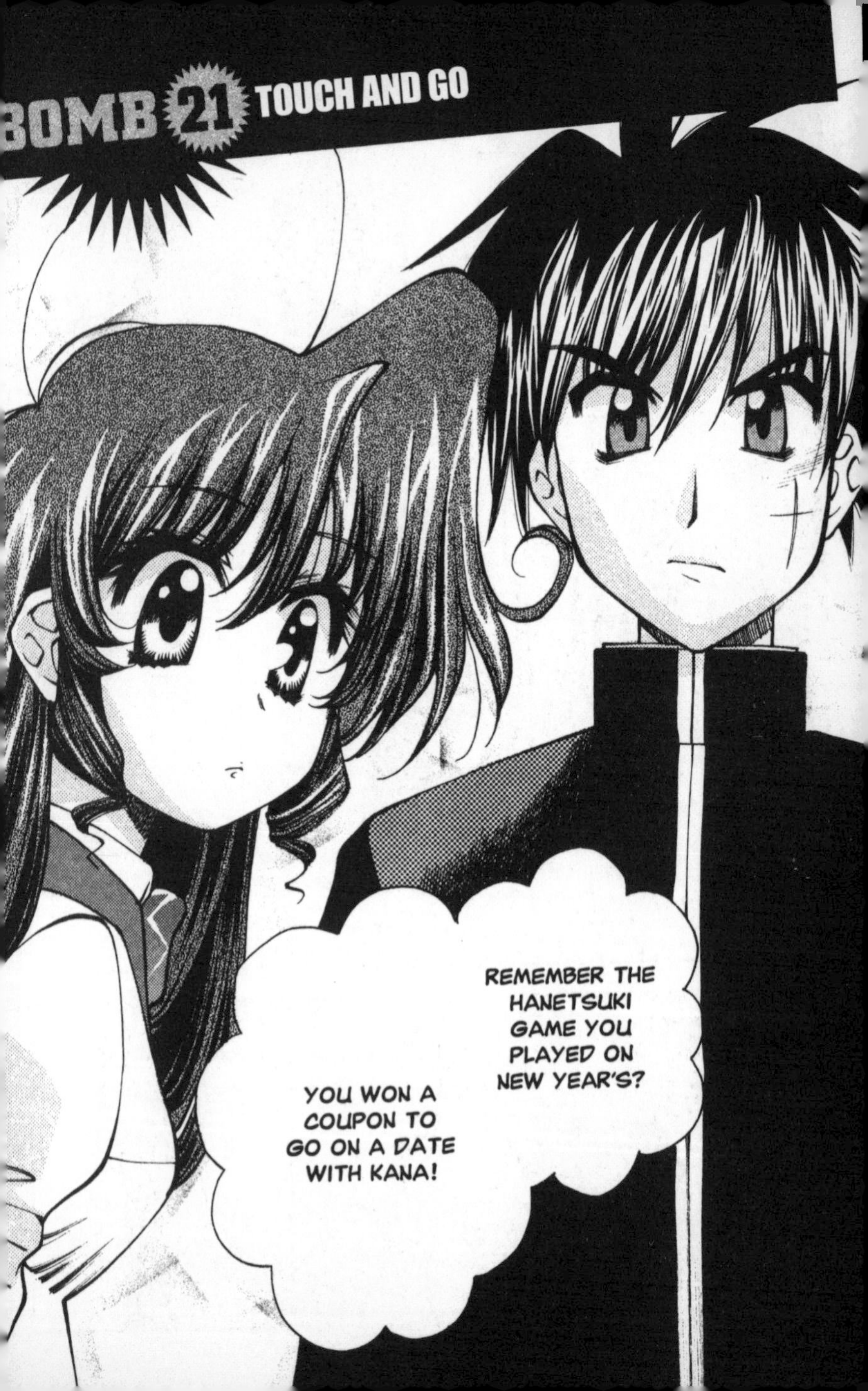
BOMB 21 TOUCH AND GO
REMEMBER THE HANETSUKI GAME YOU PLAYED ON NEW YEAR'S?
YOU WON A COUPON TO GO ON A DATE WITH KANA!

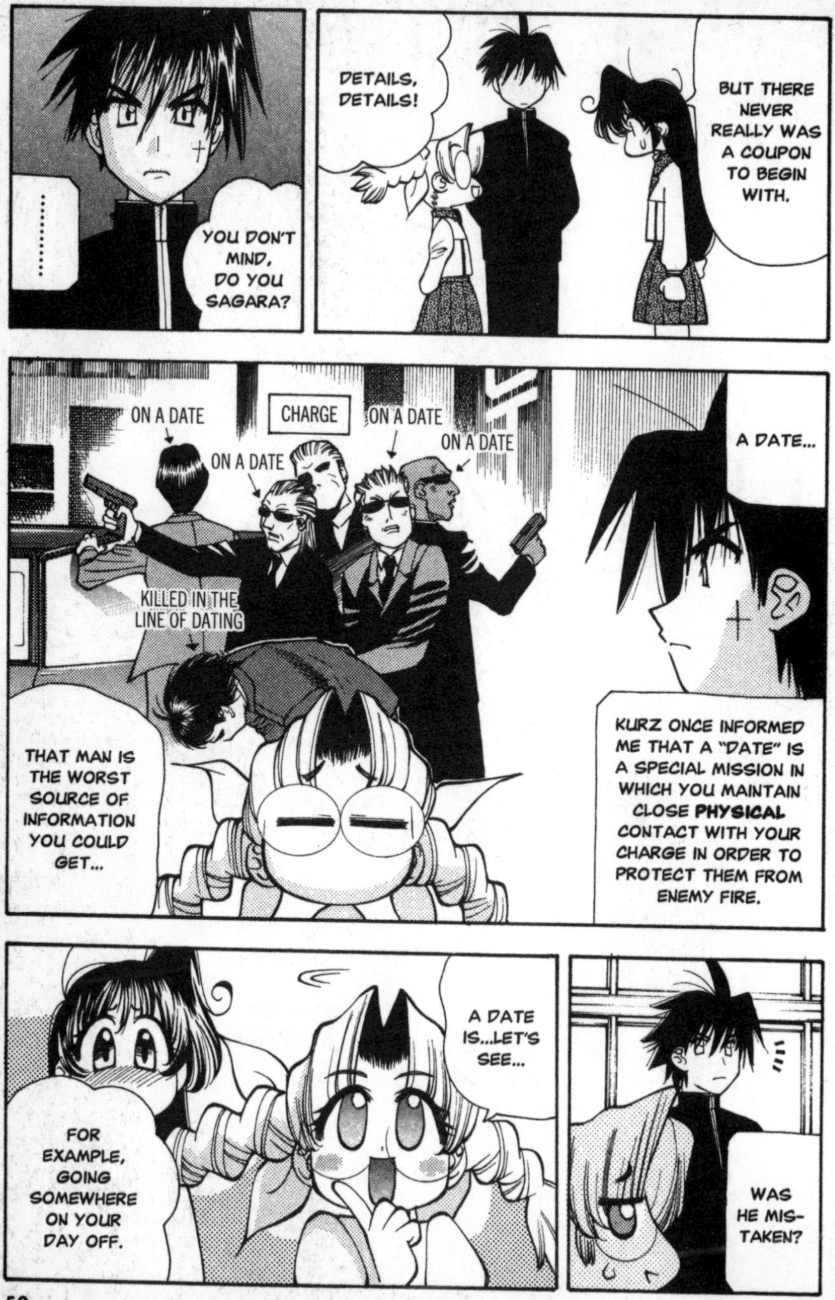
BUT THERE NEVER REALLY WAS A COUPON TO BEGIN WITH.
DETAILS, DETAILS!
YOU DON'T MIND, DO YOU SAGARA?
......
A DATE...
KURZ ONCE INFORMED ME THAT A "DATE" IS A SPECIAL MISSION IN WHICH YOU MAINTAIN CLOSE **PHYSICAL** CONTACT WITH YOUR CHARGE IN ORDER TO PROTECT THEM FROM ENEMY FIRE.
ON A DATE
CHARGE
ON A DATE
ON A DATE
ON A DATE
KILLED IN THE LINE OF DATING
THAT MAN IS THE WORST SOURCE OF INFORMATION YOU COULD GET...
WAS HE MIS-TAKEN?
A DATE IS...LET'S SEE...
FOR EXAMPLE, GOING SOMEWHERE ON YOUR DAY OFF.

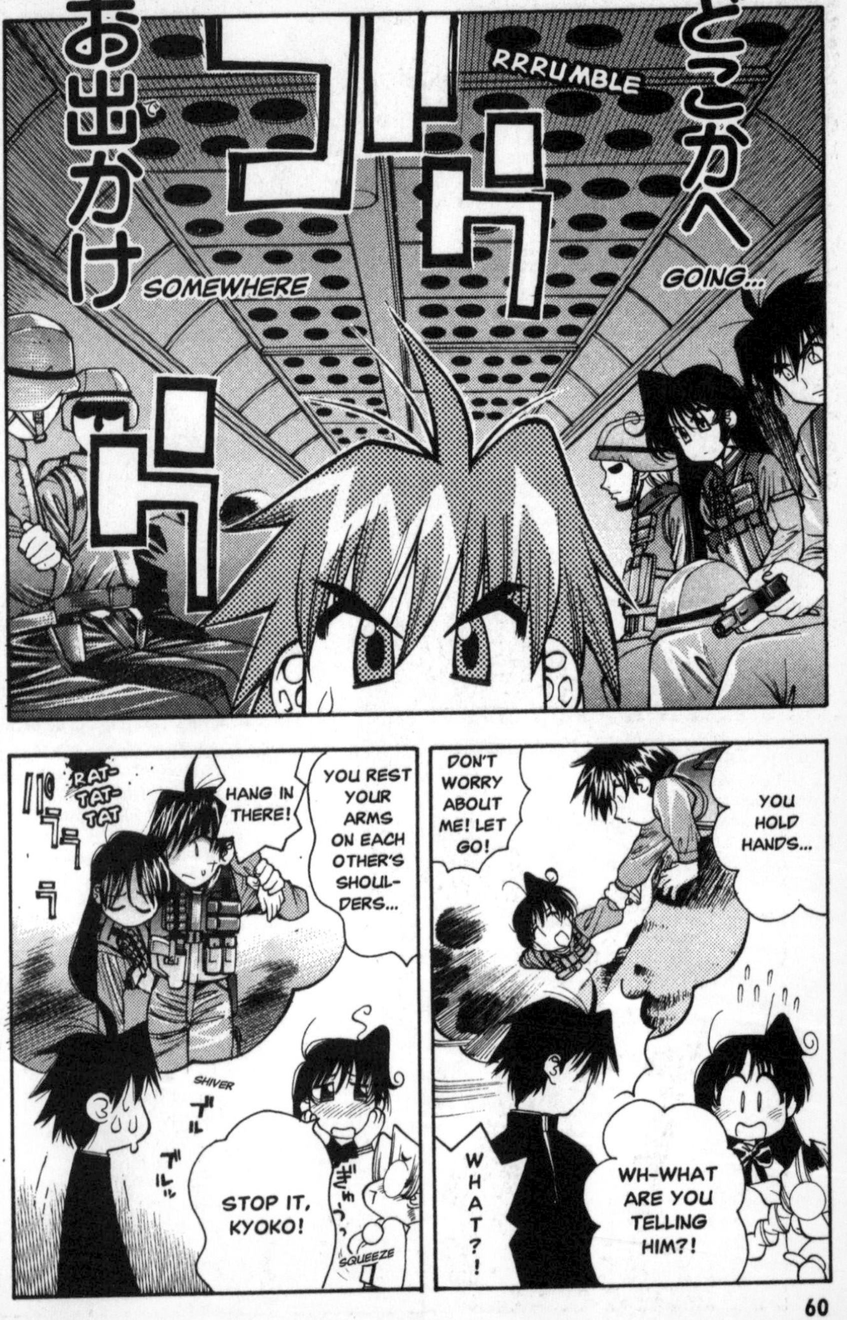
どこかへ
GOING...
ゴロゴロ
RRRUMBLE
お出かけ
SOMEWHERE
YOU HOLD HANDS...
DON'T WORRY ABOUT ME! LET GO!
WH-WHAT ARE YOU TELLING HIM?!
WHAT?!
YOU REST YOUR ARMS ON EACH OTHER'S SHOUL-DERS...
HANG IN THERE!
パラララ
RAT-TAT-TAT
ぎゅっ
SQUEEZE
STOP IT, KYOKO!
ブルブル
SHIVER

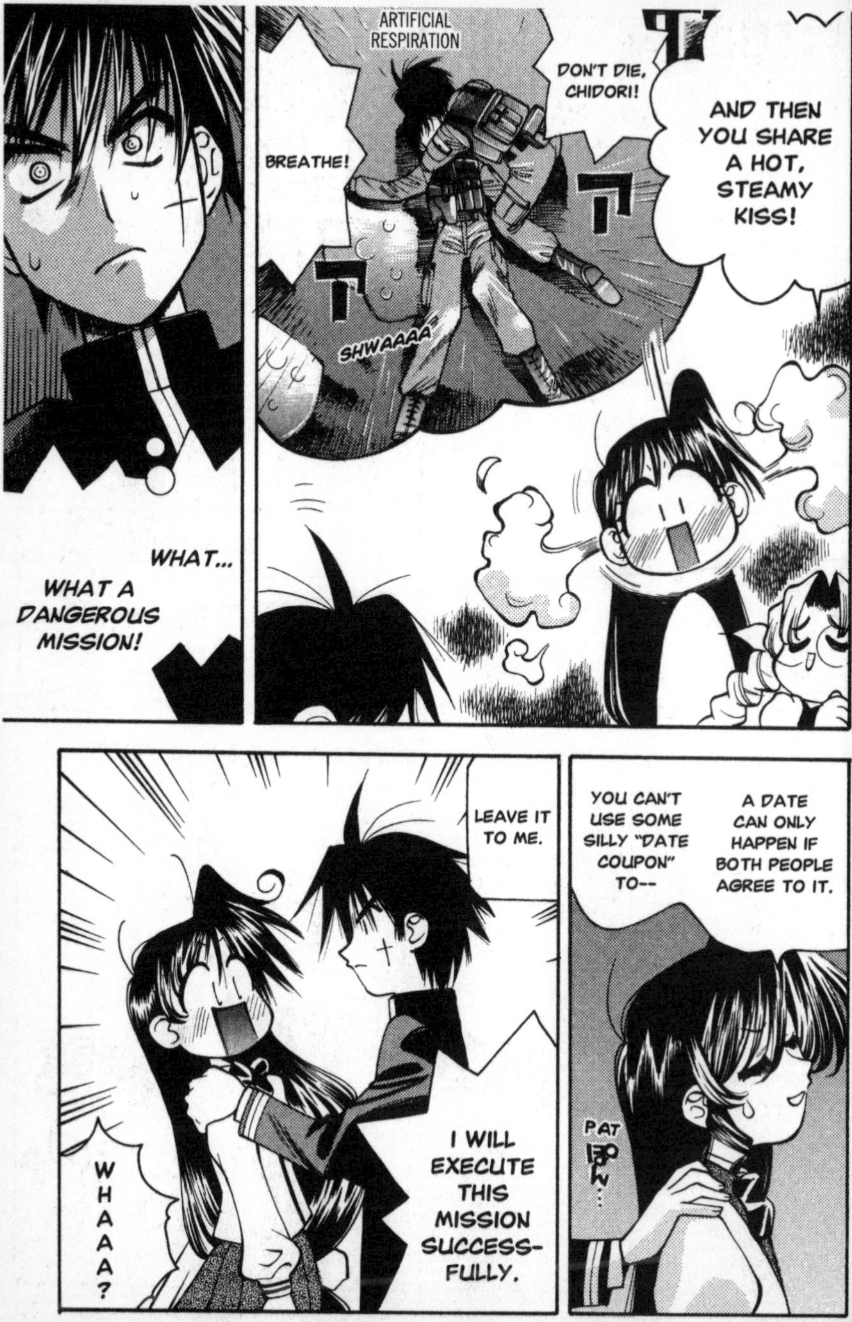
AND THEN YOU SHARE A HOT, STEAMY KISS!
ARTIFICIAL RESPIRATION
DON'T DIE, CHIDORI!
BREATHE!
SHWAAAA
WHAT...
WHAT A DANGEROUS MISSION!
A DATE CAN ONLY HAPPEN IF BOTH PEOPLE AGREE TO IT.
YOU CAN'T USE SOME SILLY "DATE COUPON" TO--
PAT
LEAVE IT TO ME.
I WILL EXECUTE THIS MISSION SUCCESS-FULLY.
WHAAAA?

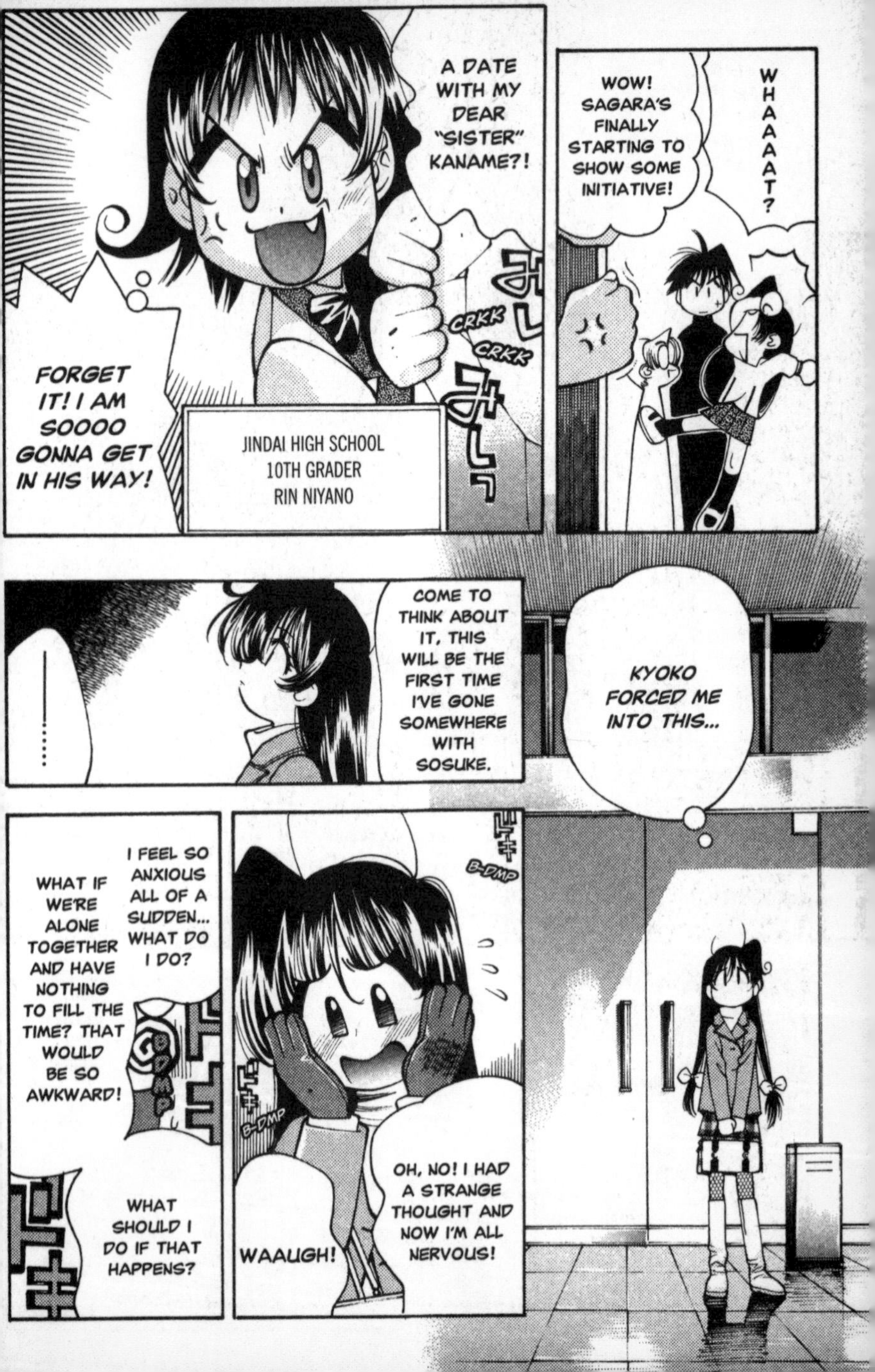
WOW! SAGARA'S FINALLY STARTING TO SHOW SOME INITIATIVE!
WHAAAAAT?
A DATE WITH MY DEAR "SISTER" KANAME?!
CRKK
CRKK
FORGET IT! I AM SOOOO GONNA GET IN HIS WAY!
JINDAI HIGH SCHOOL
10TH GRADER
RIN NIYANO
KYOKO FORCED ME INTO THIS...
COME TO THINK ABOUT IT, THIS WILL BE THE FIRST TIME I'VE GONE SOMEWHERE WITH SOSUKE.
......
B-DMP
I FEEL SO ANXIOUS ALL OF A SUDDEN... WHAT DO I DO?
WHAT IF WE'RE ALONE TOGETHER AND HAVE NOTHING TO FILL THE TIME? THAT WOULD BE SO AWKWARD!
B-DMP
OH, NO! I HAD A STRANGE THOUGHT AND NOW I'M ALL NERVOUS!
WAAUGH!
WHAT SHOULD I DO IF THAT HAPPENS?

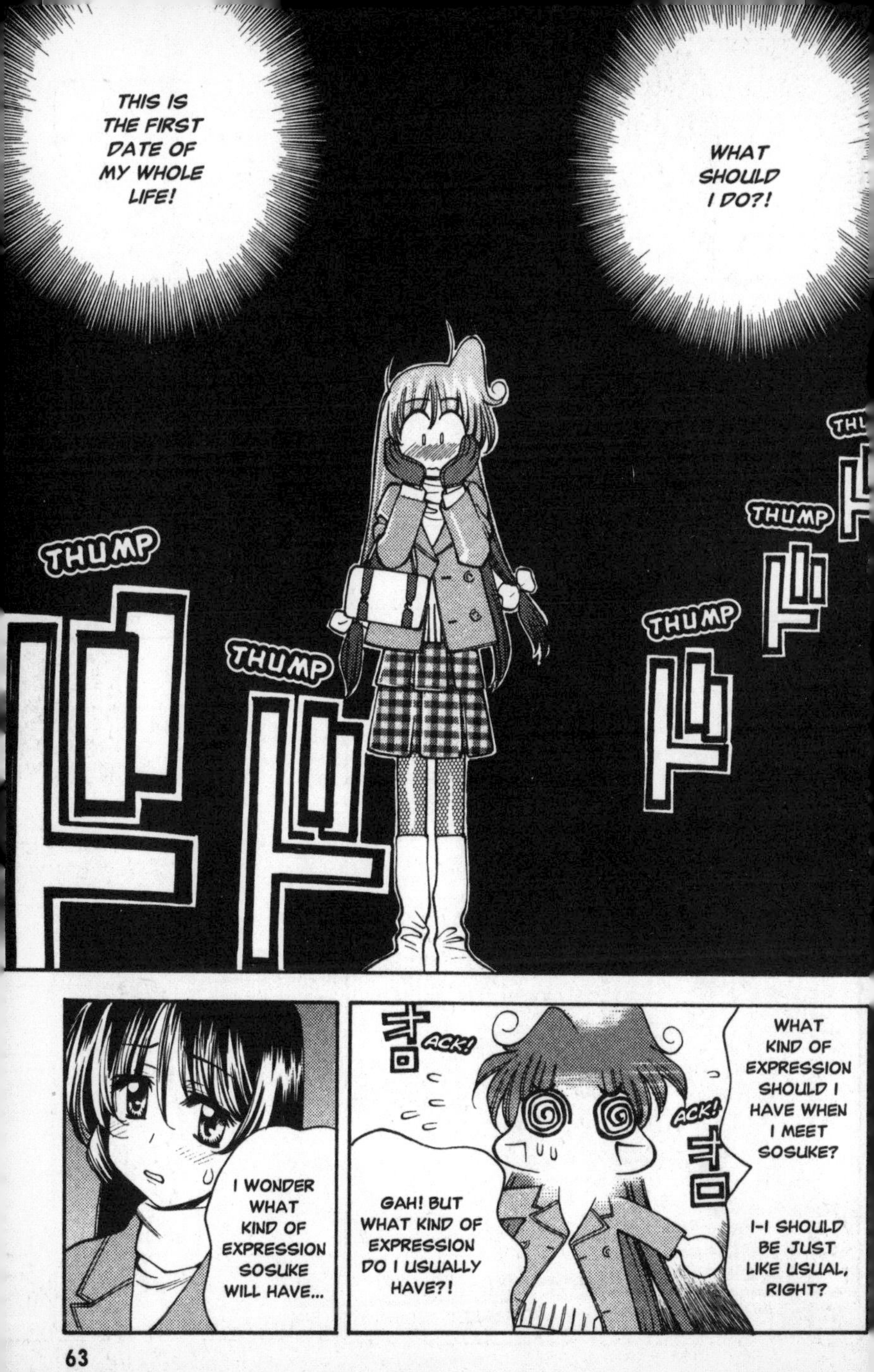
WHAT SHOULD I DO?!
THIS IS THE FIRST DATE OF MY WHOLE LIFE!
THUMP
THUMP
THUMP
THUMP
WHAT KIND OF EXPRESSION SHOULD I HAVE WHEN I MEET SOSUKE?
ACK!
ACK!
I-I SHOULD BE JUST LIKE USUAL, RIGHT?
GAH! BUT WHAT KIND OF EXPRESSION DO I USUALLY HAVE?!
I WONDER WHAT KIND OF EXPRESSION SOSUKE WILL HAVE...

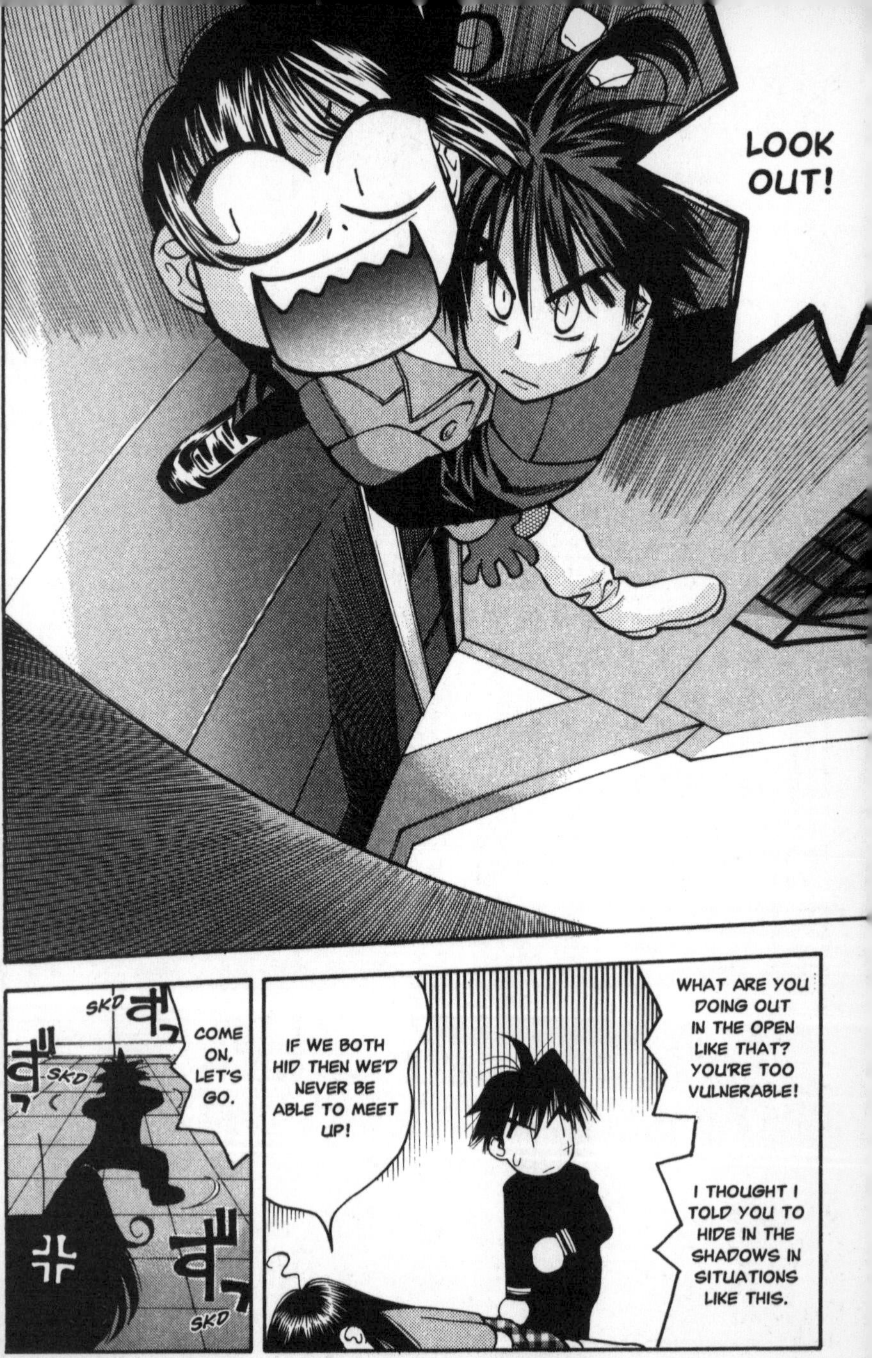
LOOK OUT!
WHAT ARE YOU DOING OUT IN THE OPEN LIKE THAT? YOU'RE TOO VULNERABLE!
I THOUGHT I TOLD YOU TO HIDE IN THE SHADOWS IN SITUATIONS LIKE THIS.
IF WE BOTH HID THEN WE'D NEVER BE ABLE TO MEET UP!
SKD
COME ON, LET'S GO.
SKD
SKD

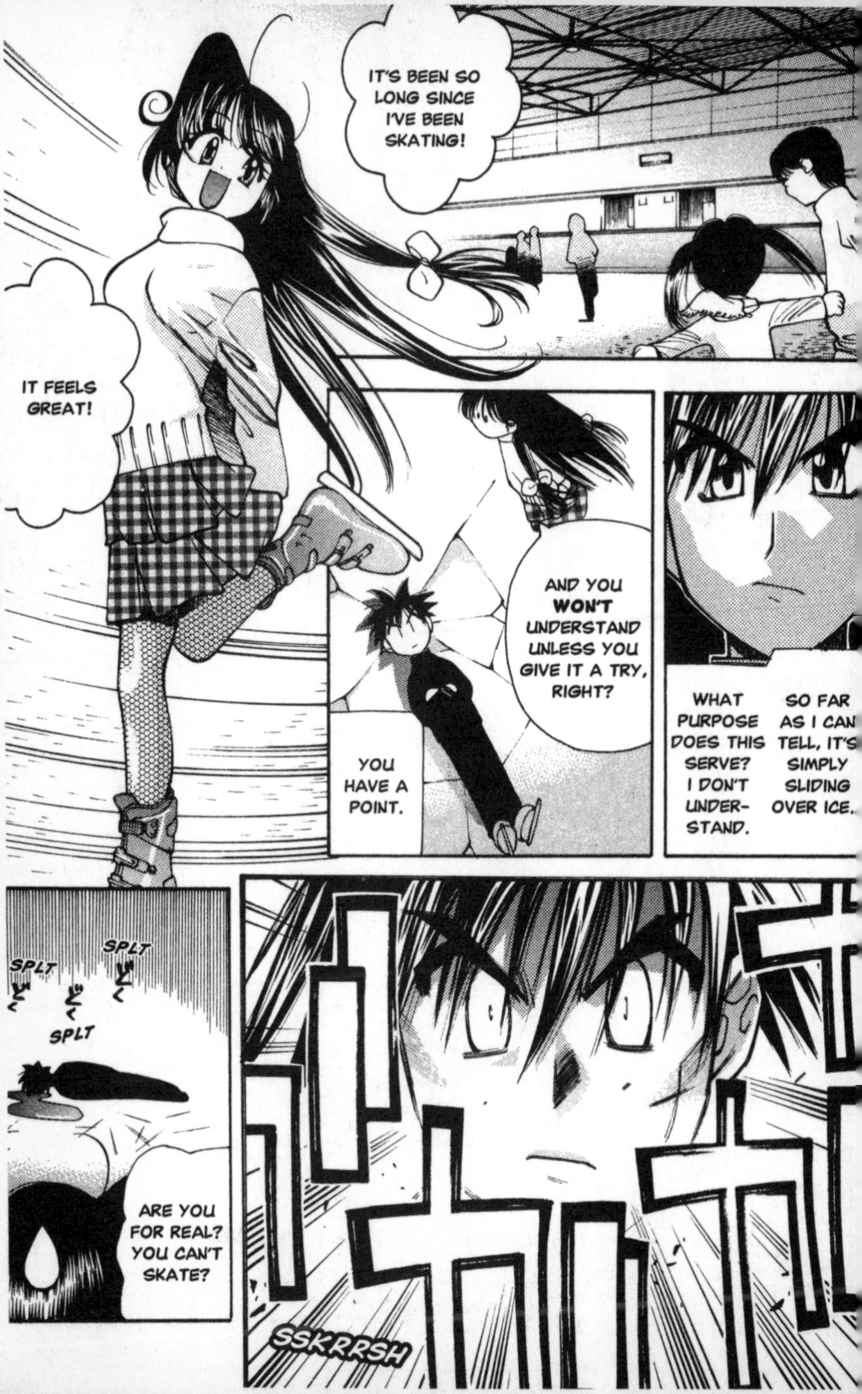
IT'S BEEN SO LONG SINCE I'VE BEEN SKATING!
IT FEELS GREAT!
SO FAR AS I CAN TELL, IT'S SIMPLY SLIDING OVER ICE..
WHAT PURPOSE DOES THIS SERVE? I DON'T UNDER-STAND.
AND YOU **WON'T** UNDERSTAND UNLESS YOU GIVE IT A TRY, RIGHT?
YOU HAVE A POINT.
SSKRRSH
SPLT
SPLT
SPLT
ARE YOU FOR REAL? YOU CAN'T SKATE?

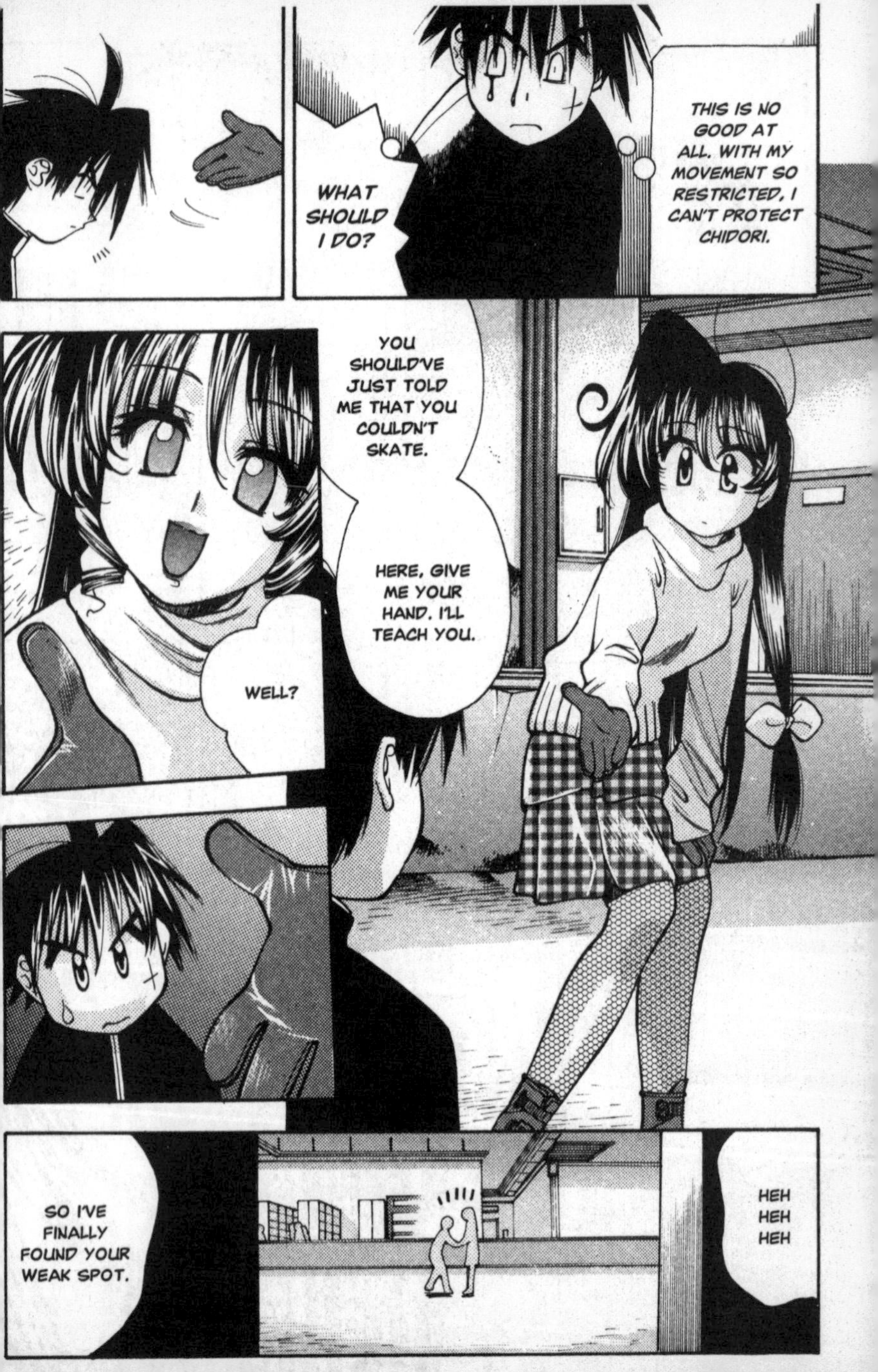
THIS IS NO GOOD AT ALL. WITH MY MOVEMENT SO RESTRICTED, I CAN'T PROTECT CHIDORI.
WHAT SHOULD I DO?
YOU SHOULD'VE JUST TOLD ME THAT YOU COULDN'T SKATE.
HERE, GIVE ME YOUR HAND. I'LL TEACH YOU.
WELL?
HEH HEH HEH
SO I'VE FINALLY FOUND YOUR WEAK SPOT.

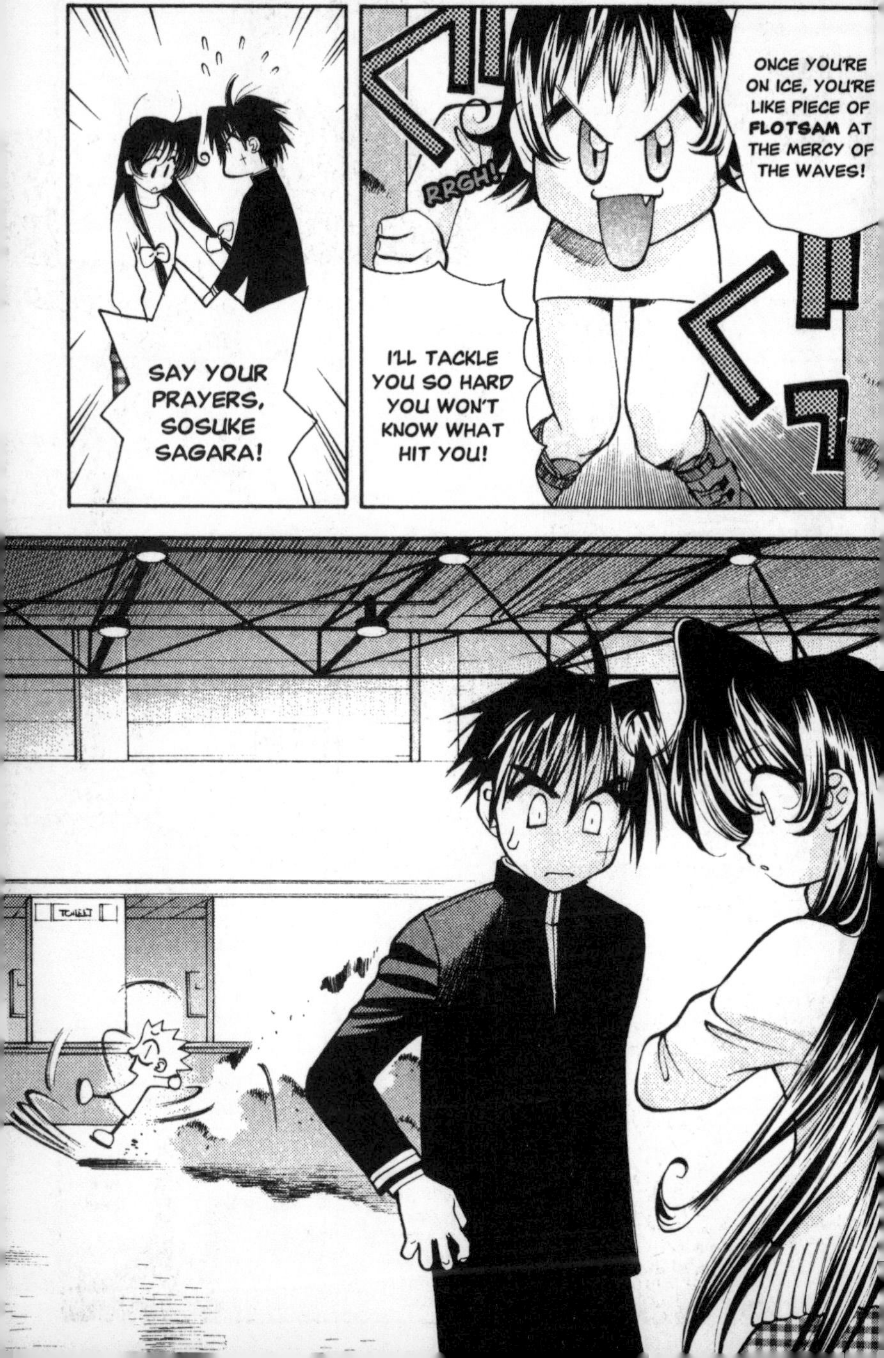
ONCE YOU'RE ON ICE, YOU'RE LIKE PIECE OF **FLOTSAM** AT THE MERCY OF THE WAVES!
RRGH!
I'LL TACKLE YOU SO HARD YOU WON'T KNOW WHAT HIT YOU!
SAY YOUR PRAYERS, SOSUKE SAGARA!

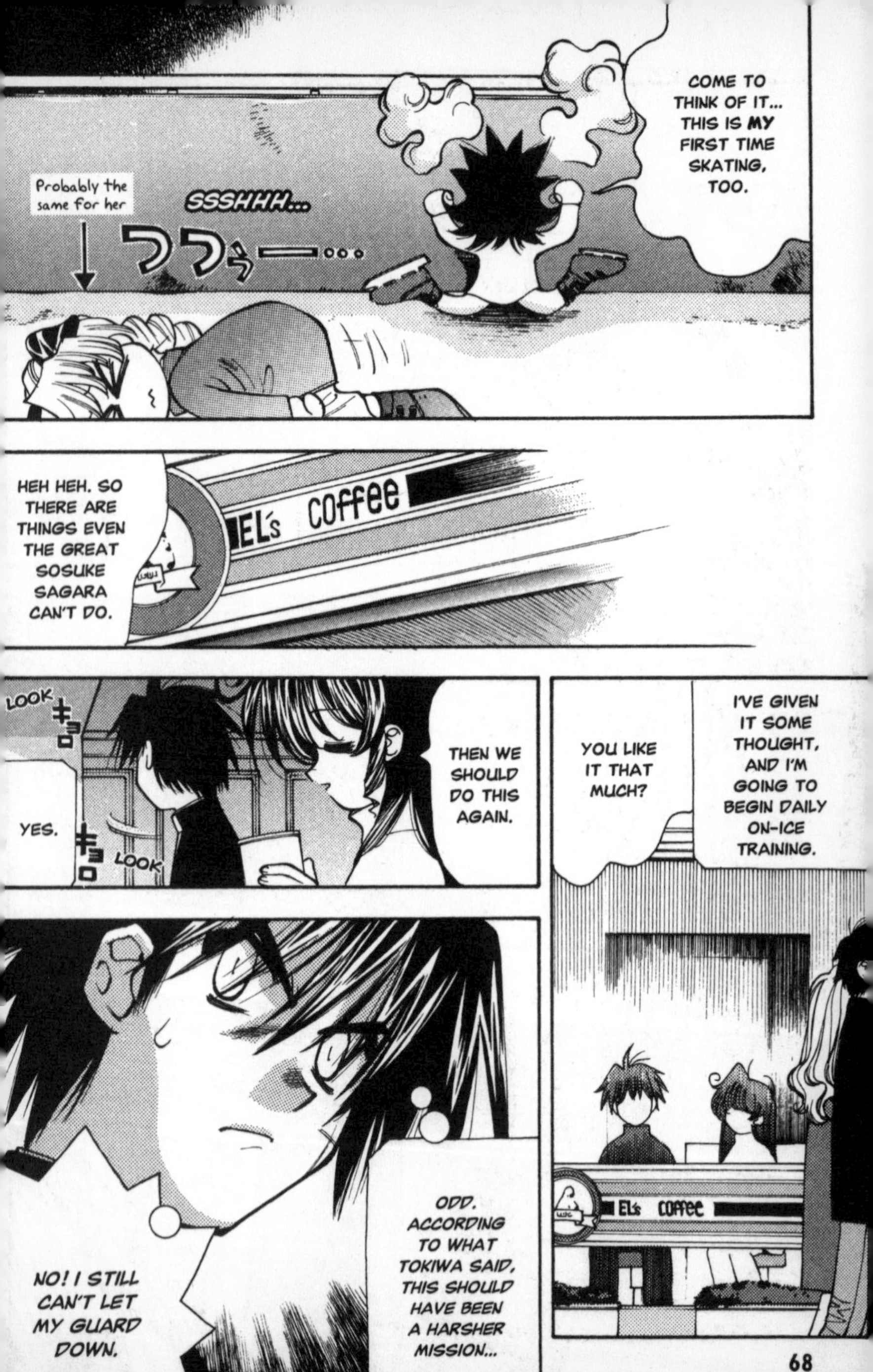

COME TO THINK OF IT... THIS IS MY FIRST TIME SKATING, TOO.
SSSHHH...
つつぅー・・・
Probably the same for her
HEH HEH. SO THERE ARE THINGS EVEN THE GREAT SOSUKE SAGARA CAN'T DO.
EL's coffee
I'VE GIVEN IT SOME THOUGHT, AND I'M GOING TO BEGIN DAILY ON-ICE TRAINING.
YOU LIKE IT THAT MUCH?
THEN WE SHOULD DO THIS AGAIN.
LOOK
キョロ
YES.
キョロ
LOOK
EL's coffee
ODD. ACCORDING TO WHAT TOKIWA SAID, THIS SHOULD HAVE BEEN A HARSHER MISSION...
NO! I STILL CAN'T LET MY GUARD DOWN.

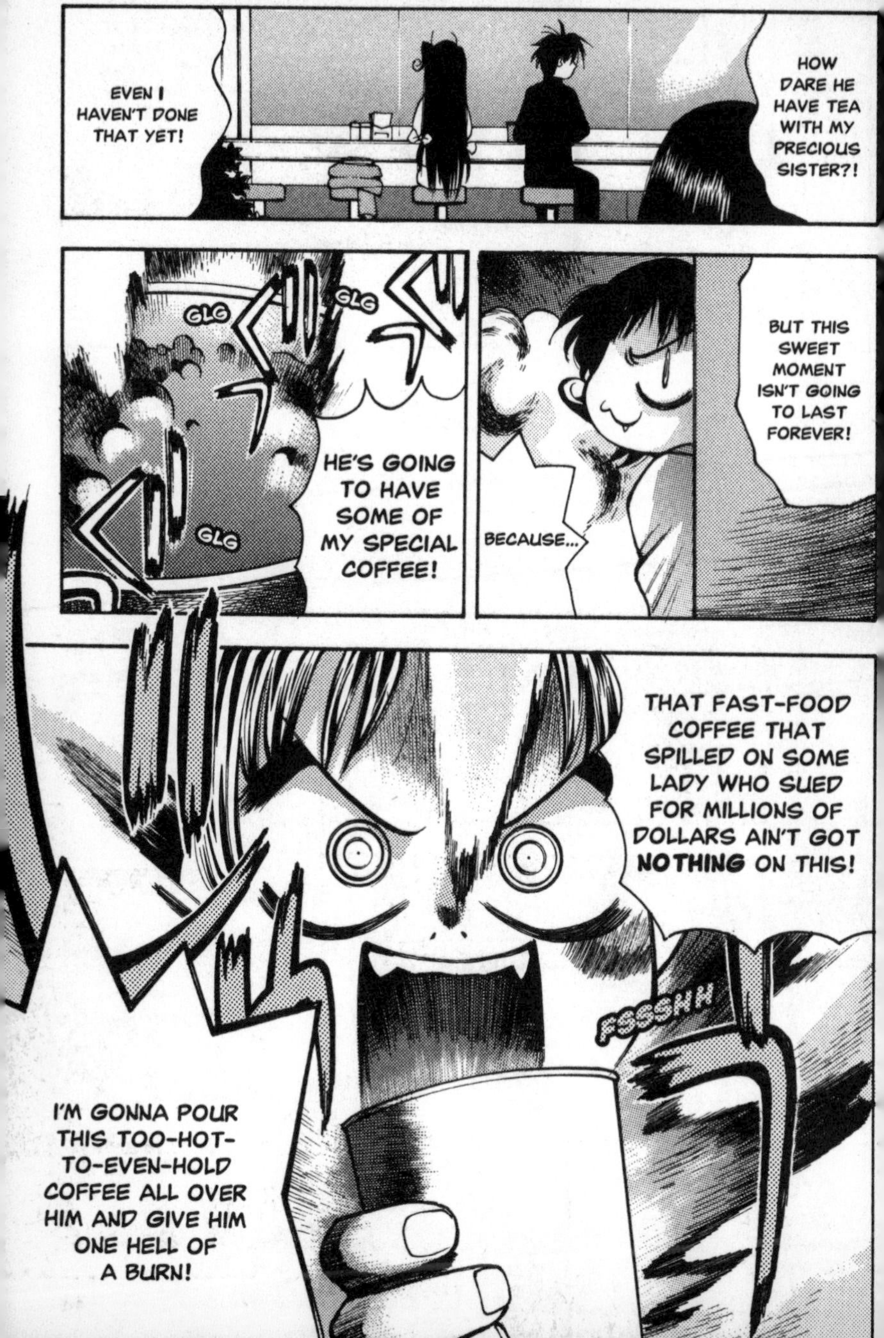
HOW DARE HE HAVE TEA WITH MY PRECIOUS SISTER?!
EVEN I HAVEN'T DONE THAT YET!
BUT THIS SWEET MOMENT ISN'T GOING TO LAST FOREVER!
BECAUSE...
GLG
GLG
GLG
HE'S GOING TO HAVE SOME OF MY SPECIAL COFFEE!
THAT FAST-FOOD COFFEE THAT SPILLED ON SOME LADY WHO SUED FOR MILLIONS OF DOLLARS AIN'T GOT NOTHING ON THIS!
FSSSHH
I'M GONNA POUR THIS TOO-HOT-TO-EVEN-HOLD COFFEE ALL OVER HIM AND GIVE HIM ONE HELL OF A BURN!

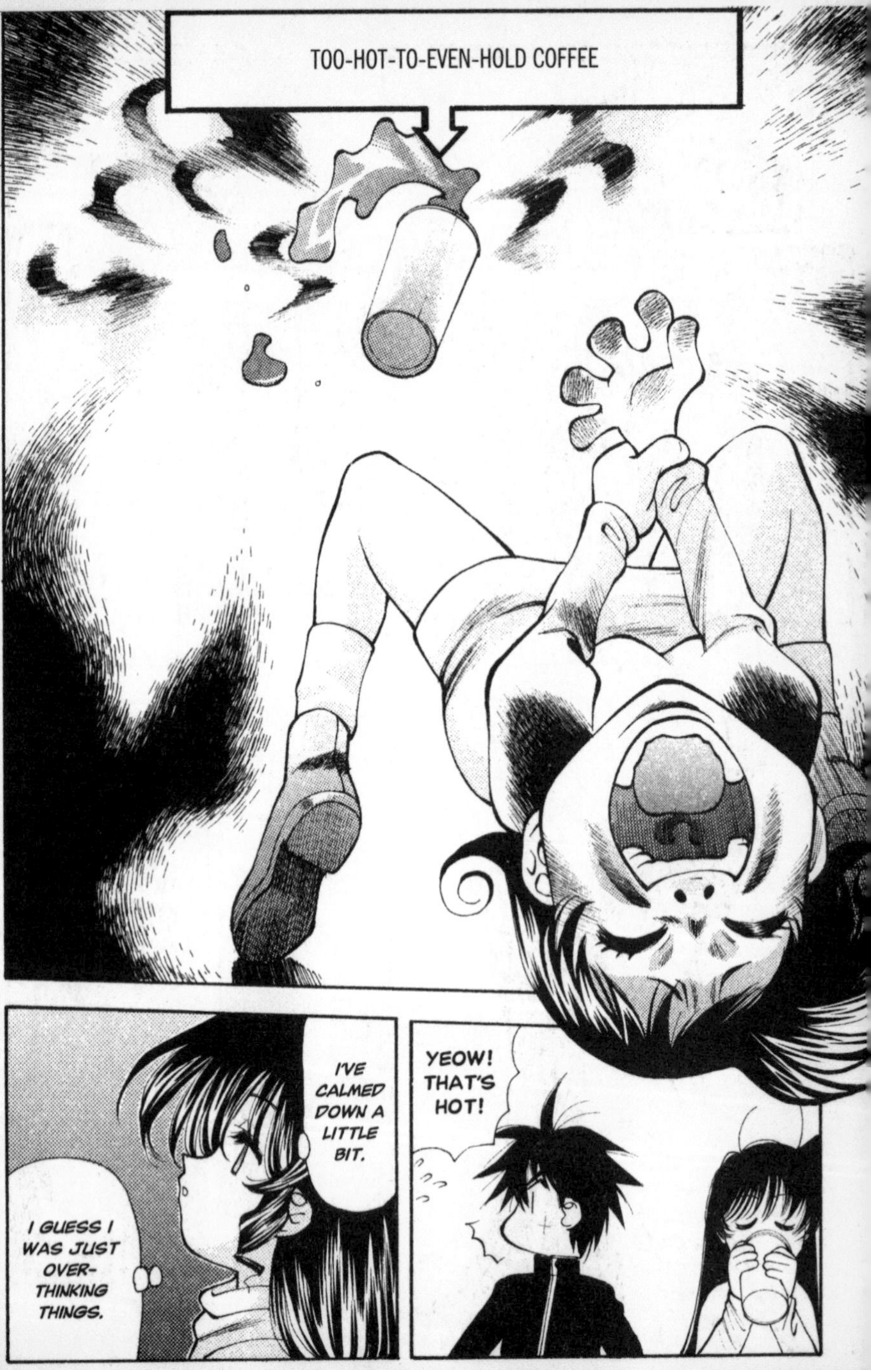
TOO-HOT-TO-EVEN-HOLD COFFEE
I'VE CALMED DOWN A LITTLE BIT.
I GUESS I WAS JUST OVER-THINKING THINGS.
YEOW! THAT'S HOT!

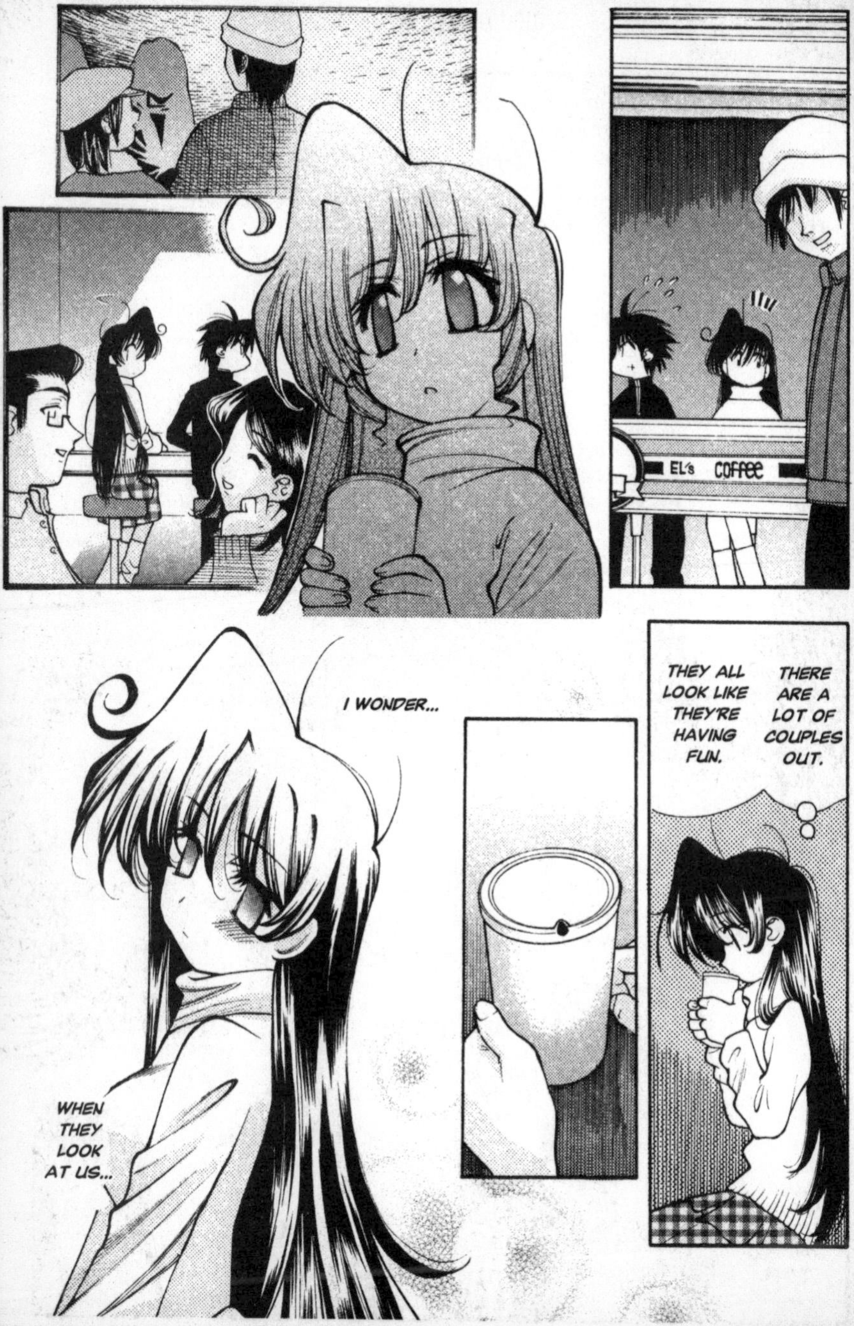
EL's COFFEE
THERE ARE A LOT OF COUPLES OUT.
THEY ALL LOOK LIKE THEY'RE HAVING FUN.
I WONDER...
WHEN THEY LOOK AT US...

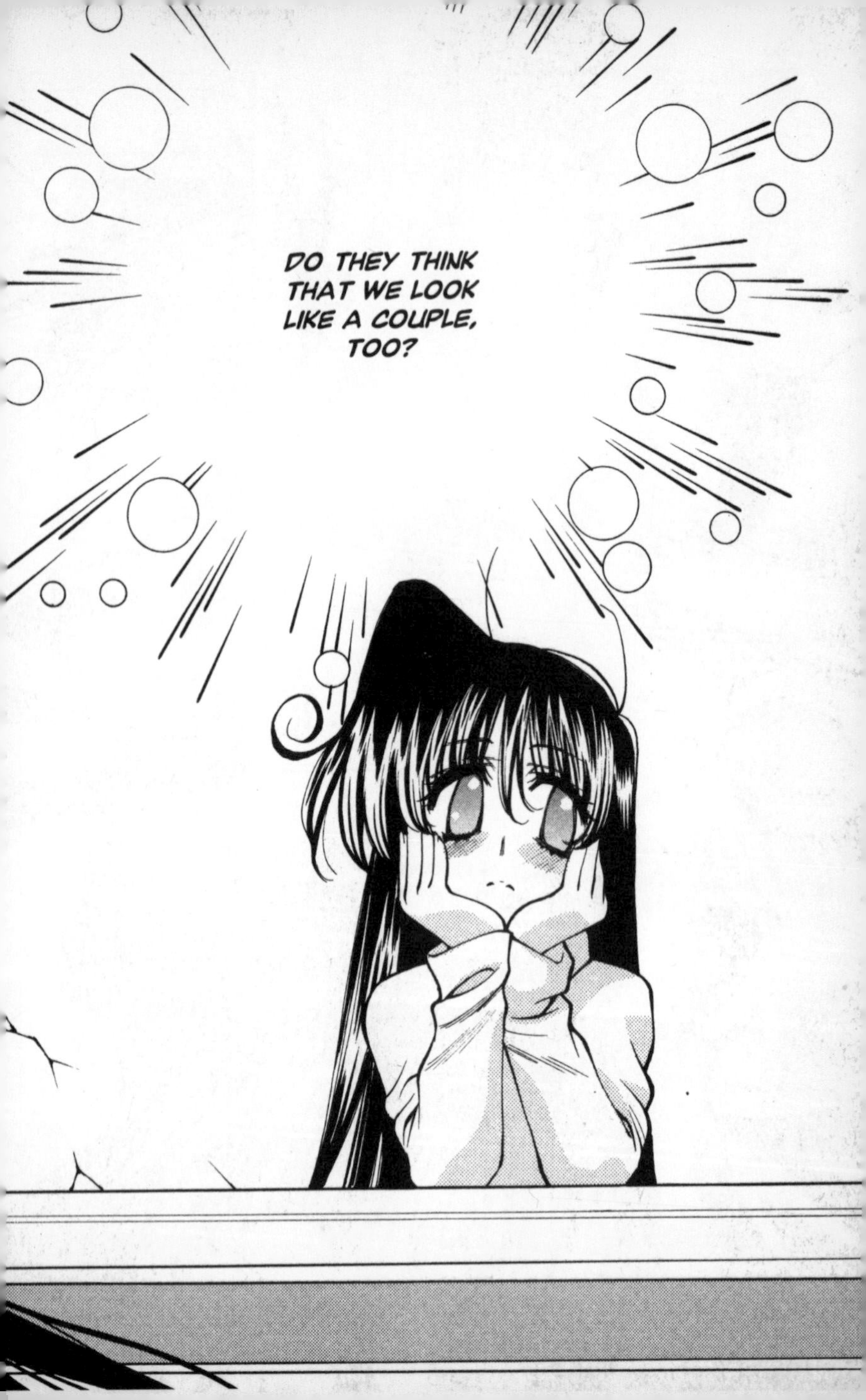
DO THEY THINK THAT WE LOOK LIKE A COUPLE, TOO?

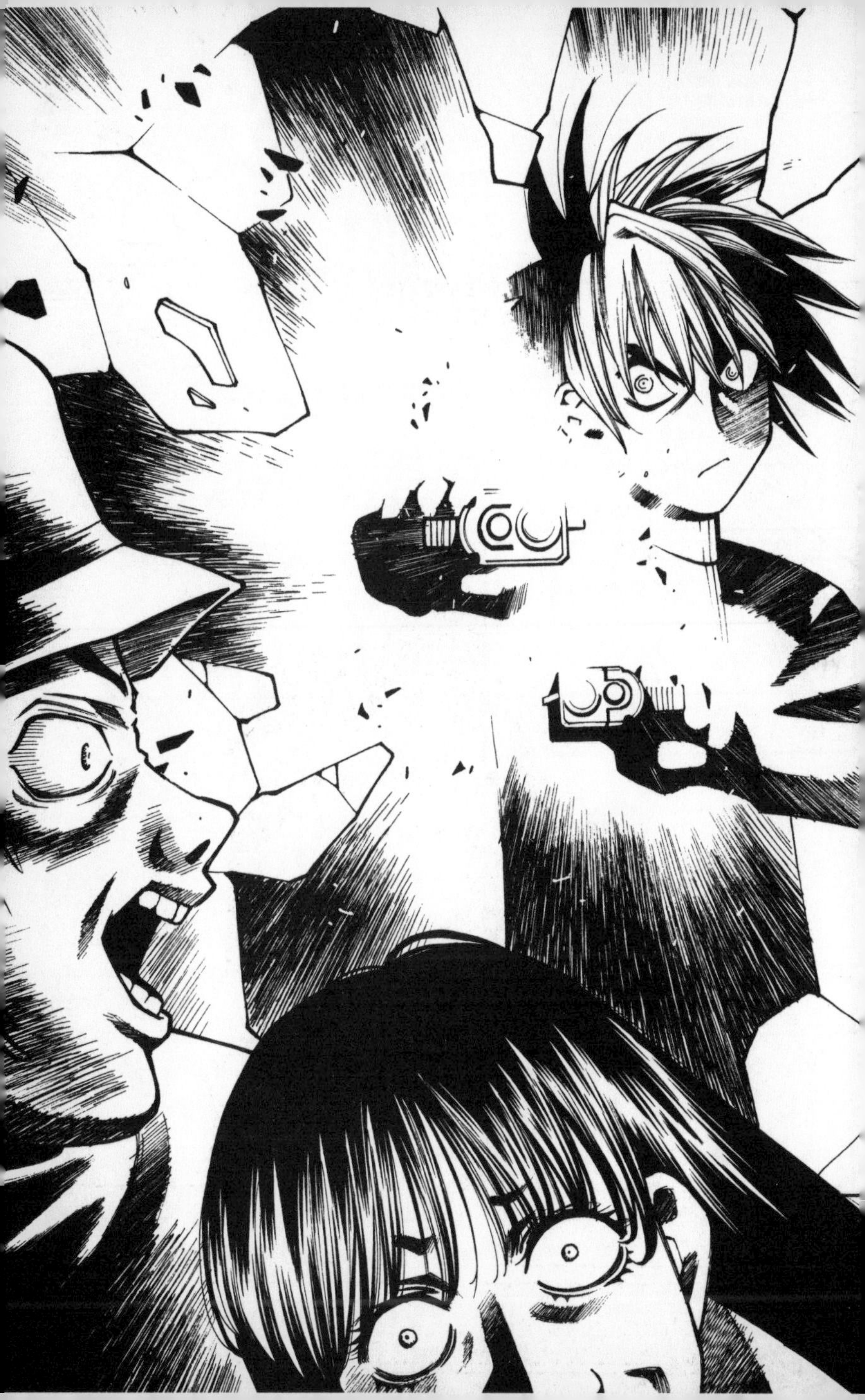

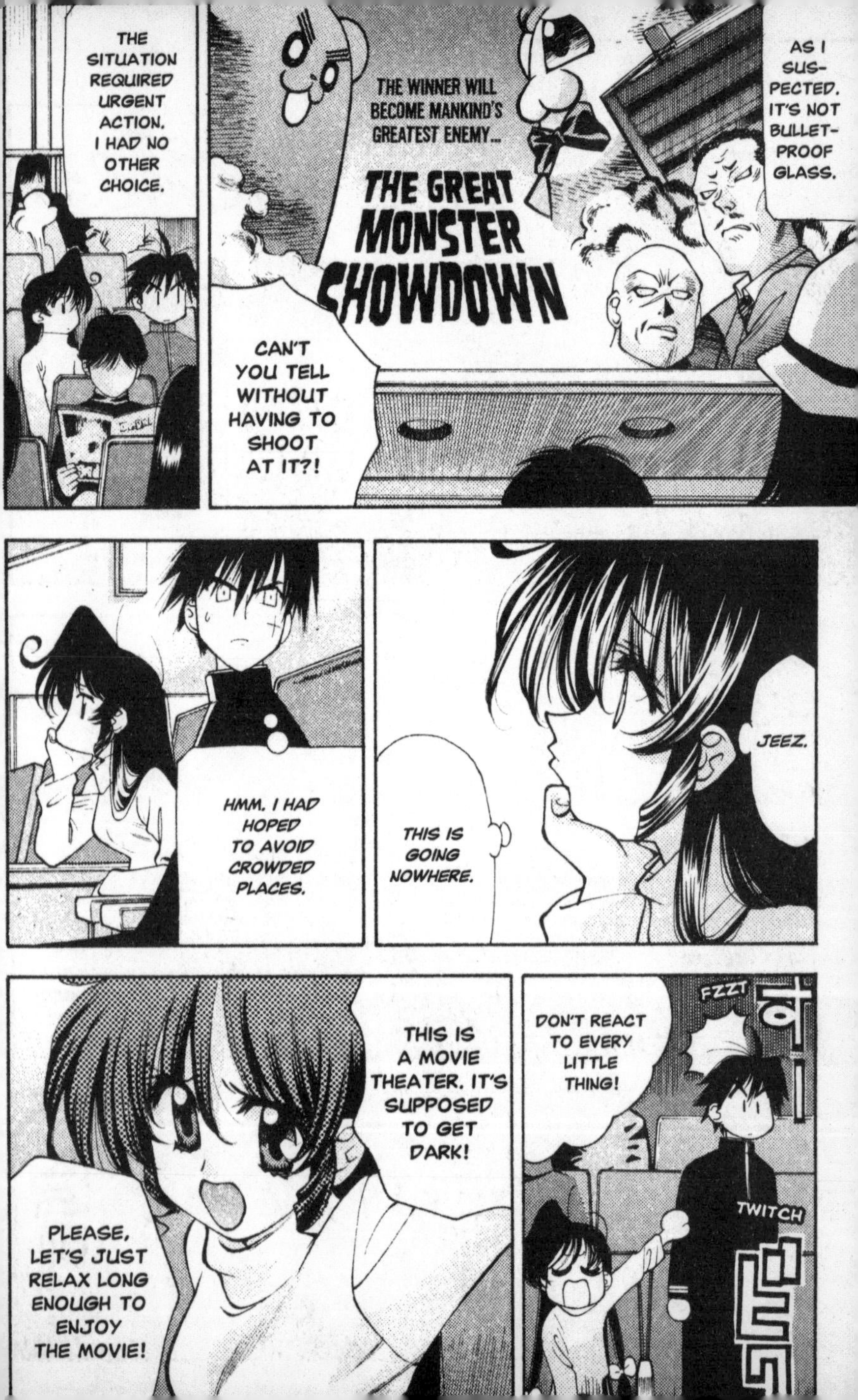
AS I SUSPECTED. IT'S NOT BULLET-PROOF GLASS.
THE WINNER WILL BECOME MANKIND'S GREATEST ENEMY...
THE GREAT MONSTER CHOWDOWN
CAN'T YOU TELL WITHOUT HAVING TO SHOOT AT IT?!
THE SITUATION REQUIRED URGENT ACTION. I HAD NO OTHER CHOICE.
JEEZ.
THIS IS GOING NOWHERE.
HMM. I HAD HOPED TO AVOID CROWDED PLACES.
FZZT
DON'T REACT TO EVERY LITTLE THING!
TWITCH
THIS IS A MOVIE THEATER. IT'S SUPPOSED TO GET DARK!
PLEASE, LET'S JUST RELAX LONG ENOUGH TO ENJOY THE MOVIE!

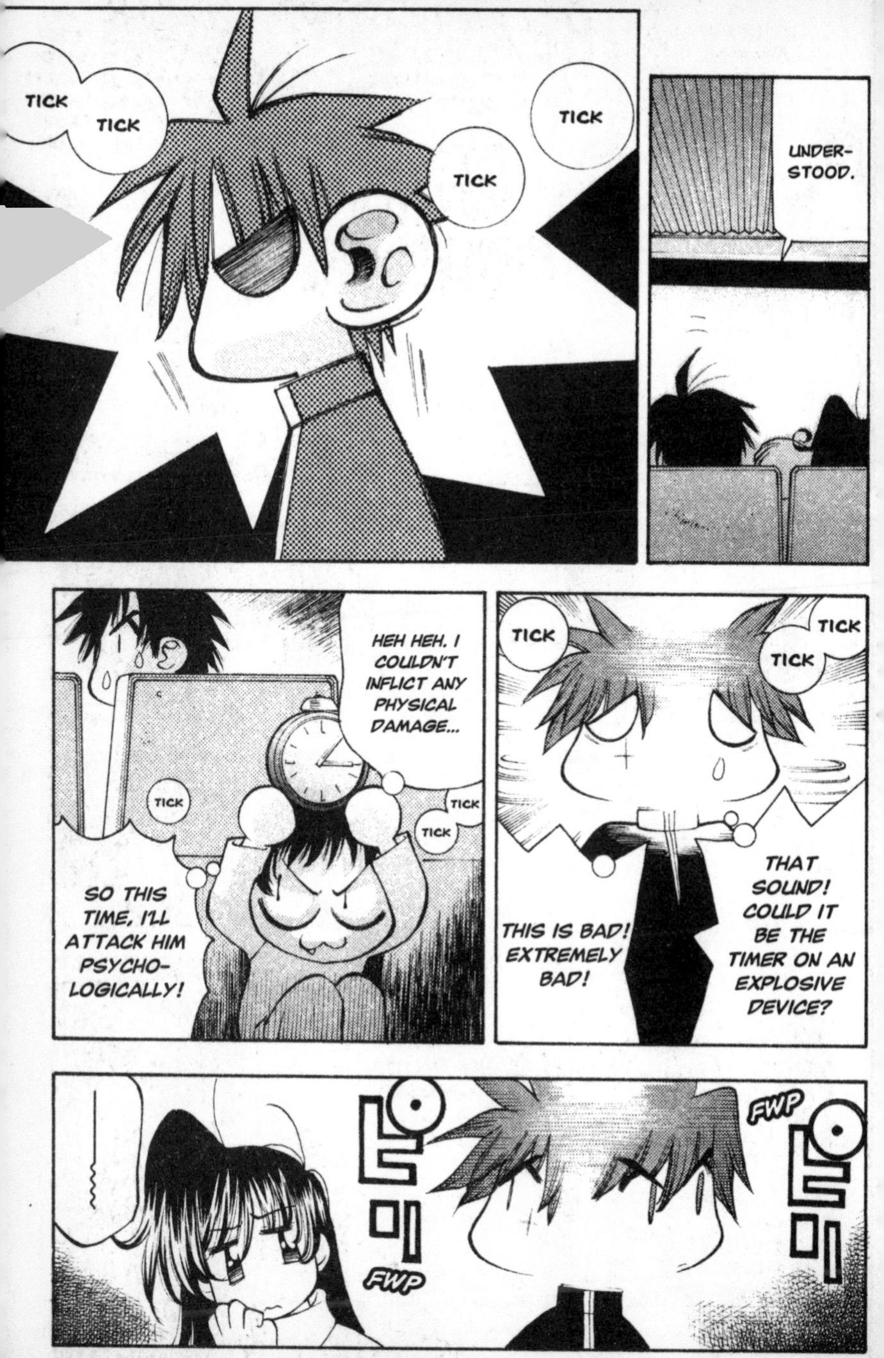
UNDER-STOOD.
TICK
TICK
TICK
TICK
TICK
TICK
TICK
TICK
THAT SOUND! COULD IT BE THE TIMER ON AN EXPLOSIVE DEVICE?
THIS IS BAD! EXTREMELY BAD!
HEH HEH. I COULDN'T INFLICT ANY PHYSICAL DAMAGE...
SO THIS TIME, I'LL ATTACK HIM PSYCHO-LOGICALLY!
TICK
TICK
TICK
FWP
FWP

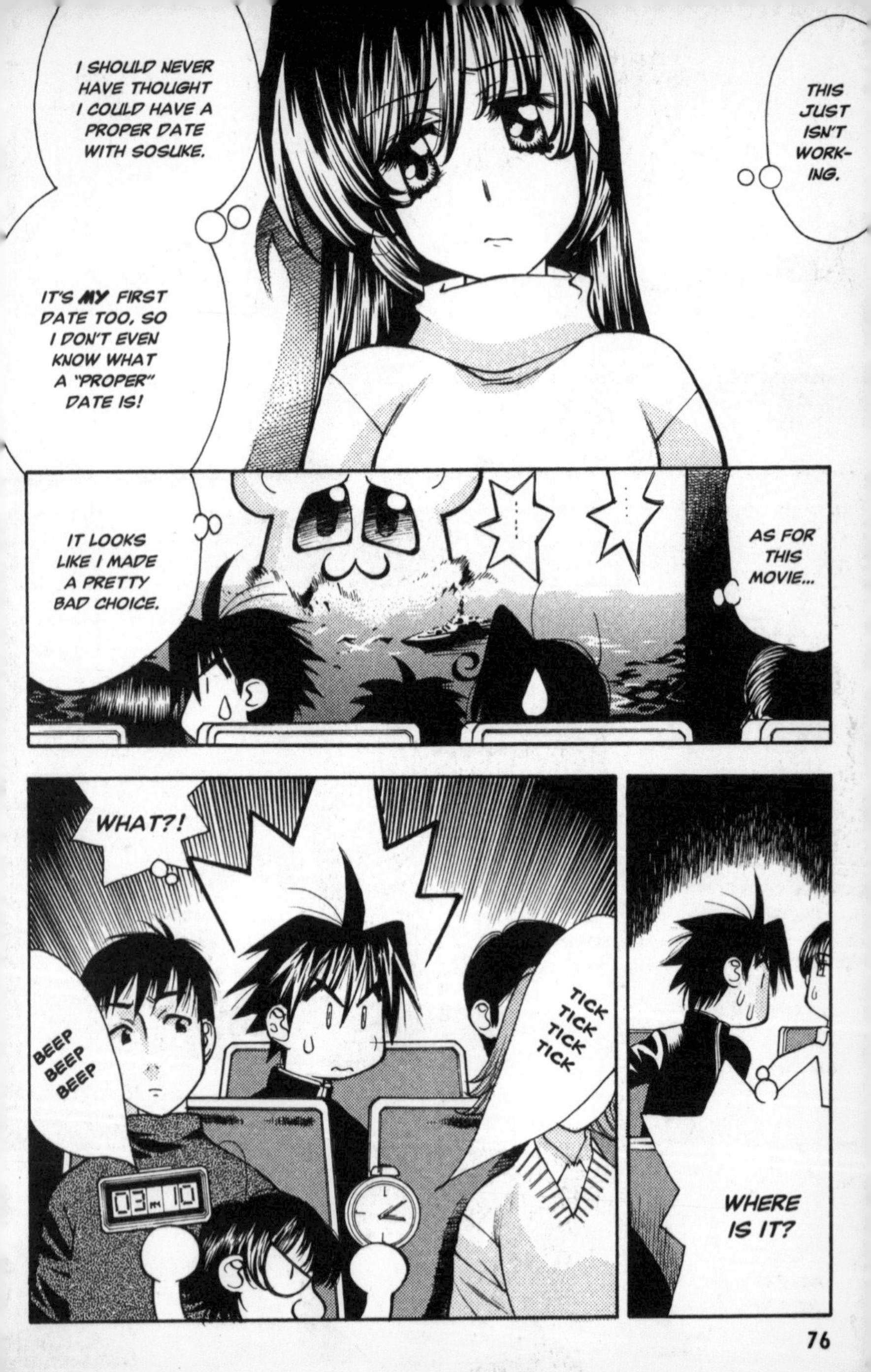
THIS JUST ISN'T WORK-ING.
I SHOULD NEVER HAVE THOUGHT I COULD HAVE A PROPER DATE WITH SOSUKE.
IT'S MY FIRST DATE TOO, SO I DON'T EVEN KNOW WHAT A "PROPER" DATE IS!
AS FOR THIS MOVIE...
IT LOOKS LIKE I MADE A PRETTY BAD CHOICE.
WHERE IS IT?
WHAT?!
TICK TICK TICK TICK
BEEP BEEP BEEP
03 10

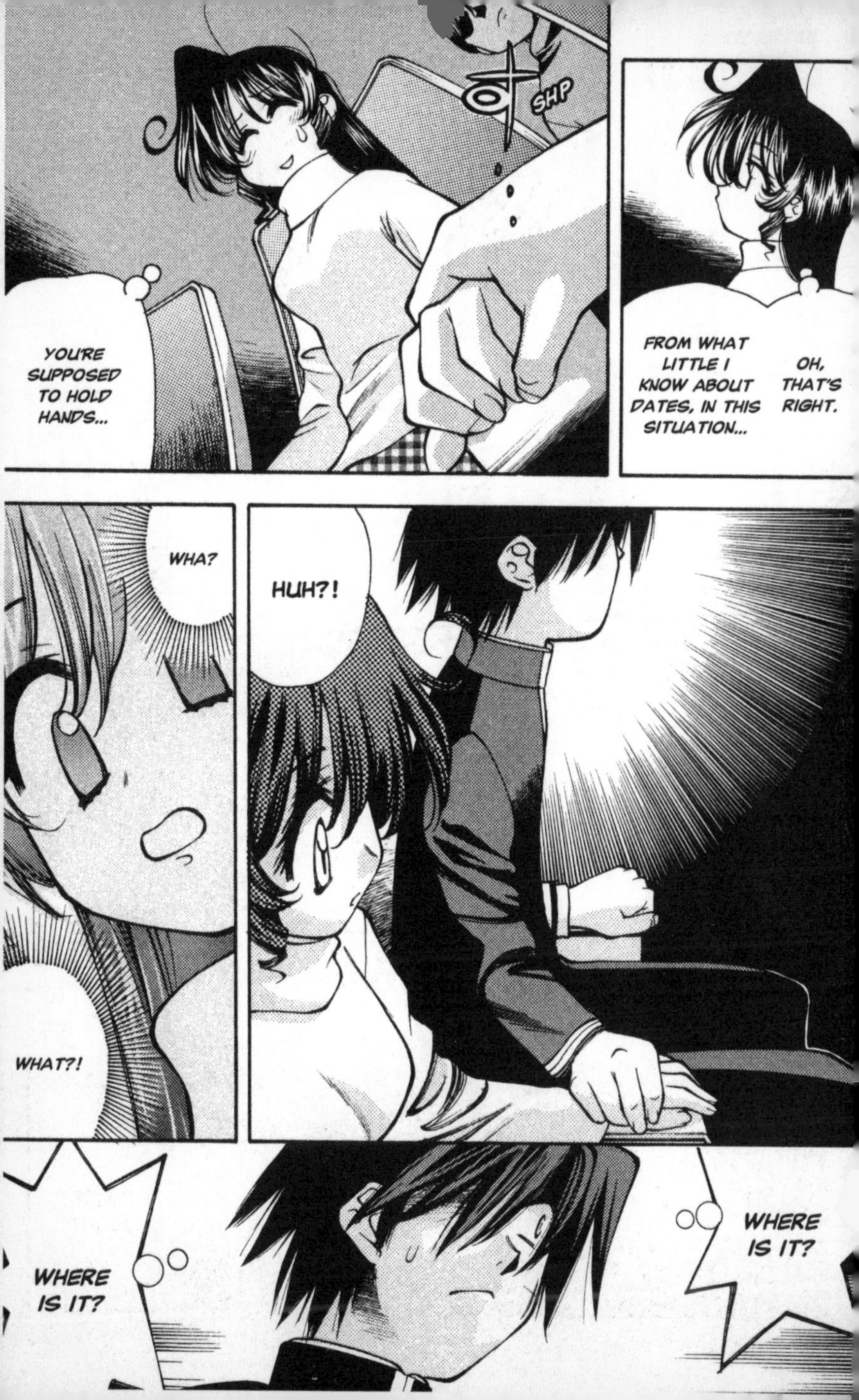
SHP
OH, THAT'S RIGHT.
FROM WHAT LITTLE I KNOW ABOUT DATES, IN THIS SITUATION...
YOU'RE SUPPOSED TO HOLD HANDS...
HUH?!
WHA?
WHAT?!
WHERE IS IT?
WHERE IS IT?

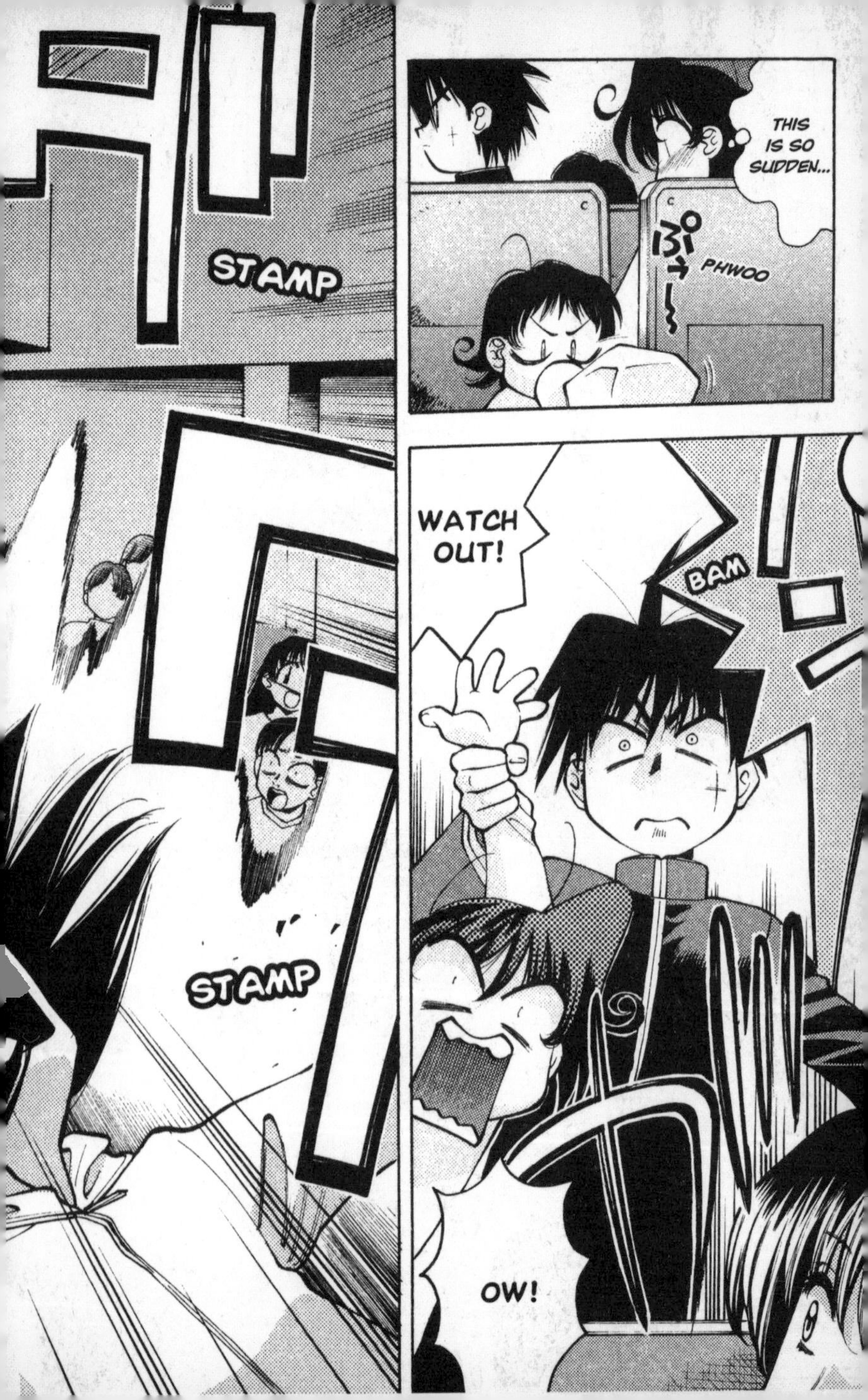
THIS IS SO SUDDEN...
PHWOO
WATCH OUT!
BAM
OW!
STAMP
STAMP

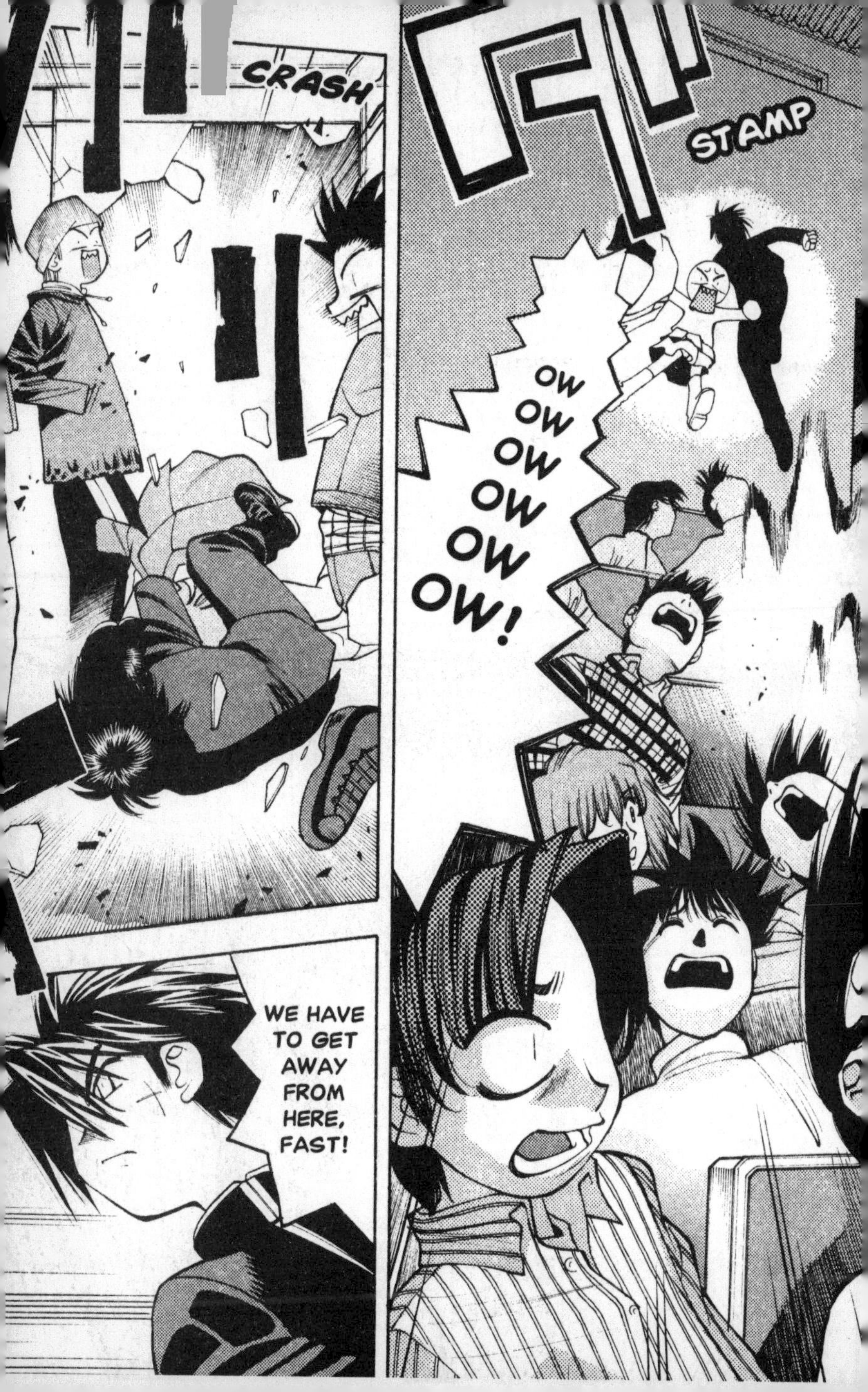
STAMP
OW OW OW OW OW OW!
CRASH
WE HAVE TO GET AWAY FROM HERE, FAST!

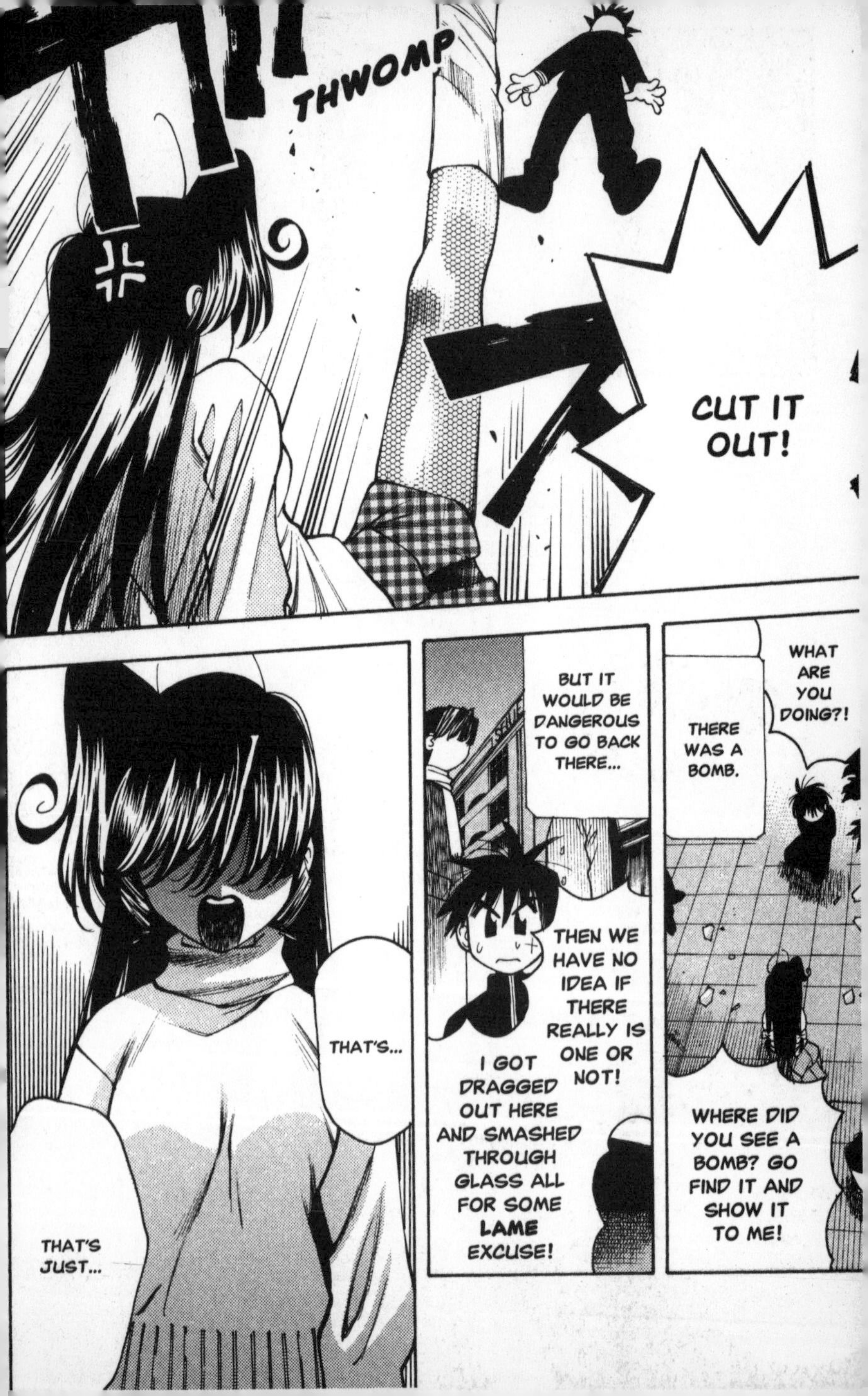
THWOMP
CUT IT OUT!
WHAT ARE YOU DOING?!
THERE WAS A BOMB.
WHERE DID YOU SEE A BOMB? GO FIND IT AND SHOW IT TO ME!
BUT IT WOULD BE DANGEROUS TO GO BACK THERE...
THEN WE HAVE NO IDEA IF THERE REALLY IS ONE OR NOT!
I GOT DRAGGED OUT HERE AND SMASHED THROUGH GLASS ALL FOR SOME LAME EXCUSE!
THAT'S...
THAT'S JUST...

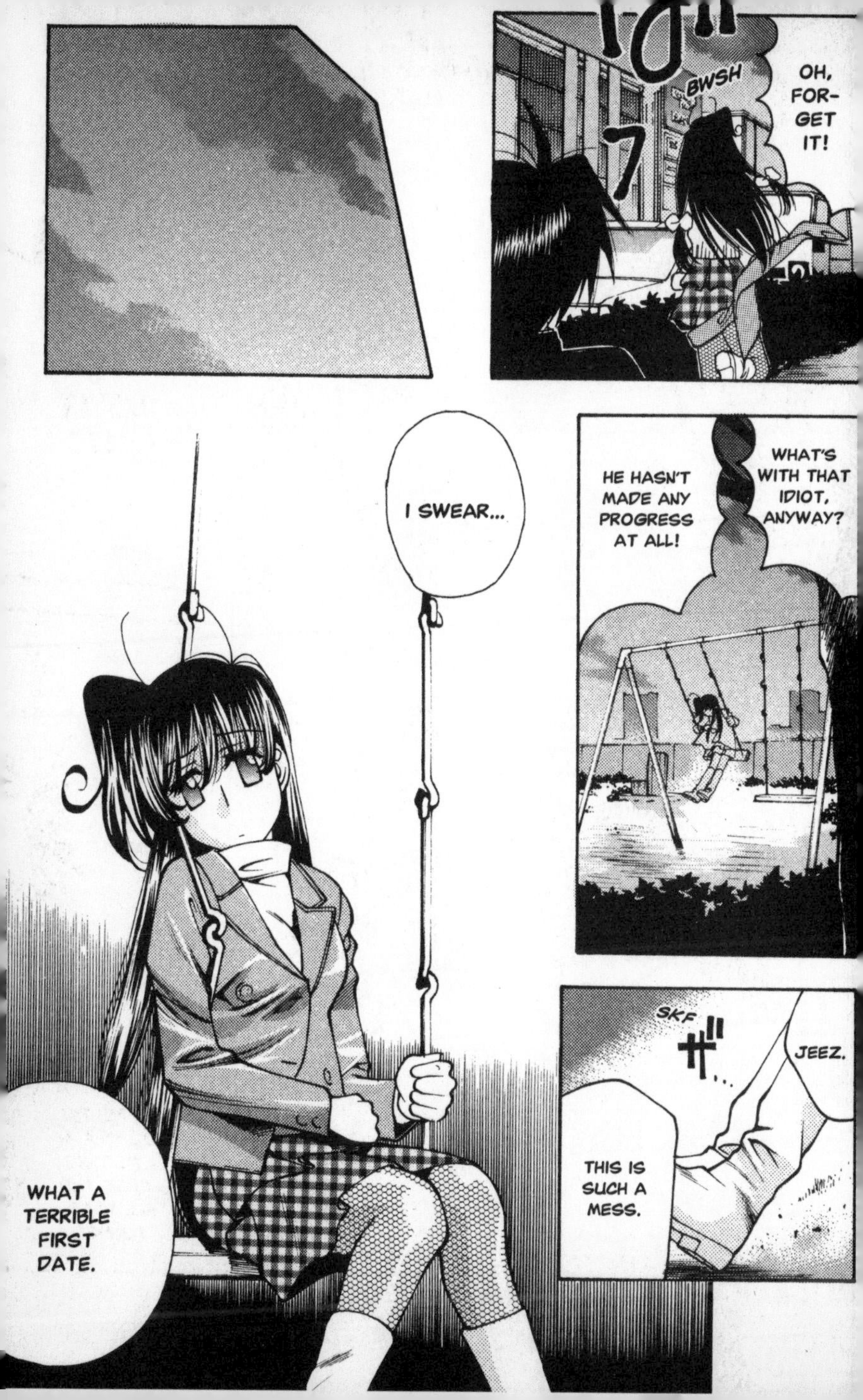
BWSH
OH, FOR-GET IT!
WHAT'S WITH THAT IDIOT, ANYWAY?
HE HASN'T MADE ANY PROGRESS AT ALL!
SKF
JEEZ.
THIS IS SUCH A MESS.
I SWEAR...
WHAT A TERRIBLE FIRST DATE.

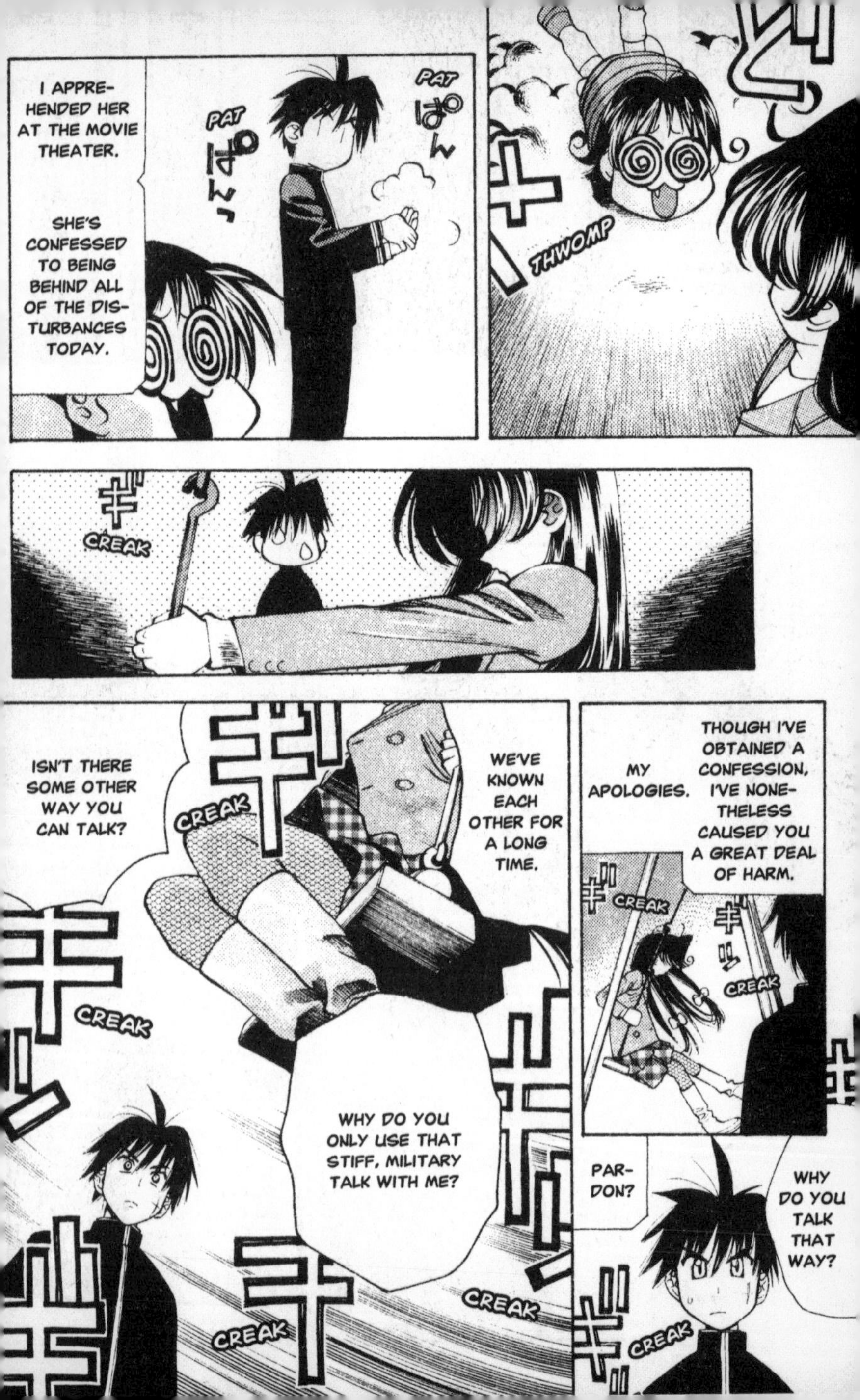
THWOMP
PAT ぱん
PAT ぱん
I APPREHENDED HER AT THE MOVIE THEATER.
SHE'S CONFESSED TO BEING BEHIND ALL OF THE DISTURBANCES TODAY.
CREAK
THOUGH I'VE OBTAINED A CONFESSION, I'VE NONETHELESS CAUSED YOU A GREAT DEAL OF HARM.
MY APOLOGIES.
CREAK
CREAK
WHY DO YOU TALK THAT WAY?
PARDON?
CREAK
WE'VE KNOWN EACH OTHER FOR A LONG TIME.
ISN'T THERE SOME OTHER WAY YOU CAN TALK?
CREAK
CREAK
WHY DO YOU ONLY USE THAT STIFF, MILITARY TALK WITH ME?
CREAK
CREAK

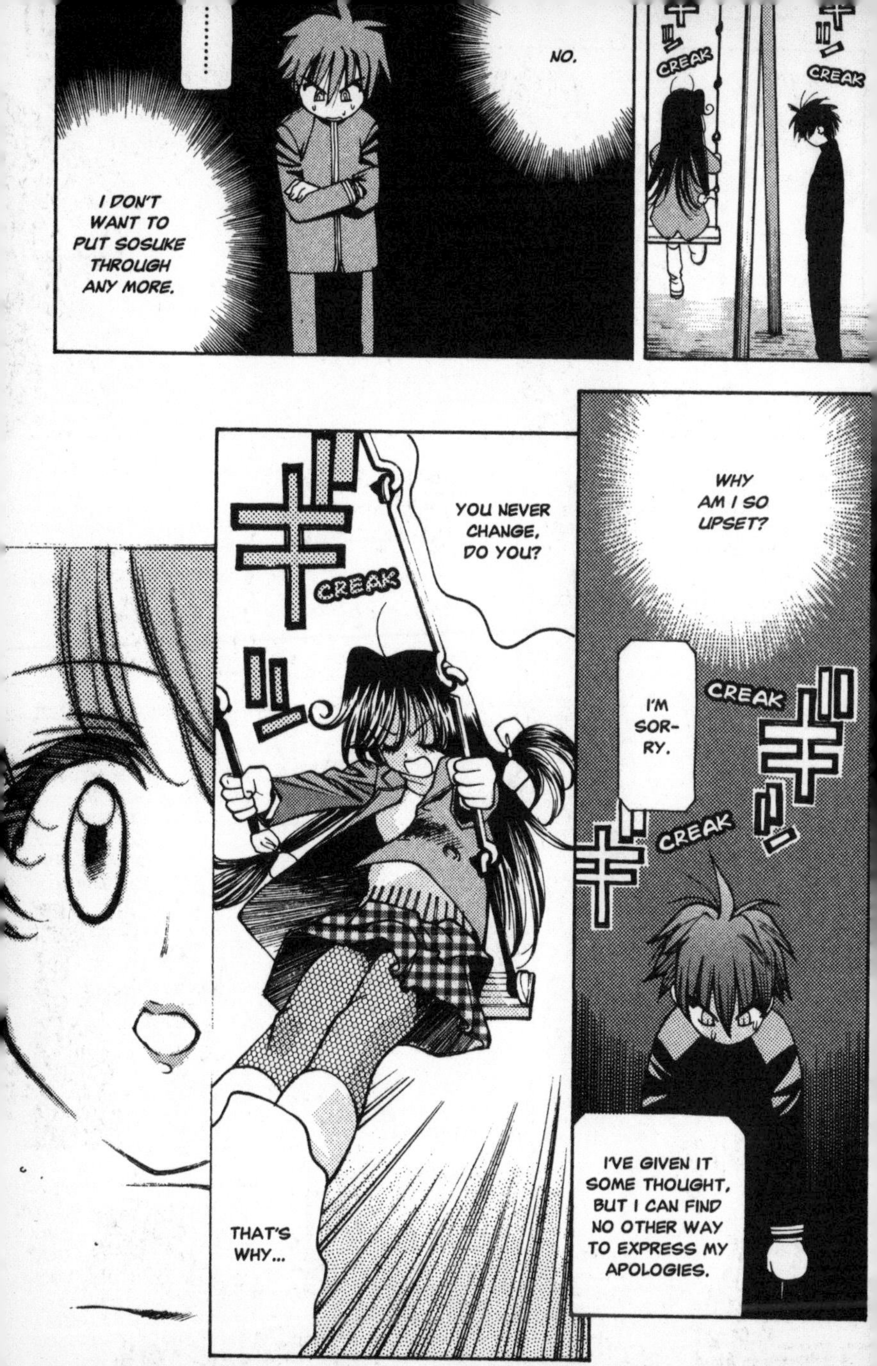
CREAK
CREAK
……
NO.
I DON'T WANT TO PUT SOSUKE THROUGH ANY MORE.
WHY AM I SO UPSET?
I'M SOR-RY.
CREAK
CREAK
I'VE GIVEN IT SOME THOUGHT, BUT I CAN FIND NO OTHER WAY TO EXPRESS MY APOLOGIES.
YOU NEVER CHANGE, DO YOU?
CREAK
THAT'S WHY...

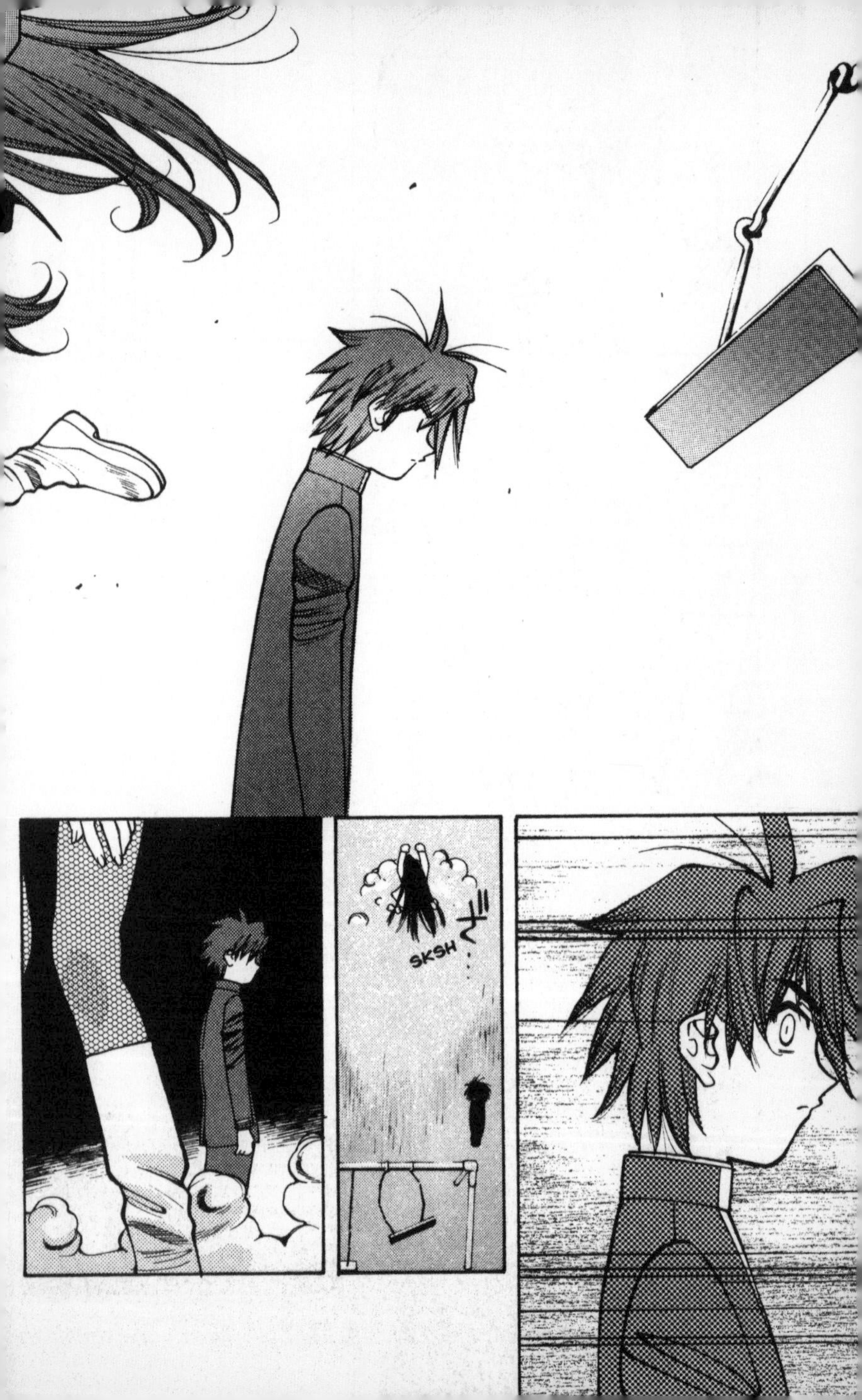
SKSH

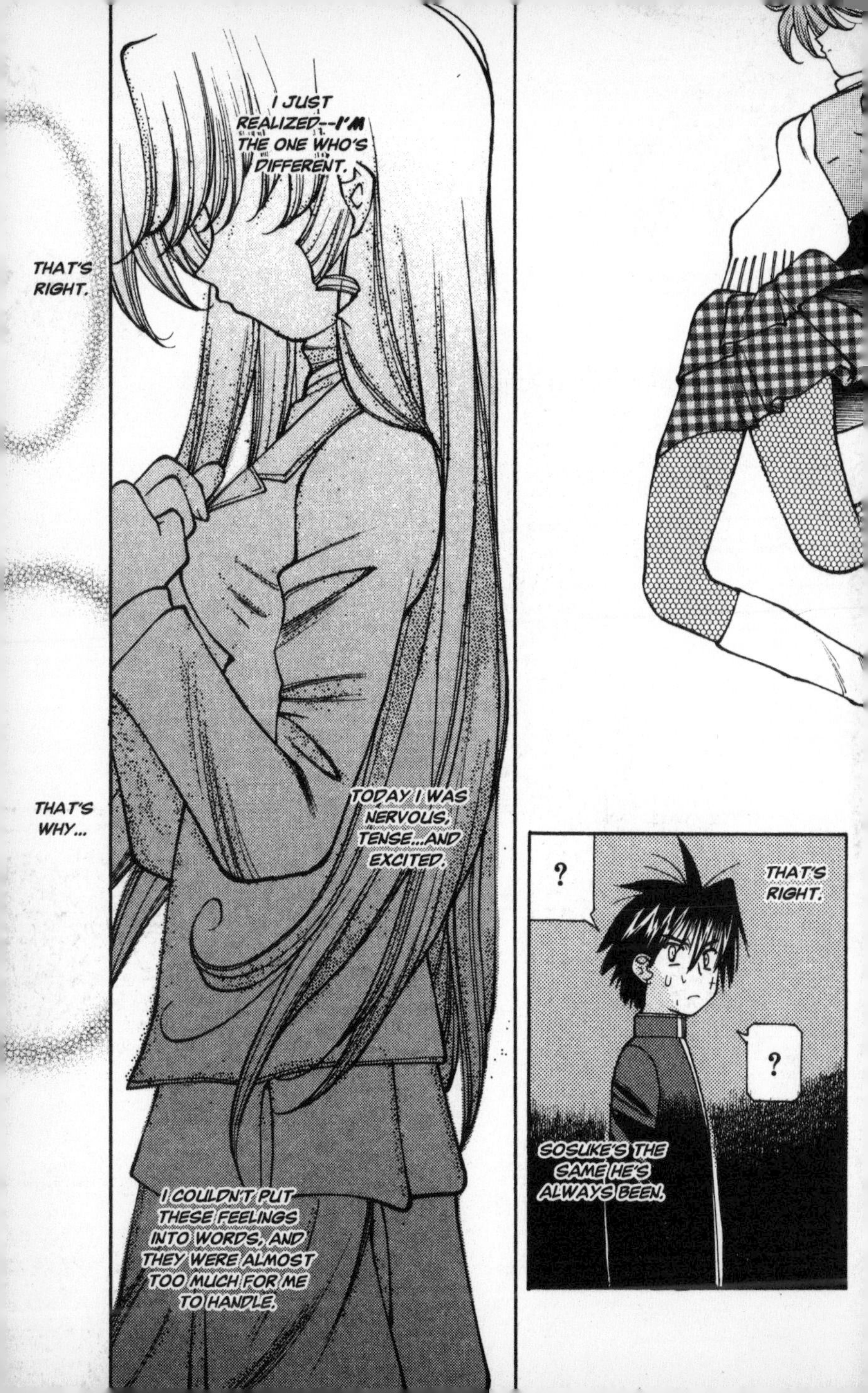
?
THAT'S RIGHT.
?
SOSUKE'S THE SAME HE'S ALWAYS BEEN.
I JUST REALIZED--I'M THE ONE WHO'S DIFFERENT.
THAT'S RIGHT.
TODAY I WAS NERVOUS, TENSE...AND EXCITED.
THAT'S WHY...
I COULDN'T PUT THESE FEELINGS INTO WORDS, AND THEY WERE ALMOST TOO MUCH FOR ME TO HANDLE.

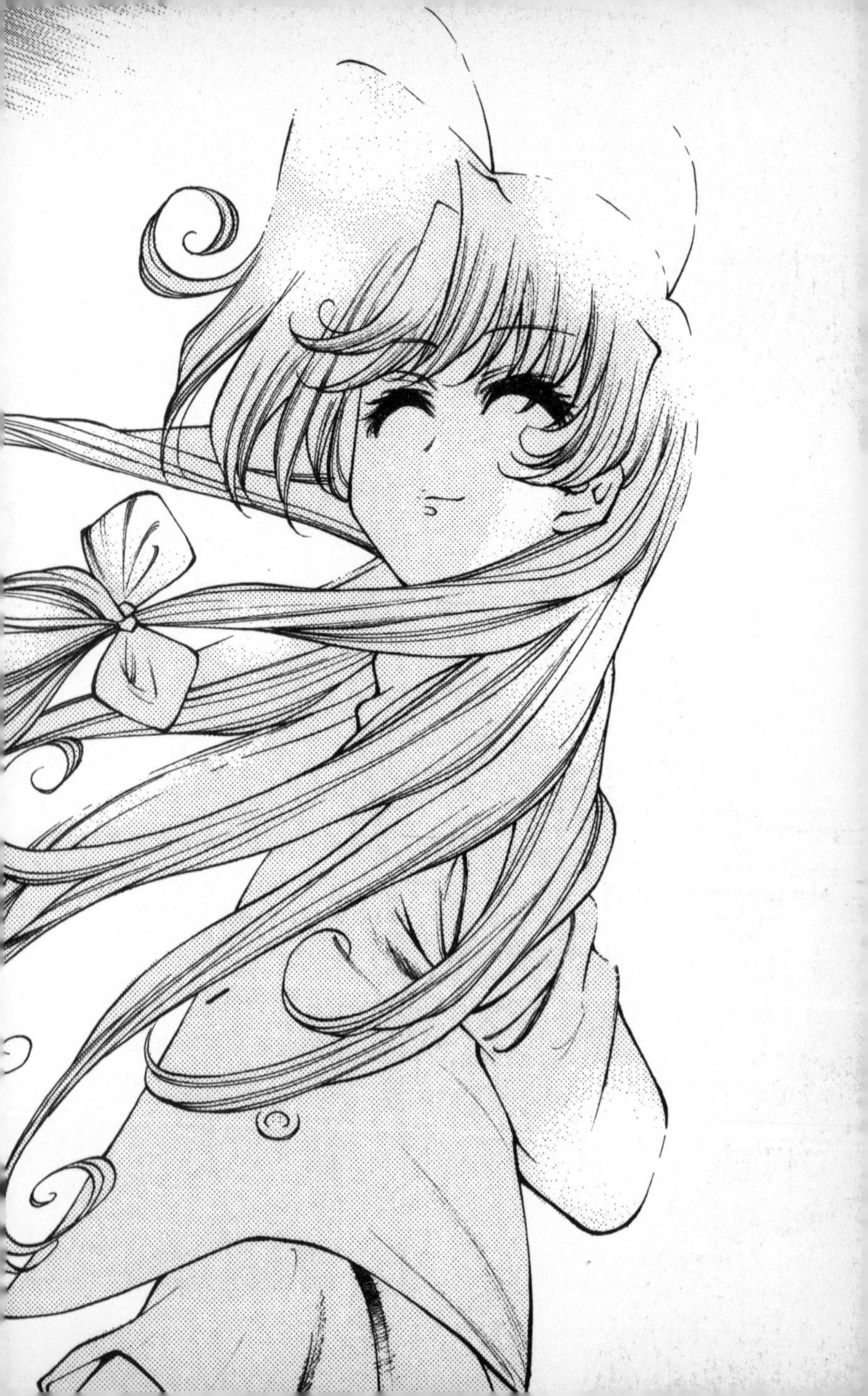

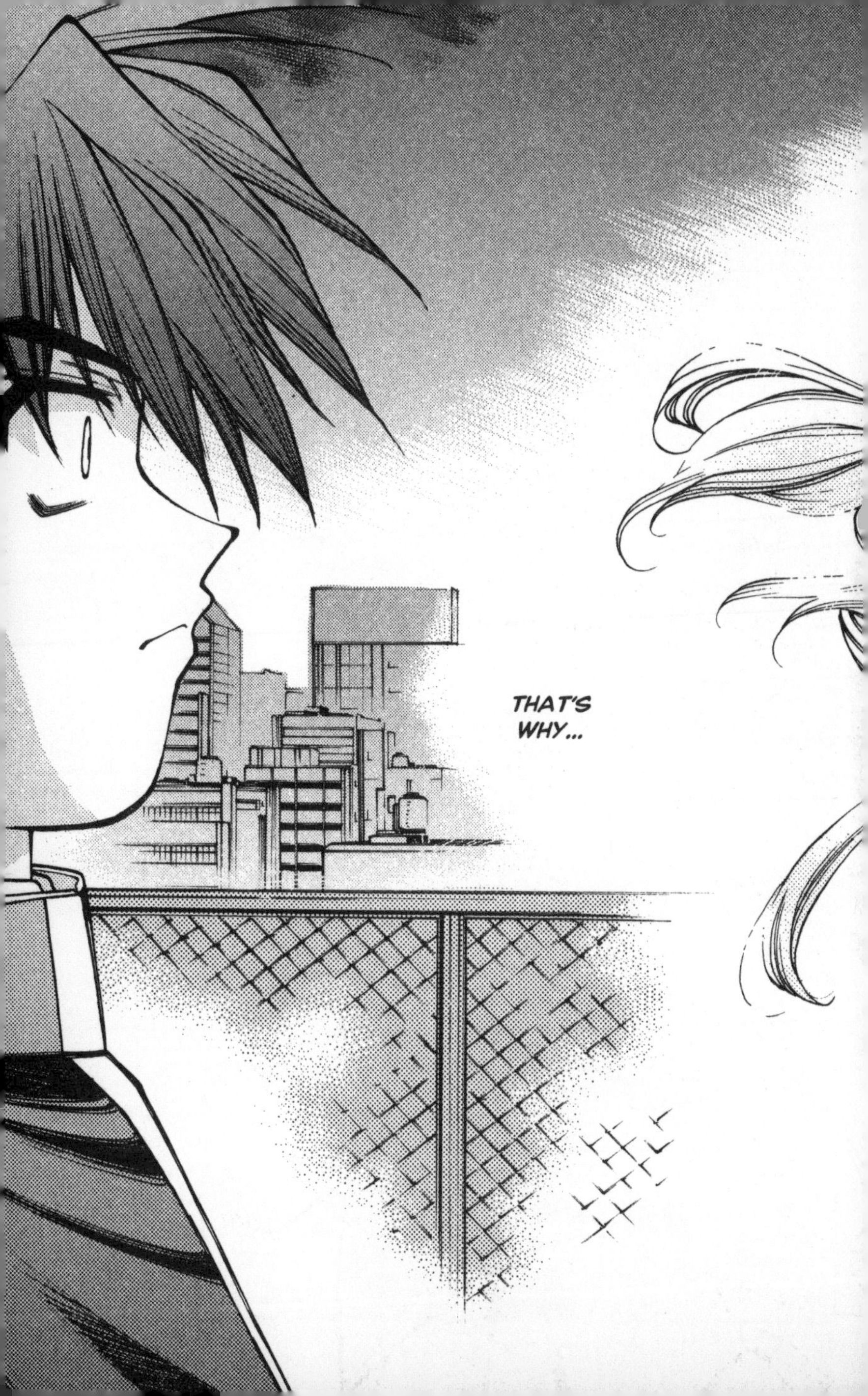
THAT'S WHY...

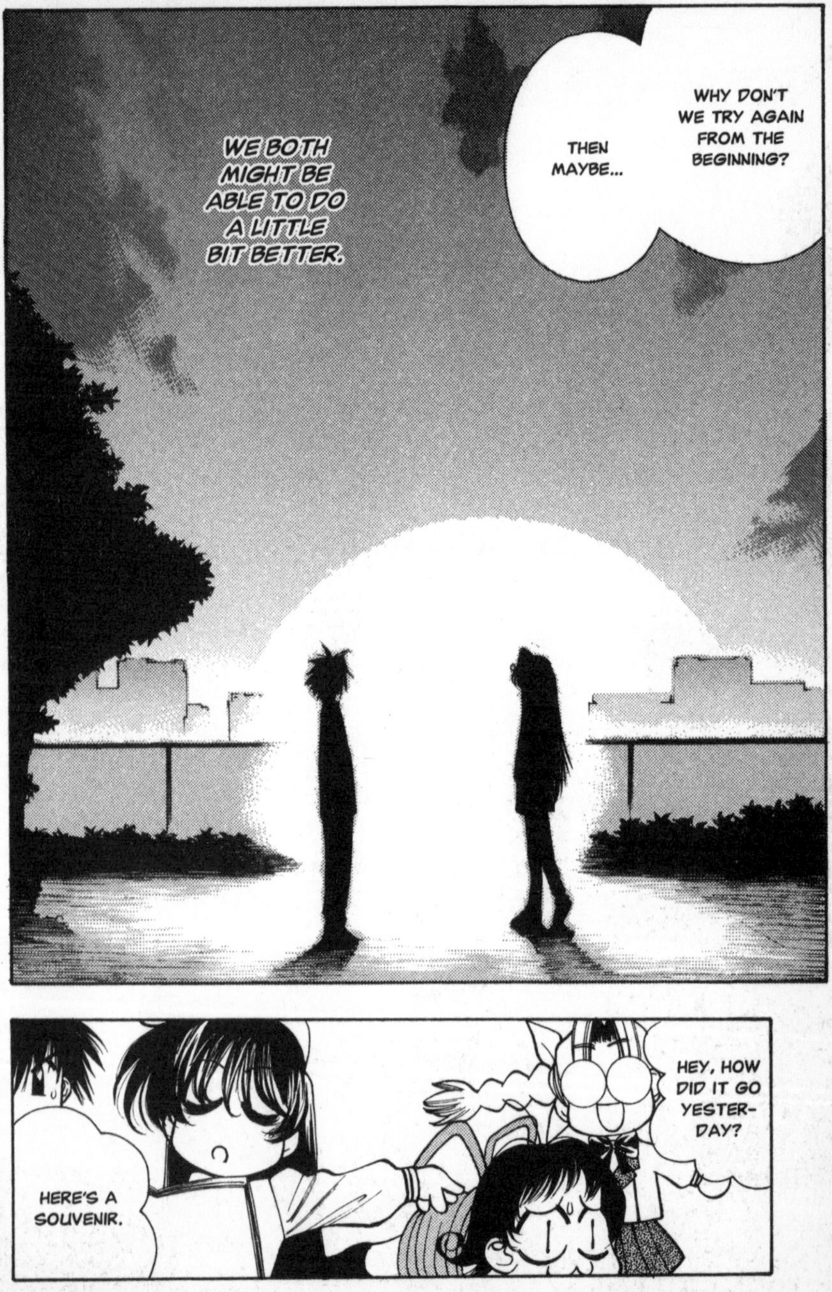
WHY DON'T WE TRY AGAIN FROM THE BEGINNING?
THEN MAYBE...
WE BOTH MIGHT BE ABLE TO DO A LITTLE BIT BETTER.
HEY, HOW DID IT GO YESTER-DAY?
HERE'S A SOUVENIR.

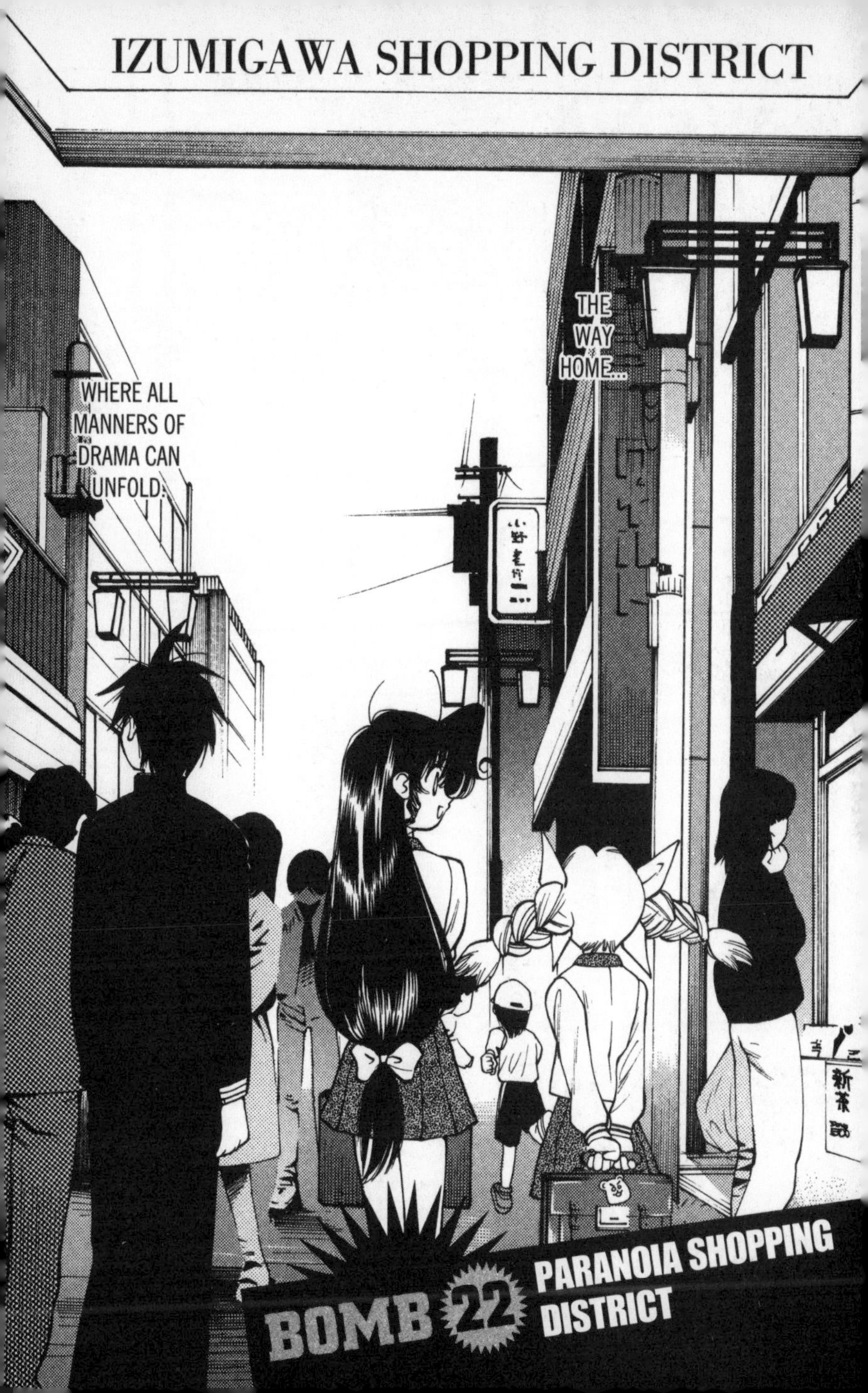
IZUMIGAWA SHOPPING DISTRICT
THE WAY HOME...
WHERE ALL MANNERS OF DRAMA CAN UNFOLD.
BOMB 22
PARANOIA SHOPPING DISTRICT

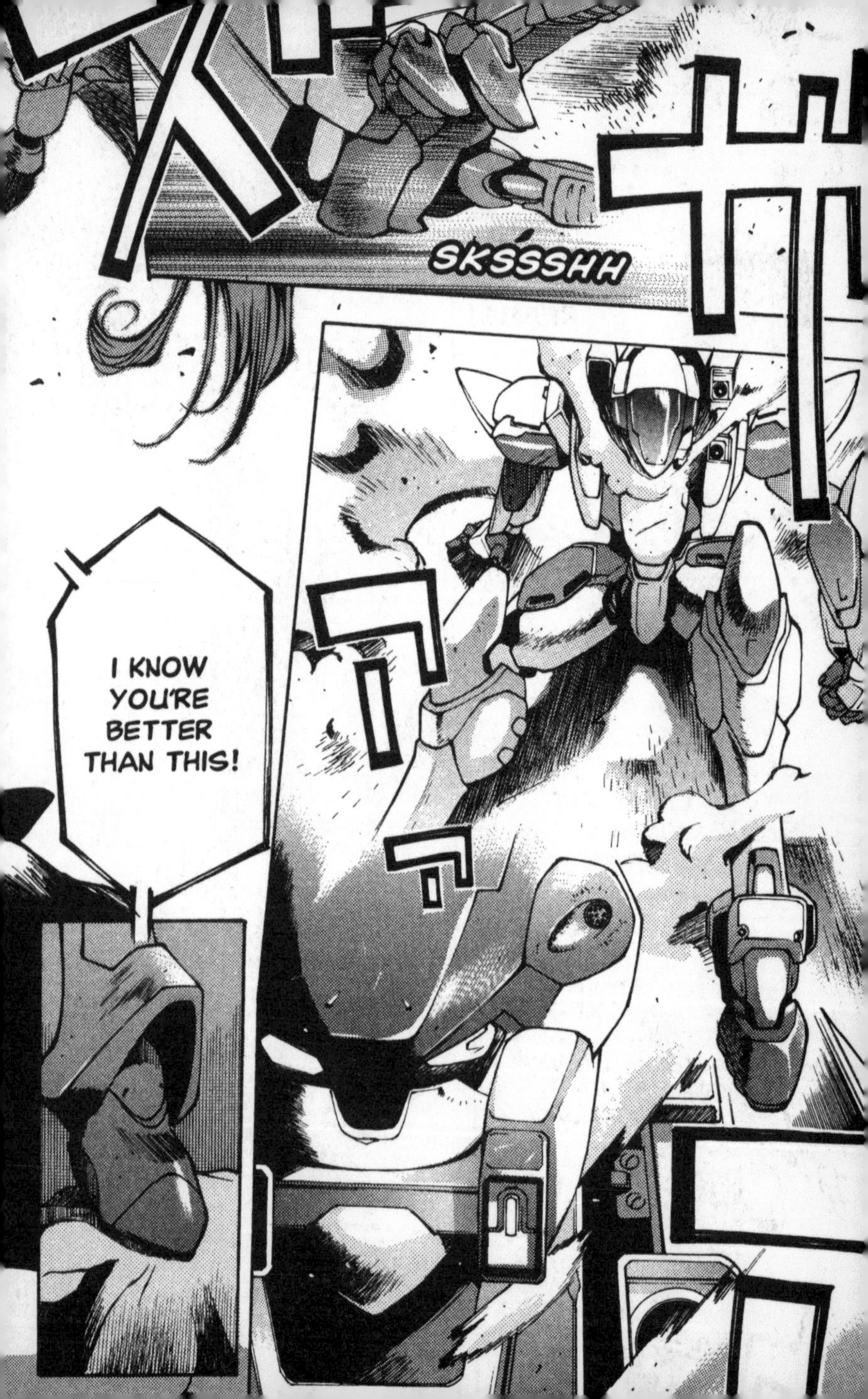
SKSSSHH
I KNOW YOU'RE BETTER THAN THIS!

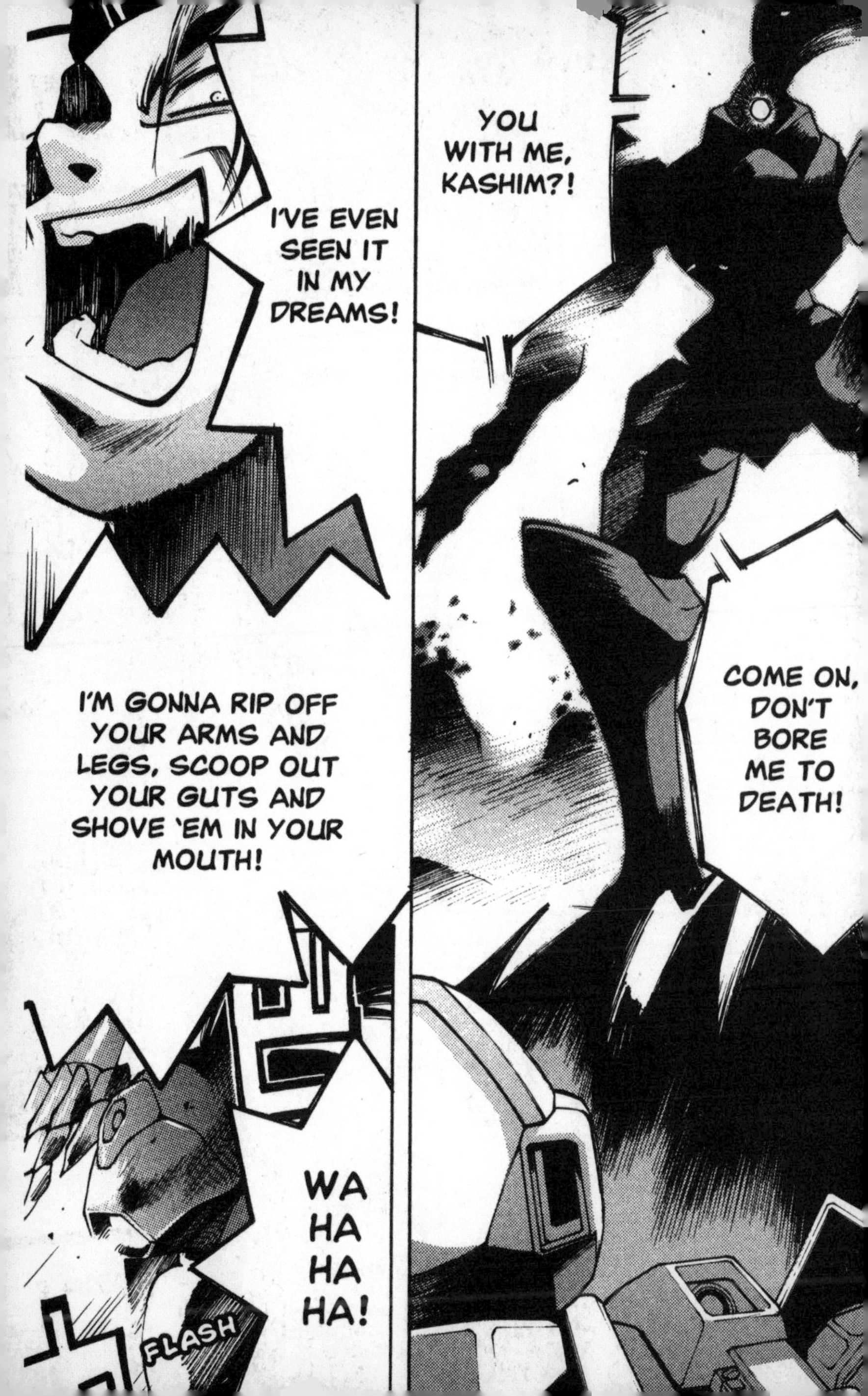
YOU WITH ME, KASHIM?!
COME ON, DON'T BORE ME TO DEATH!
I'VE EVEN SEEN IT IN MY DREAMS!
I'M GONNA RIP OFF YOUR ARMS AND LEGS, SCOOP OUT YOUR GUTS AND SHOVE 'EM IN YOUR MOUTH!
WA HA HA HA!
FLASH

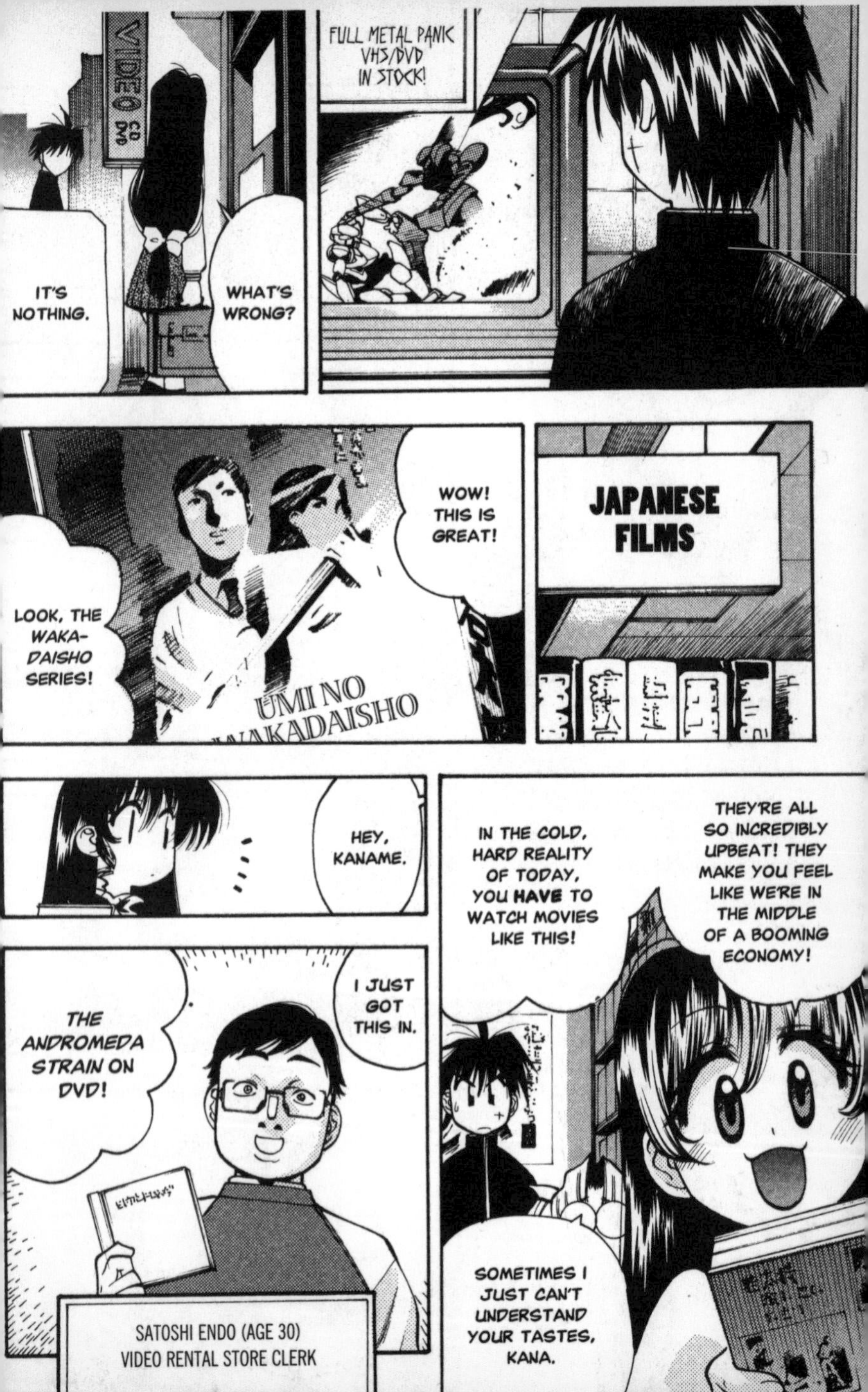
FULL METAL PANIC VHS/DVD IN STOCK!
VIDEO CD DVD
WHAT'S WRONG?
IT'S NOTHING.
JAPANESE FILMS
WOW! THIS IS GREAT!
LOOK, THE WAKA-DAISHO SERIES!
UMI NO WAKADAISHO
THEY'RE ALL SO INCREDIBLY UPBEAT! THEY MAKE YOU FEEL LIKE WE'RE IN THE MIDDLE OF A BOOMING ECONOMY!
IN THE COLD, HARD REALITY OF TODAY, YOU **HAVE** TO WATCH MOVIES LIKE THIS!
HEY, KANAME.
...
SOMETIMES I JUST CAN'T UNDERSTAND YOUR TASTES, KANA.
I JUST GOT THIS IN.
THE ANDROMEDA STRAIN ON DVD!
SATOSHI ENDO (AGE 30)
VIDEO RENTAL STORE CLERK

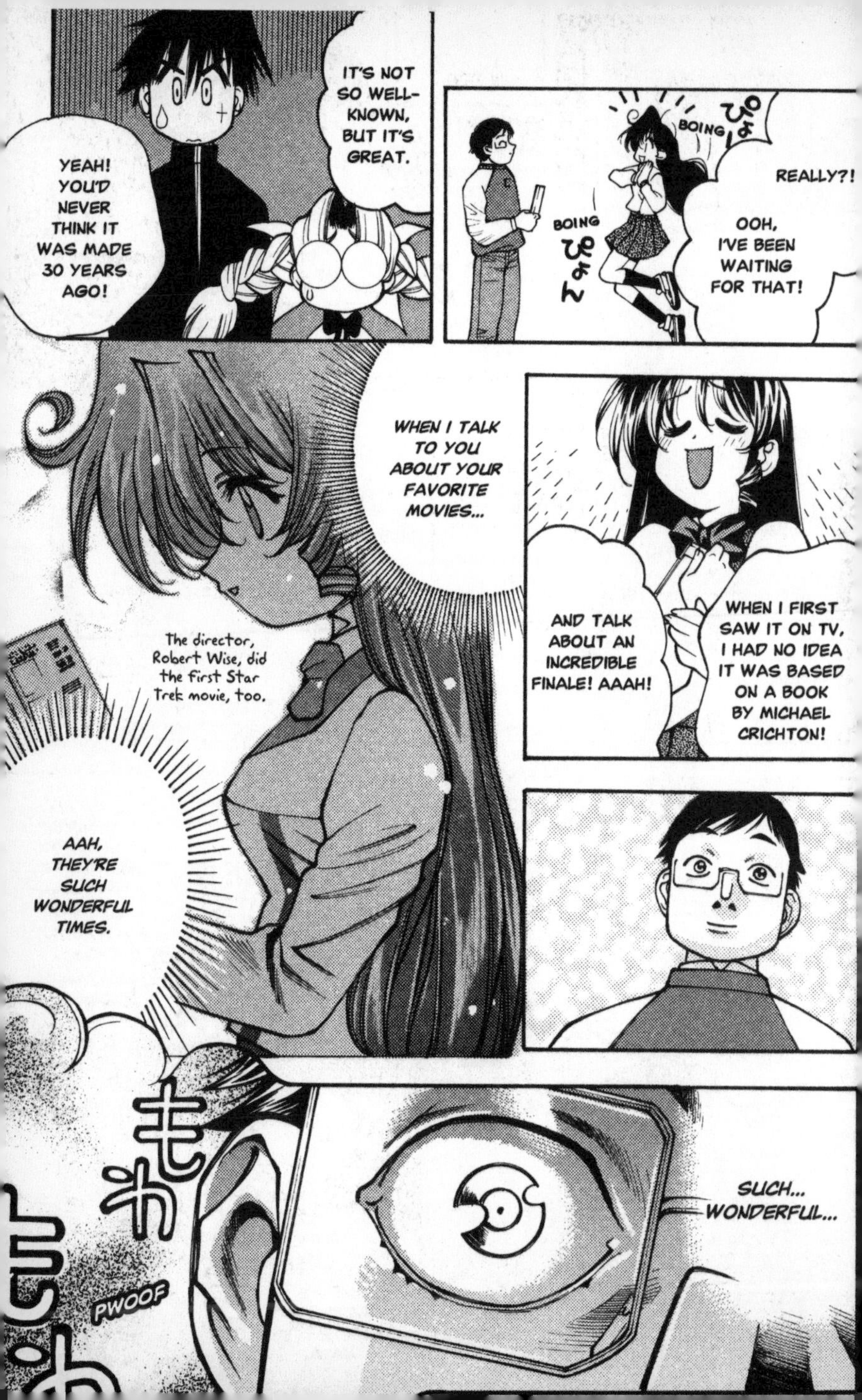
REALLY?!
OOH, I'VE BEEN WAITING FOR THAT!
BOING
BOING
IT'S NOT SO WELL-KNOWN, BUT IT'S GREAT.
YEAH! YOU'D NEVER THINK IT WAS MADE 30 YEARS AGO!
WHEN I FIRST SAW IT ON TV, I HAD NO IDEA IT WAS BASED ON A BOOK BY MICHAEL CRICHTON!
AND TALK ABOUT AN INCREDIBLE FINALE! AAAH!
WHEN I TALK TO YOU ABOUT YOUR FAVORITE MOVIES...
The director, Robert Wise, did the first Star Trek movie, too.
AAH, THEY'RE SUCH WONDERFUL TIMES.
SUCH... WONDERFUL...
PWOOF

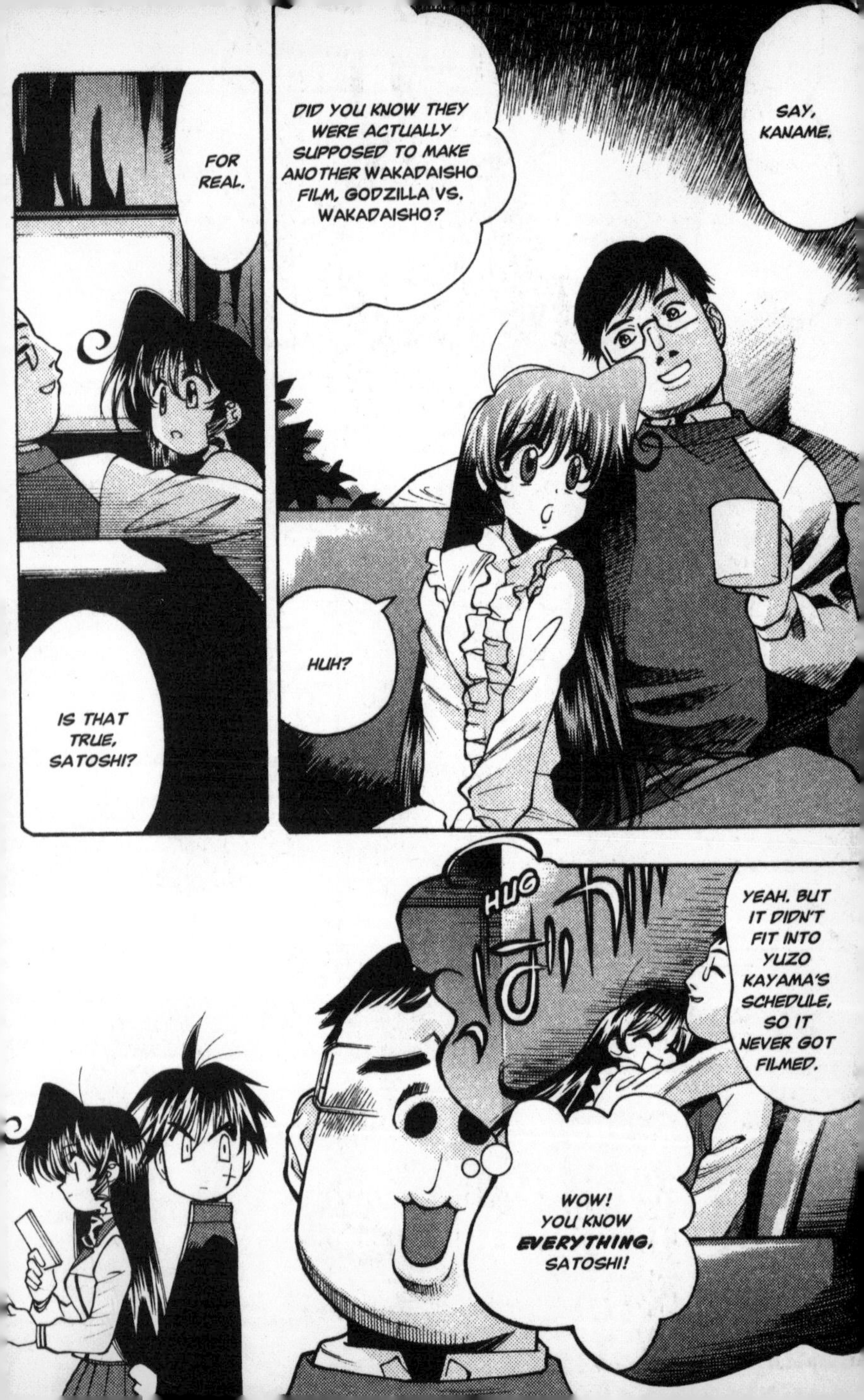
SAY, KANAME.
DID YOU KNOW THEY WERE ACTUALLY SUPPOSED TO MAKE ANOTHER WAKADAISHO FILM, GODZILLA VS. WAKADAISHO?
HUH?
FOR REAL.
IS THAT TRUE, SATOSHI?
YEAH. BUT IT DIDN'T FIT INTO YUZO KAYAMA'S SCHEDULE, SO IT NEVER GOT FILMED.
HUG
WOW! YOU KNOW **EVERYTHING**, SATOSHI!

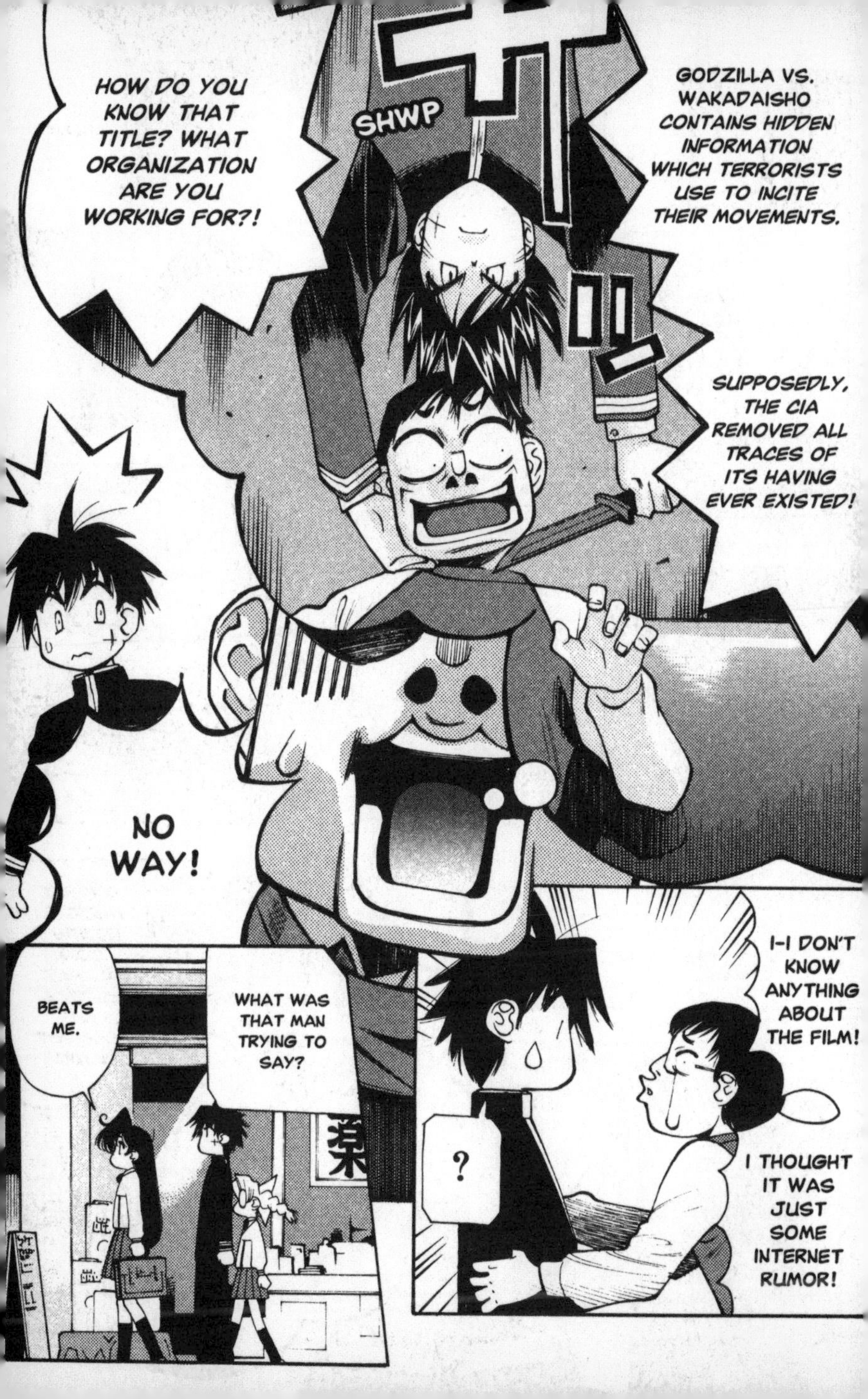
GODZILLA VS. WAKADAISHO CONTAINS HIDDEN INFORMATION WHICH TERRORISTS USE TO INCITE THEIR MOVEMENTS.
SHWP
HOW DO YOU KNOW THAT TITLE? WHAT ORGANIZATION ARE YOU WORKING FOR?!
SUPPOSEDLY, THE CIA REMOVED ALL TRACES OF ITS HAVING EVER EXISTED!
NO WAY!
I-I DON'T KNOW ANYTHING ABOUT THE FILM!
I THOUGHT IT WAS JUST SOME INTERNET RUMOR!
?
WHAT WAS THAT MAN TRYING TO SAY?
BEATS ME.

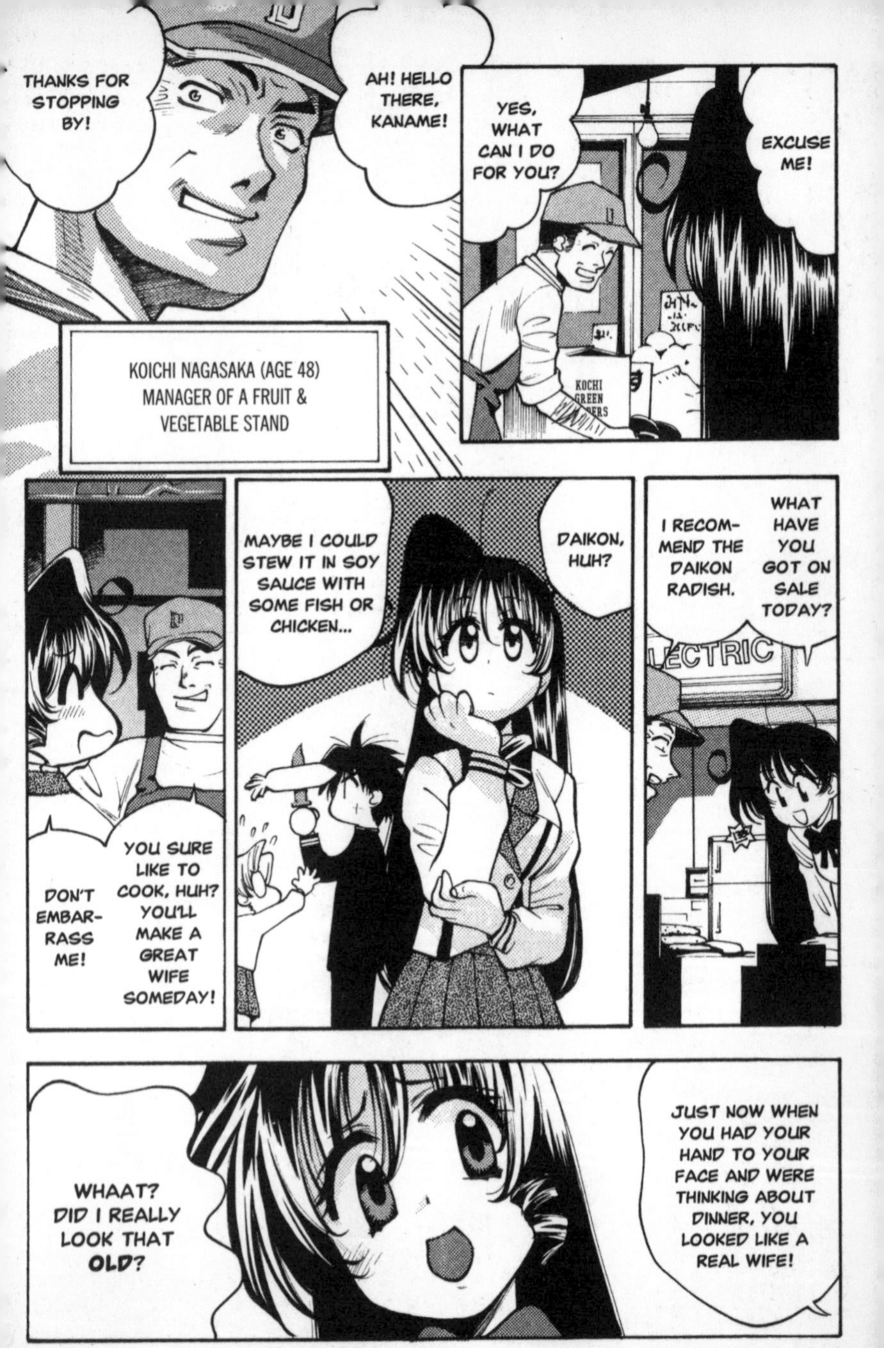
EXCUSE ME!
YES, WHAT CAN I DO FOR YOU?
AH! HELLO THERE, KANAME!
THANKS FOR STOPPING BY!
KOICHI NAGASAKA (AGE 48) MANAGER OF A FRUIT & VEGETABLE STAND
KOCHI GREEN
WHAT HAVE YOU GOT ON SALE TODAY?
I RECOM-MEND THE DAIKON RADISH.
LECTRIC
DAIKON, HUH?
MAYBE I COULD STEW IT IN SOY SAUCE WITH SOME FISH OR CHICKEN...
YOU SURE LIKE TO COOK, HUH? YOU'LL MAKE A GREAT WIFE SOMEDAY!
DON'T EMBAR-RASS ME!
JUST NOW WHEN YOU HAD YOUR HAND TO YOUR FACE AND WERE THINKING ABOUT DINNER, YOU LOOKED LIKE A REAL WIFE!
WHAAT? DID I REALLY LOOK THAT **OLD**?

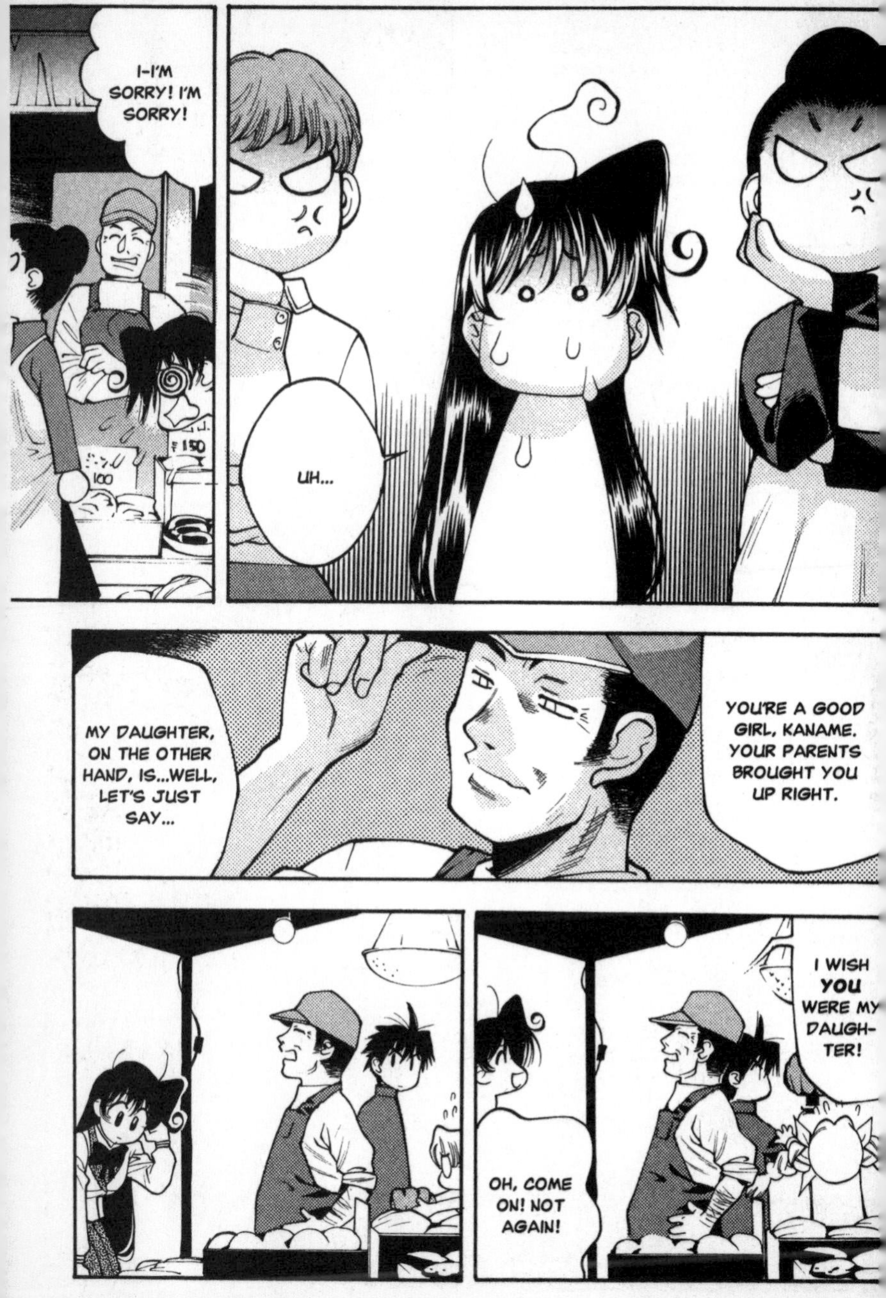
UH...
I-I'M SORRY! I'M SORRY!
¥150
100
YOU'RE A GOOD GIRL, KANAME. YOUR PARENTS BROUGHT YOU UP RIGHT.
MY DAUGHTER, ON THE OTHER HAND, IS...WELL, LET'S JUST SAY...
I WISH YOU WERE MY DAUGHTER!
OH, COME ON! NOT AGAIN!

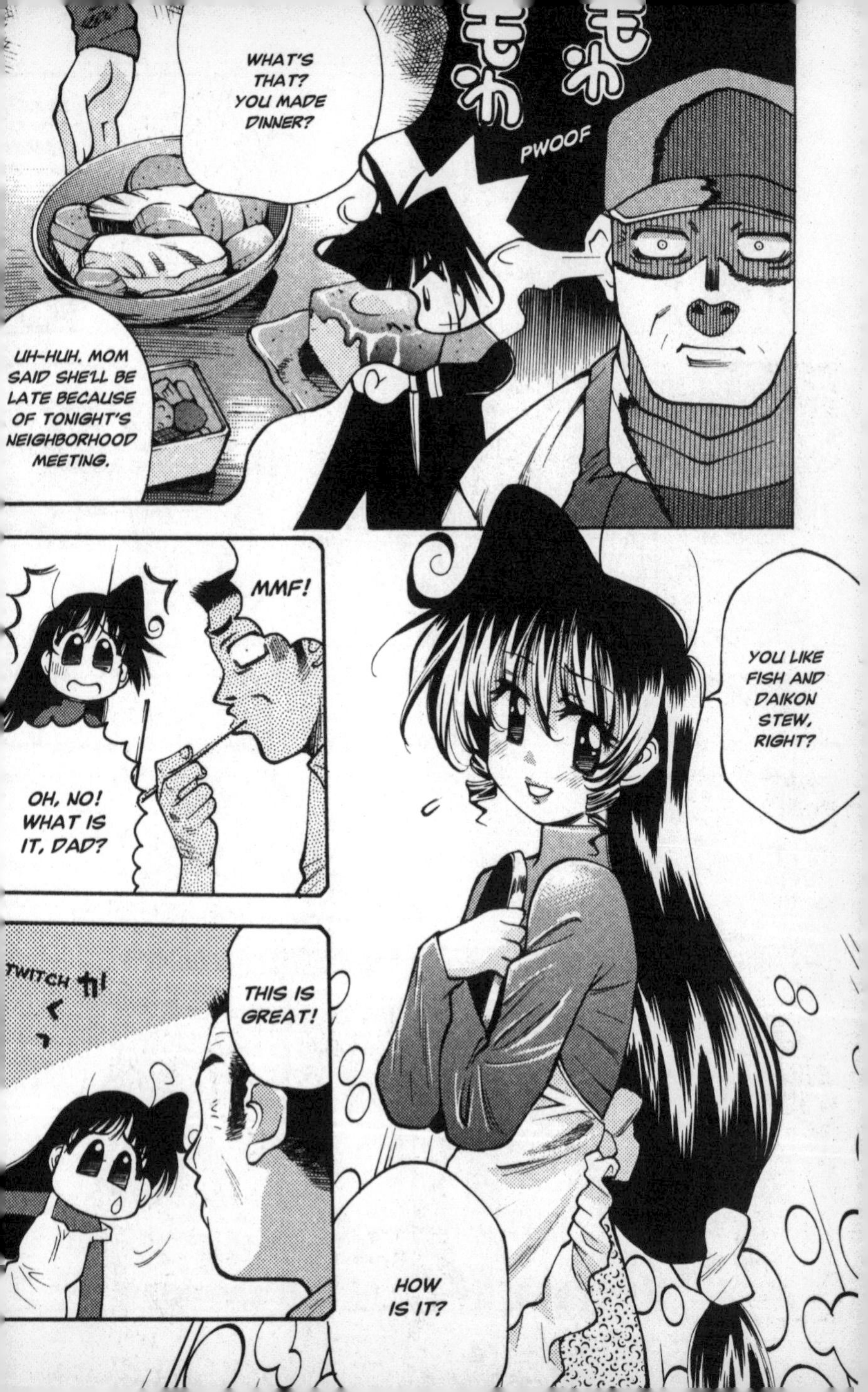
もわもわ
PWOOF
WHAT'S THAT? YOU MADE DINNER?
UH-HUH. MOM SAID SHE'LL BE LATE BECAUSE OF TONIGHT'S NEIGHBORHOOD MEETING.
YOU LIKE FISH AND DAIKON STEW, RIGHT?
HOW IS IT?
MMF!
OH, NO! WHAT IS IT, DAD?
TWITCH
THIS IS GREAT!

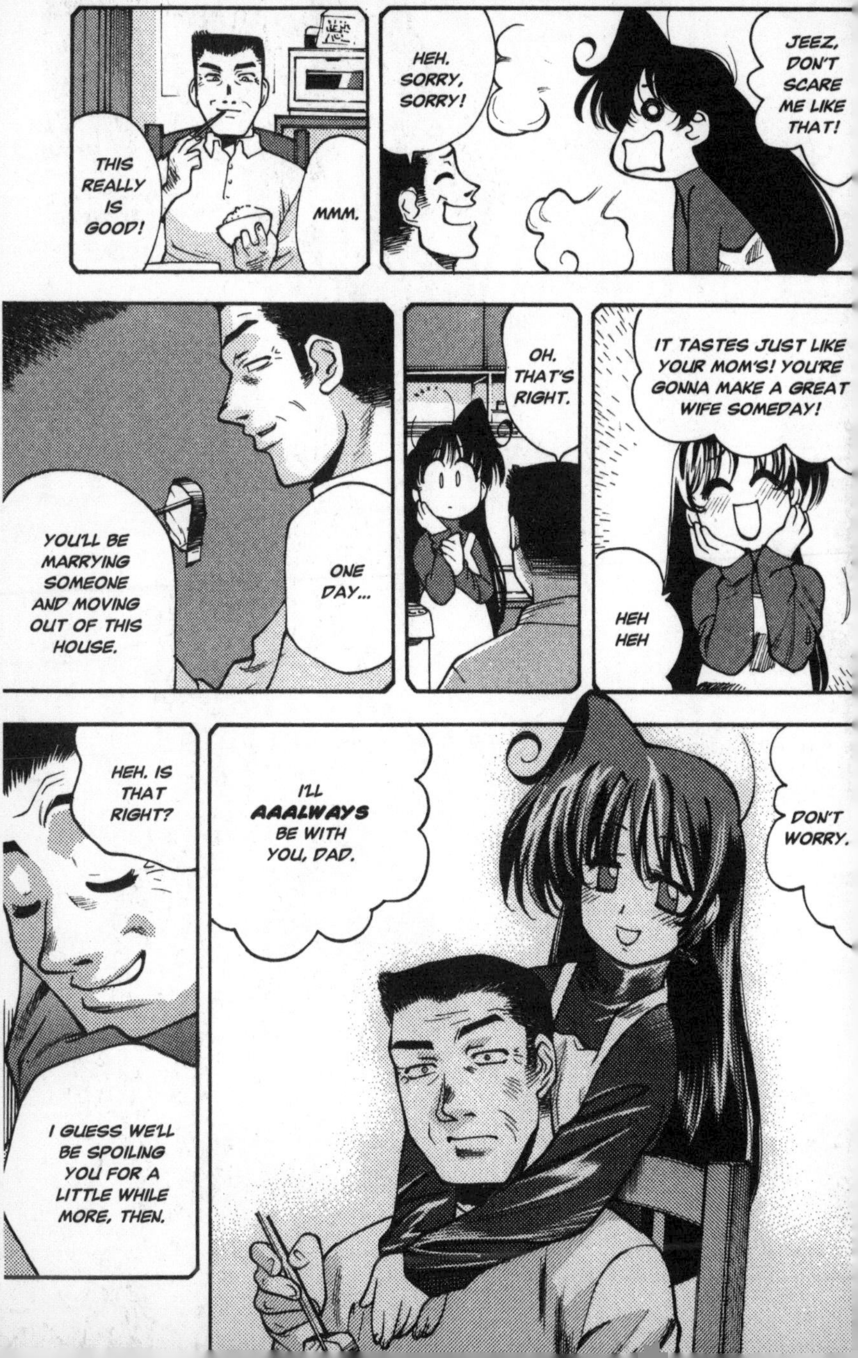
JEEZ, DON'T SCARE ME LIKE THAT!
HEH. SORRY, SORRY!
MMM.
THIS REALLY IS GOOD!
IT TASTES JUST LIKE YOUR MOM'S! YOU'RE GONNA MAKE A GREAT WIFE SOMEDAY!
HEH HEH
OH. THAT'S RIGHT.
ONE DAY...
YOU'LL BE MARRYING SOMEONE AND MOVING OUT OF THIS HOUSE.
DON'T WORRY.
I'LL AAALWAYS BE WITH YOU, DAD.
HEH. IS THAT RIGHT?
I GUESS WE'LL BE SPOILING YOU FOR A LITTLE WHILE MORE, THEN.

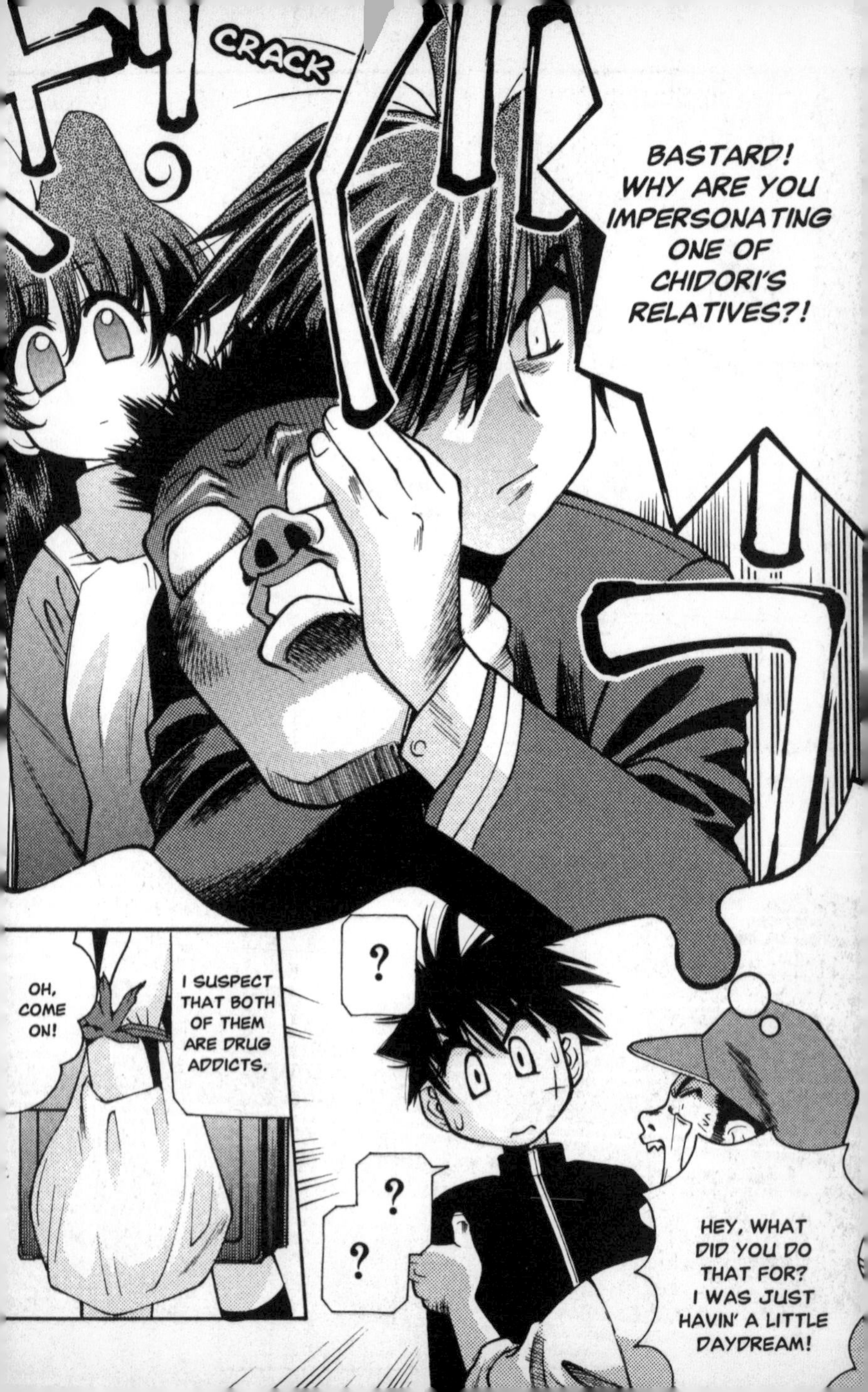

CRACK
BASTARD! WHY ARE YOU IMPERSONATING ONE OF CHIDORI'S RELATIVES?!
HEY, WHAT DID YOU DO THAT FOR? I WAS JUST HAVIN' A LITTLE DAYDREAM!
?
? ?
I SUSPECT THAT BOTH OF THEM ARE DRUG ADDICTS.
OH, COME ON!

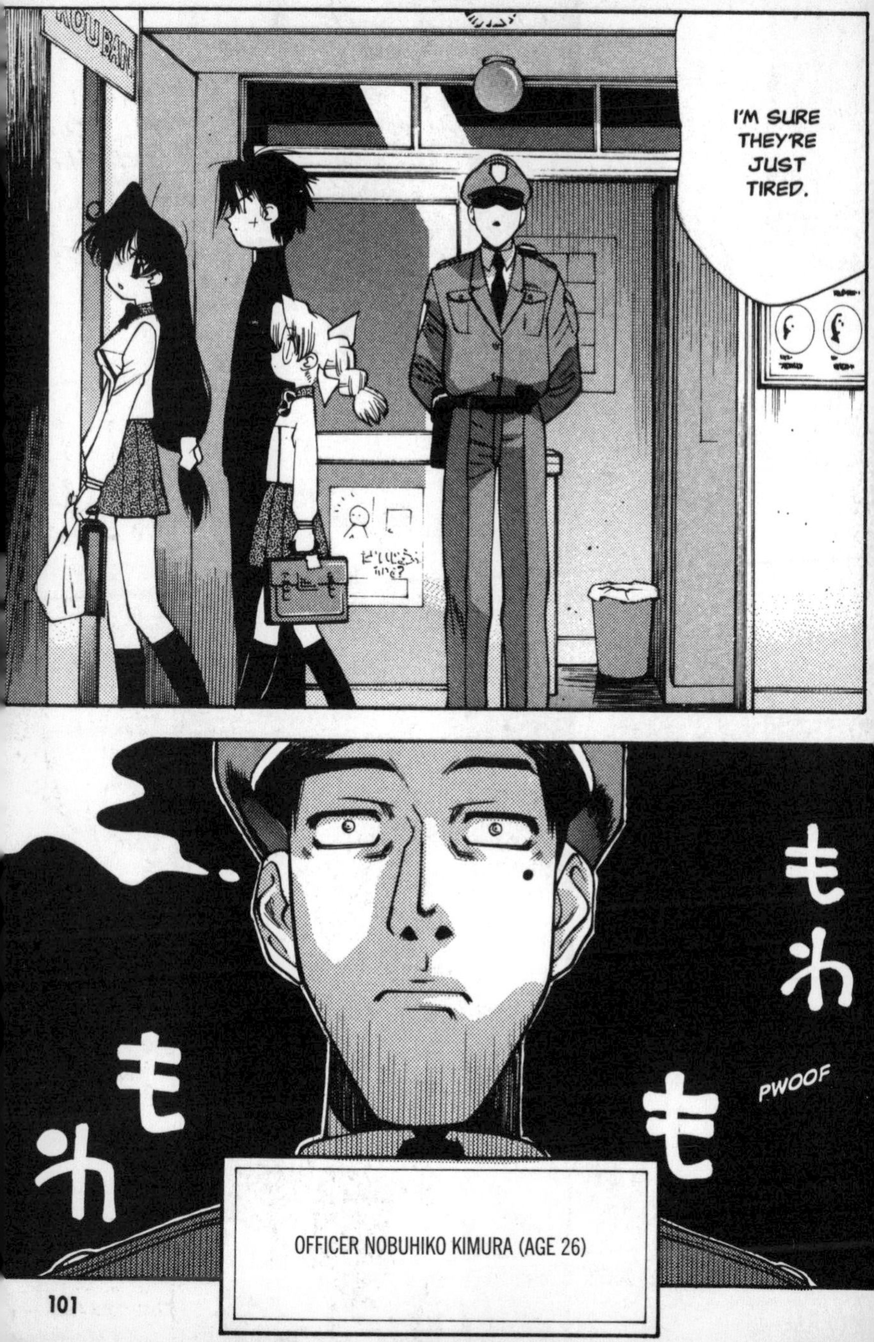
KOUBAN
I'M SURE THEY'RE JUST TIRED.
もわ
も
PWOOF
もわ
OFFICER NOBUHIKO KIMURA (AGE 26)

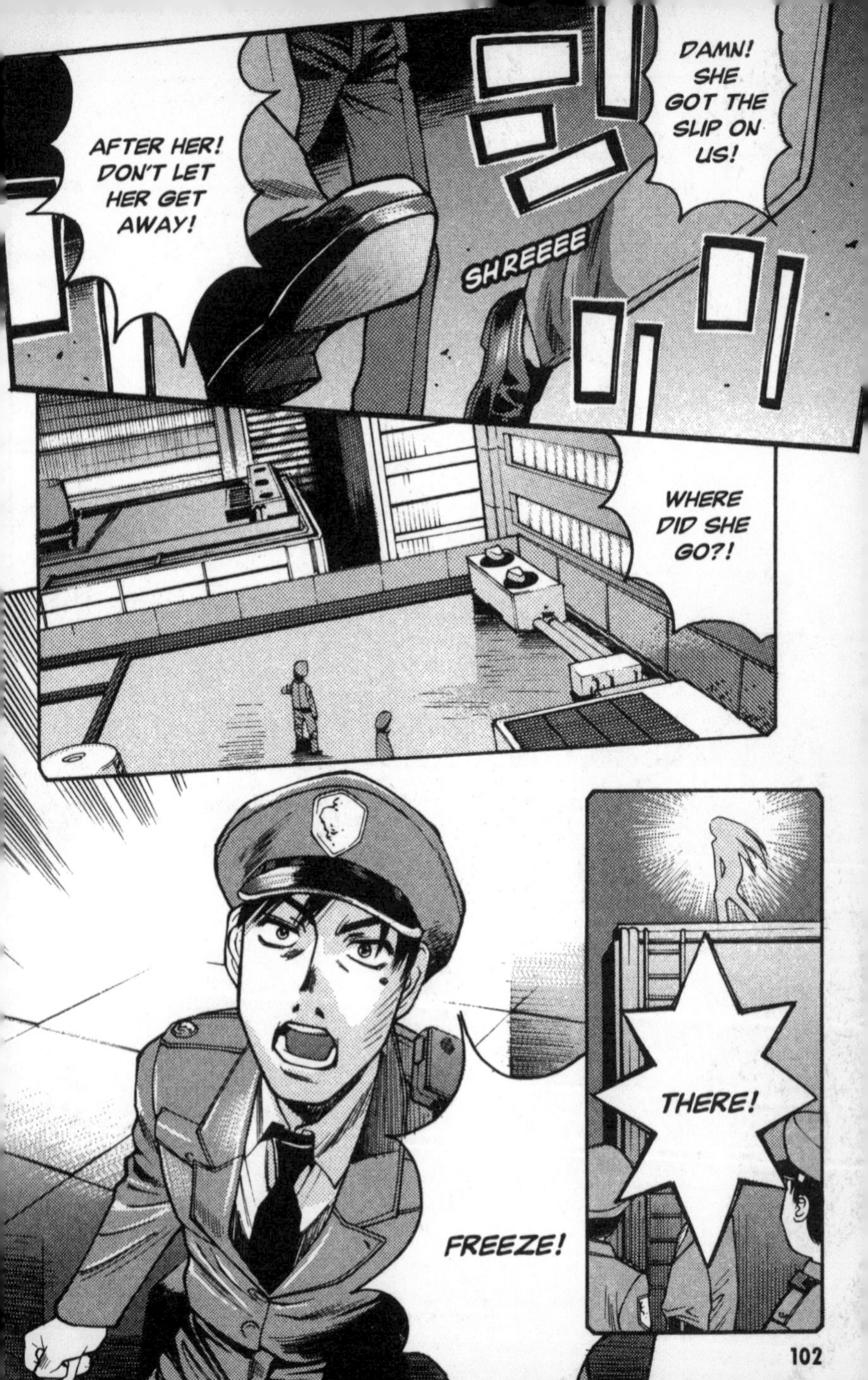
DAMN! SHE GOT THE SLIP ON US!
AFTER HER! DON'T LET HER GET AWAY!
SHREEEE
WHERE DID SHE GO?!
THERE!
FREEZE!

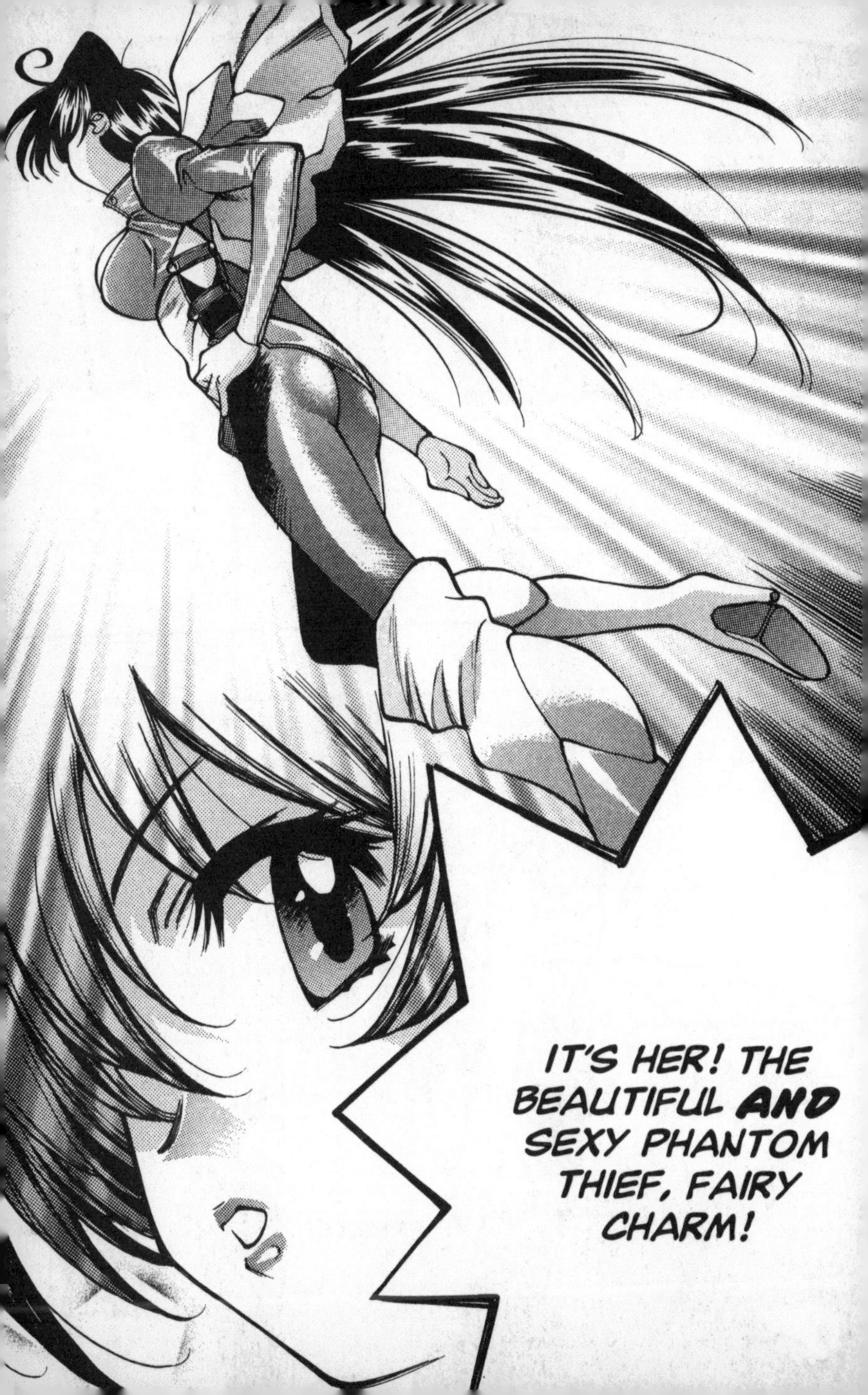
IT'S HER! THE BEAUTIFUL AND SEXY PHANTOM THIEF, FAIRY CHARM!

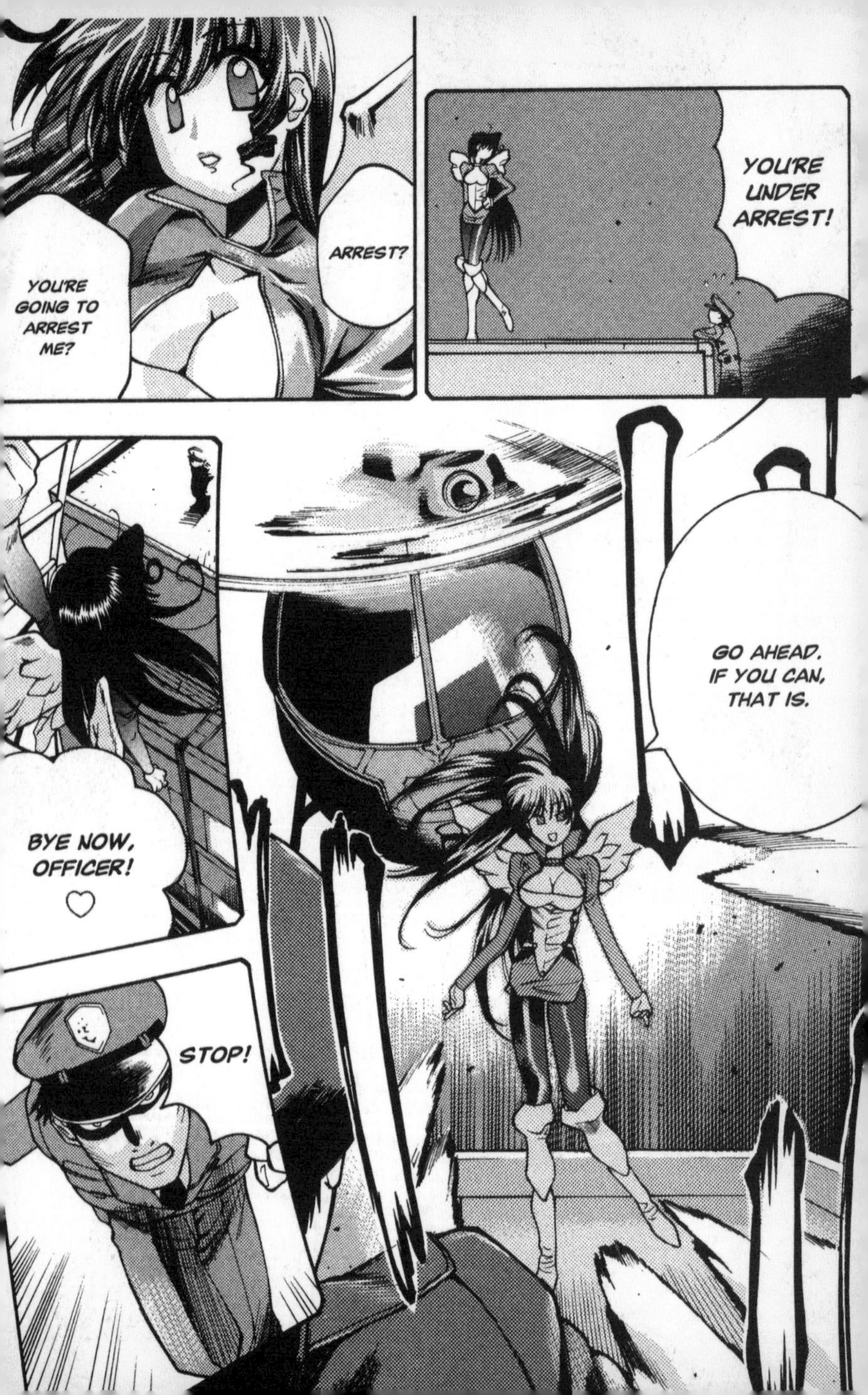
YOU'RE UNDER ARREST!
ARREST?
YOU'RE GOING TO ARREST ME?
GO AHEAD. IF YOU CAN, THAT IS.
BYE NOW, OFFICER! ♡
STOP!

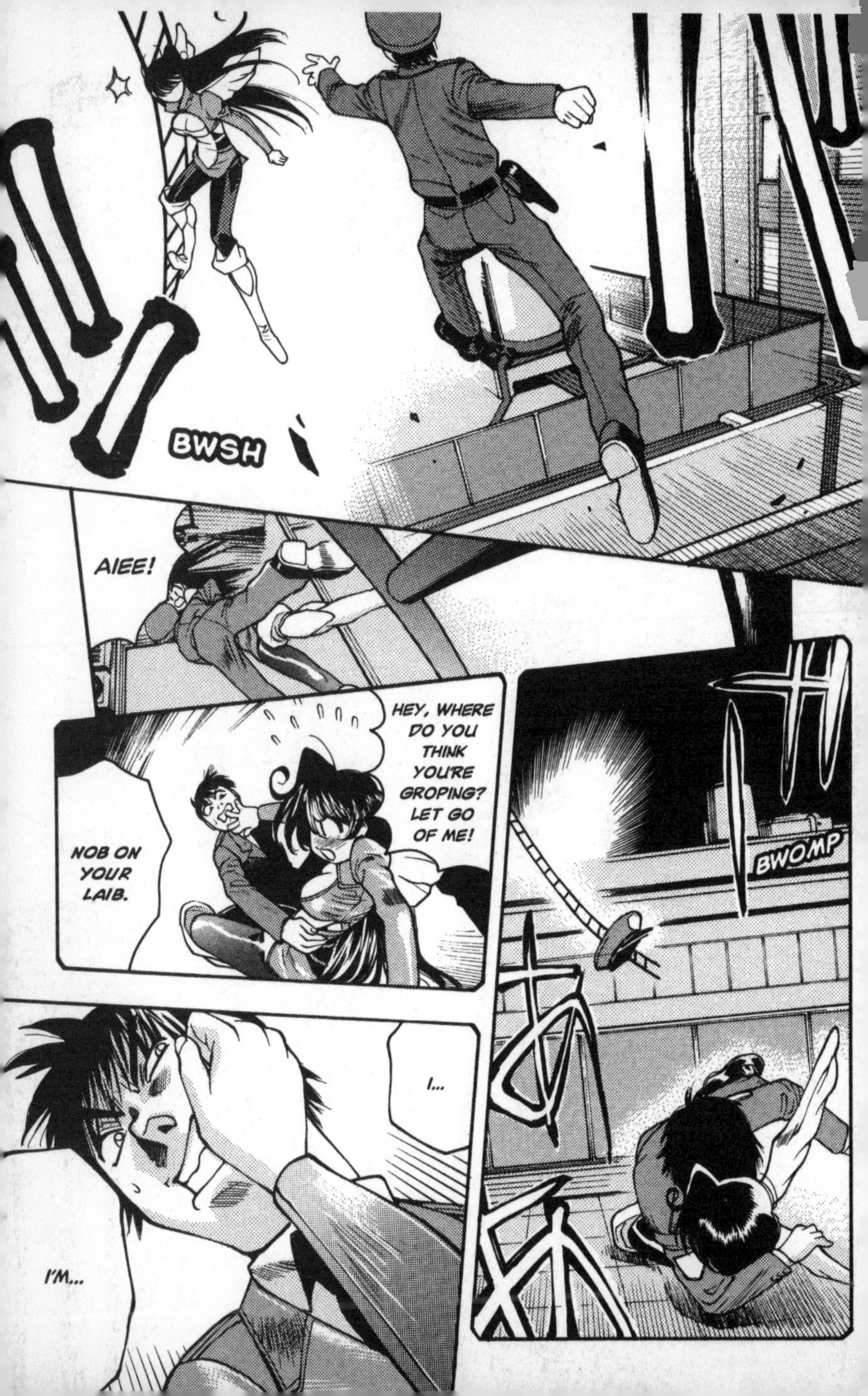
BWSH
AIEE!
BWOMP
HEY, WHERE DO YOU THINK YOU'RE GROPING? LET GO OF ME!
NOB ON YOUR LAIB.
I...
I'M...

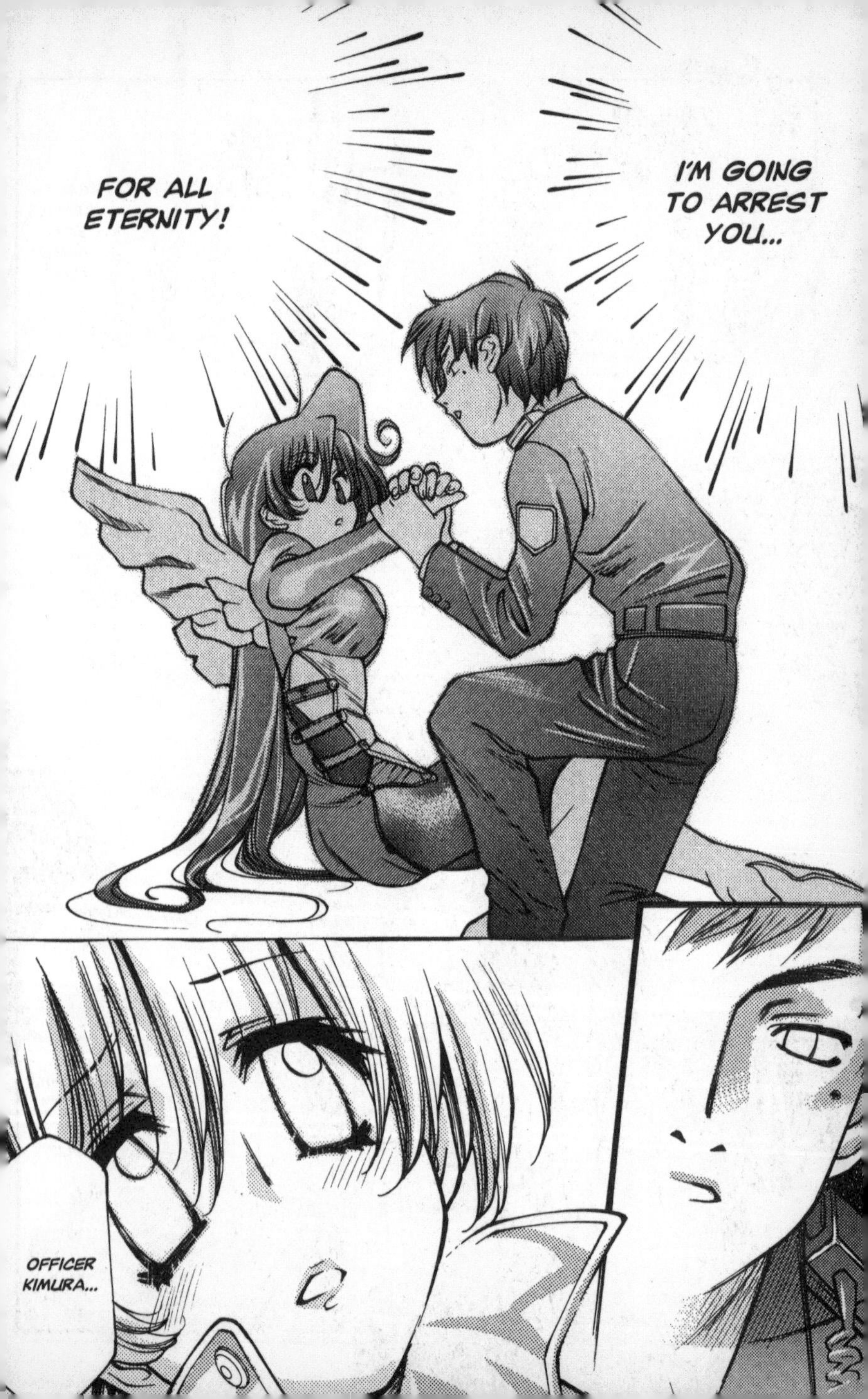
I'M GOING TO ARREST YOU...
FOR ALL ETERNITY!
OFFICER KIMURA...

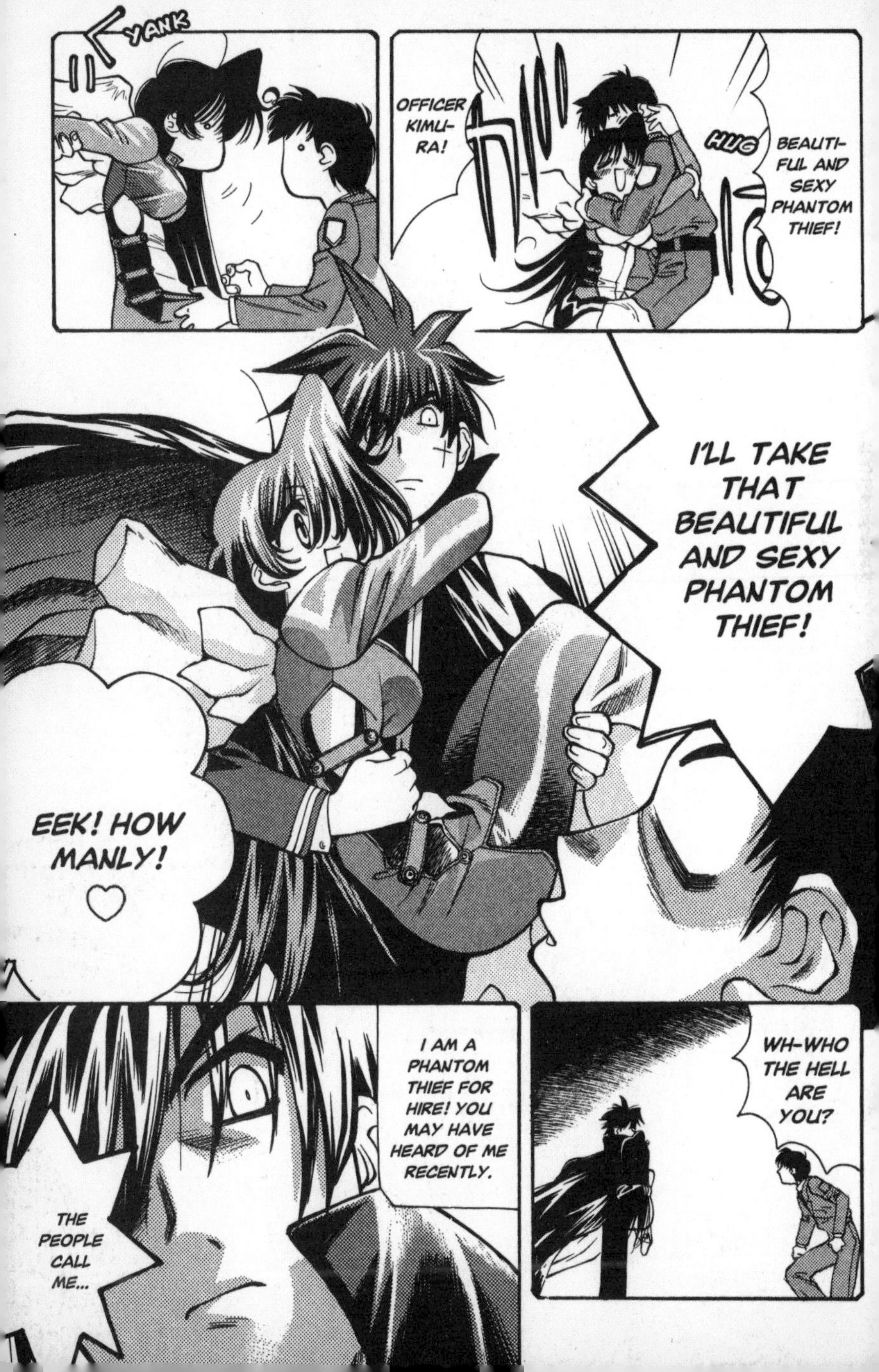
YANK
OFFICER KIMURA!
HUG
BEAUTIFUL AND SEXY PHANTOM THIEF!
I'LL TAKE THAT BEAUTIFUL AND SEXY PHANTOM THIEF!
EEK! HOW MANLY! ♡
WH-WHO THE HELL ARE YOU?
I AM A PHANTOM THIEF FOR HIRE! YOU MAY HAVE HEARD OF ME RECENTLY.
THE PEOPLE CALL ME...

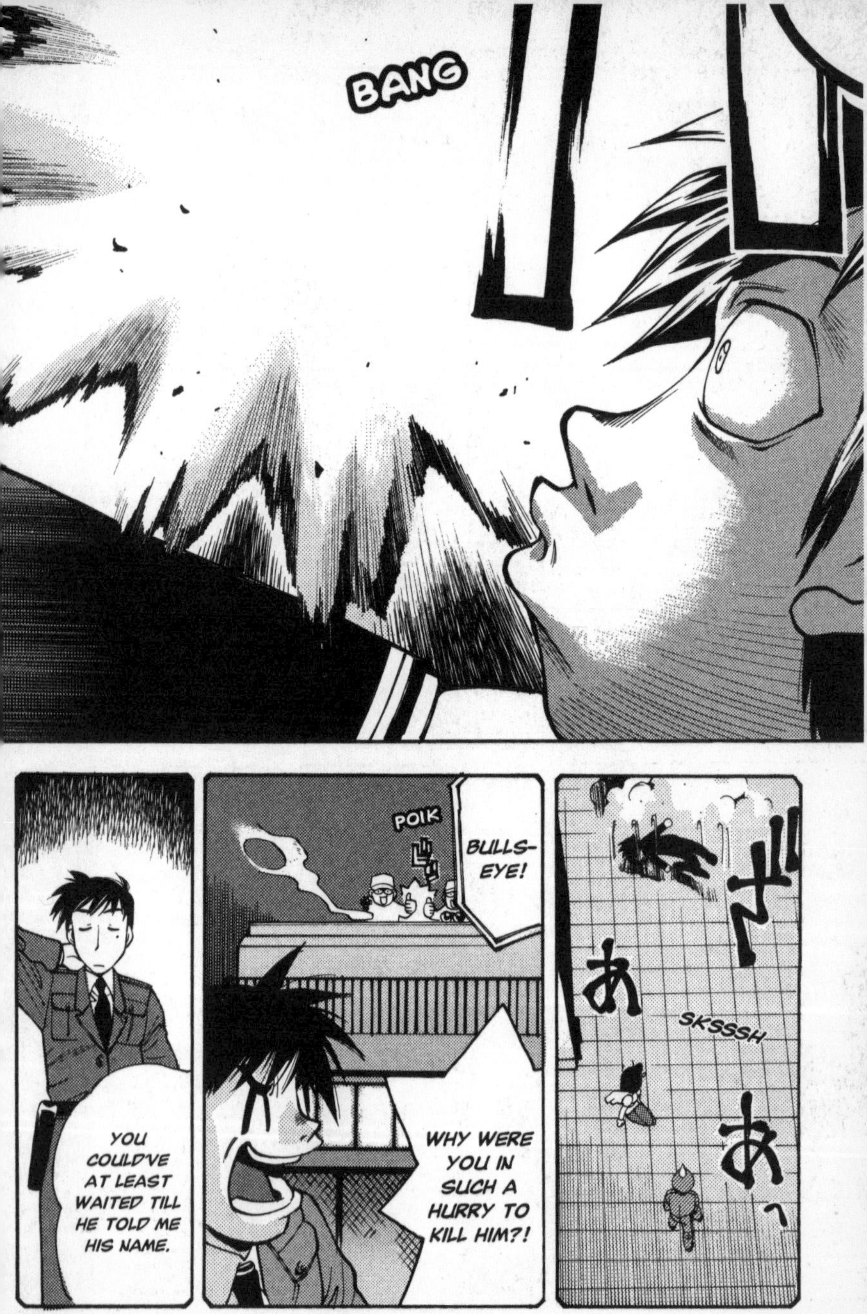
BANG
ざ
SKSSSH
あ
あ
POIK
BULLS-EYE!
WHY WERE YOU IN SUCH A HURRY TO KILL HIM?!
YOU COULD'VE AT LEAST WAITED TILL HE TOLD ME HIS NAME.

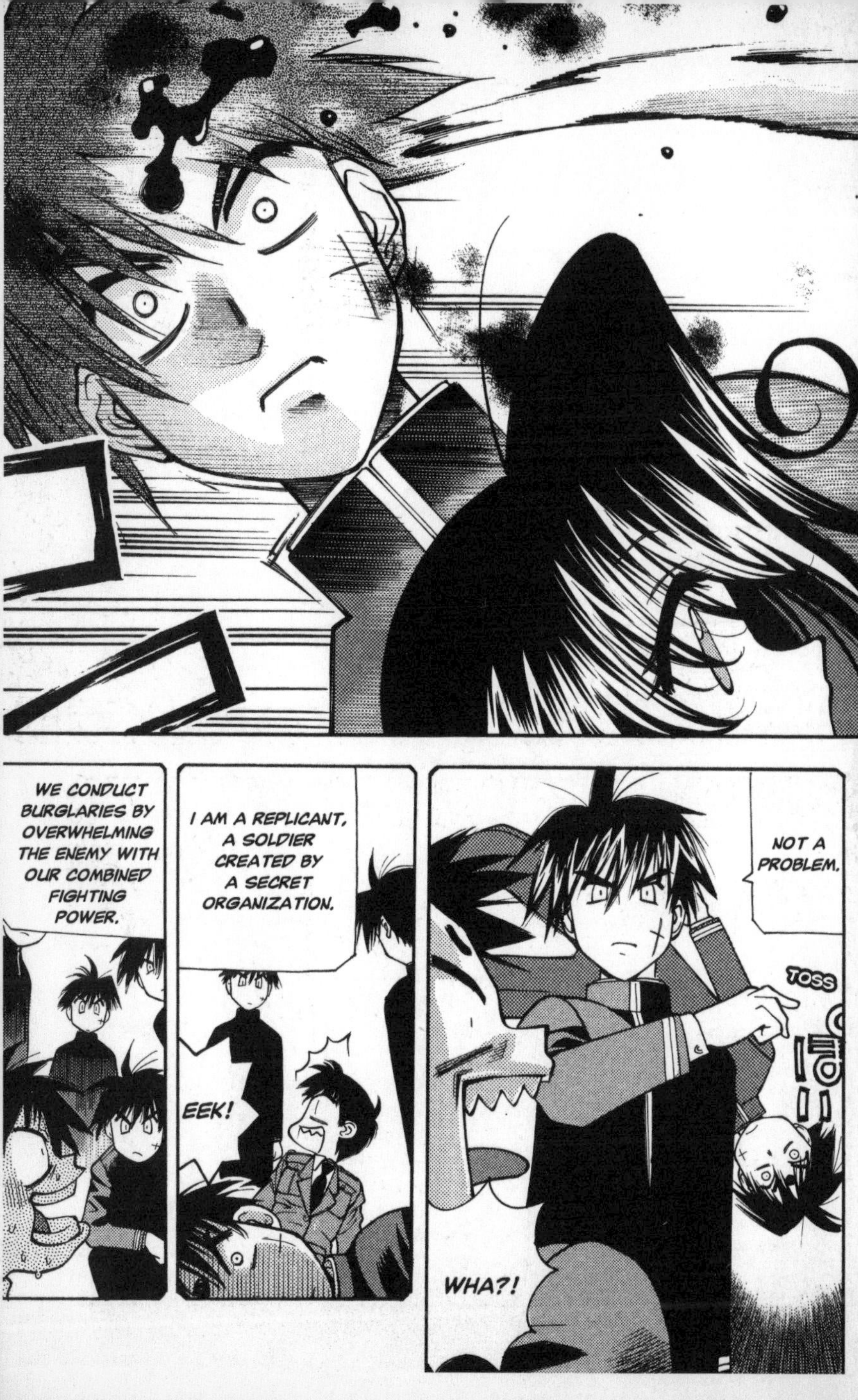

NOT A PROBLEM.
TOSS
WHA?!
I AM A REPLICANT, A SOLDIER CREATED BY A SECRET ORGANIZATION.
EEK!
WE CONDUCT BURGLARIES BY OVERWHELMING THE ENEMY WITH OUR COMBINED FIGHTING POWER.

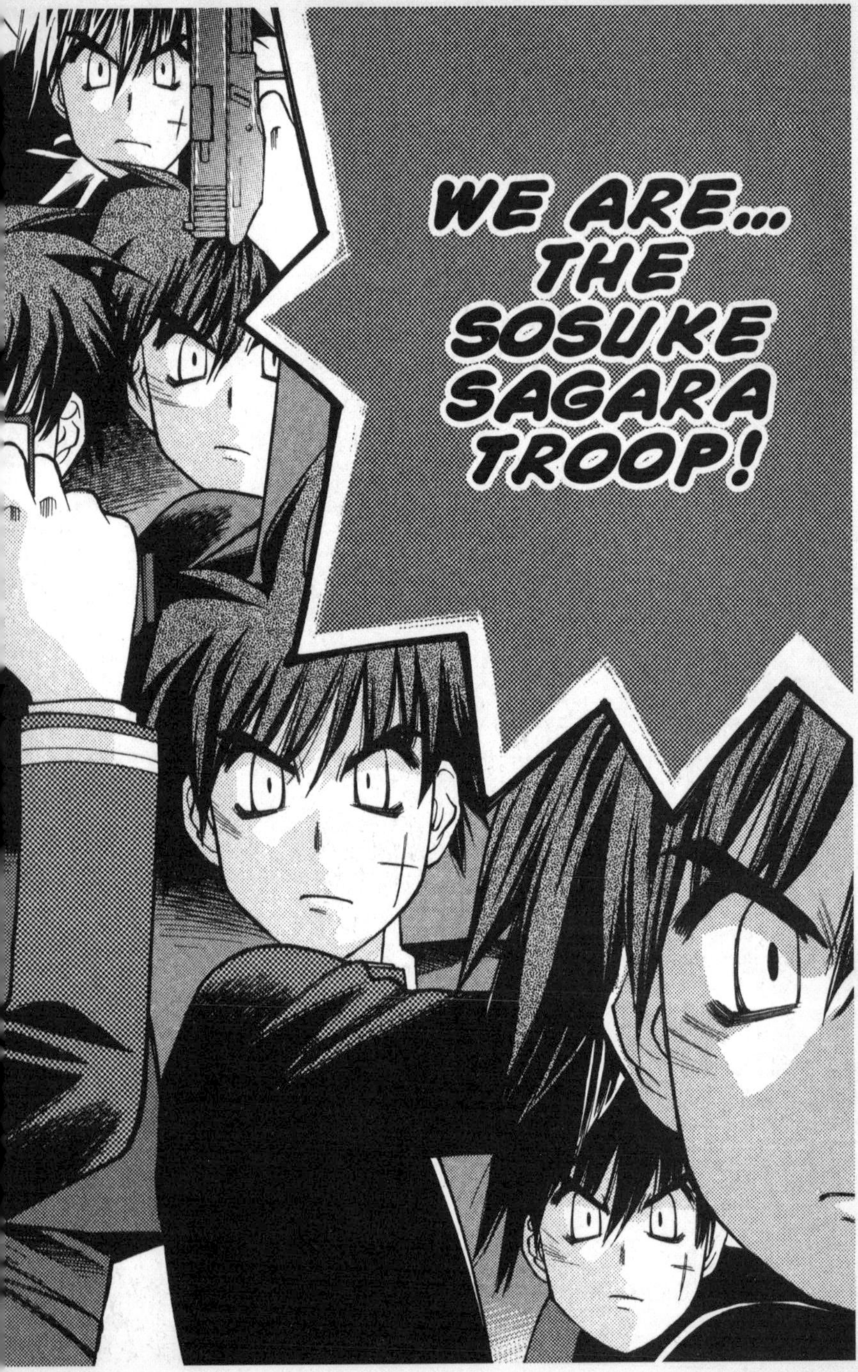
WE ARE... THE SOSUKE SAGARA TROOP!

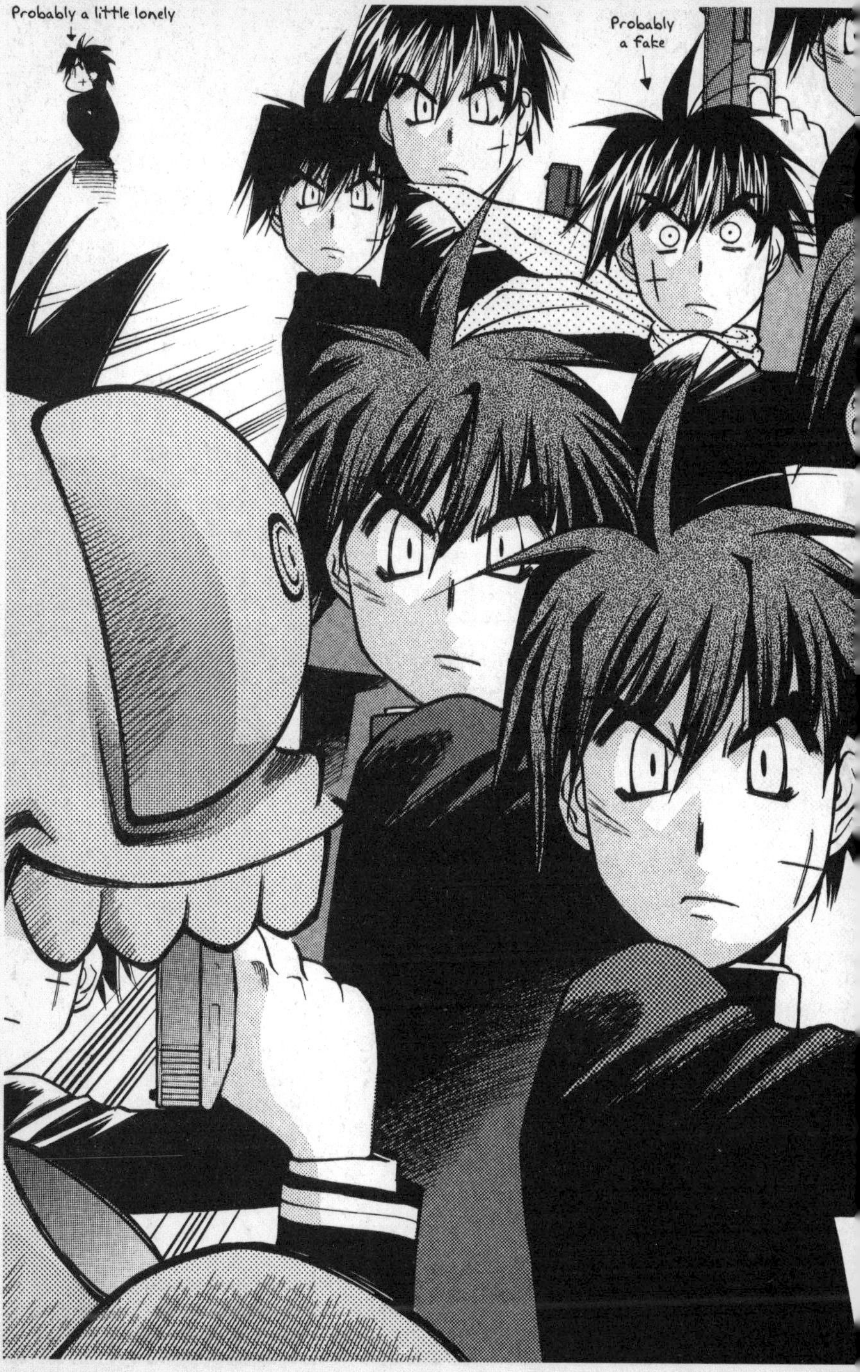
Probably a fake
Probably a little lonely

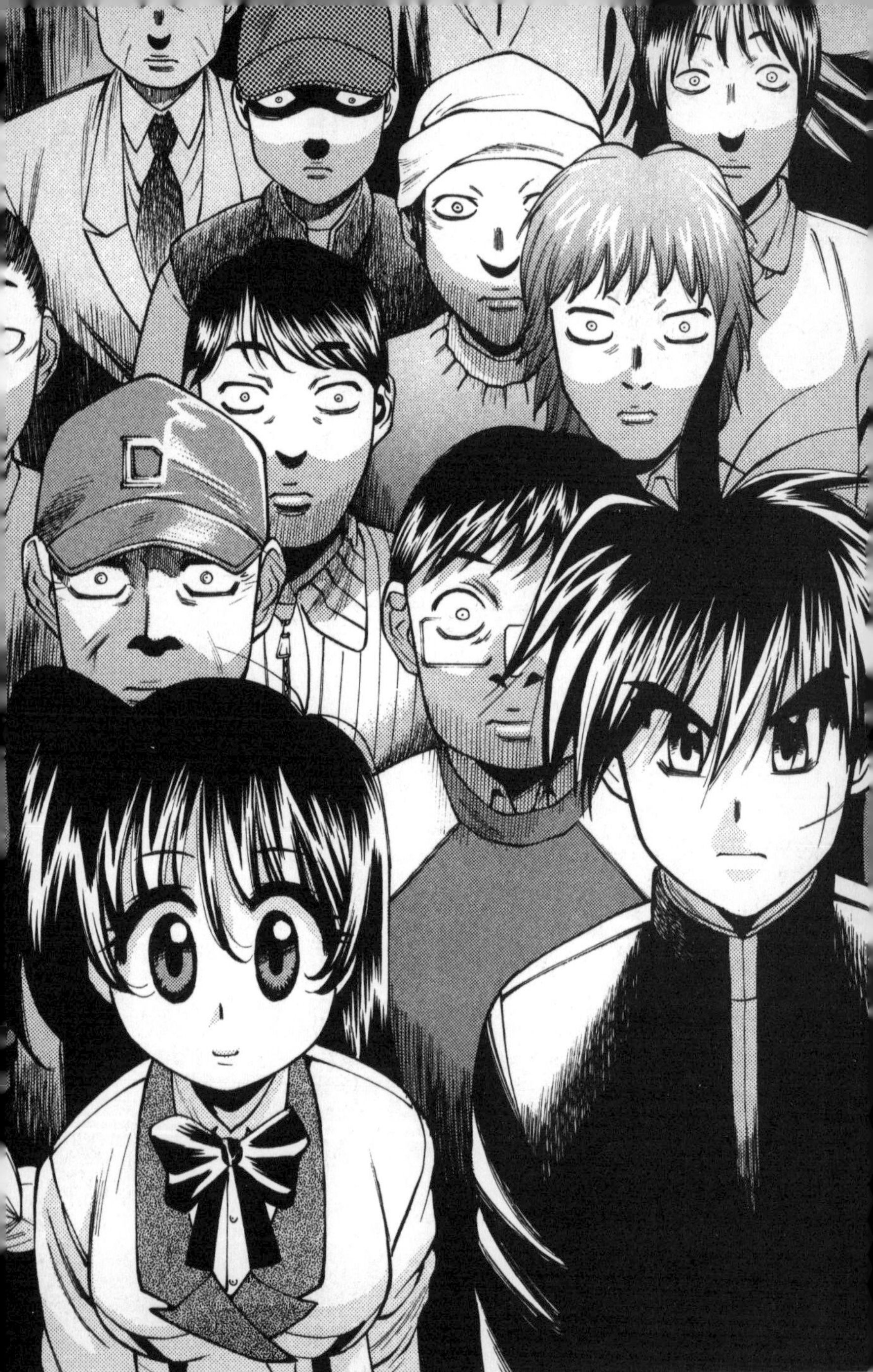

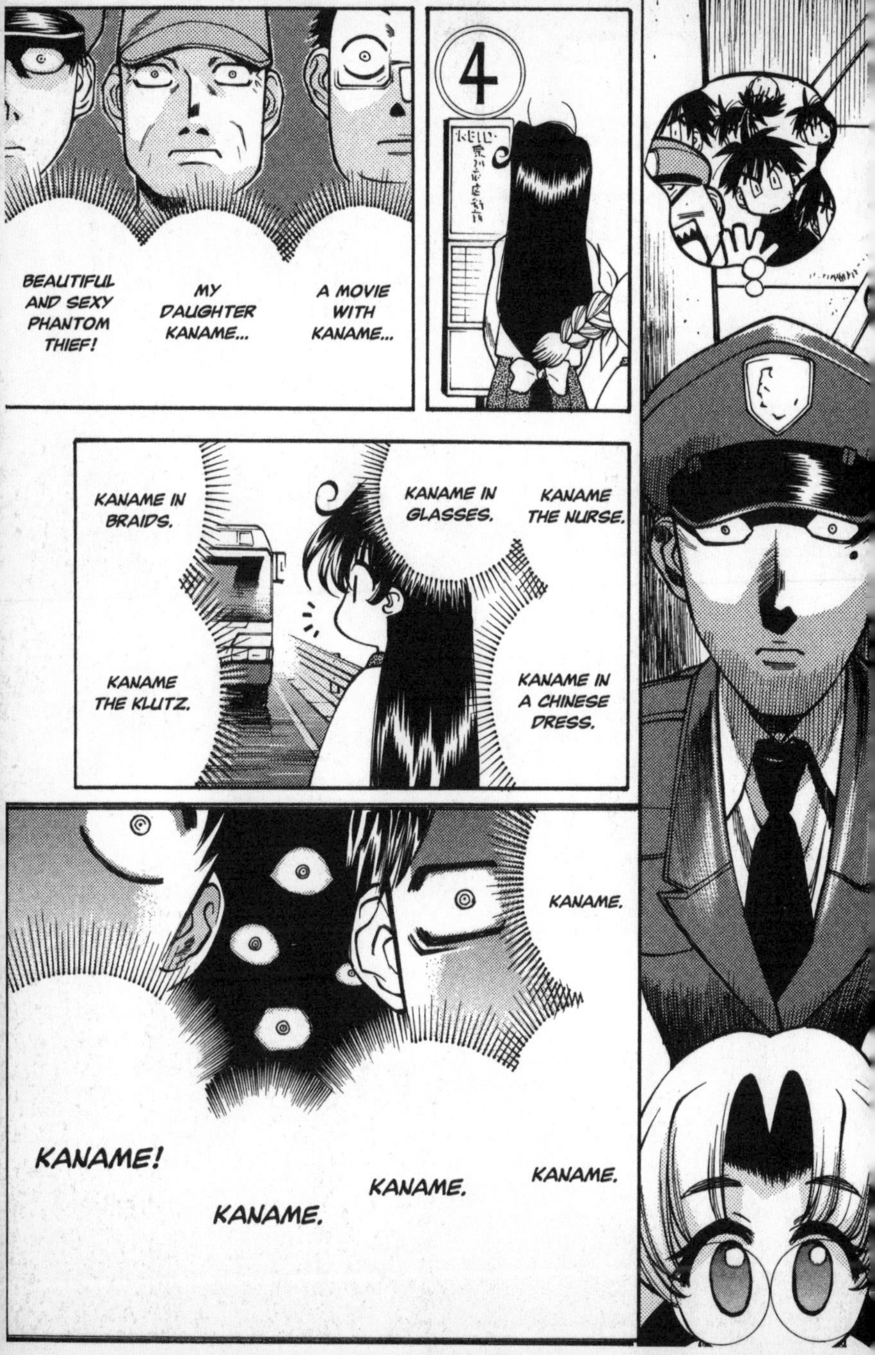
4
A MOVIE WITH KANAME...
MY DAUGHTER KANAME...
BEAUTIFUL AND SEXY PHANTOM THIEF!
KANAME THE NURSE.
KANAME IN GLASSES.
KANAME IN BRAIDS.
KANAME IN A CHINESE DRESS.
KANAME THE KLUTZ.
KANAME.
KANAME.
KANAME.
KANAME.
KANAME!

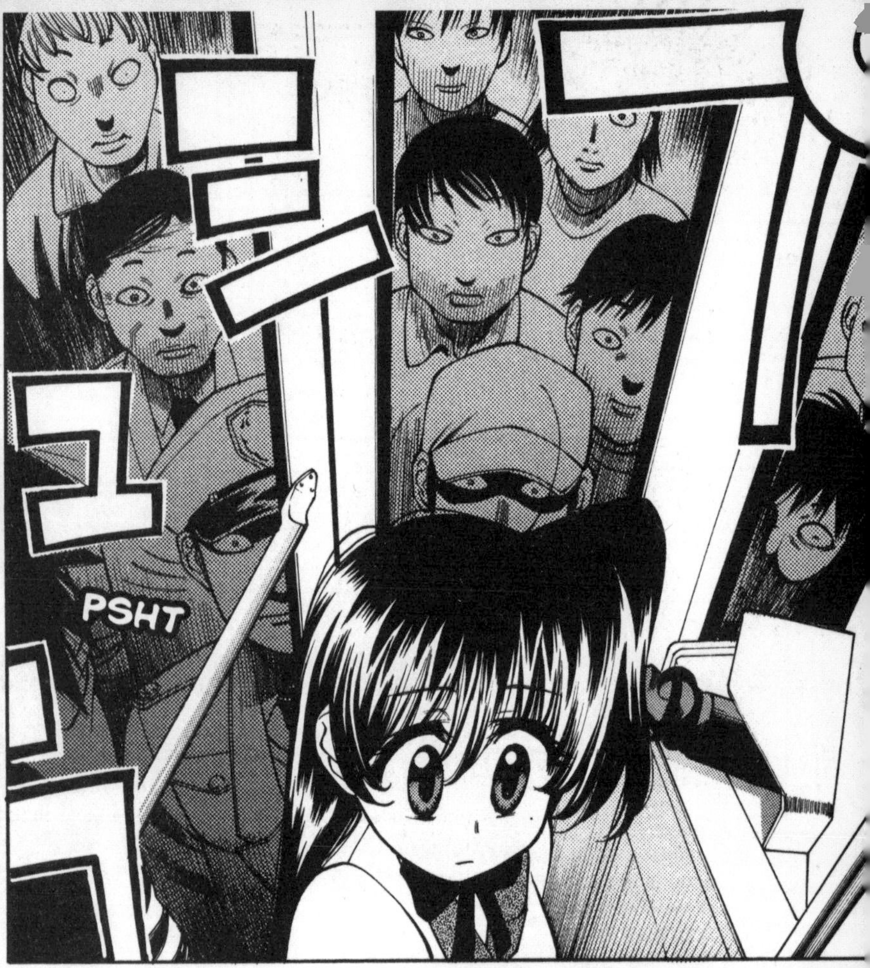
PSHT

THE PARANOIA SHOPPING DISTRICT IS WAITING FOR YOU.

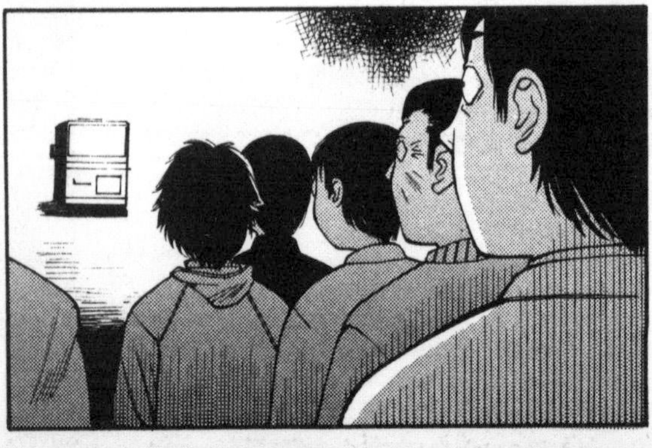

THE WAY HOME... WHERE ALL MANNERS OF DRAMA CAN UNFOLD.

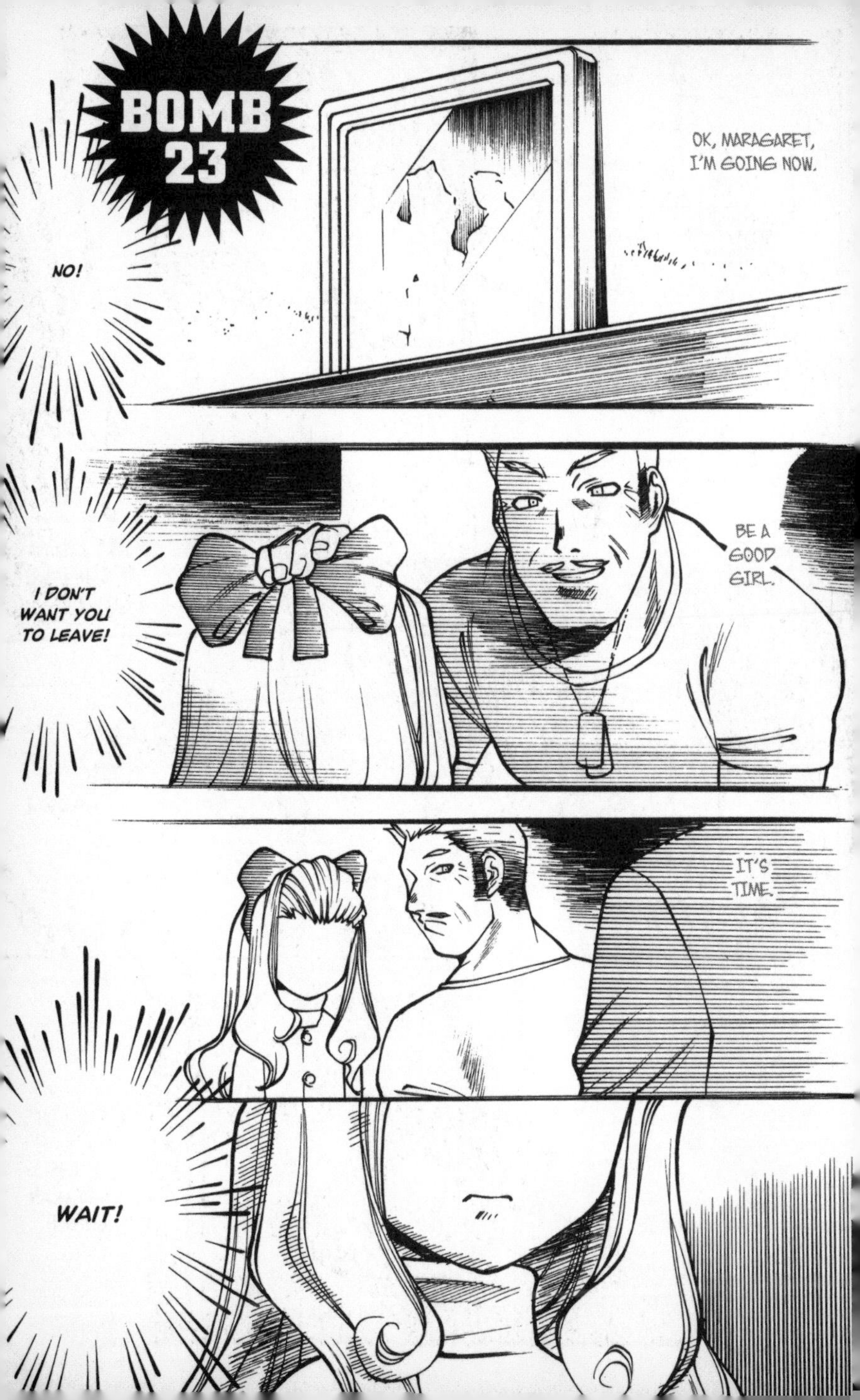
BOMB 23
OK, MARAGARET, I'M GOING NOW.
NO!
BE A GOOD GIRL.
I DON'T WANT YOU TO LEAVE!
IT'S TIME.
WAIT!

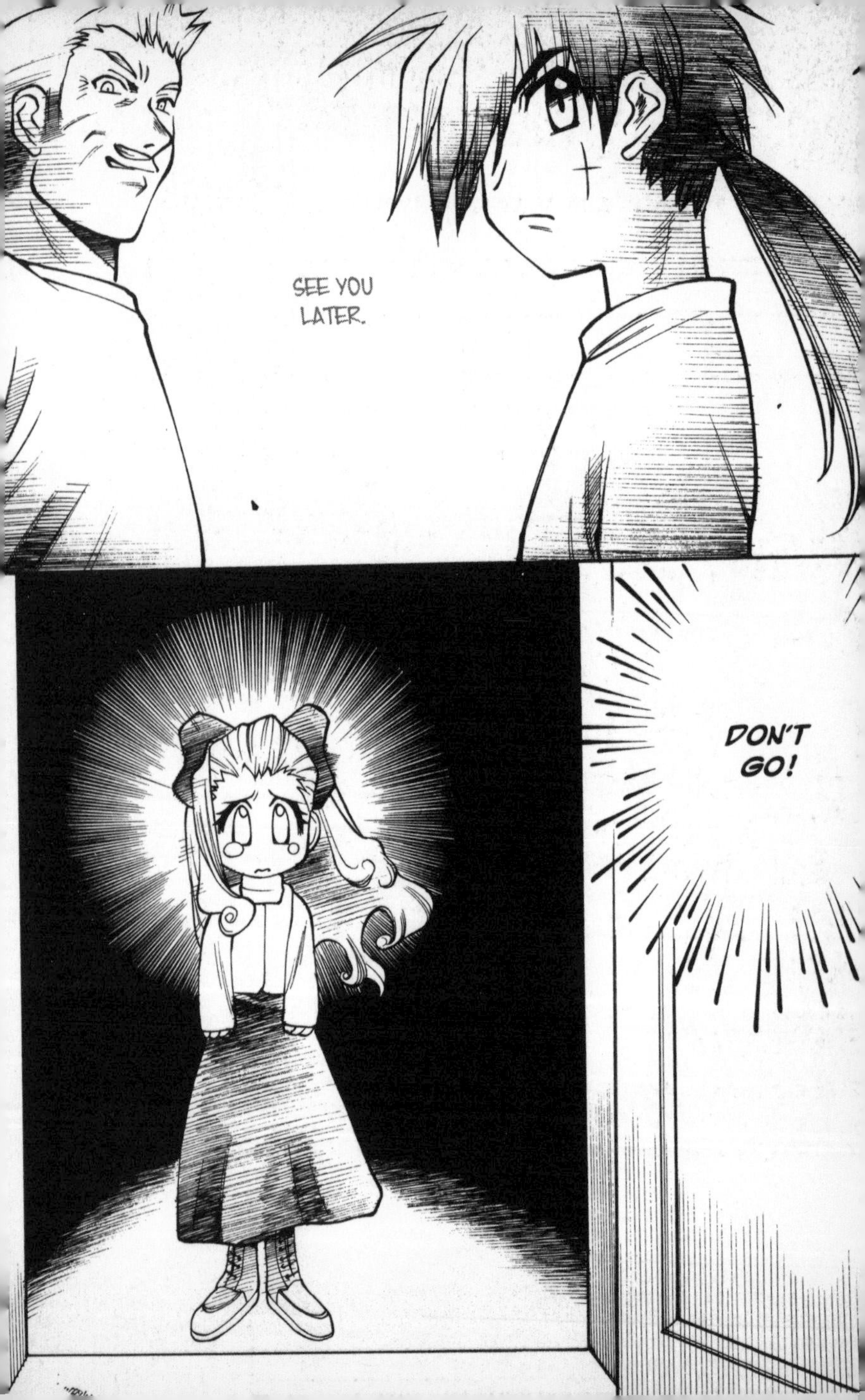
SEE YOU
LATER.
DON'T
GO!

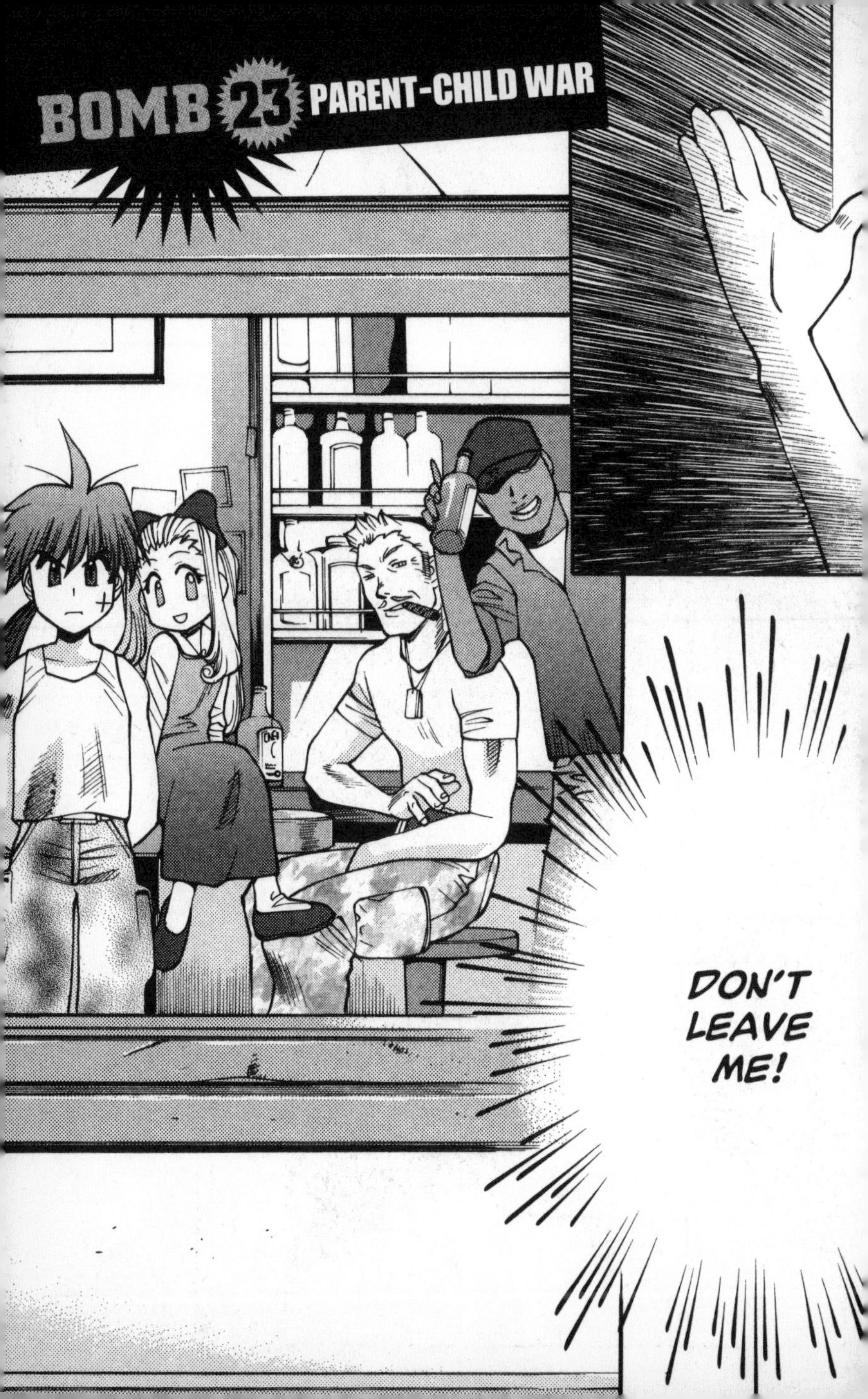
BOMB 23 PARENT-CHILD WAR
DON'T LEAVE ME!

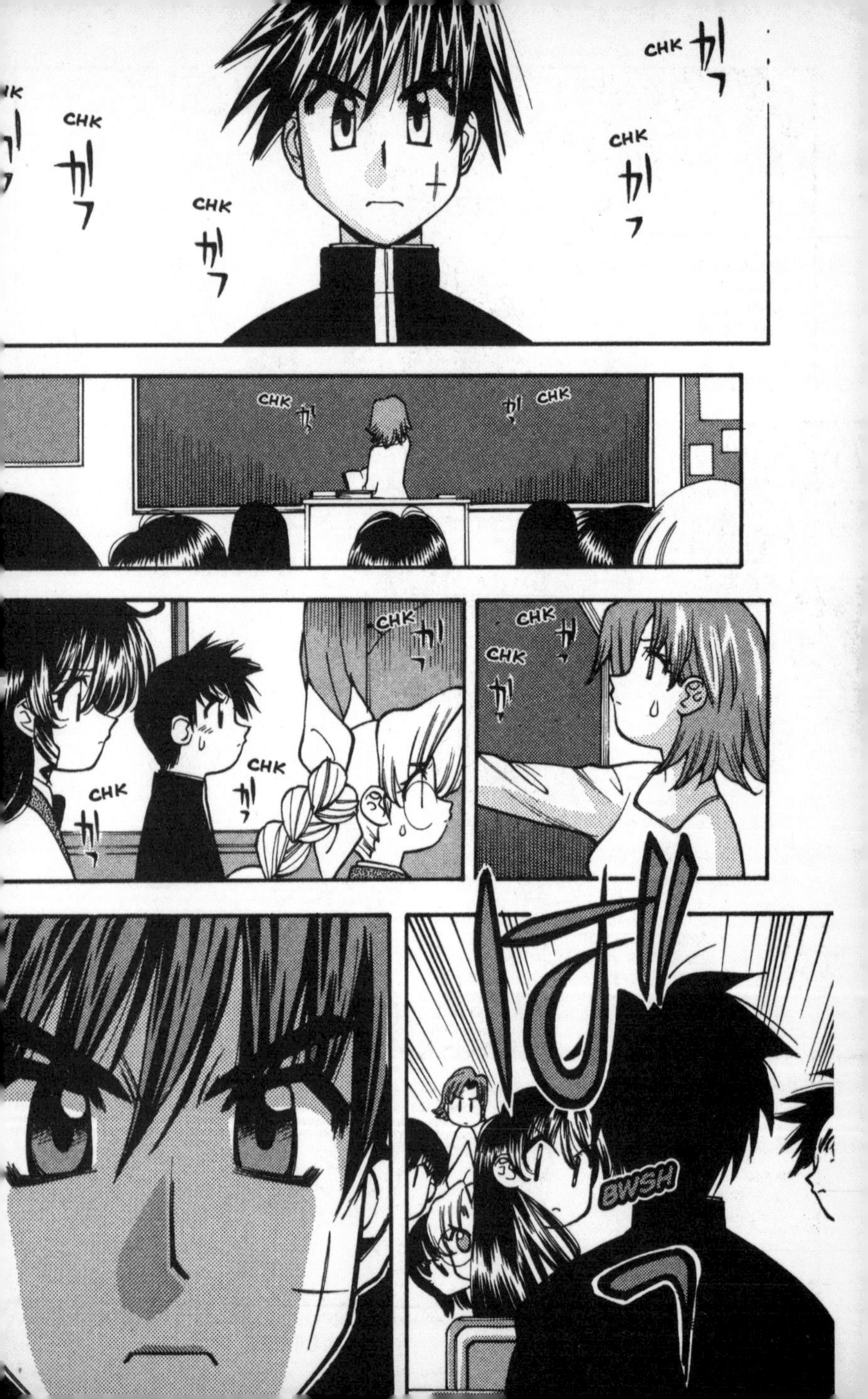
CHK
CHK
CHK
CHK
CHK
CHK
CHK
CHK
CHK
CHK
CHK
CHK
BWSH

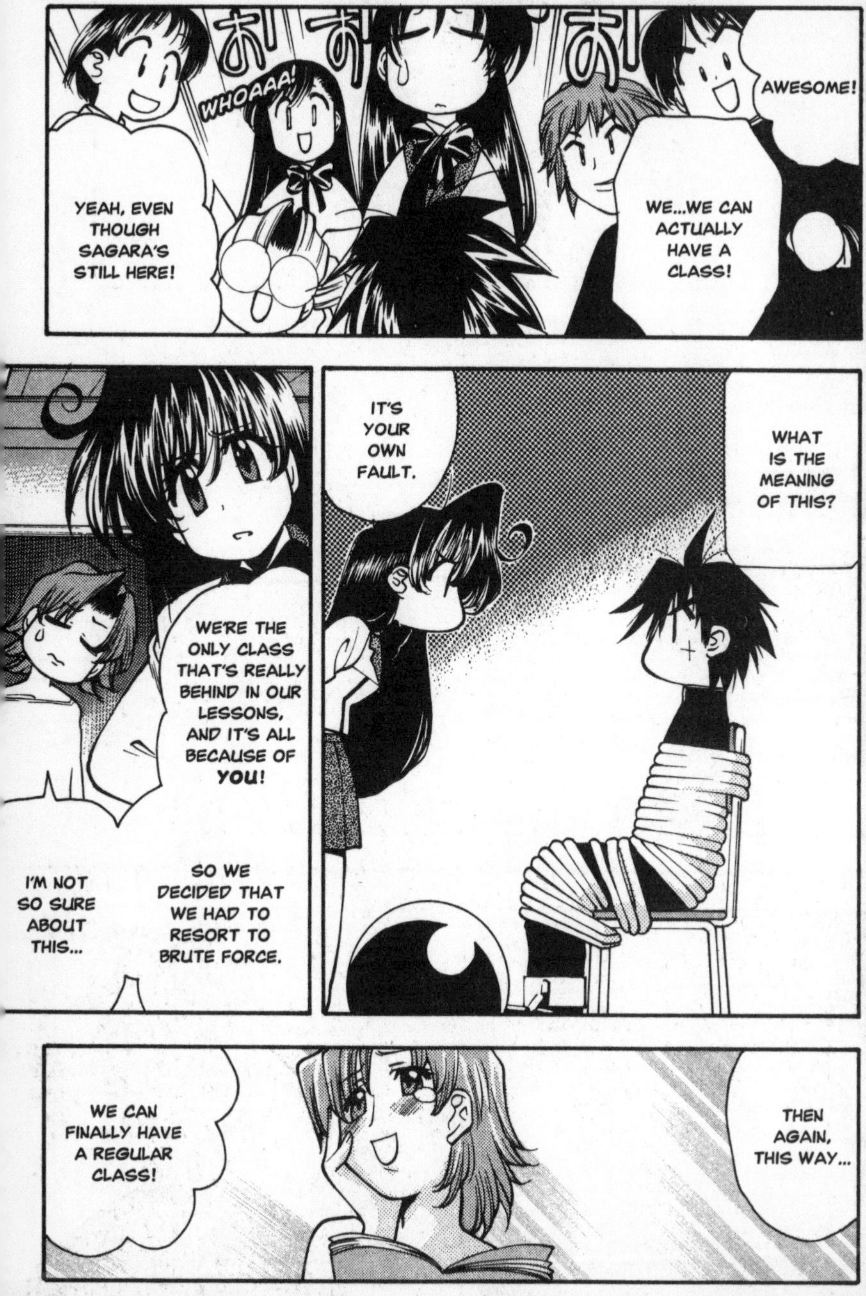
AWESOME!
WE...WE CAN ACTUALLY HAVE A CLASS!
おおお
WHOAAA!
YEAH, EVEN THOUGH SAGARA'S STILL HERE!
WHAT IS THE MEANING OF THIS?
IT'S YOUR OWN FAULT.
WE'RE THE ONLY CLASS THAT'S REALLY BEHIND IN OUR LESSONS, AND IT'S ALL BECAUSE OF YOU!
SO WE DECIDED THAT WE HAD TO RESORT TO BRUTE FORCE.
I'M NOT SO SURE ABOUT THIS...
THEN AGAIN, THIS WAY...
WE CAN FINALLY HAVE A REGULAR CLASS!

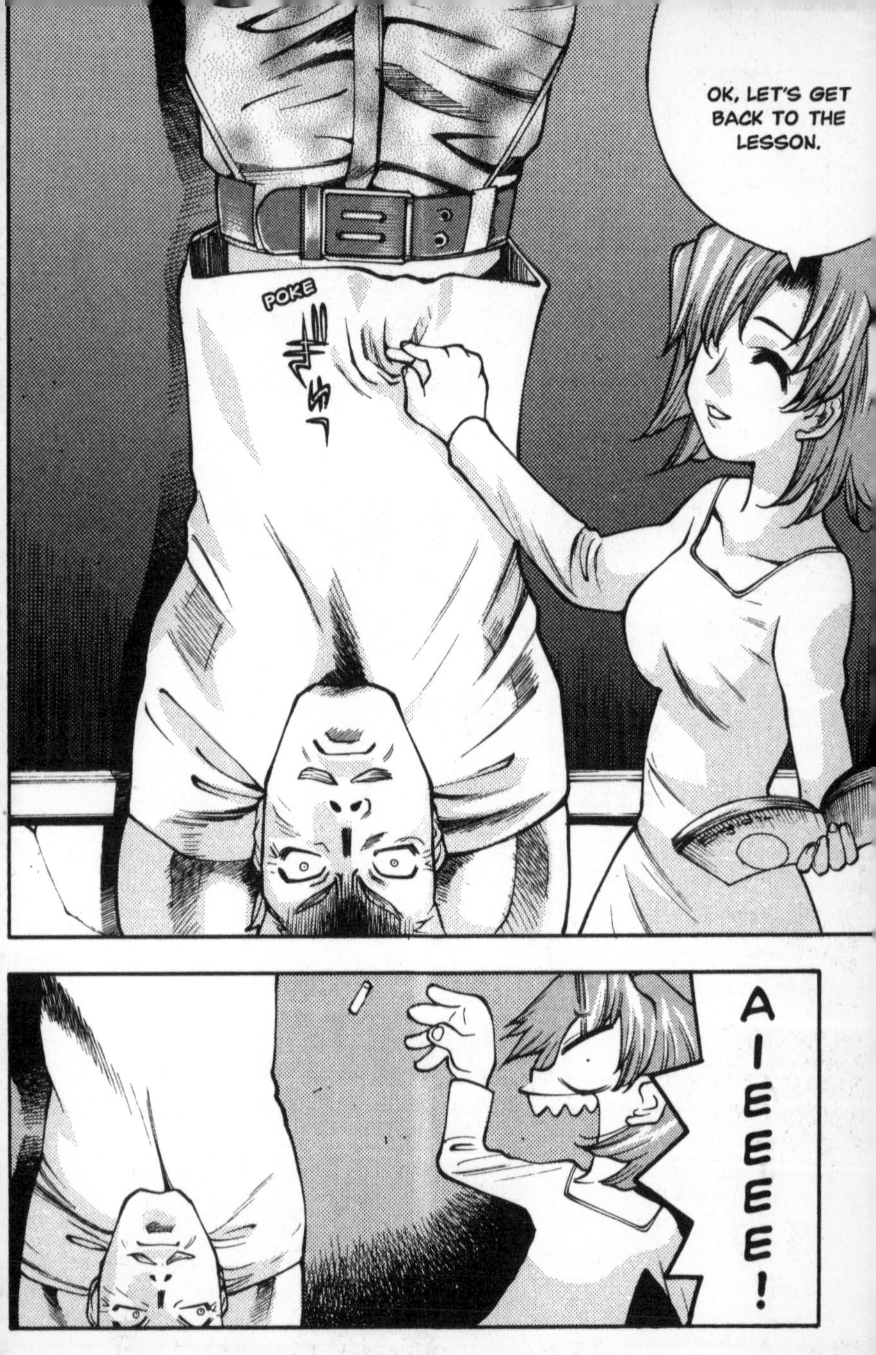
OK, LET'S GET BACK TO THE LESSON.
POKE
AIEEEE!

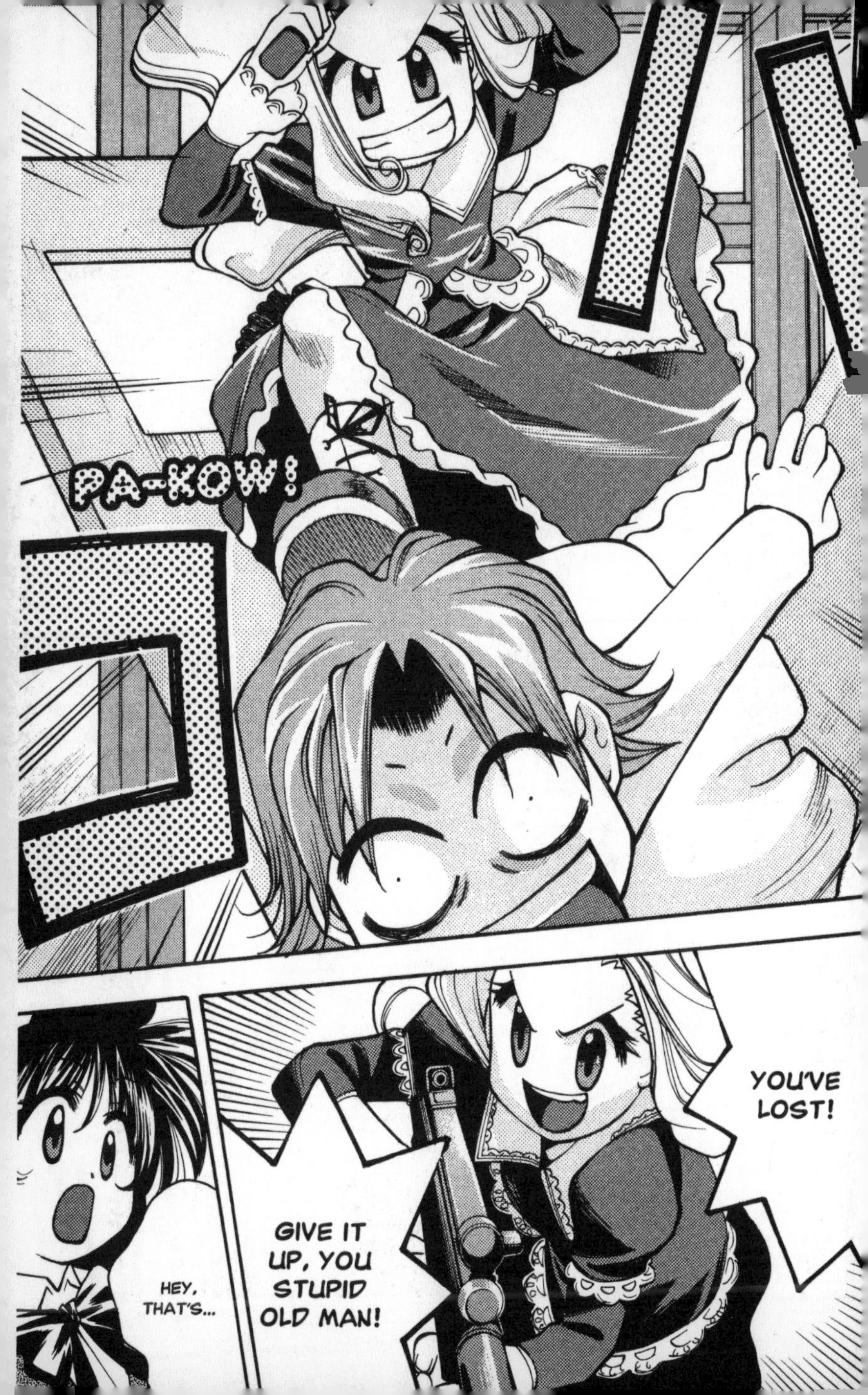
PA-KOW!
YOU'VE LOST!
GIVE IT UP, YOU STUPID OLD MAN!
HEY, THAT'S...

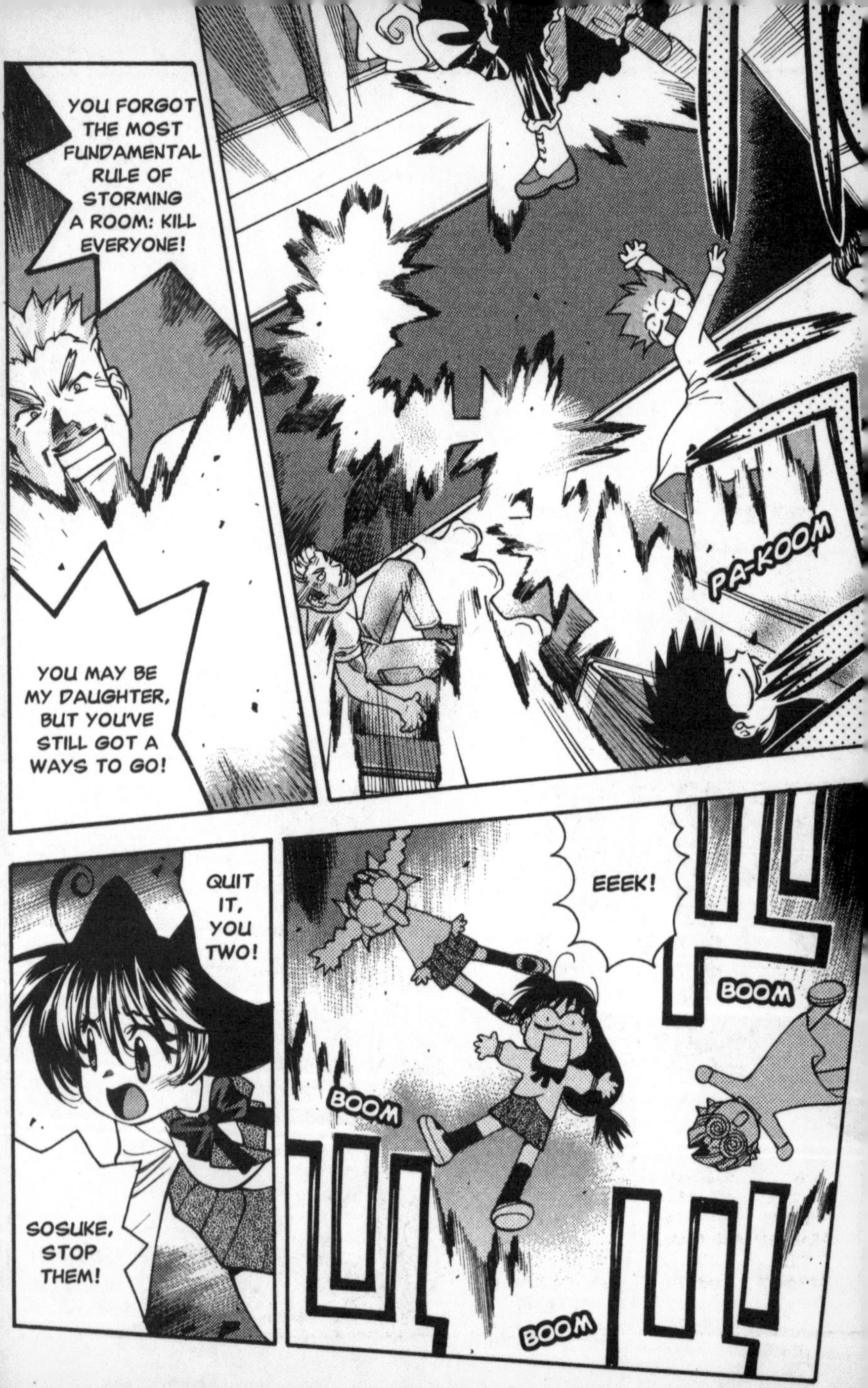
PA-KOOM
YOU FORGOT THE MOST FUNDAMENTAL RULE OF STORMING A ROOM: KILL EVERYONE!
YOU MAY BE MY DAUGHTER, BUT YOU'VE STILL GOT A WAYS TO GO!
EEEK!
BOOM
BOOM
BOOM
QUIT IT, YOU TWO!
SOSUKE, STOP THEM!

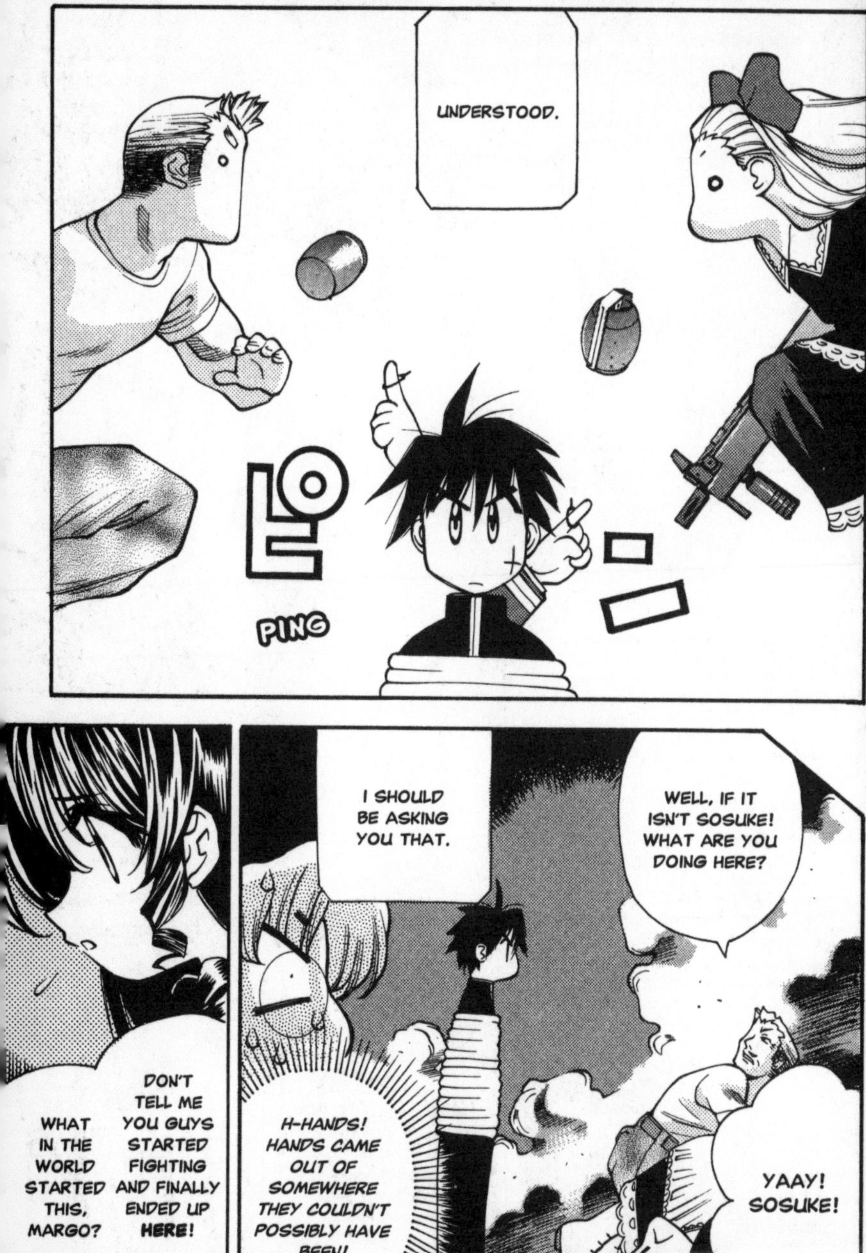
UNDERSTOOD.
PING
WELL, IF IT ISN'T SOSUKE! WHAT ARE YOU DOING HERE?
I SHOULD BE ASKING YOU THAT.
YAAY! SOSUKE!
H-HANDS! HANDS CAME OUT OF SOMEWHERE THEY COULDN'T POSSIBLY HAVE BEEN!
DON'T TELL ME YOU GUYS STARTED FIGHTING AND FINALLY ENDED UP HERE!
WHAT IN THE WORLD STARTED THIS, MARGO?

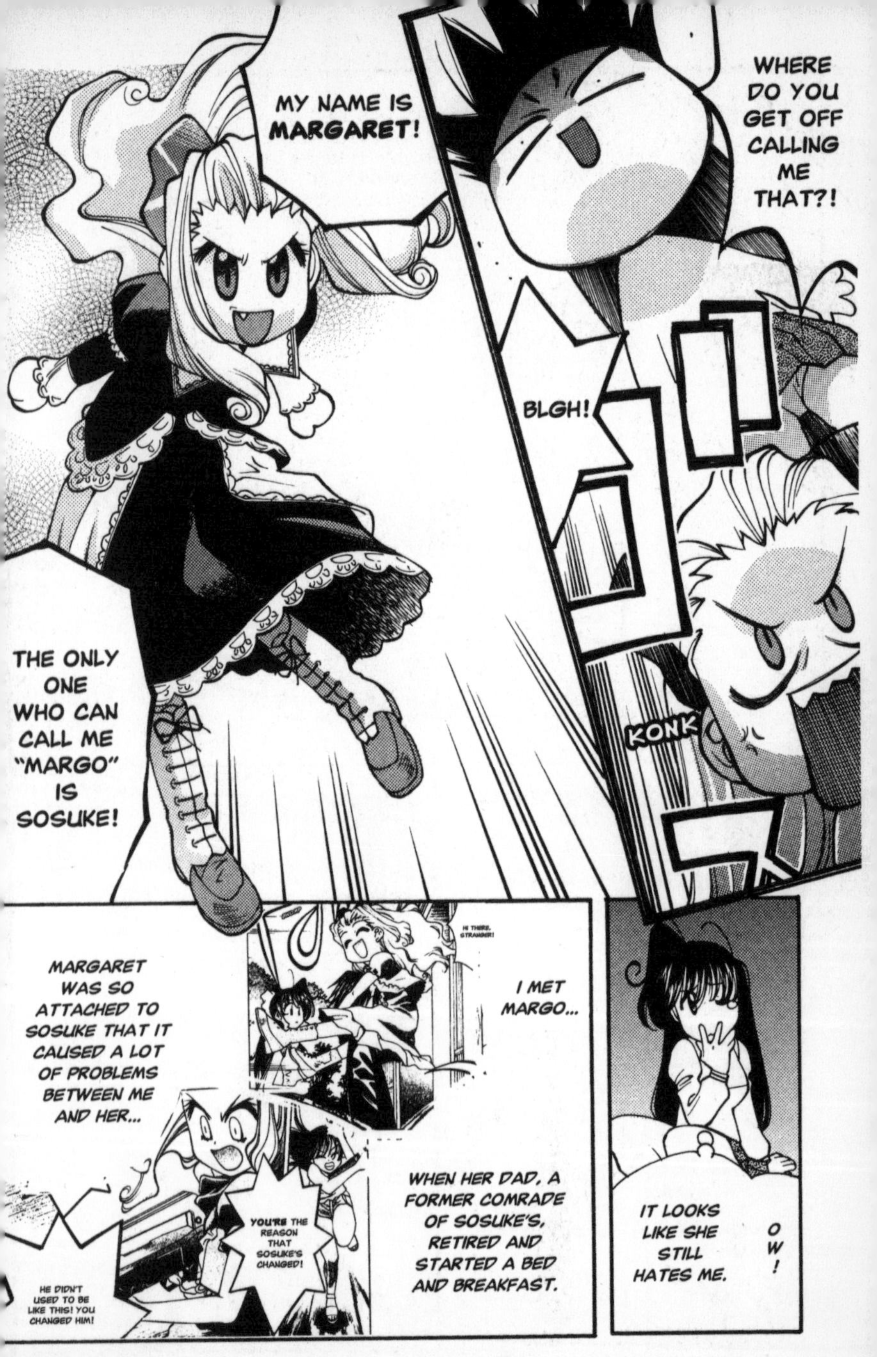
WHERE DO YOU GET OFF CALLING ME THAT?!
MY NAME IS MARGARET!
BLGH!
KONK
THE ONLY ONE WHO CAN CALL ME "MARGO" IS SOSUKE!
IT LOOKS LIKE SHE STILL HATES ME.
OW!
I MET MARGO...
HI THERE, STRANGER!
WHEN HER DAD, A FORMER COMRADE OF SOSUKE'S, RETIRED AND STARTED A BED AND BREAKFAST.
MARGARET WAS SO ATTACHED TO SOSUKE THAT IT CAUSED A LOT OF PROBLEMS BETWEEN ME AND HER...
YOU'RE THE REASON THAT SOSUKE'S CHANGED!
HE DIDN'T USED TO BE LIKE THIS! YOU CHANGED HIM!

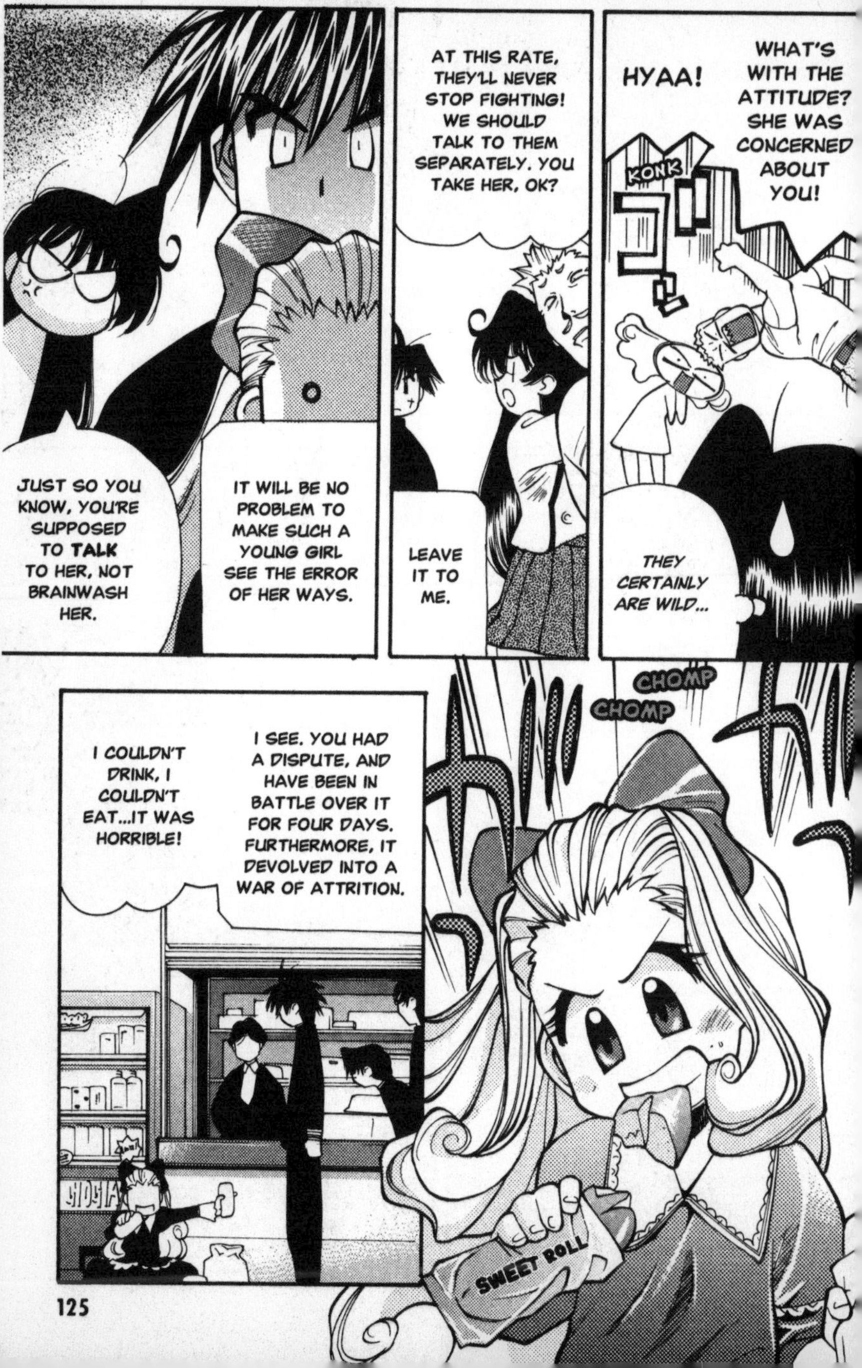
WHAT'S WITH THE ATTITUDE? SHE WAS CONCERNED ABOUT YOU!
HYAA!
KONK
THEY CERTAINLY ARE WILD...
AT THIS RATE, THEY'LL NEVER STOP FIGHTING! WE SHOULD TALK TO THEM SEPARATELY. YOU TAKE HER, OK?
LEAVE IT TO ME.
IT WILL BE NO PROBLEM TO MAKE SUCH A YOUNG GIRL SEE THE ERROR OF HER WAYS.
JUST SO YOU KNOW, YOU'RE SUPPOSED TO **TALK** TO HER, NOT BRAINWASH HER.
CHOMP
CHOMP
SWEET ROLL
I SEE. YOU HAD A DISPUTE, AND HAVE BEEN IN BATTLE OVER IT FOR FOUR DAYS. FURTHERMORE, IT DEVOLVED INTO A WAR OF ATTRITION.
I COULDN'T DRINK, I COULDN'T EAT...IT WAS HORRIBLE!

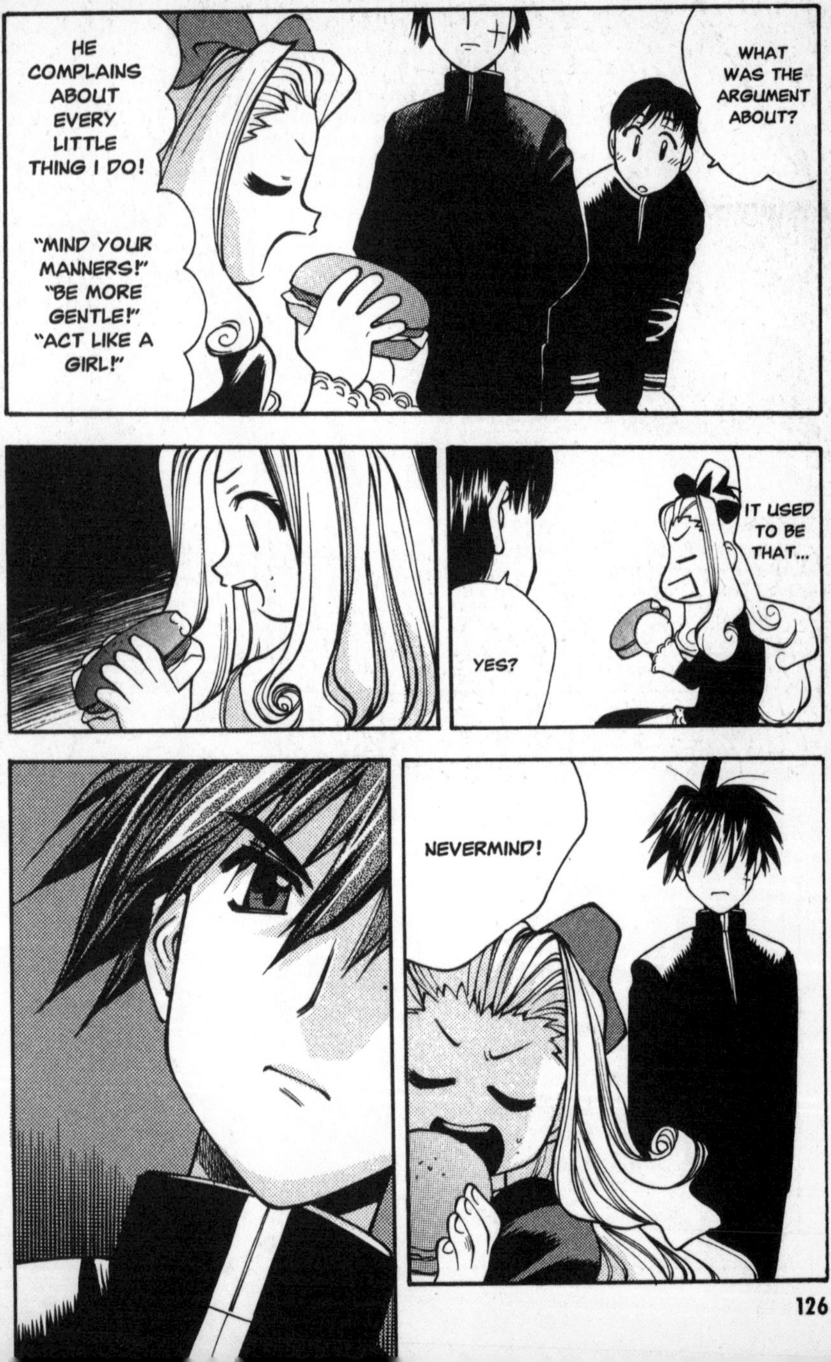
WHAT WAS THE ARGUMENT ABOUT?
HE COMPLAINS ABOUT EVERY LITTLE THING I DO!
"MIND YOUR MANNERS!" "BE MORE GENTLE!" "ACT LIKE A GIRL!"
IT USED TO BE THAT...
YES?
NEVERMIND!

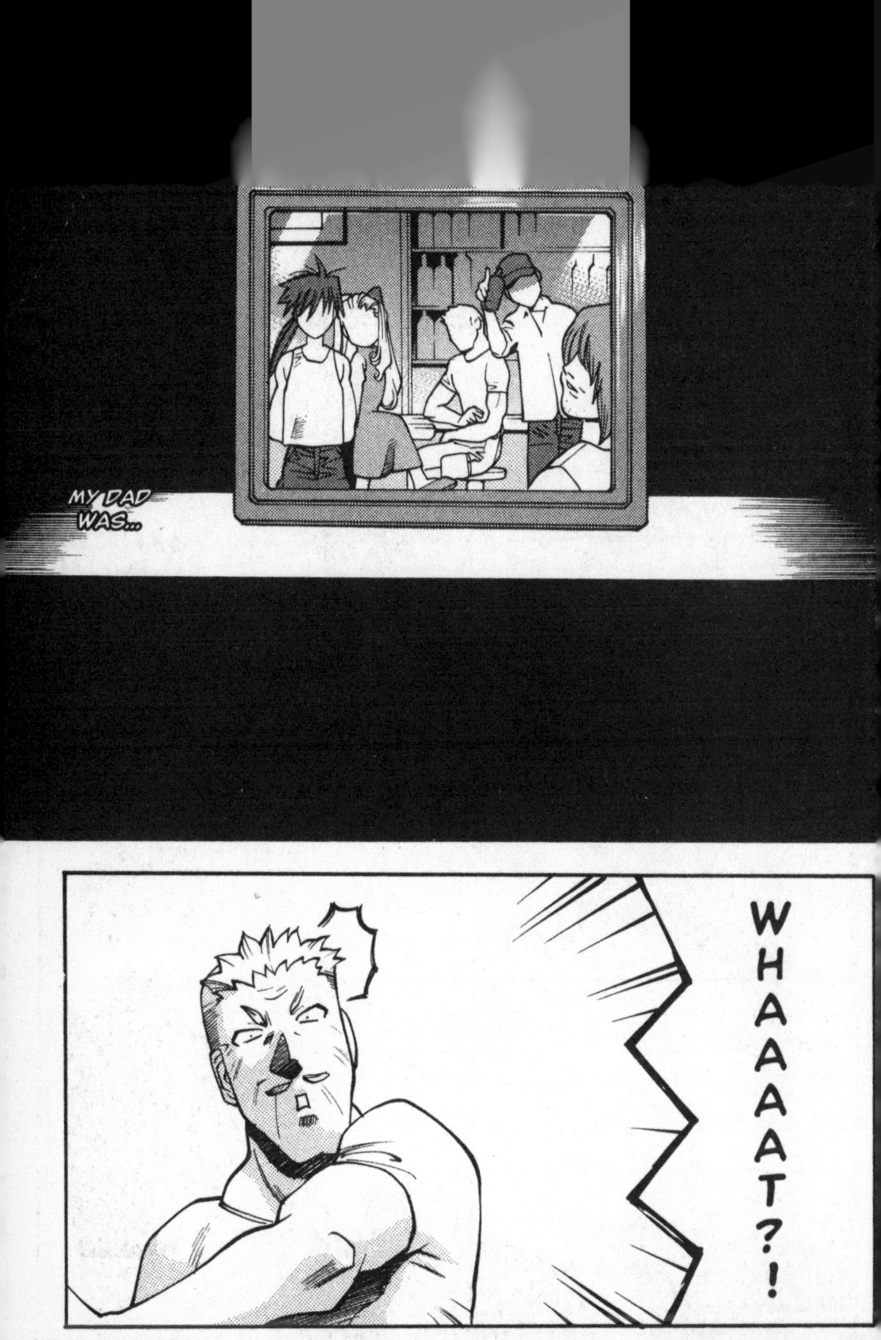
MY DAD WAS...
WHAAAAT?!

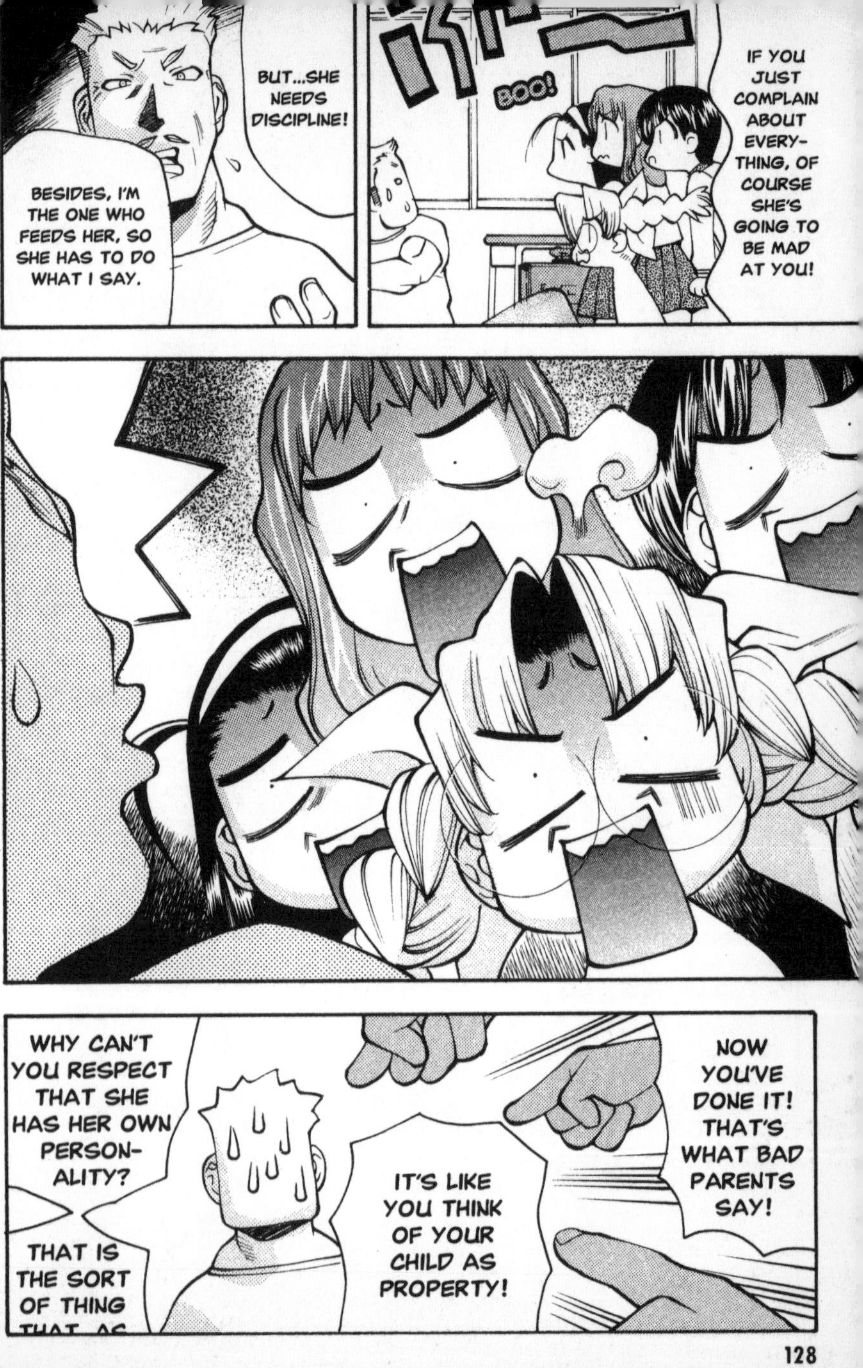
IF YOU JUST COMPLAIN ABOUT EVERY-THING, OF COURSE SHE'S GOING TO BE MAD AT YOU!
BOO!
BUT...SHE NEEDS DISCIPLINE!
BESIDES, I'M THE ONE WHO FEEDS HER, SO SHE HAS TO DO WHAT I SAY.
NOW YOU'VE DONE IT! THAT'S WHAT BAD PARENTS SAY!
IT'S LIKE YOU THINK OF YOUR CHILD AS PROPERTY!
WHY CAN'T YOU RESPECT THAT SHE HAS HER OWN PERSON-ALITY?
THAT IS THE SORT OF THING

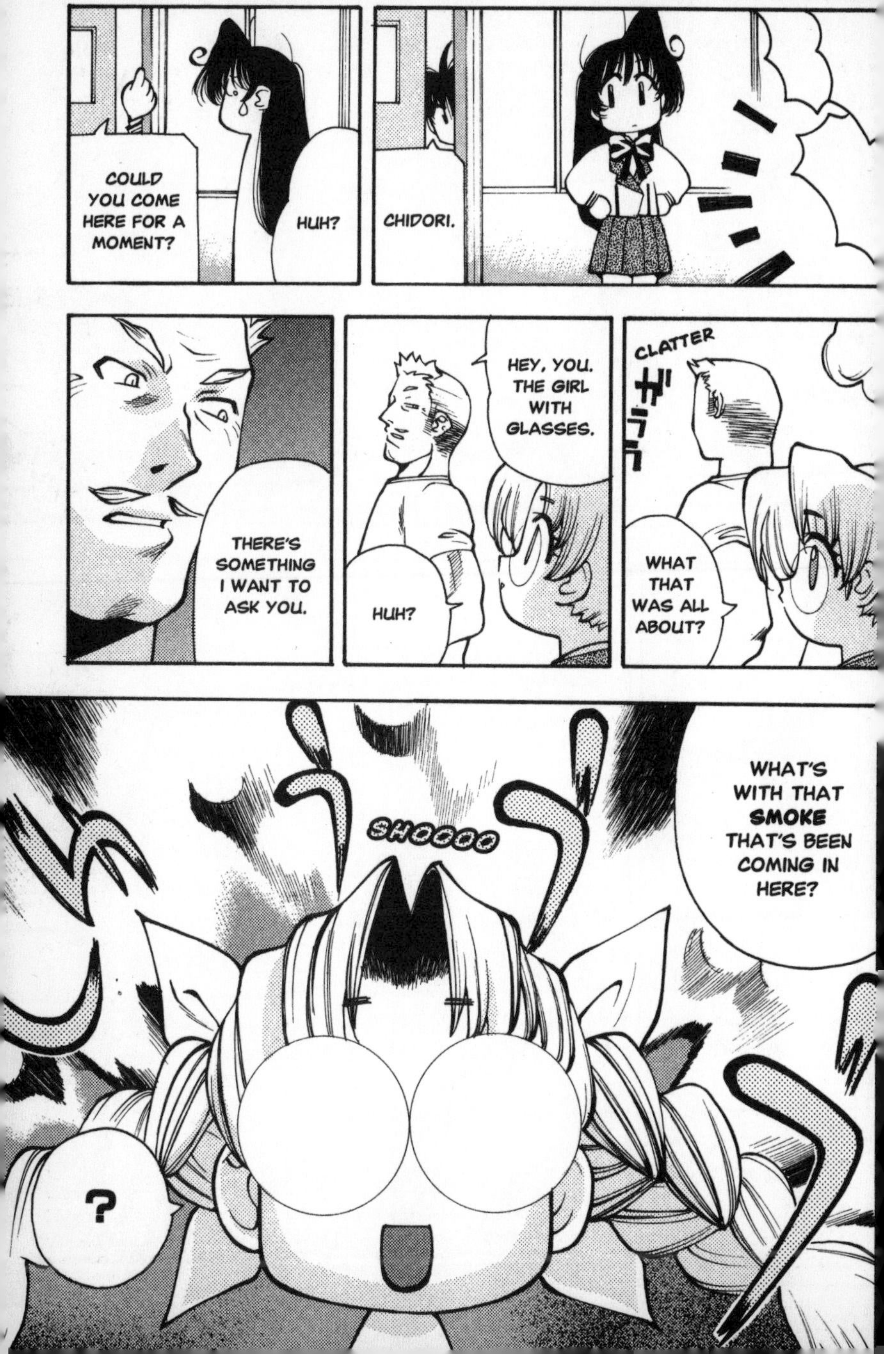
COULD YOU COME HERE FOR A MOMENT?
HUH?
CHIDORI.
THERE'S SOMETHING I WANT TO ASK YOU.
HEY, YOU. THE GIRL WITH GLASSES.
HUH?
CLATTER
WHAT THAT WAS ALL ABOUT?
WHAT'S WITH THAT **SMOKE** THAT'S BEEN COMING IN HERE?
SHOOOOO
?

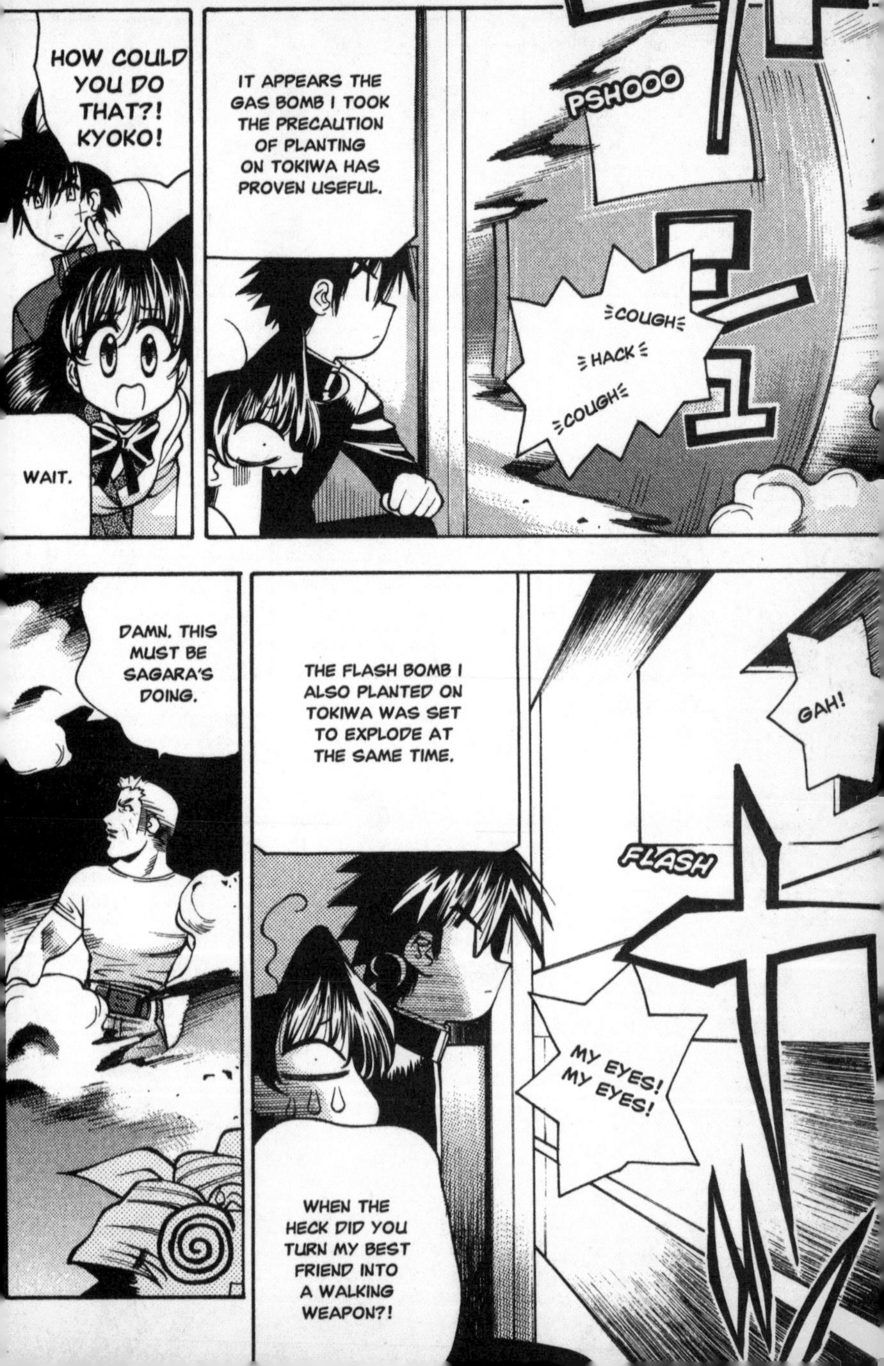
PSHOOO
COUGH
HACK
COUGH
IT APPEARS THE GAS BOMB I TOOK THE PRECAUTION OF PLANTING ON TOKIWA HAS PROVEN USEFUL.
HOW COULD YOU DO THAT?! KYOKO!
WAIT.
GAH!
FLASH
MY EYES! MY EYES!
THE FLASH BOMB I ALSO PLANTED ON TOKIWA WAS SET TO EXPLODE AT THE SAME TIME.
WHEN THE HECK DID YOU TURN MY BEST FRIEND INTO A WALKING WEAPON?!
DAMN. THIS MUST BE SAGARA'S DOING.

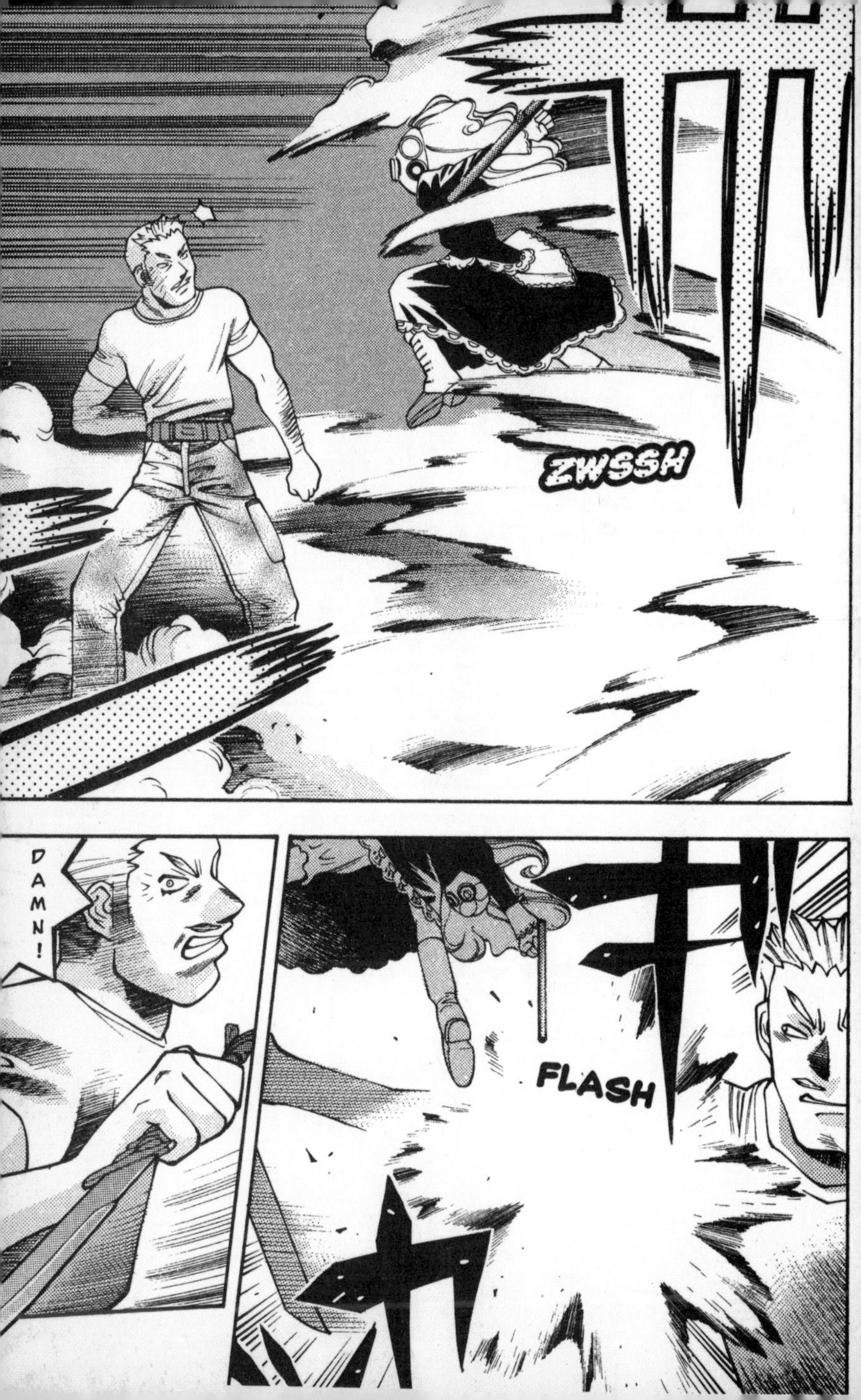
ZWSSH
DAMN!
FLASH

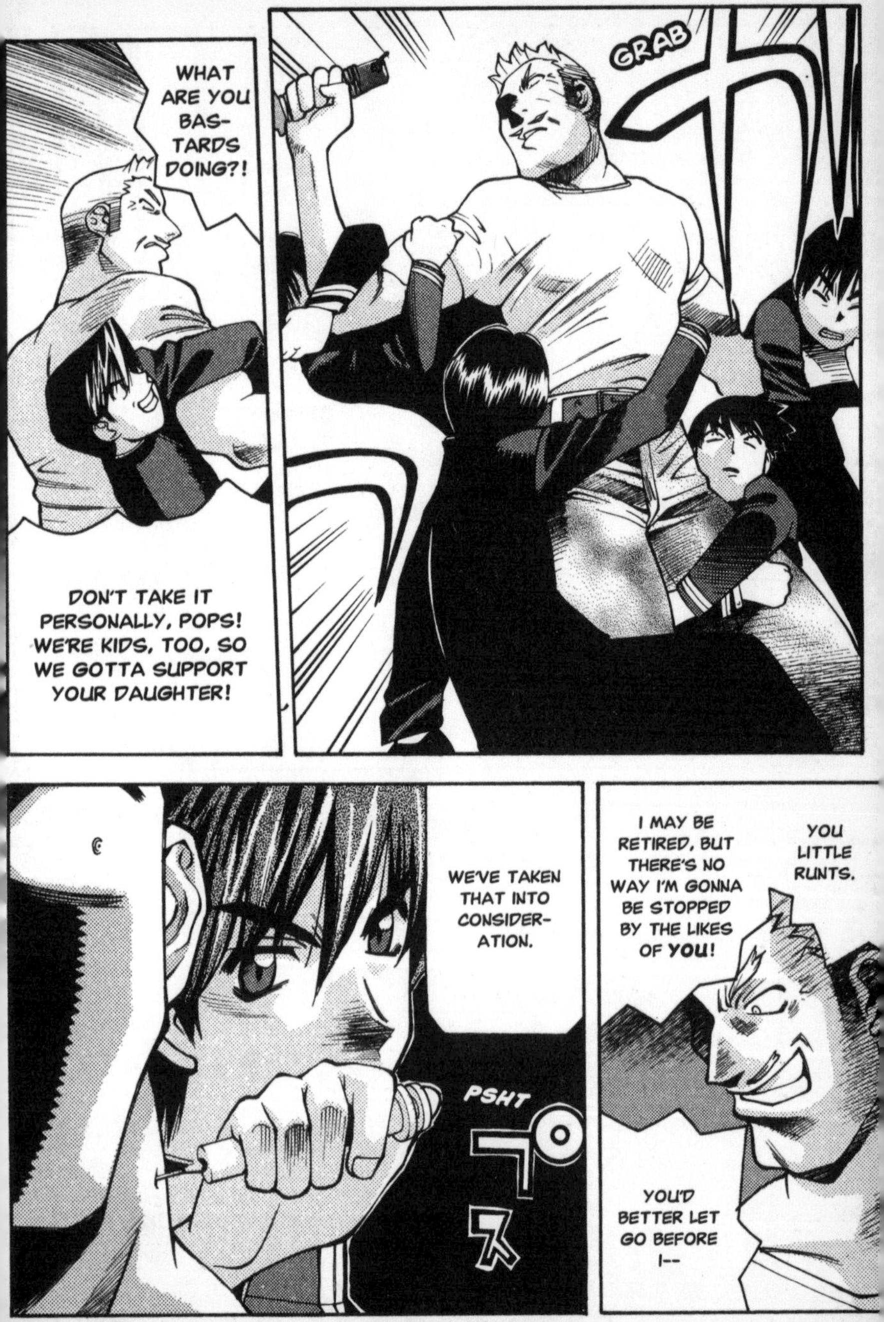
GRAB
WHAT ARE YOU BASTARDS DOING?!
DON'T TAKE IT PERSONALLY, POPS! WE'RE KIDS, TOO, SO WE GOTTA SUPPORT YOUR DAUGHTER!
YOU LITTLE RUNTS.
I MAY BE RETIRED, BUT THERE'S NO WAY I'M GONNA BE STOPPED BY THE LIKES OF **YOU**!
YOU'D BETTER LET GO BEFORE I--
WE'VE TAKEN THAT INTO CONSIDERATION.
PSHT

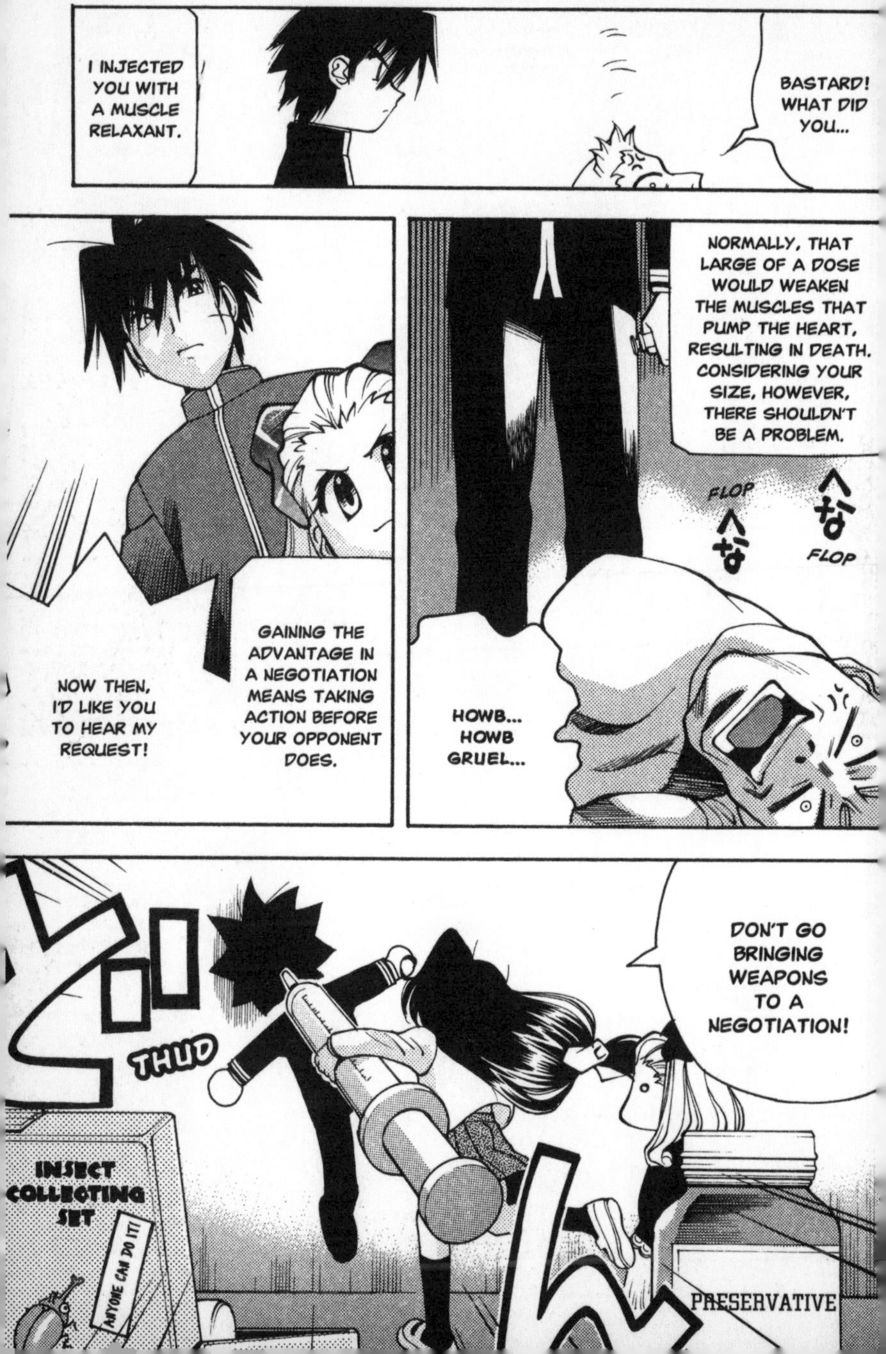
BASTARD! WHAT DID YOU...
I INJECTED YOU WITH A MUSCLE RELAXANT.
NORMALLY, THAT LARGE OF A DOSE WOULD WEAKEN THE MUSCLES THAT PUMP THE HEART, RESULTING IN DEATH. CONSIDERING YOUR SIZE, HOWEVER, THERE SHOULDN'T BE A PROBLEM.
FLOP
な
FLOP
な
HOWB... HOWB GRUEL...
GAINING THE ADVANTAGE IN A NEGOTIATION MEANS TAKING ACTION BEFORE YOUR OPPONENT DOES.
NOW THEN, I'D LIKE YOU TO HEAR MY REQUEST!
DON'T GO BRINGING WEAPONS TO A NEGOTIATION!
THUD
INSECT COLLECTING SET
ANYONE CAN DO IT!
PRESERVATIVE

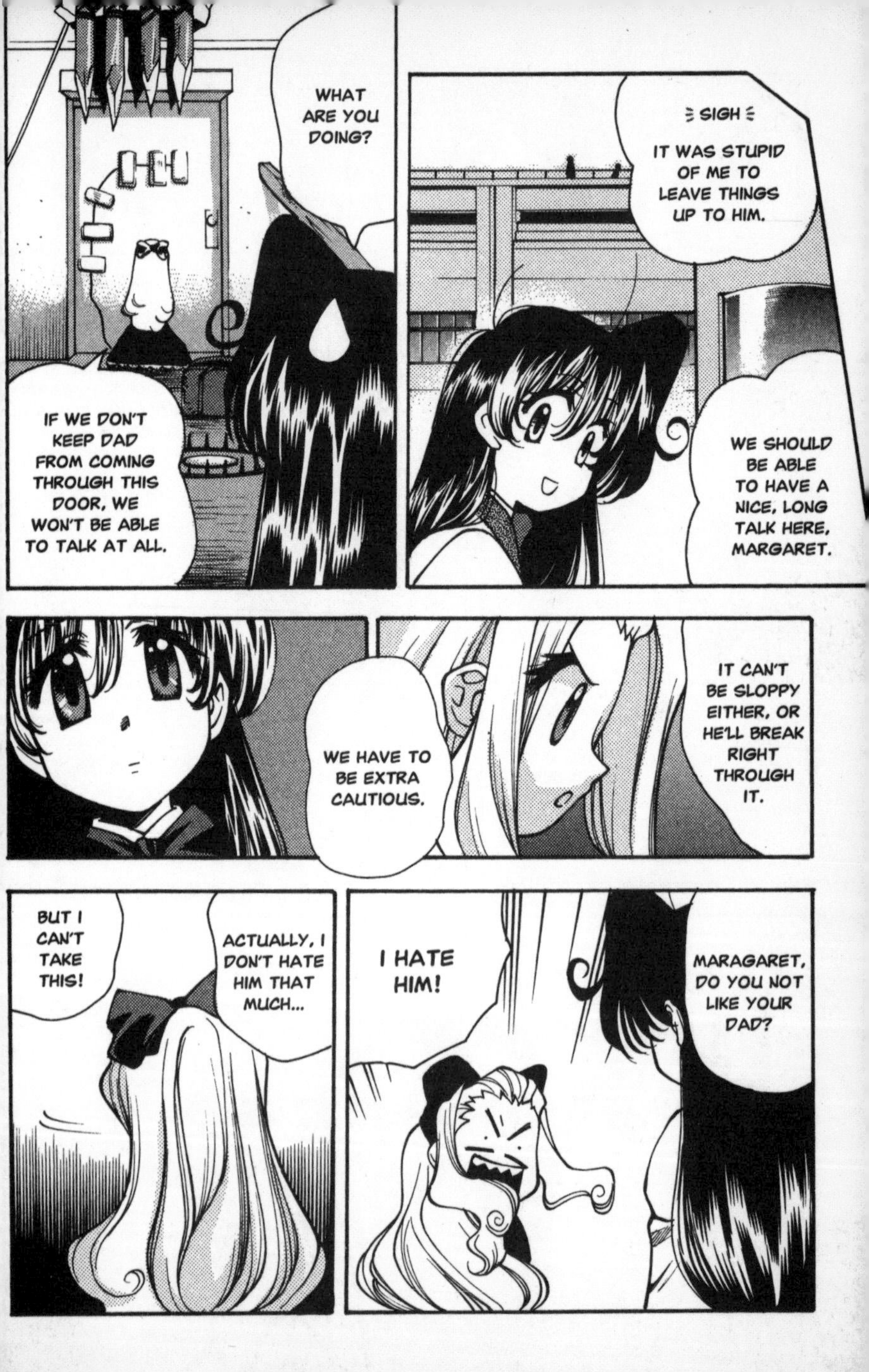

≡ SIGH ≡
IT WAS STUPID OF ME TO LEAVE THINGS UP TO HIM.
WE SHOULD BE ABLE TO HAVE A NICE, LONG TALK HERE, MARGARET.
WHAT ARE YOU DOING?
IF WE DON'T KEEP DAD FROM COMING THROUGH THIS DOOR, WE WON'T BE ABLE TO TALK AT ALL.
WE HAVE TO BE EXTRA CAUTIOUS.
IT CAN'T BE SLOPPY EITHER, OR HE'LL BREAK RIGHT THROUGH IT.
MARAGARET, DO YOU NOT LIKE YOUR DAD?
I HATE HIM!
ACTUALLY, I DON'T HATE HIM THAT MUCH...
BUT I CAN'T TAKE THIS!

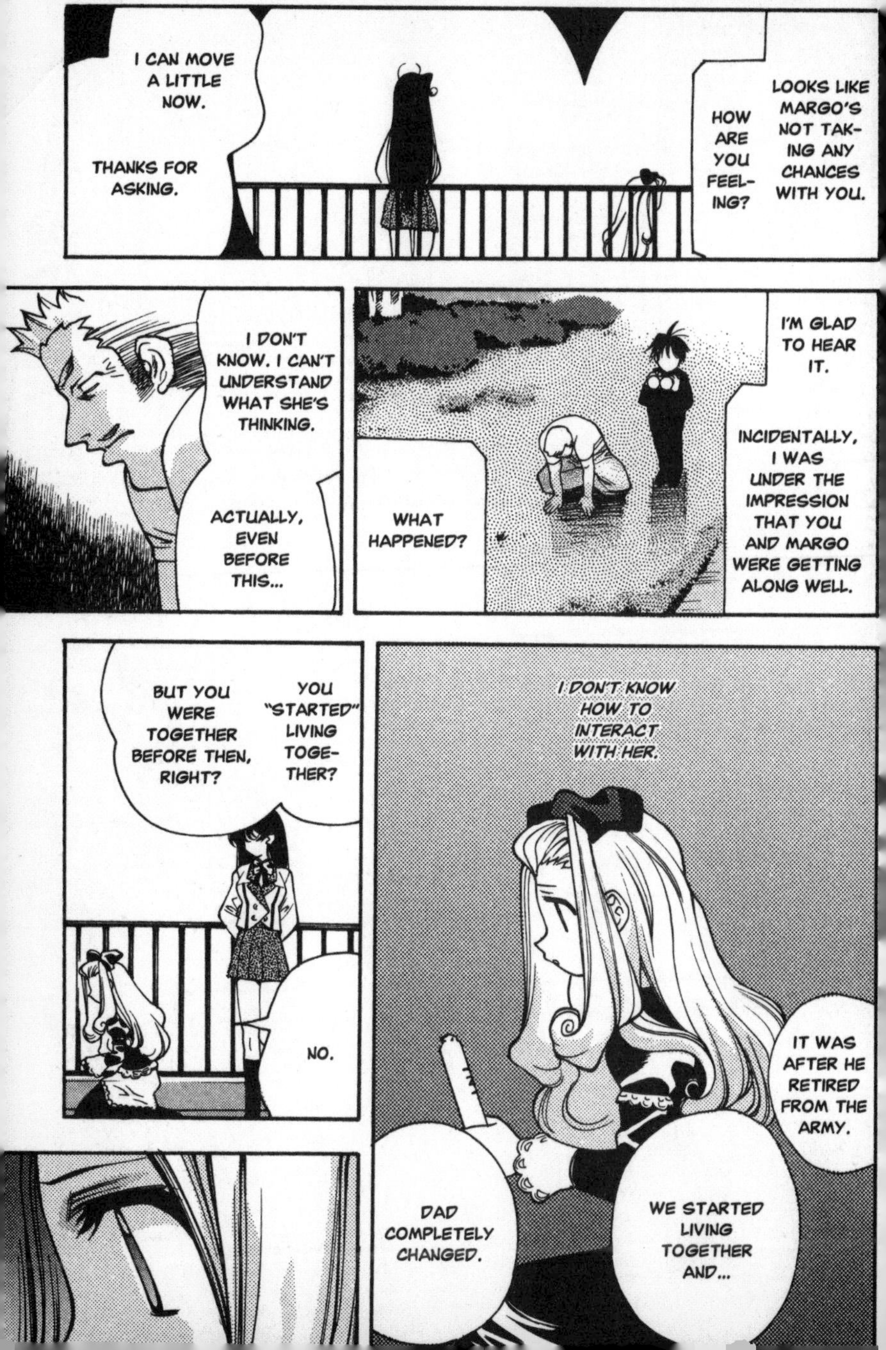
LOOKS LIKE MARGO'S NOT TAKING ANY CHANCES WITH YOU.
HOW ARE YOU FEELING?
I CAN MOVE A LITTLE NOW.
THANKS FOR ASKING.
I'M GLAD TO HEAR IT.
INCIDENTALLY, I WAS UNDER THE IMPRESSION THAT YOU AND MARGO WERE GETTING ALONG WELL.
WHAT HAPPENED?
I DON'T KNOW. I CAN'T UNDERSTAND WHAT SHE'S THINKING.
ACTUALLY, EVEN BEFORE THIS...
I DON'T KNOW HOW TO INTERACT WITH HER.
IT WAS AFTER HE RETIRED FROM THE ARMY.
WE STARTED LIVING TOGETHER AND...
DAD COMPLETELY CHANGED.
YOU "STARTED" LIVING TOGETHER?
BUT YOU WERE TOGETHER BEFORE THEN, RIGHT?
NO.

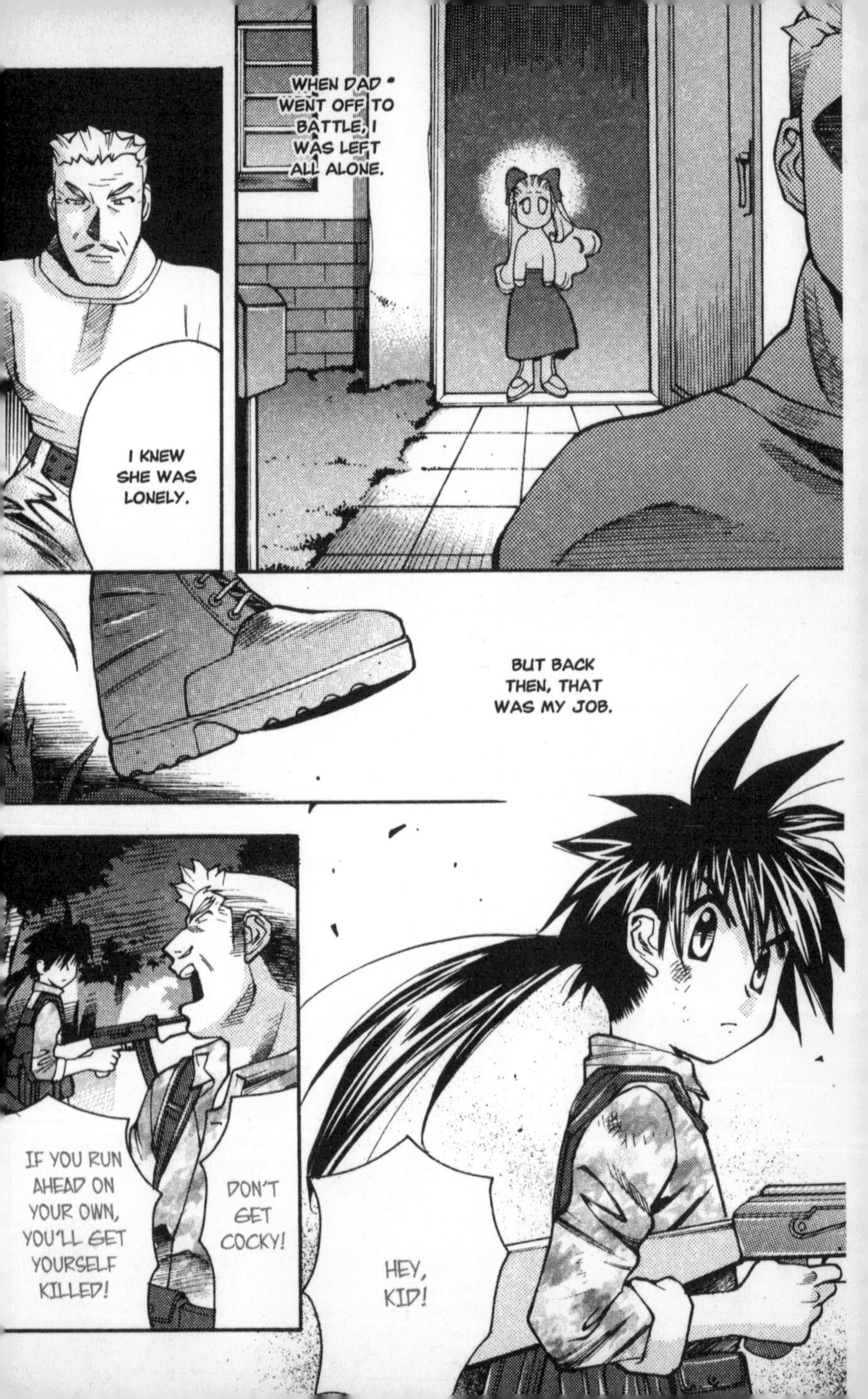
WHEN DAD WENT OFF TO BATTLE, I WAS LEFT ALL ALONE.
I KNEW SHE WAS LONELY.
BUT BACK THEN, THAT WAS MY JOB.
HEY, KID!
DON'T GET COCKY!
IF YOU RUN AHEAD ON YOUR OWN, YOU'LL GET YOURSELF KILLED!

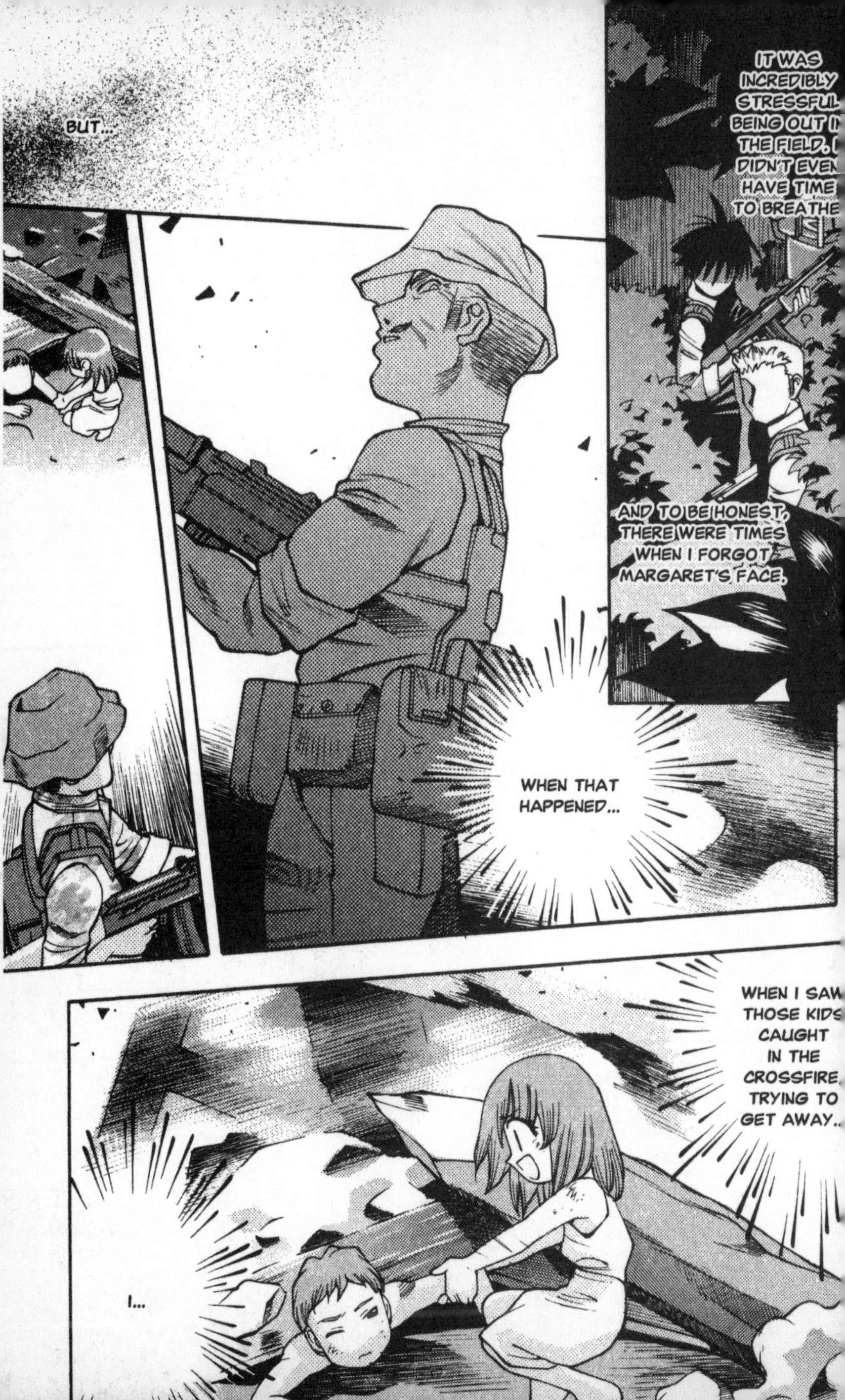
IT WAS INCREDIBLY STRESSFUL BEING OUT IN THE FIELD. I DIDN'T EVEN HAVE TIME TO BREATHE
AND TO BE HONEST, THERE WERE TIMES WHEN I FORGOT MARGARET'S FACE.
BUT...
WHEN THAT HAPPENED...
WHEN I SAW THOSE KIDS CAUGHT IN THE CROSSFIRE, TRYING TO GET AWAY...
I...

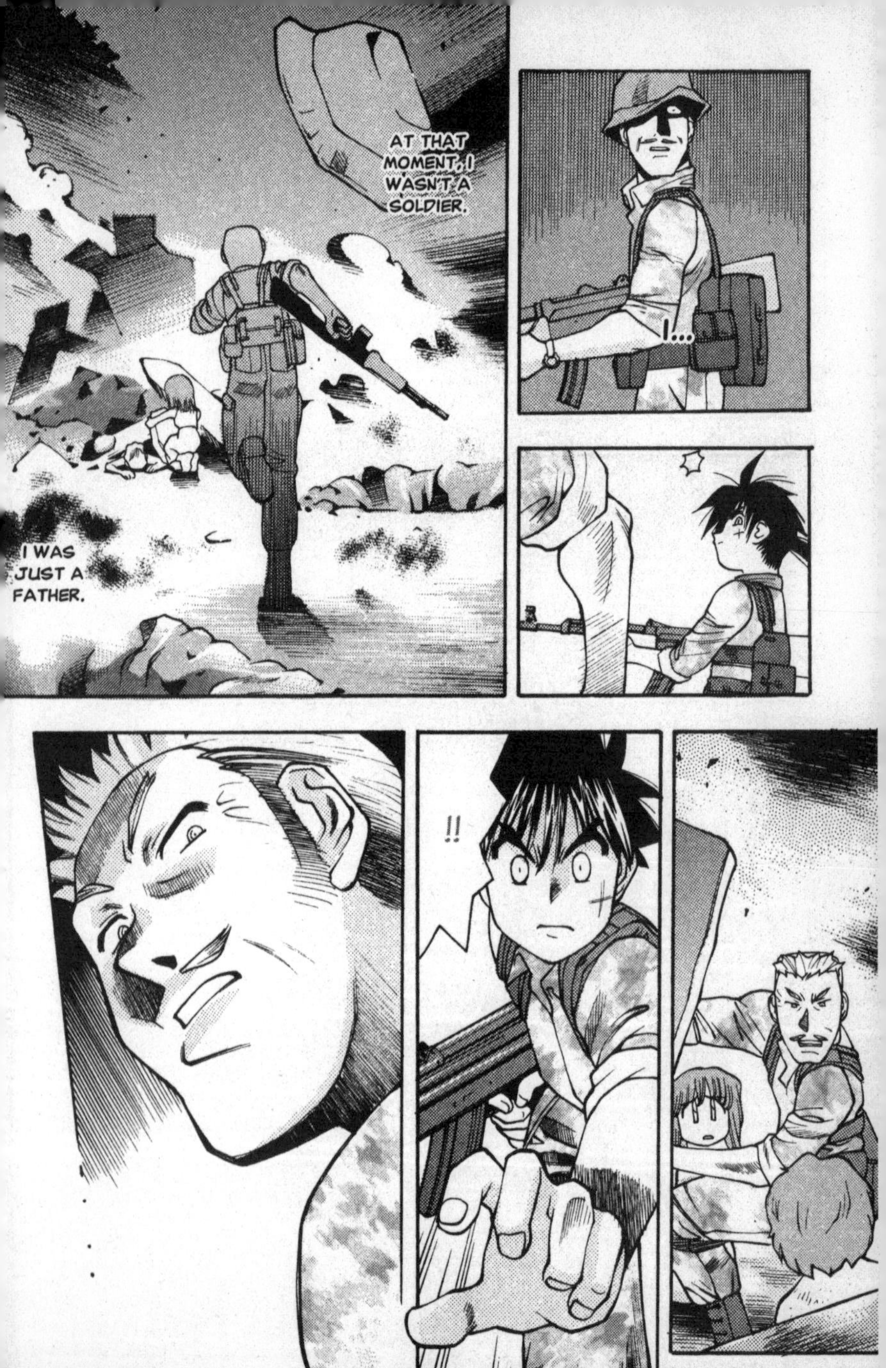
AT THAT MOMENT, I WASN'T A SOLDIER.
I WAS JUST A FATHER.
I...
!!

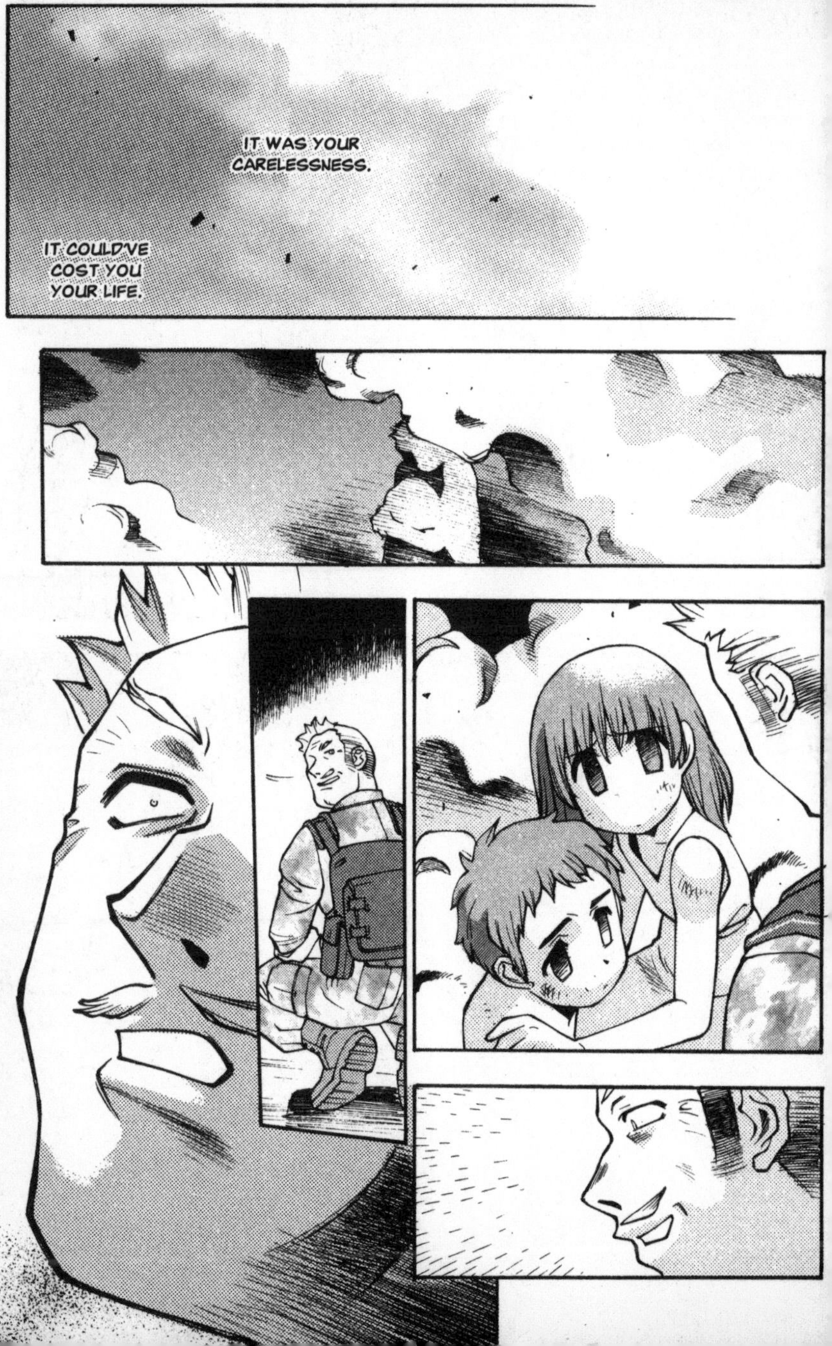
IT WAS YOUR CARELESSNESS.
IT COULD'VE COST YOU YOUR LIFE.

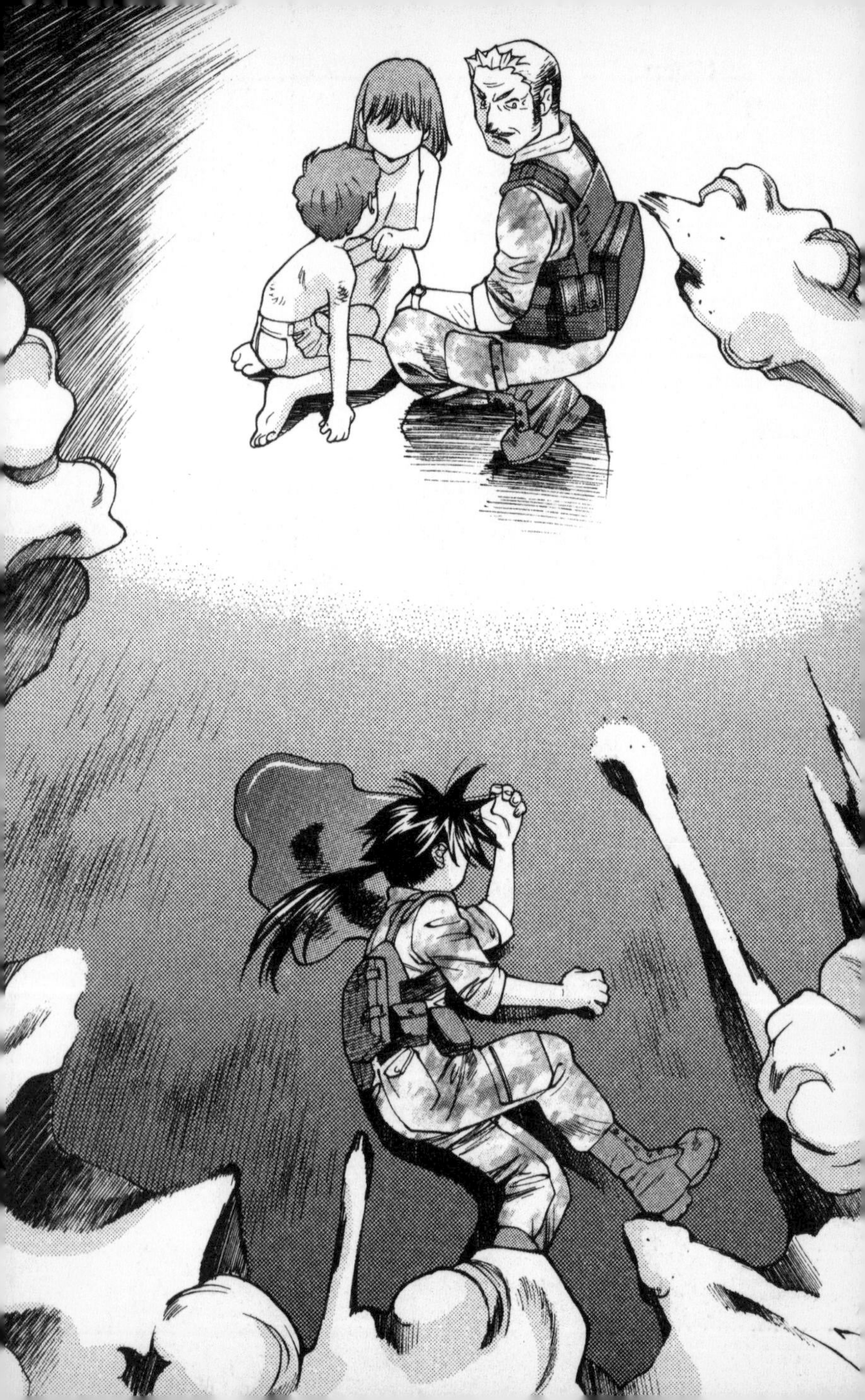

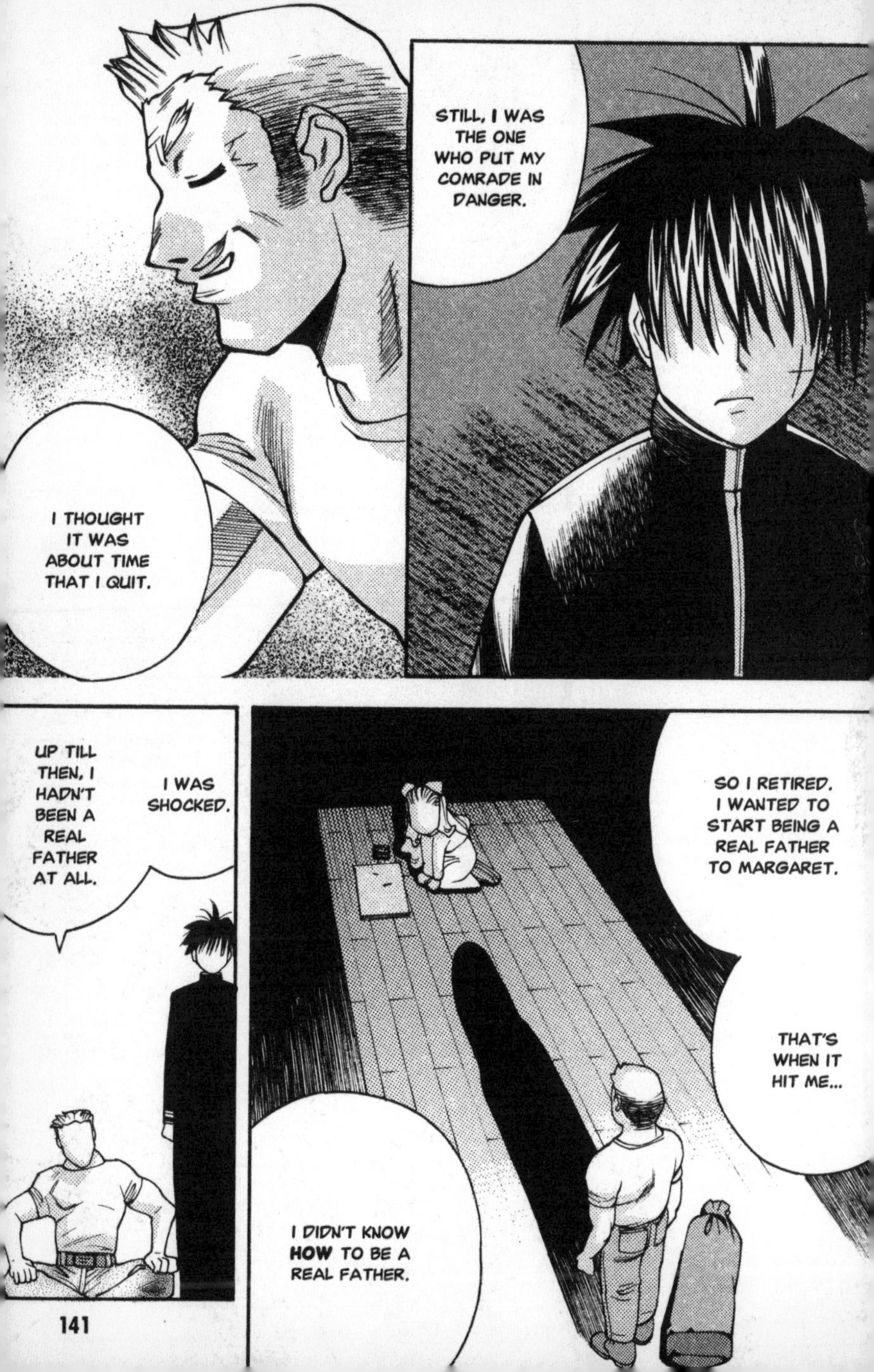

STILL, I WAS THE ONE WHO PUT MY COMRADE IN DANGER.
I THOUGHT IT WAS ABOUT TIME THAT I QUIT.
SO I RETIRED. I WANTED TO START BEING A REAL FATHER TO MARGARET.
THAT'S WHEN IT HIT ME...
I DIDN'T KNOW **HOW** TO BE A REAL FATHER.
I WAS SHOCKED.
UP TILL THEN, I HADN'T BEEN A REAL FATHER AT ALL.

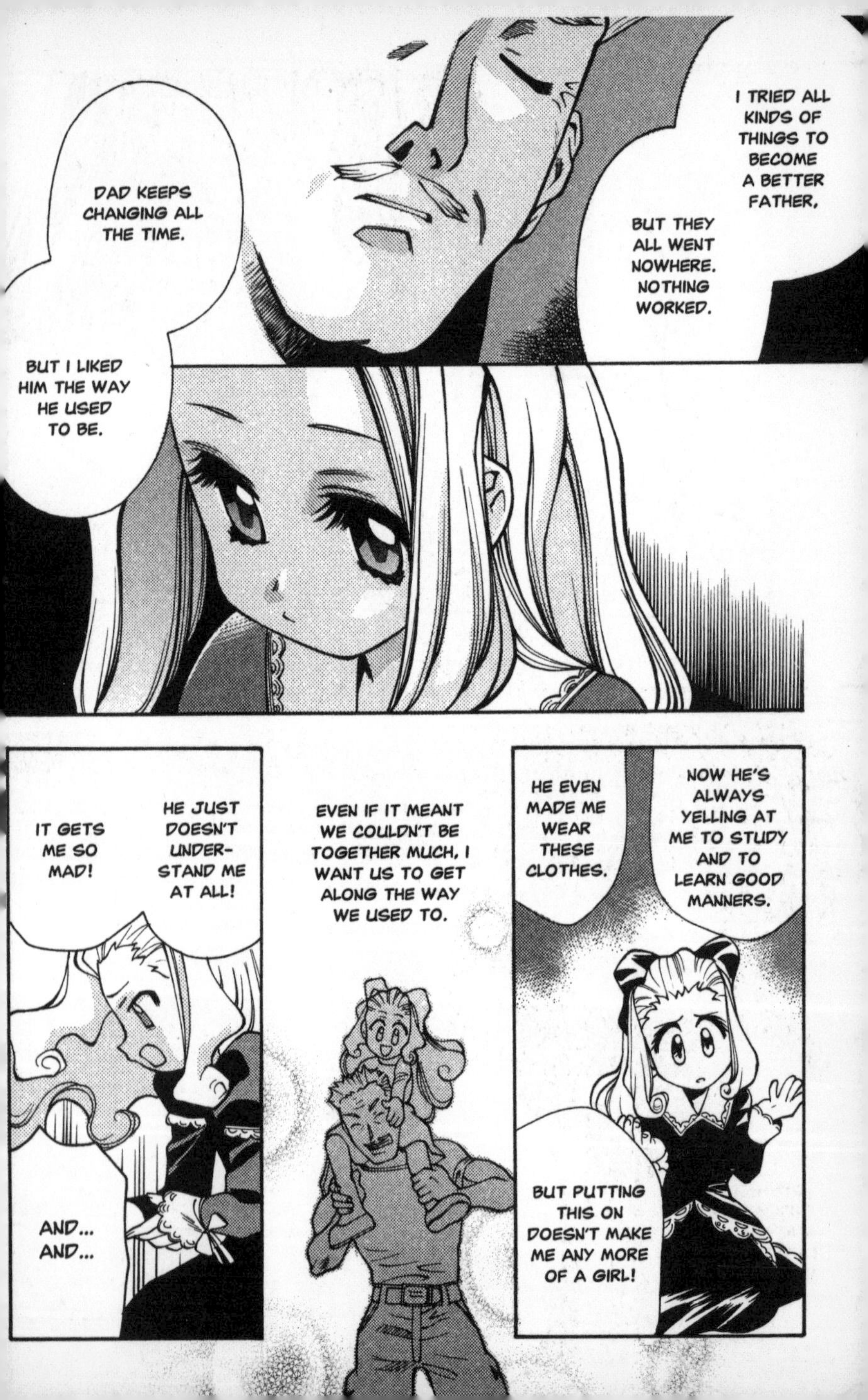
I TRIED ALL KINDS OF THINGS TO BECOME A BETTER FATHER,
BUT THEY ALL WENT NOWHERE. NOTHING WORKED.
DAD KEEPS CHANGING ALL THE TIME.
BUT I LIKED HIM THE WAY HE USED TO BE.
NOW HE'S ALWAYS YELLING AT ME TO STUDY AND TO LEARN GOOD MANNERS.
HE EVEN MADE ME WEAR THESE CLOTHES.
BUT PUTTING THIS ON DOESN'T MAKE ME ANY MORE OF A GIRL!
EVEN IF IT MEANT WE COULDN'T BE TOGETHER MUCH, I WANT US TO GET ALONG THE WAY WE USED TO.
HE JUST DOESN'T UNDER-STAND ME AT ALL!
IT GETS ME SO MAD!
AND... AND...

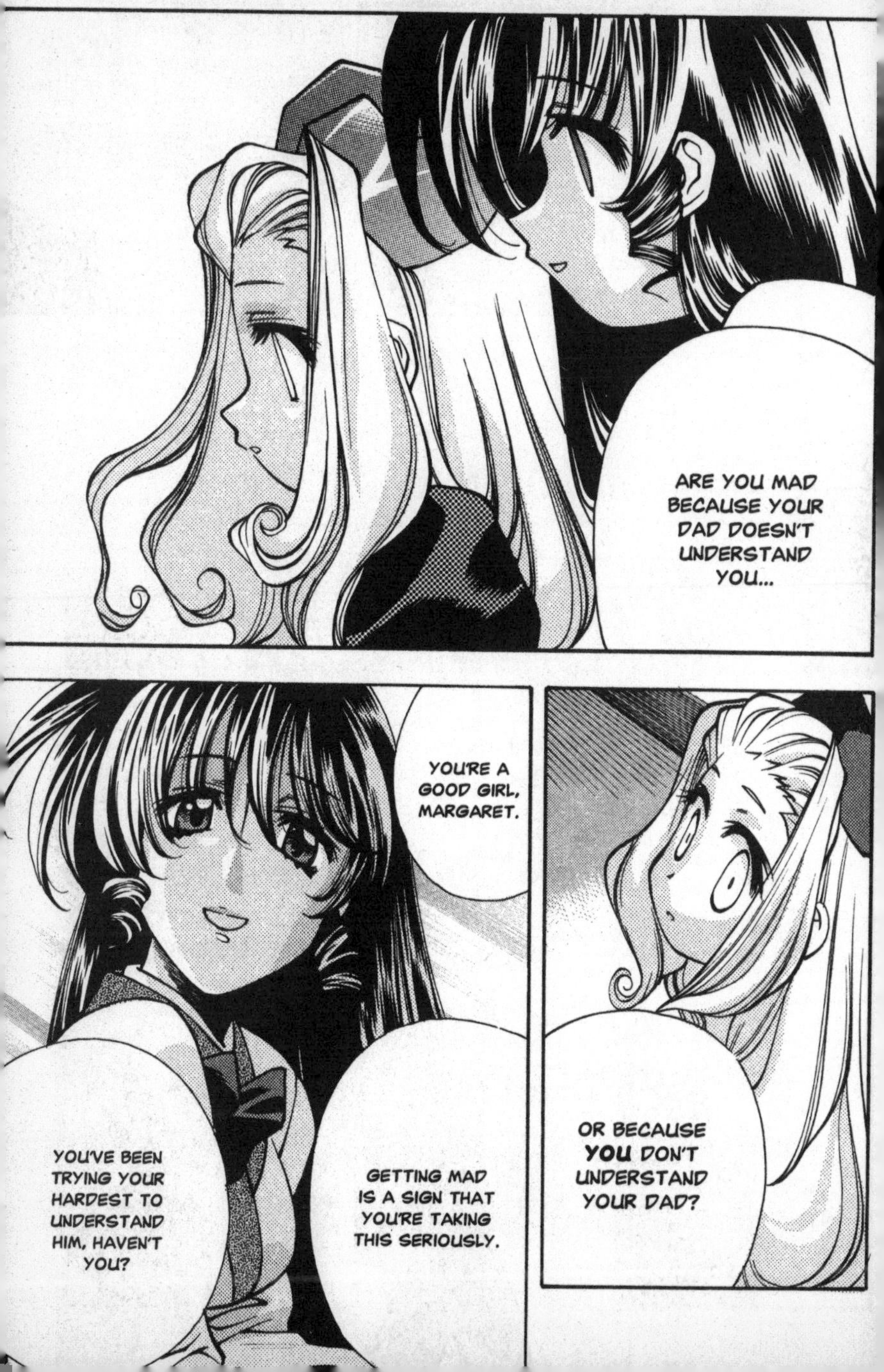
ARE YOU MAD BECAUSE YOUR DAD DOESN'T UNDERSTAND YOU...
OR BECAUSE YOU DON'T UNDERSTAND YOUR DAD?
YOU'RE A GOOD GIRL, MARGARET.
GETTING MAD IS A SIGN THAT YOU'RE TAKING THIS SERIOUSLY.
YOU'VE BEEN TRYING YOUR HARDEST TO UNDERSTAND HIM, HAVEN'T YOU?

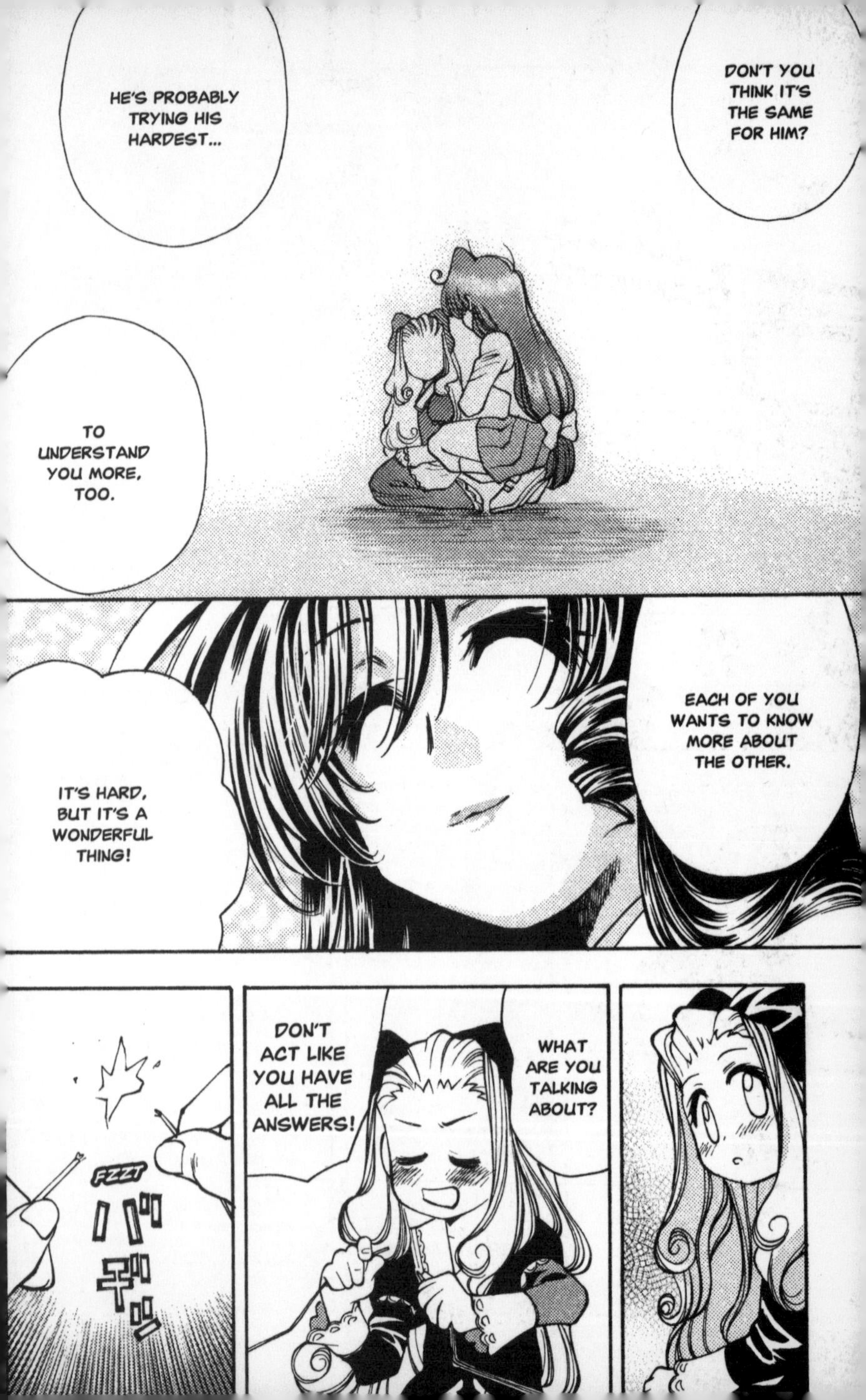

DON'T YOU THINK IT'S THE SAME FOR HIM?
HE'S PROBABLY TRYING HIS HARDEST...
TO UNDERSTAND YOU MORE, TOO.
EACH OF YOU WANTS TO KNOW MORE ABOUT THE OTHER.
IT'S HARD, BUT IT'S A WONDERFUL THING!
WHAT ARE YOU TALKING ABOUT?
DON'T ACT LIKE YOU HAVE ALL THE ANSWERS!
FZZT

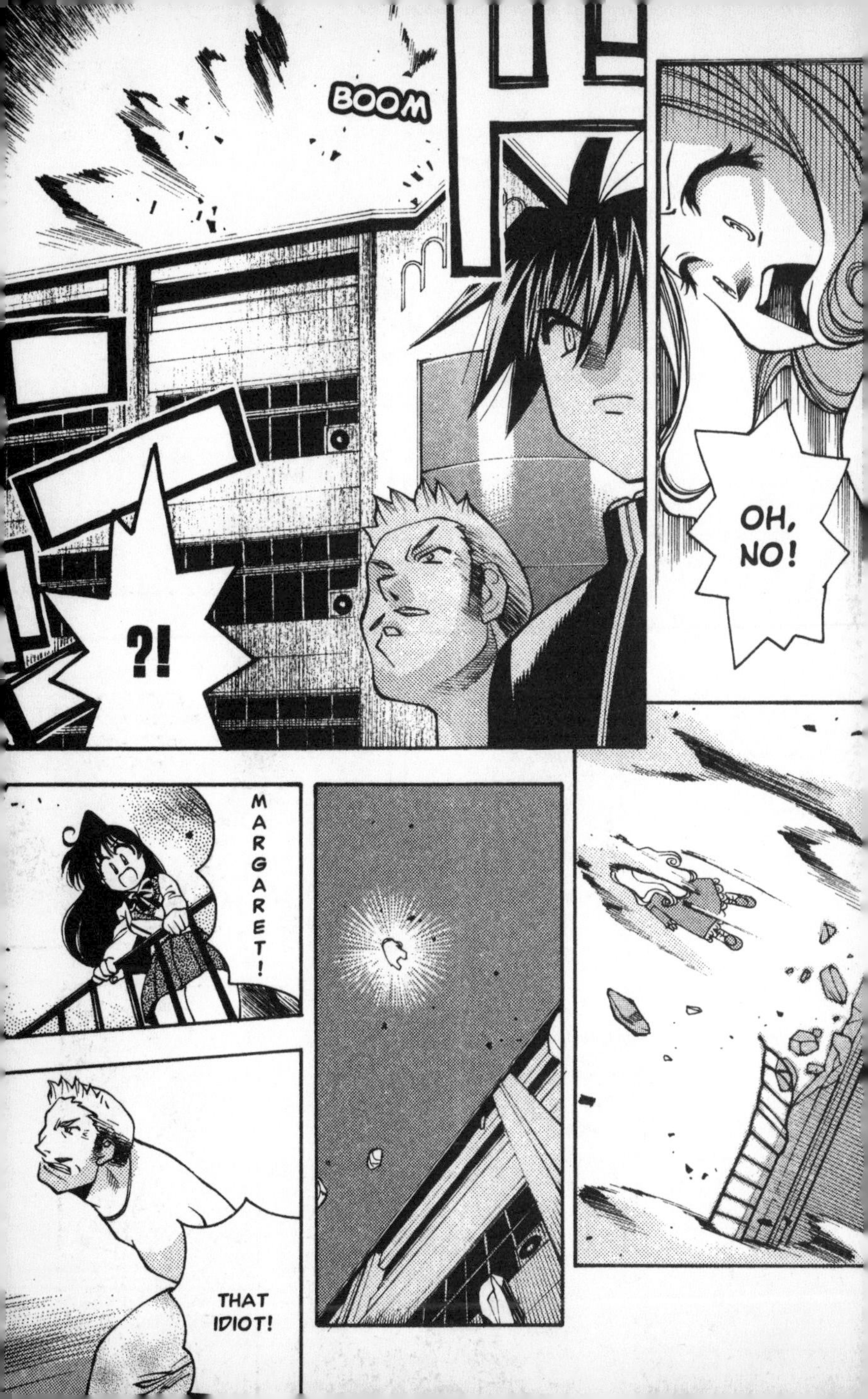
BOOM
OH, NO!
?!
MARGARET!
THAT IDIOT!

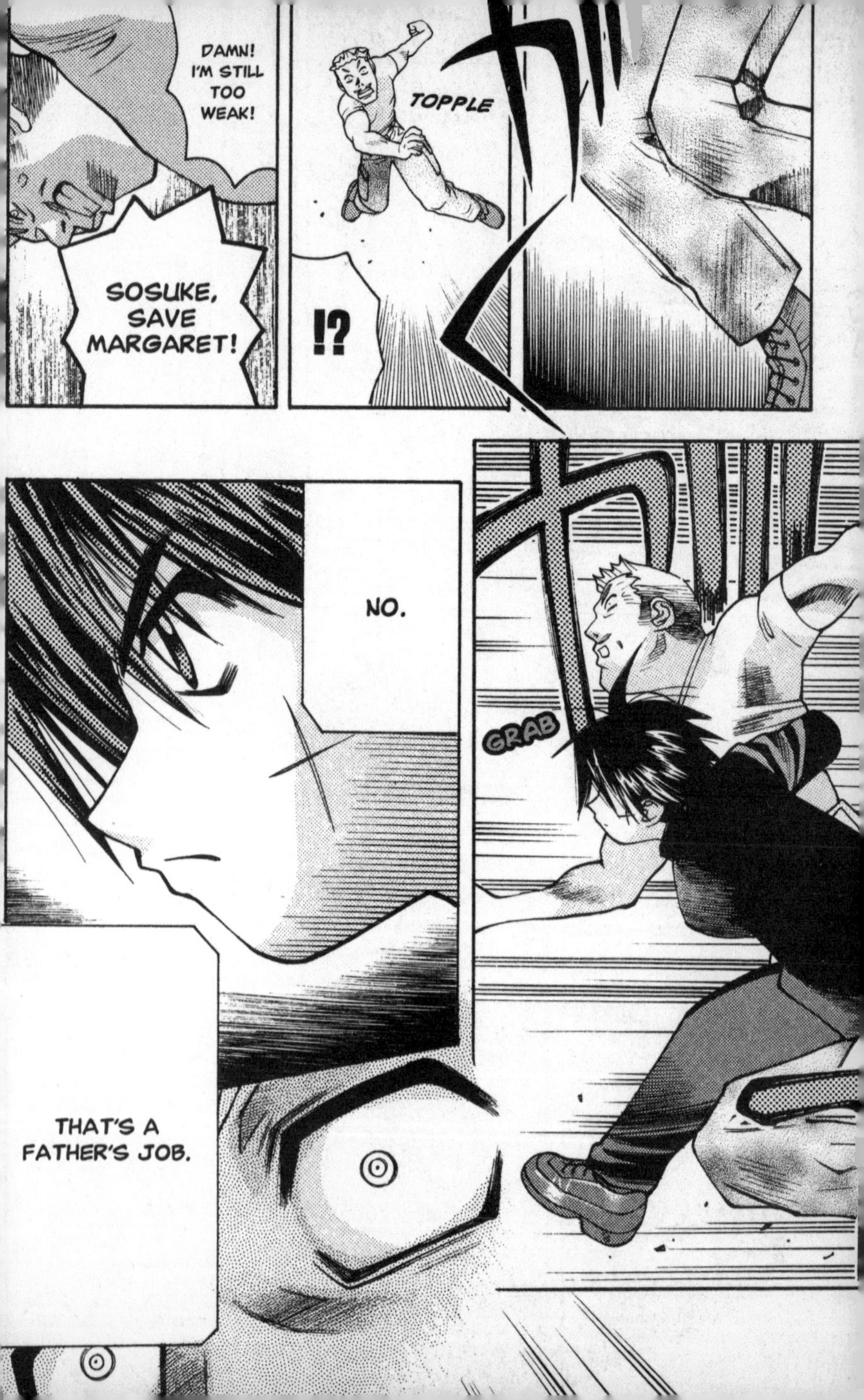
DAMN! I'M STILL TOO WEAK!
SOSUKE, SAVE MARGARET!
TOPPLE
!?
NO.
GRAB
THAT'S A FATHER'S JOB.

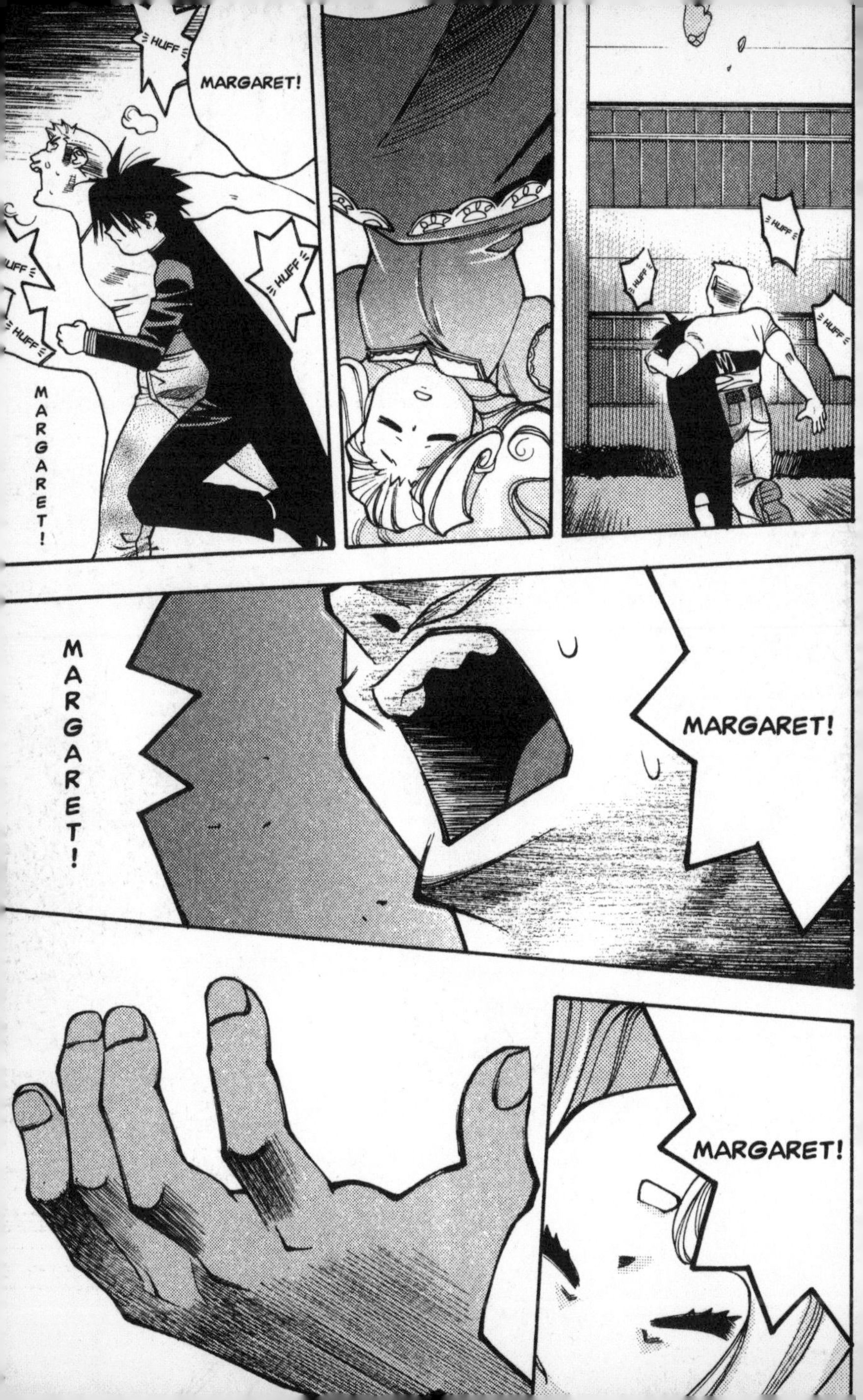

HUFF
MARGARET!
HUFF
HUFF
HUFF
MARGARET!
HUFF
HUFF
HUFF
MARGARET!
MARGARET!
MARGARET!

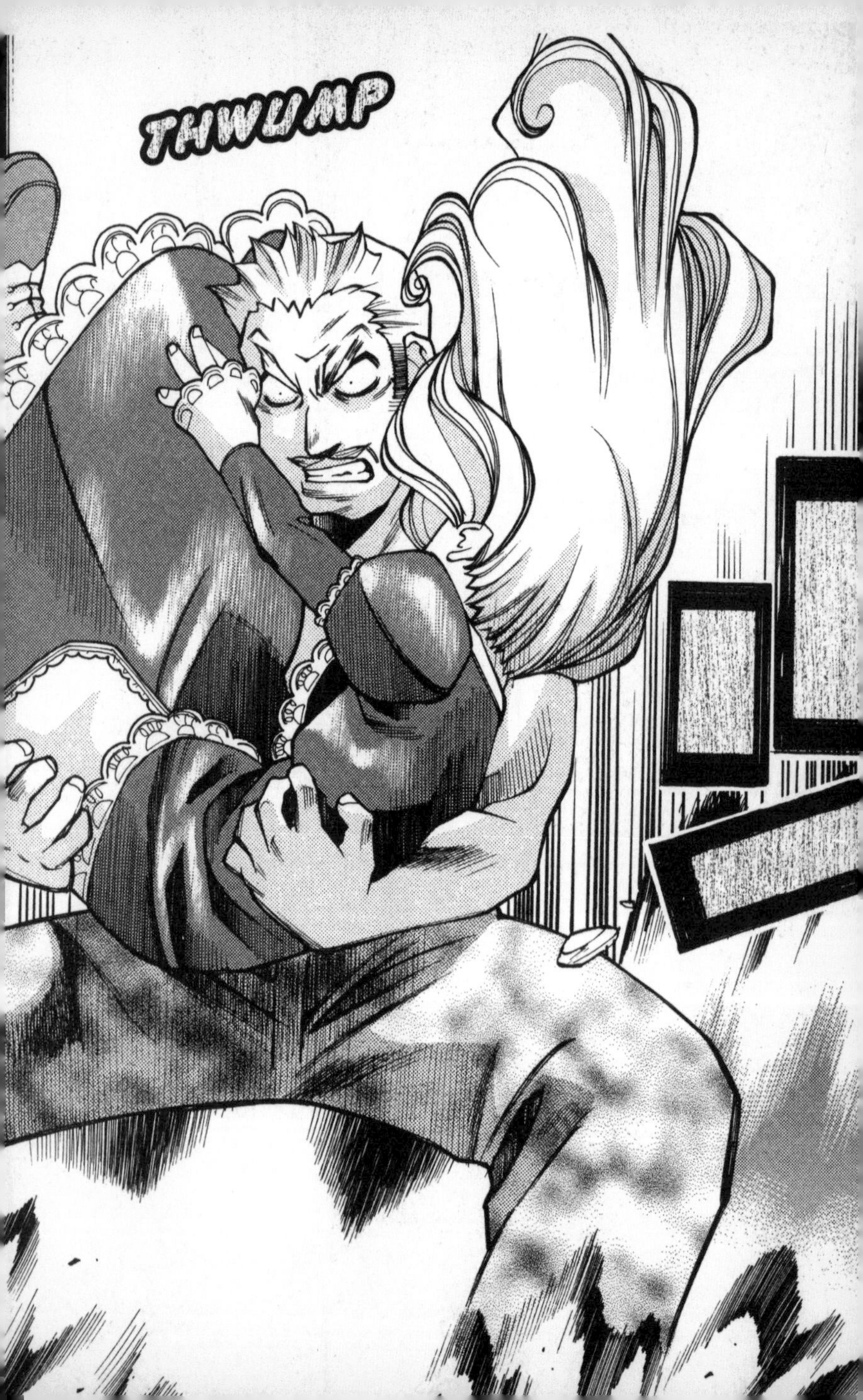
THWUMP

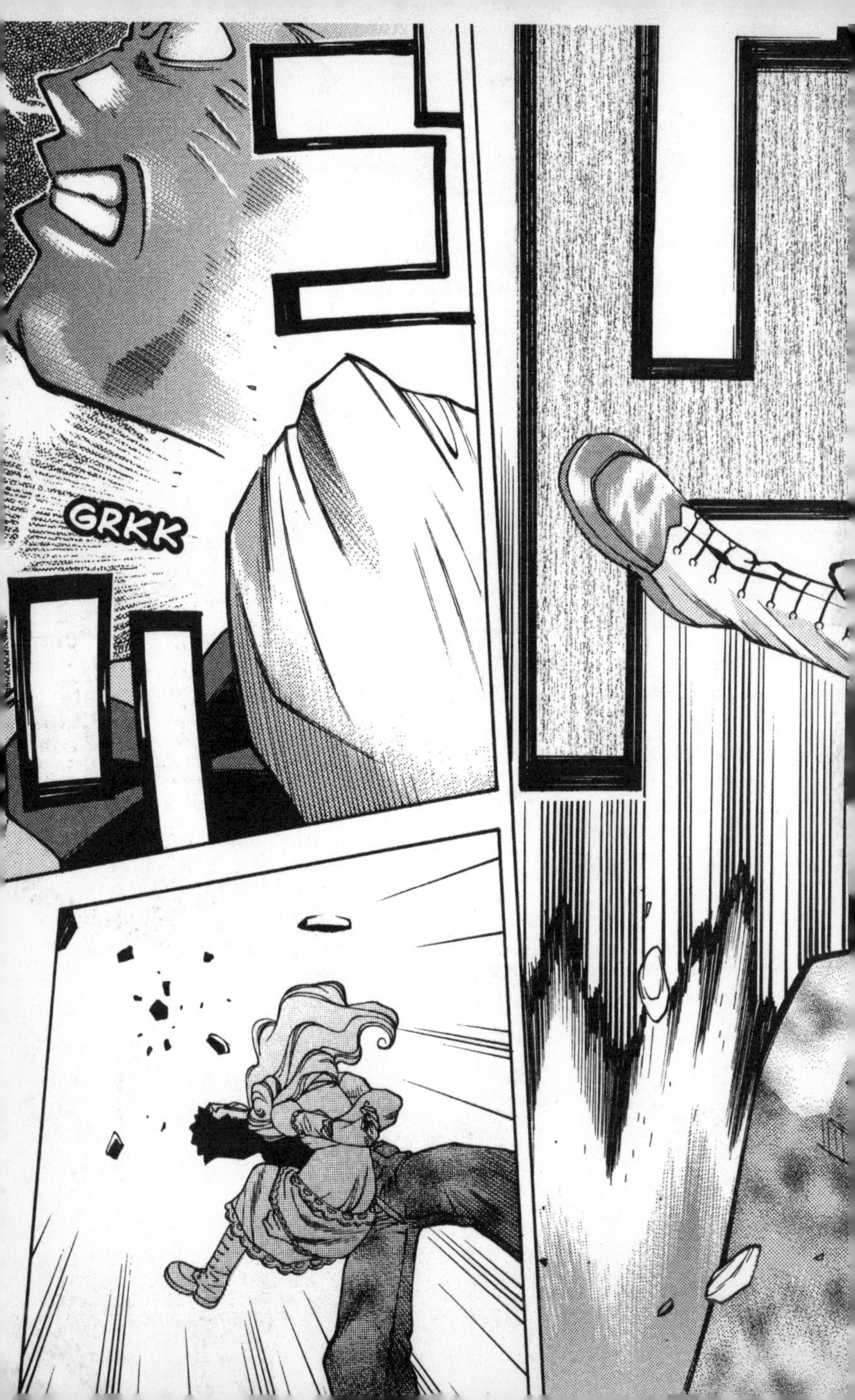
GRKK

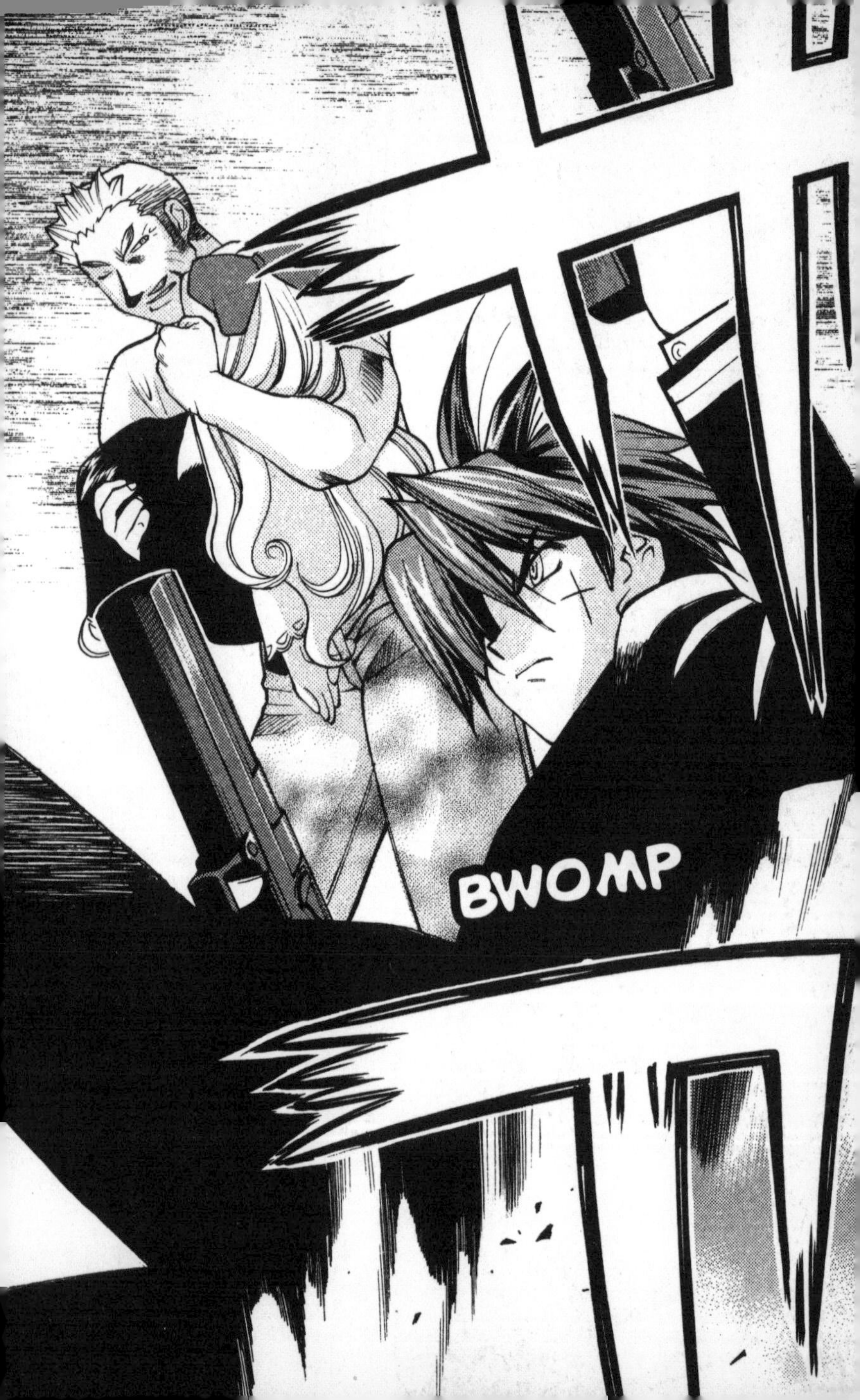
BWOMP

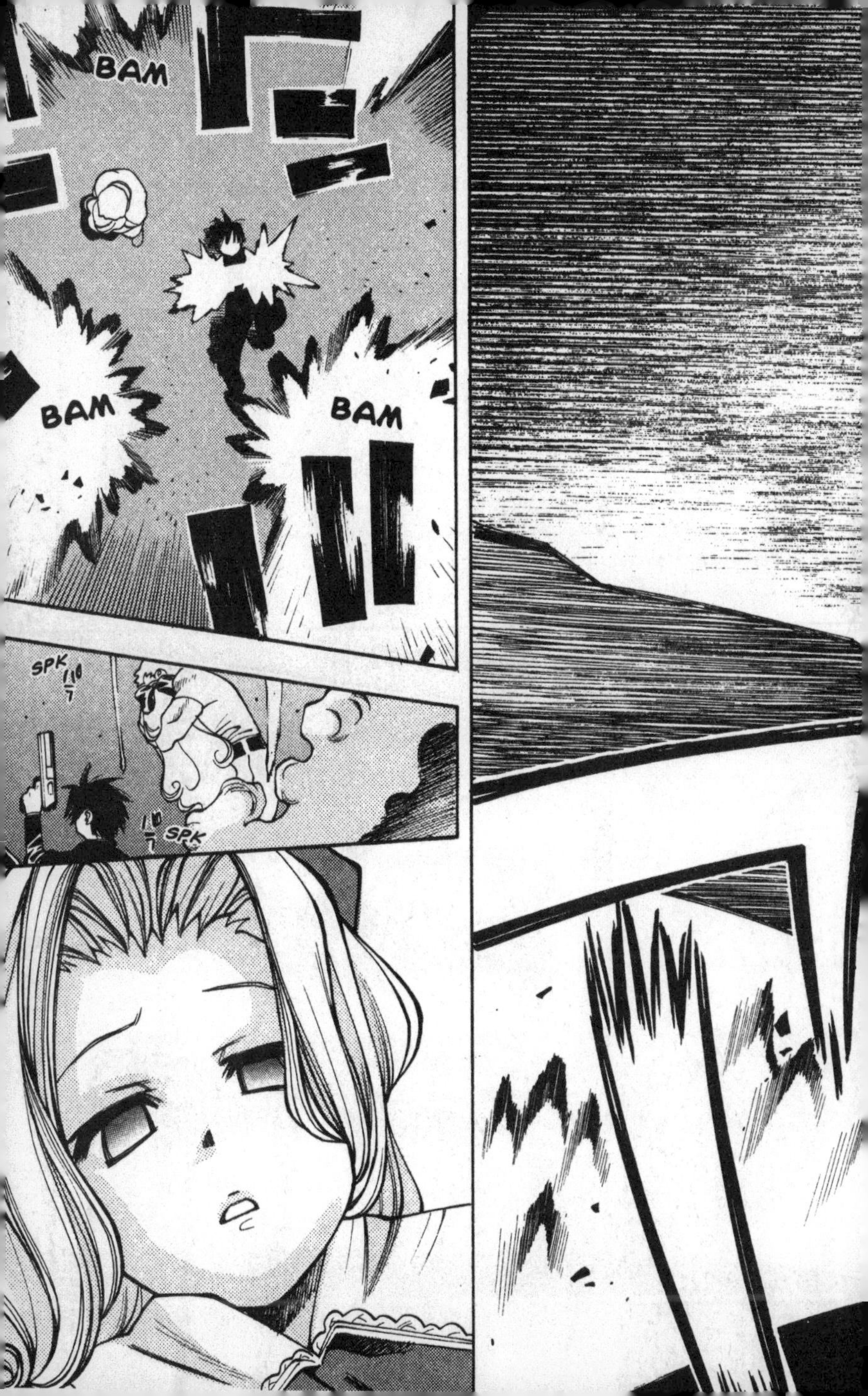
BAM
BAM
BAM
SPK
SPK

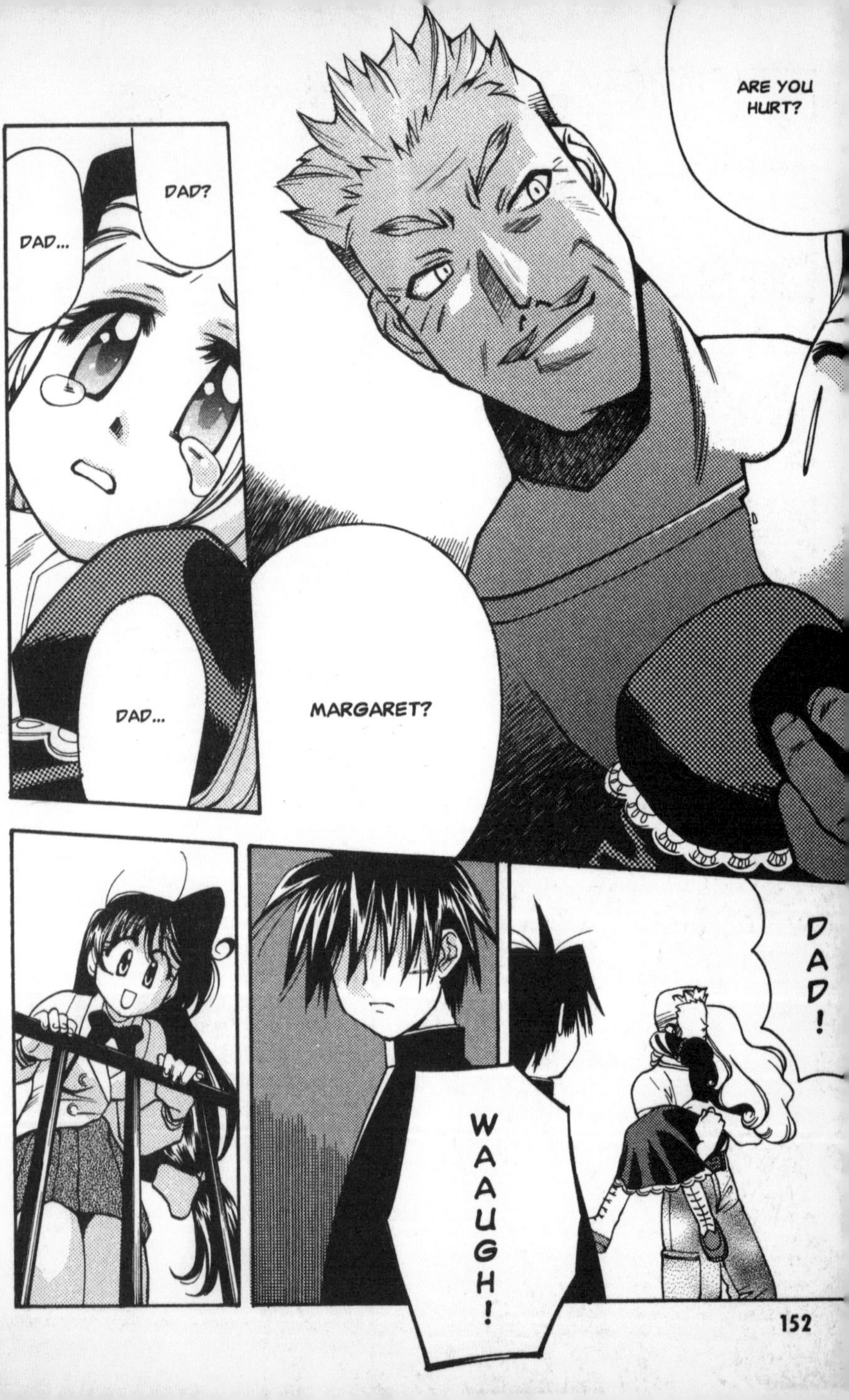
ARE YOU HURT?
DAD?
DAD...
MARGARET?
DAD...
DAD!
WAAAUGH!

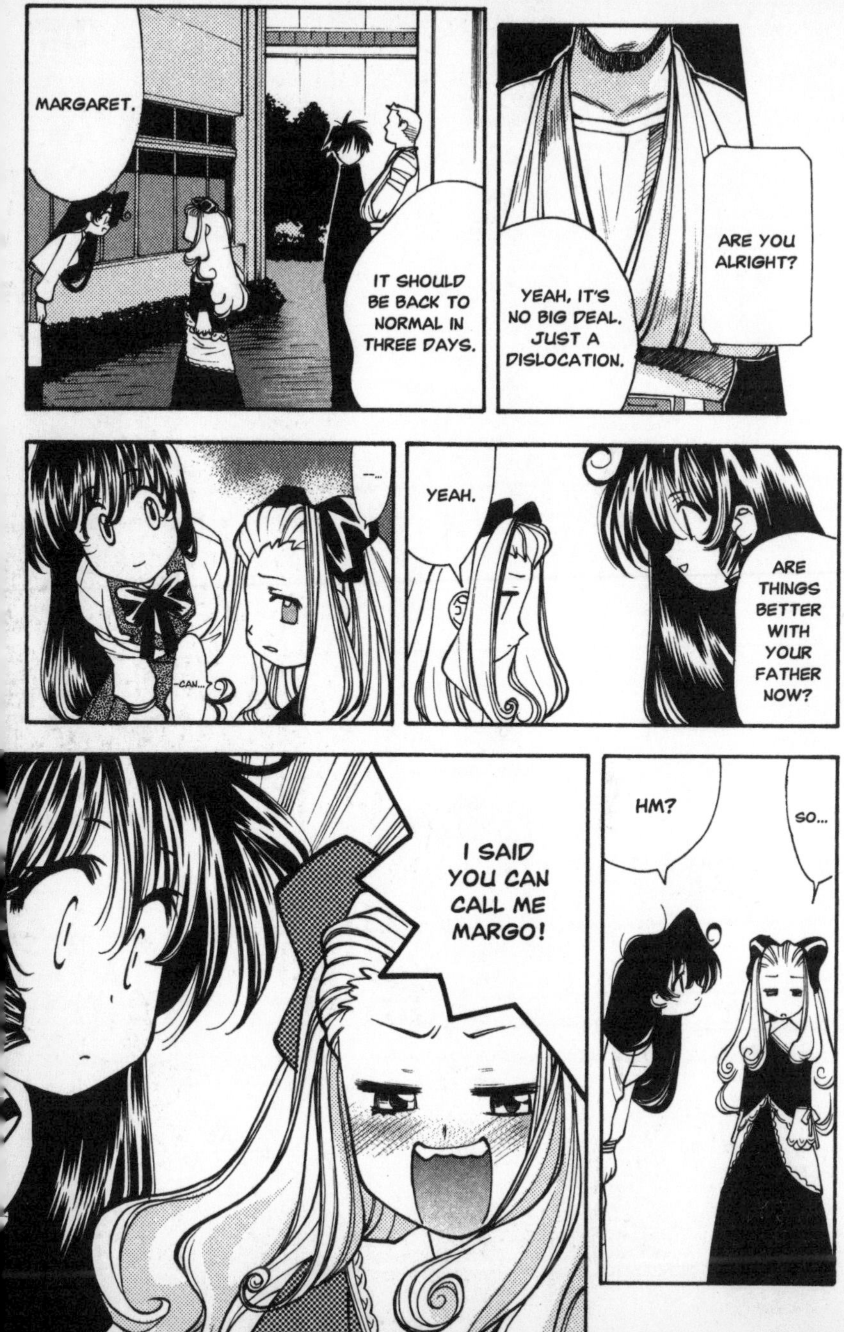
ARE YOU ALRIGHT?
YEAH, IT'S NO BIG DEAL. JUST A DISLOCATION.
IT SHOULD BE BACK TO NORMAL IN THREE DAYS.
MARGARET.
ARE THINGS BETTER WITH YOUR FATHER NOW?
YEAH.
--...
-CAN...
SO...
HM?
I SAID YOU CAN CALL ME MARGO!

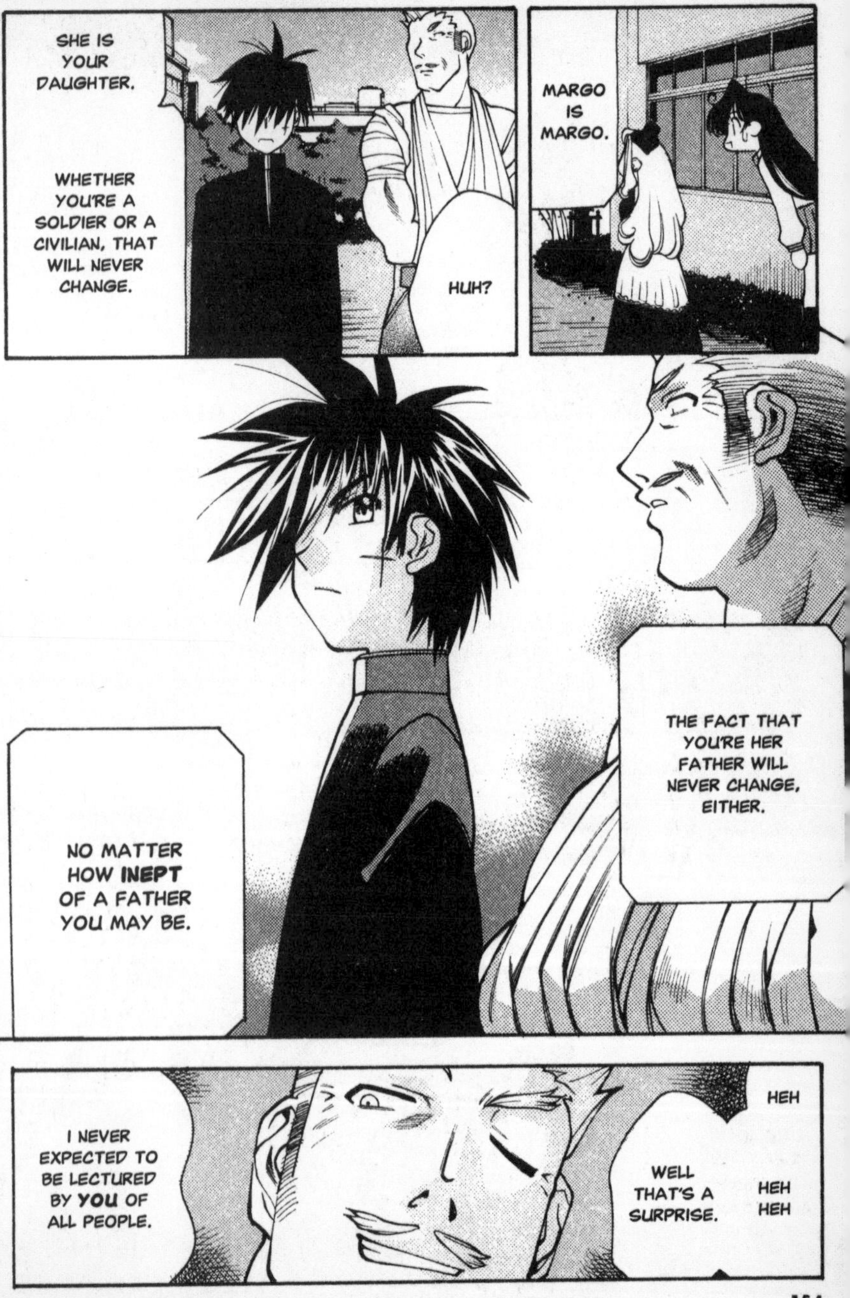
SHE IS YOUR DAUGHTER.
WHETHER YOU'RE A SOLDIER OR A CIVILIAN, THAT WILL NEVER CHANGE.
HUH?
MARGO IS MARGO.
THE FACT THAT YOU'RE HER FATHER WILL NEVER CHANGE, EITHER.
NO MATTER HOW **INEPT** OF A FATHER YOU MAY BE.
I NEVER EXPECTED TO BE LECTURED BY **YOU** OF ALL PEOPLE.
WELL THAT'S A SURPRISE.
HEH
HEH HEH

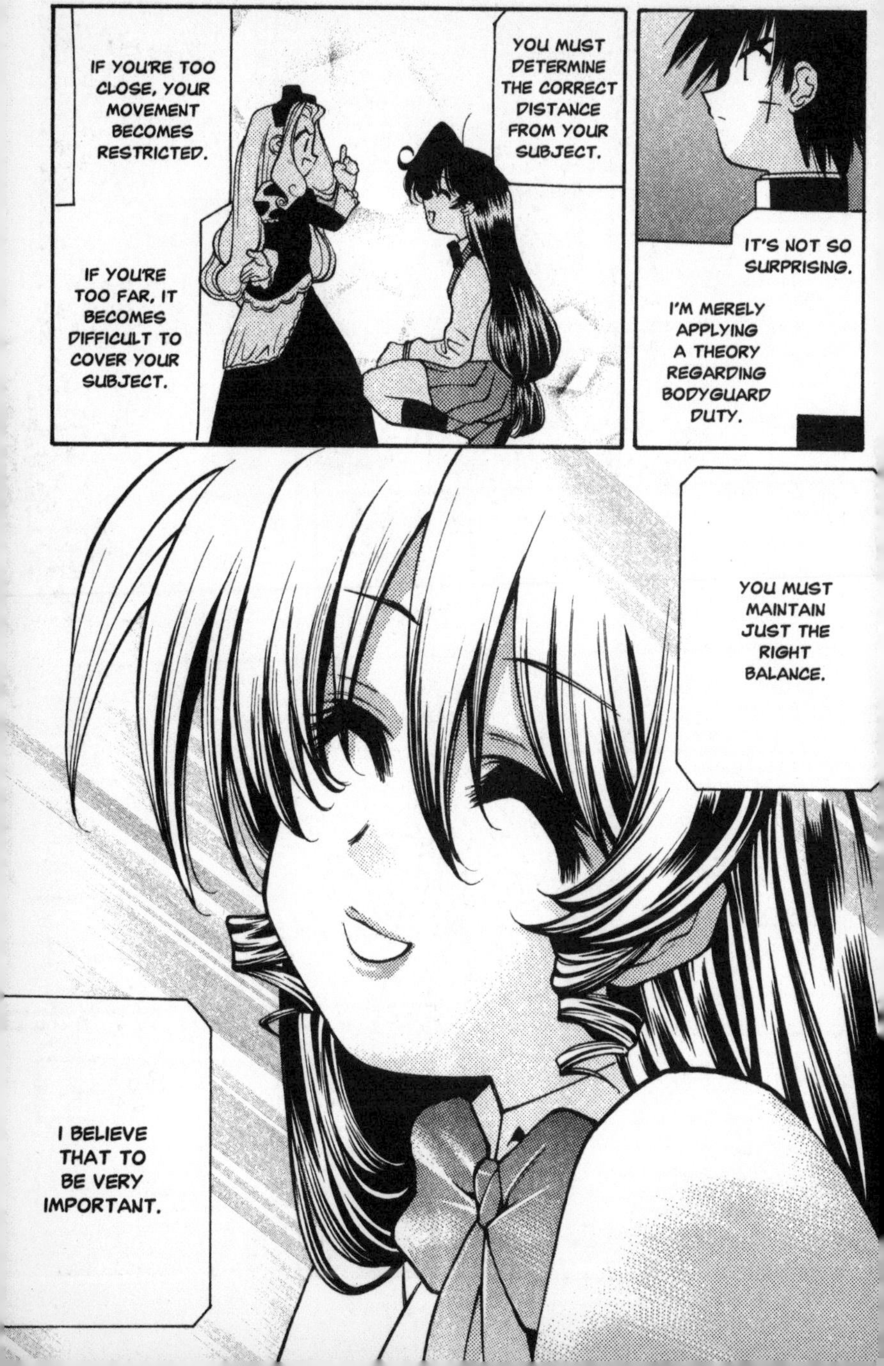
IT'S NOT SO SURPRISING.
I'M MERELY APPLYING A THEORY REGARDING BODYGUARD DUTY.
YOU MUST DETERMINE THE CORRECT DISTANCE FROM YOUR SUBJECT.
IF YOU'RE TOO CLOSE, YOUR MOVEMENT BECOMES RESTRICTED.
IF YOU'RE TOO FAR, IT BECOMES DIFFICULT TO COVER YOUR SUBJECT.
YOU MUST MAINTAIN JUST THE RIGHT BALANCE.
I BELIEVE THAT TO BE VERY IMPORTANT.

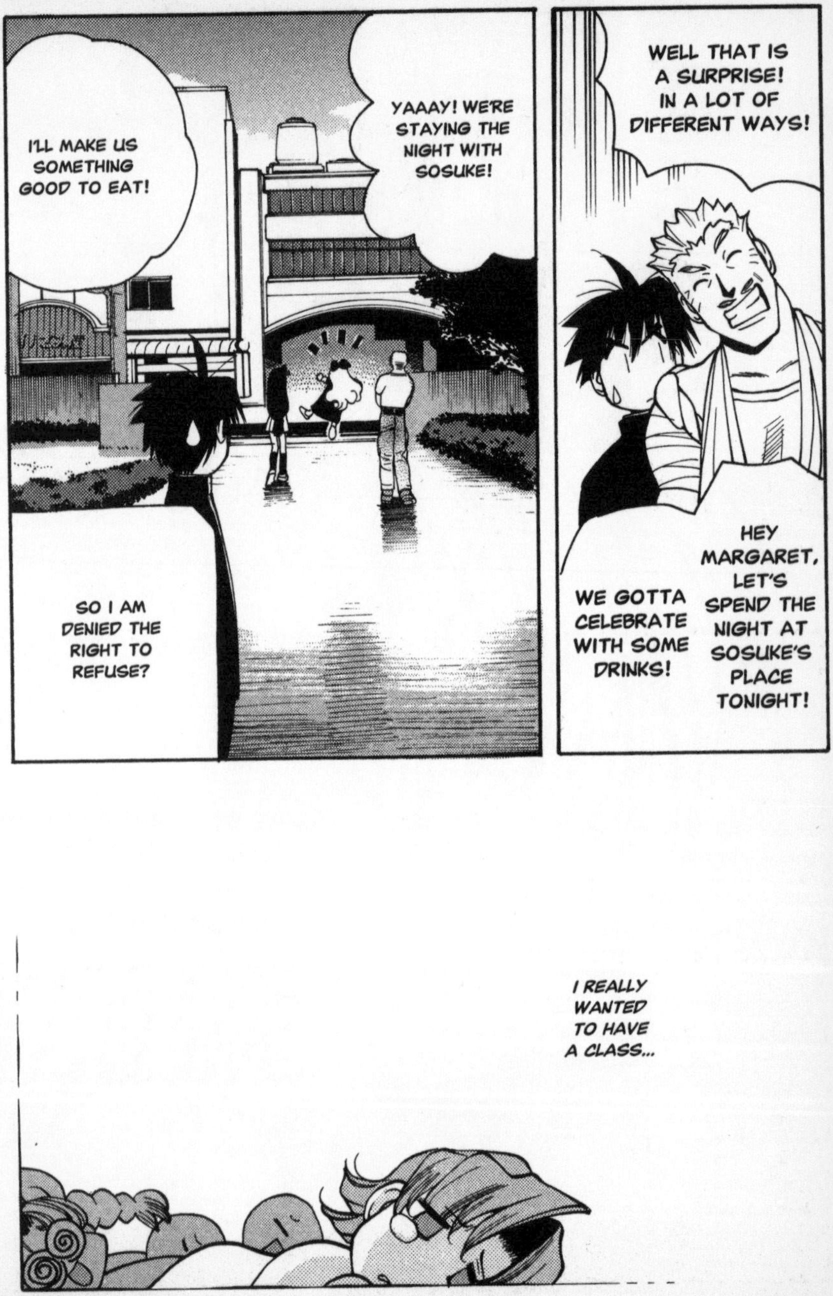
WELL THAT IS A SURPRISE! IN A LOT OF DIFFERENT WAYS!
HEY MARGARET, LET'S SPEND THE NIGHT AT SOSUKE'S PLACE TONIGHT!
WE GOTTA CELEBRATE WITH SOME DRINKS!
YAAAY! WE'RE STAYING THE NIGHT WITH SOSUKE!
I'LL MAKE US SOMETHING GOOD TO EAT!
SO I AM DENIED THE RIGHT TO REFUSE?
I REALLY WANTED TO HAVE A CLASS...

CONTINUED IN VOLUME 5

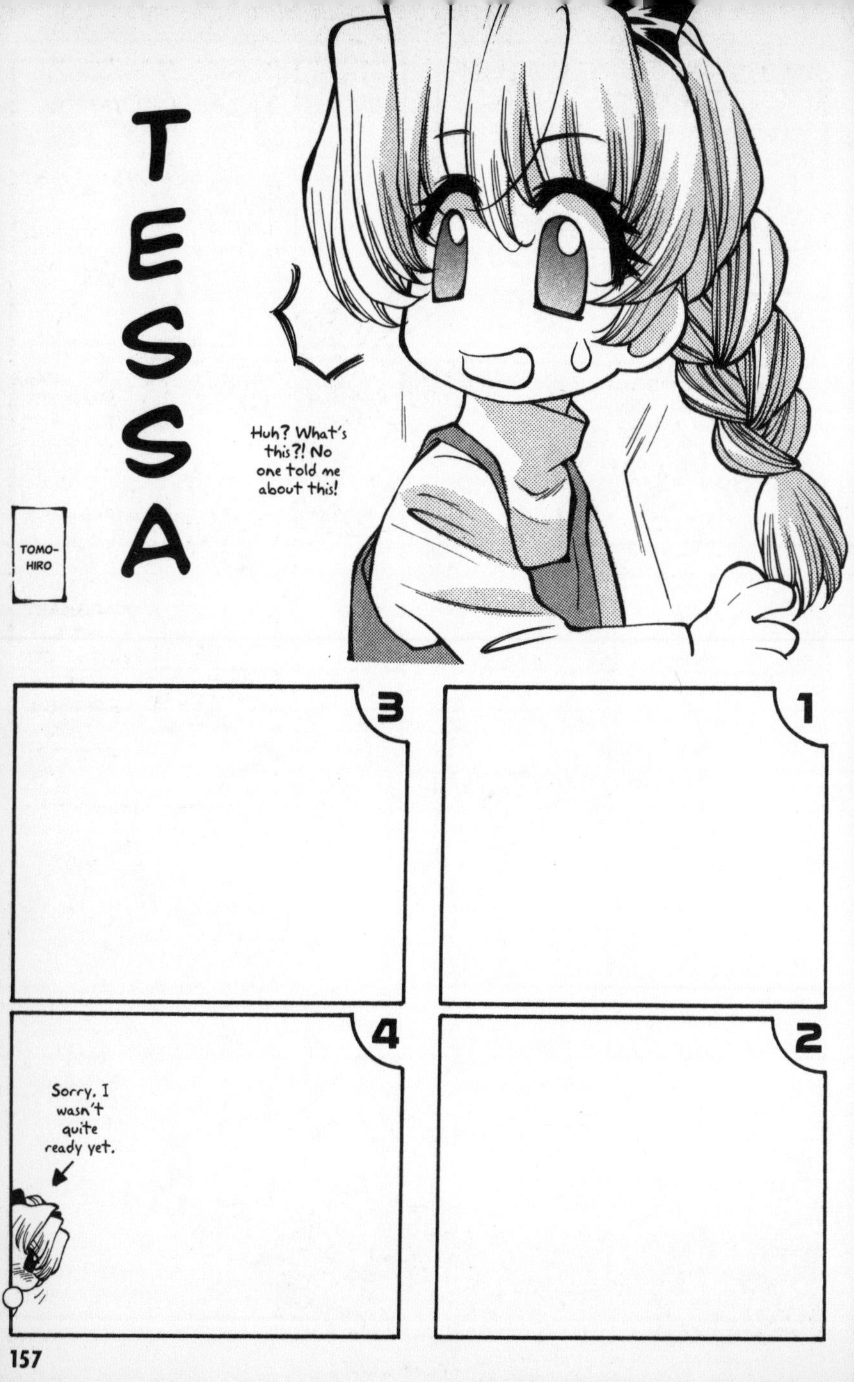
TESSA
TOMO-HIRO
Huh? What's this?! No one told me about this!
1
2
3
4
Sorry. I wasn't quite ready yet.

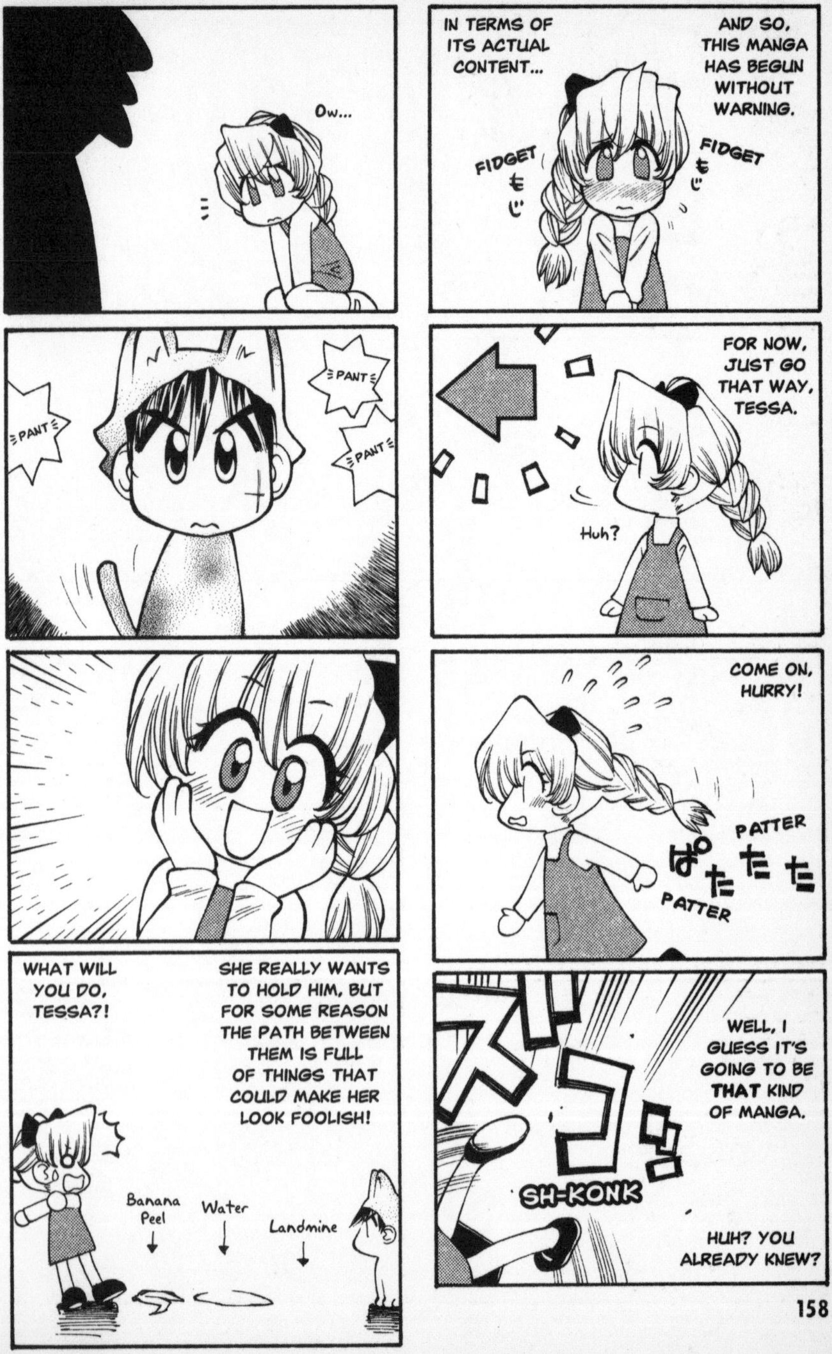

AND SO, THIS MANGA HAS BEGUN WITHOUT WARNING.
IN TERMS OF ITS ACTUAL CONTENT...
FIDGET もじ
FIDGET もじ
FOR NOW, JUST GO THAT WAY, TESSA.
Huh?
COME ON, HURRY!
PATTER
ぱたたた
PATTER
WELL, I GUESS IT'S GOING TO BE THAT KIND OF MANGA.
SH-KONK
HUH? YOU ALREADY KNEW?
Ow...
PANT
PANT
PANT
SHE REALLY WANTS TO HOLD HIM, BUT FOR SOME REASON THE PATH BETWEEN THEM IS FULL OF THINGS THAT COULD MAKE HER LOOK FOOLISH!
WHAT WILL YOU DO, TESSA?!
Banana Peel
Water
Landmine

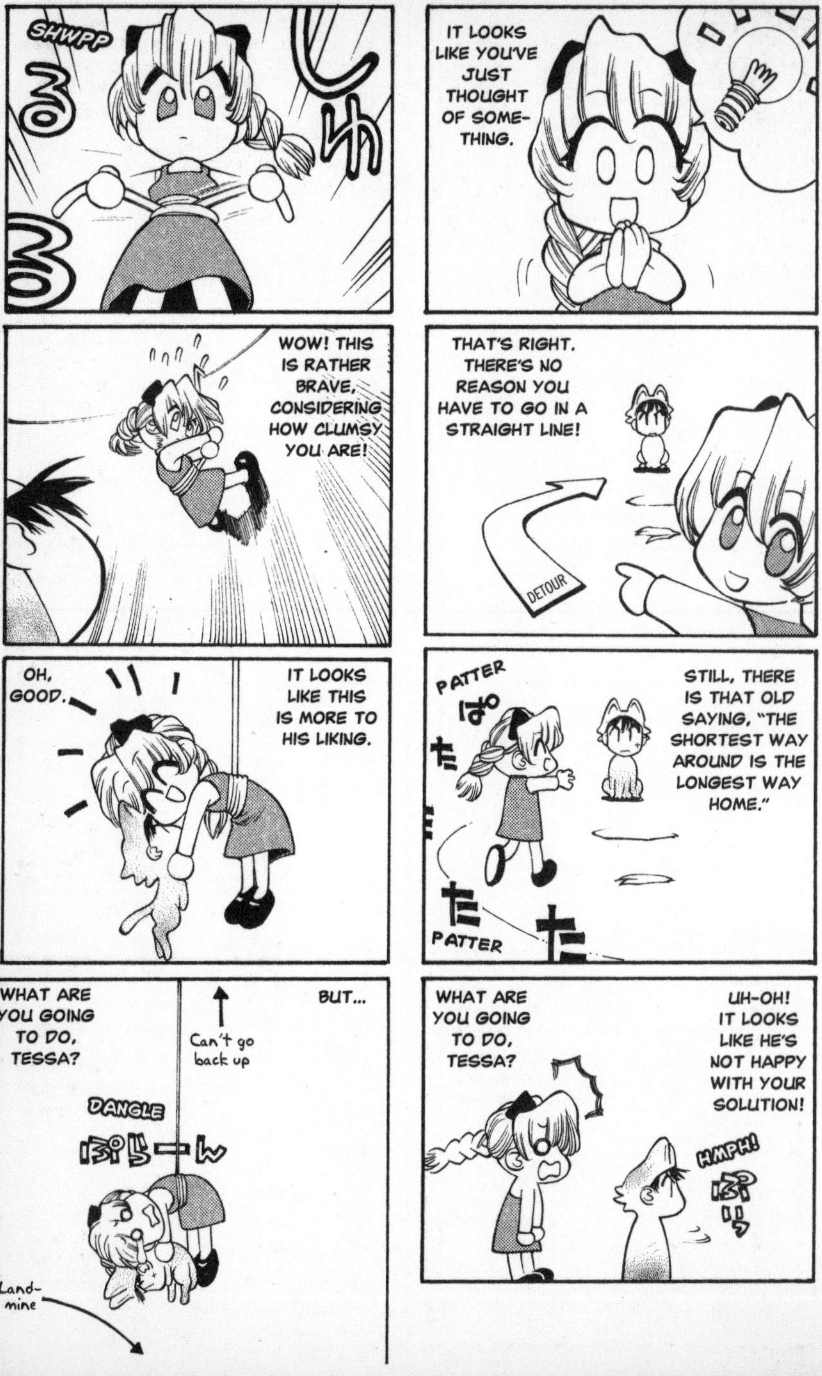
IT LOOKS LIKE YOU'VE JUST THOUGHT OF SOME-THING.
THAT'S RIGHT. THERE'S NO REASON YOU HAVE TO GO IN A STRAIGHT LINE!
DETOUR
PATTER
STILL, THERE IS THAT OLD SAYING, "THE SHORTEST WAY AROUND IS THE LONGEST WAY HOME."
PATTER
WHAT ARE YOU GOING TO DO, TESSA?
UH-OH! IT LOOKS LIKE HE'S NOT HAPPY WITH YOUR SOLUTION!
HMPH!
SHWPP
WOW! THIS IS RATHER BRAVE, CONSIDERING HOW CLUMSY YOU ARE!
OH, GOOD.
IT LOOKS LIKE THIS IS MORE TO HIS LIKING.
WHAT ARE YOU GOING TO DO, TESSA?
BUT...
Can't go back up
DANGLE
Land-mine

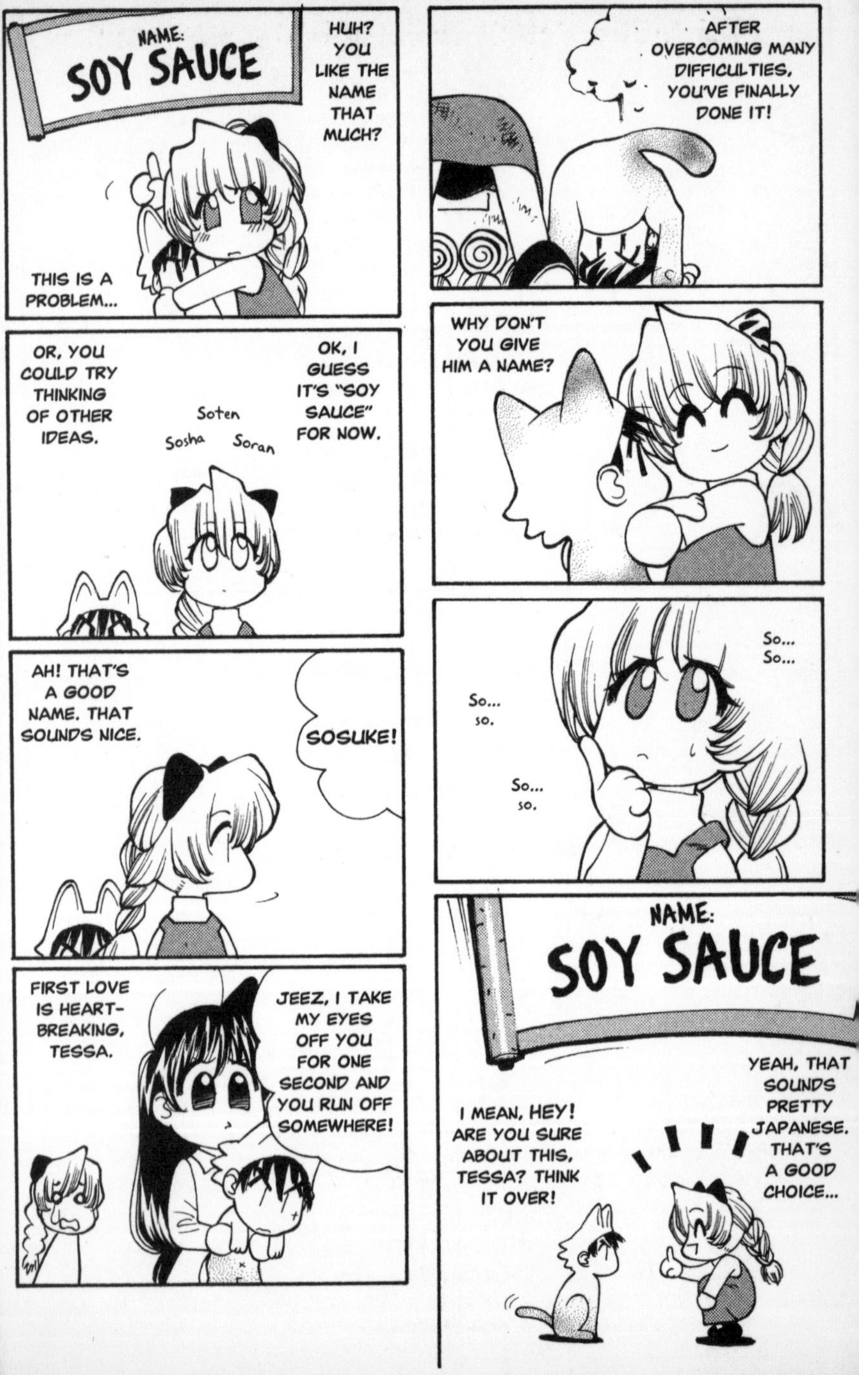

AFTER OVERCOMING MANY DIFFICULTIES, YOU'VE FINALLY DONE IT!
WHY DON'T YOU GIVE HIM A NAME?
So... So...
So... so.
So... so.
NAME:
SOY SAUCE
YEAH, THAT SOUNDS PRETTY JAPANESE. THAT'S A GOOD CHOICE...
I MEAN, HEY! ARE YOU SURE ABOUT THIS, TESSA? THINK IT OVER!
HUH? YOU LIKE THE NAME THAT MUCH?
NAME:
SOY SAUCE
THIS IS A PROBLEM...
OK, I GUESS IT'S "SOY SAUCE" FOR NOW.
Soten
Sosha
Soran
OR, YOU COULD TRY THINKING OF OTHER IDEAS.
SOSUKE!
AH! THAT'S A GOOD NAME. THAT SOUNDS NICE.
JEEZ, I TAKE MY EYES OFF YOU FOR ONE SECOND AND YOU RUN OFF SOMEWHERE!
FIRST LOVE IS HEART-BREAKING, TESSA.

FULL METAL PANIC! OVERLOAD! VOLUME FOUR

© 2002 Tomohiro NAGAI • Shouji GATOU
© 2002 Shikidouji
Originally published in Japan in 2002 by
KADOKAWA SHOTEN PUBLISHING CO., LTD., Tokyo.
English translation rights arranged with
KADOKAWA SHOTEN PUBLISHING CO., LTD., Tokyo.

Editor **JAVIER LOPEZ**
Translator **AMY FORSYTH**
Graphic Artist **SCOTT HOWARD**

Editorial Director **GARY STEINMAN**
Creative Director **JASON BABLER**
Print Production Manager **BRIDGETT JANOTA**
Production Coordinator **MARISA KREITZ**

International Coordinators **TORU IWAKAMI & MIYUKI KAMIYA**

President, CEO & Publisher **JOHN LEDFORD**

Email: editor@adv-manga.com
www.adv-manga.com

www.advfilms.com

For sales and distribution inquiries please call 1.800.282.7202

ADV ™
MANGA
is a division of A.D. Vision, Inc.
5750 Bintliff Drive, Suite 210, Houston, Texas 77036

English text © 2006 published by A.D. Vision, Inc. under exclusive license.
ADV MANGA is a trademark of A.D. Vision, Inc.

ISBN: 1-4139-0340-1
First printing, March 2006
10 9 8 7 6 5 4 3 2 1
Printed in Canada

Full Metal Panic! Overload! Vol. 04

P. 12 **LVTP**

LVTP stands for "Landing Vehicle, Tracked, Personnel." This (somewhat outdated) term refers to a class of armored vehicles that, as Sagara explains, are designed to transport soldiers from offshore onto land. They are now known by the term AAV (Amphibious Assault Vehicle).

P. 16 **1) Chobham Armor**

The exact composition of Chobham Armor remains a secret, but it is believed to be a composite of different metals, ceramics and plastics layered in a specific sequence. It is used on tanks such as the M1 series, the Leopard 2 and the Challenger.

2) HEAT Rounds

HEAT stands for "High Explosive Anti-Tank," and they are explosive charges capable of punching through armor. The development of HEAT rounds sparked the development of new tank armor to defend against it, such as the Chobham armor mentioned above.

P. 24 **1) OTH RADAR**

OTH RADAR stands for "Over The Horizon RAdio Detection And Ranging." It uses radio waves that reflect off the ionosphere to detect targets beyond the visible horizon.

2) Bell "Huey Cobra"

The AH-1S, also known as the "Huey Cobra," is an assault helicopter designed by Bell Helicopter Textron.

P. 29 **First visit to the shrine**

It is a Japanese tradition to visit a shrine during the first days of the New Year.

P. 43 **Hanetsuki**

Hanetsuki is a traditional Japanese game often played by girls during the New Year. It is similar to badminton, with the object being to keep the shuttlecock in the air as long as possible.

P. 92 **Umi no Wakadaisho**

Informally known in English as "Young Guy at the Sea," *Umi no Wakadaisho* is one in a series of popular *Wakadaisho* films made during the 1960s-'70s. The Yuzo Kayama mentioned by the rental video clerk in this manga is the star of this series.

FULL METAL PANIC OVERLOAD! 5

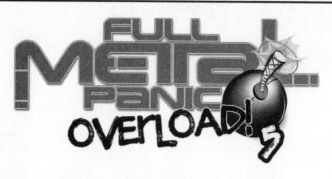

MISSION COMPLETE!

SOSUKE GETS ORDERED BACK TO BASE, BUT INSTEAD OF REPORTING IN, HE PLACES JINDAI HIGH UNDER LOCKDOWN AND FILLS THE CLASSROOMS WITH GUN-TOTING TEDDY BEARS! TENSIONS ARE HIGH, AND WHEN A FAMILIAR FACE SHOWS UP WITH A TEDDY BEAR ARMY OF HIS OWN, THE WALLS COME CRASHING DOWN IN AN ALL-OUT BATTLE OF BEAR VS. BAZOOKA!

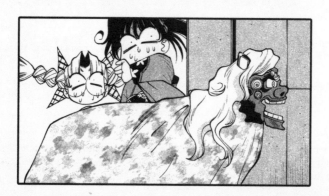

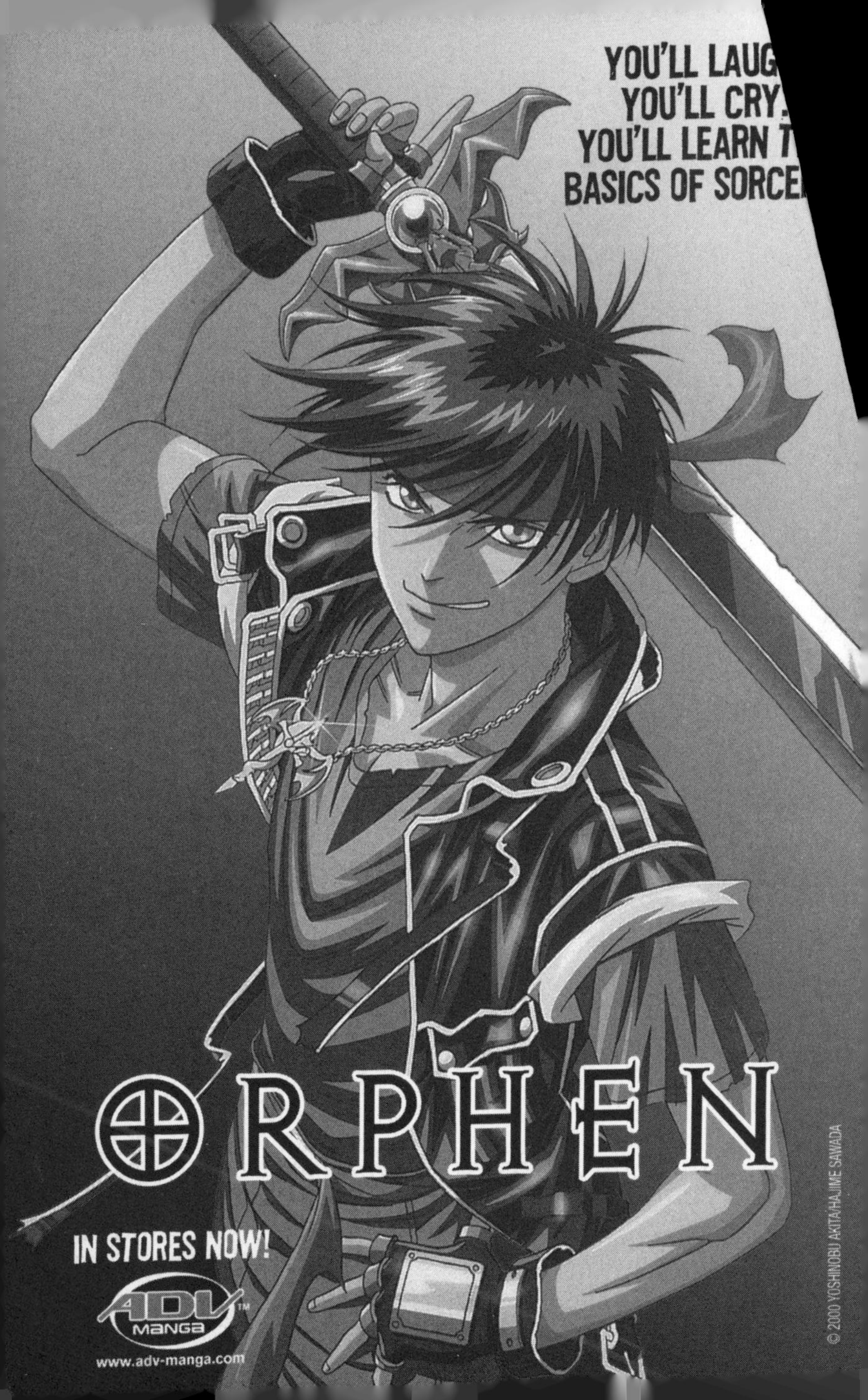
YOU'LL LAUG
YOU'LL CRY.
YOU'LL LEARN T
BASICS OF SORCE
ORPHEN
IN STORES NOW!
ADV Manga
www.adv-manga.com
© 2000 YOSHINOBU AKITA/HAJIME SAWADA

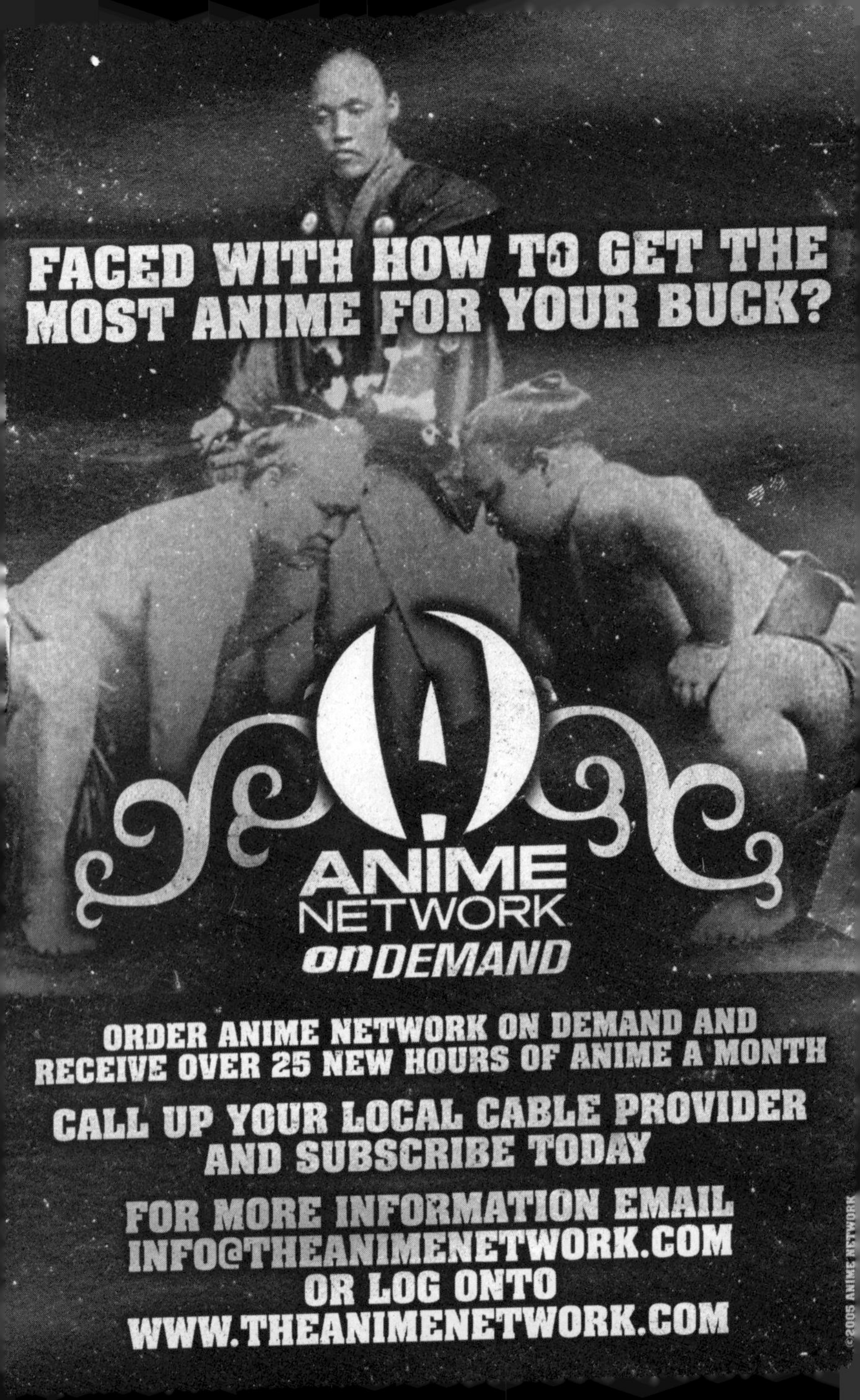

FACED WITH HOW TO GET THE MOST ANIME FOR YOUR BUCK?
ANIME NETWORK
onDEMAND
ORDER ANIME NETWORK ON DEMAND AND RECEIVE OVER 25 NEW HOURS OF ANIME A MONTH
CALL UP YOUR LOCAL CABLE PROVIDER AND SUBSCRIBE TODAY
FOR MORE INFORMATION EMAIL INFO@THEANIMENETWORK.COM OR LOG ONTO WWW.THEANIMENETWORK.COM
©2005 ANIME NETWORK